1,2,4,5,4/2

Counseling for Career Development

Carl McDaniels
Norman C. Gysbers

Counseling for Career Development

Theories, Resources, and Practice

Jossey-Bass Publishers • San Francisco

For international orders, please contact your local Paramount Publishing International office.

Printed on acid-free paper and manufactured in the United States of America

 The paper used in this book meets the State of California requirements for recycled paper (50 percent recycled waste, including 10 percent postconsumer waste), which are the strictest guidelines for recycled paper currently in use in the United States.

Library of Congress Cataloging-in-Publication Data

McDaniels, Carl, date.
   Counseling for career development : theories, resources, and practice / Carl McDaniels, Norman C. Gysbers.
       p.   cm. — (The Jossey-Bass social and behavioral science series)
   Includes bibliographical references and index.
   ISBN 1-55542-399-X
   1. Career development. 2. Employee counseling. I. Gysbers, Norman C. II. Title. III. Series.
   HF5549.5.C35M38   1992
   158.6—dc20   91-25851
                                                                          CIP

Credits are on p. 463

FIRST EDITION
HB Printing   10 9 8 7 6 5 4 3   *Code 9204*

The Jossey-Bass
Social and Behavioral Science Series

*To one of the early pioneers,
Frank Parsons*

Contents

Preface   xi

The Authors   xvii

Part One: The Important Role of Career Theory in Counseling

1. Careers and Career Development   3

2. Understanding Career Theories   27

3. Using Theory to Counsel Clients   65

Part Two: Building the Foundations for Career Development

4. The World of Work   91

5. The World of Education and Training   114

6. The Importance of Leisure in Career Development   135

7.   Integrating Career and Family   158

**Part Three:
Resources for Career Development**

8.   Resources for the World of Work   185

9.   Resources for Education and Leisure   214

10. Working with Career Information Delivery
     Systems   239

11. Renewing and Evaluating Career Information   256

**Part Four: Using Career Resources
and Information**

12. Focusing on Populations with Special Needs   279

13. Designing and Managing Career Development
     Centers   298

14. Using Techniques for Individual Counseling   324

15. Working with Structured Groups   368

**Resource: National Career
Development Association Guidelines**

Guidelines for the Preparation and Evaluation
of Career and Occupational Information
Literature   387

Career Software Review Guidelines   400

References   415

Index   443

Preface

Whether your current or intended work setting as a counselor is a public or private agency, an elementary or secondary school, a hospital, a private practice, a community college, a four-year college, a university, or a business, some of your clients will need and want assistance with their career development. In some settings, this may mean helping clients find jobs immediately. You may be called on to provide them with assistance in career exploration, planning, and decision making. In other settings, the emphasis may be on clients' personal or social concerns as these interact with career issues. Or you may find yourself working with displaced homemakers or workers who need immediate job placement help and longer-term counseling, career exploration, and decision-making assistance.

The kind of counseling for career development done with clients with these diverse goals and problems can vary substantially. Some clients may be capable of reaching their goals or solving their problems with a minimum of counseling assistance once they have been helped to obtain and process the information they require. Other clients, however, may need help with a wide variety of tasks, including self-understanding, career decision making, obtaining and processing information, and making transitions. Emotional issues may sometimes be central with these clients and may block or inhibit progress, and thus they may need to be responded to directly. Figler (1989, p. 1) made this point clearly when he stated that "emotions are the genie in the bottle of career development, the winds whipping around inside a client, while s/he wears the polite mask of reasonableness. For career counselors to be fully effective, they must unbottle the emotions that often accompany clients' struggles toward career goals."

Purpose of the Book

The purpose of this book is to help you develop or expand the knowledge and skills you use in counseling for career development. It is intended to identify and describe the indispensable roles career theory and information play in counseling for career development. It is designed to be a theory-based, professional source of ideas, concepts, techniques, and resources to help you counsel more effectively with clients whatever their ages, circumstances, or career goals or concerns. In short, our focus is on career development over the life span.

To accomplish this purpose, *Counseling for Career Development: Theories, Resources, and Practice* begins with an overview of selected career theories, highlighting their use in counseling. Because of the indispensable role of information in this process, up-to-date and authoritative foundation knowledge about the worlds of work, education and training, leisure, and the family are presented next. Then we describe key information resources used to assist clients in their career planning and decision making. The specifics of gathering, evaluating, and organizing these resources follow. Finally, we present illustrative and innovative practices, tools, and techniques for use with clients. The fifteen chapters are grouped into four major parts, each of which offers in-depth presentations and analyses of key life-career development topics, issues, and practices.

Overview of the Contents

Part One, "The Important Role of Career Theory in Counseling," provides you with theoretical concepts and a counseling framework to use in working with clients, whether they require short-term counseling and information or longer-term counseling concerning emotional issues that may be intertwined with career issues. Chapter One first covers the evolution of the concept of life-career development, and then reviews the implications of this evolution for the practice of counseling. It also describes the counseling process from the standpoint of life-career development. In Chapter Two, we sum up selected theories of career behavior and development. Chapter Three emphasizes the constructs in these theories that may be useful in counseling clients individually and in structured groups. The focus is on how constructs from theories that explain career behavior and development can be used to assist clients with their life-career development.

Part Two, "Building the Foundations for Career Development," supplies necessary foundation knowledge about the nature and structure of the worlds of work, education and training, leisure, and the family. This is foundation knowledge that will help you understand the contexts in which clients' career goals and problems unfold. It also is foundation knowledge that you will need to draw on directly as you help clients achieve their goals and resolve their career problems. Chapter Four sketches the past, present, and possible future of the world of work and discusses the role of work in one's life-career development over the life span. Then, in Chapter Five, we provide an in-depth review of education and training. Chapter Six discusses leisure as an important component of life-career development and reviews the multiple leisure options open to individuals of all ages, stages, and circumstances. Finally, Chapter Seven provides an extensive review of today's family structures and the influence they may have on life-career development. (Chapters Six and Seven present topics not normally included in a book of this type.)

Part Three, "Resources for Career Development," presents the "how to" of gathering, organizing, and evaluating career information resources and systems. Chapter Eight reveals where to find the resources needed to counsel clients with respect to the world of work. Chapter Nine discusses resources for education and leisure. In Chapter Ten, we devote special attention to state and commercial career information delivery systems. Finally, the "when" and "how" of gathering and evaluating all types of career information are highlighted in Chapter Eleven, with specific emphasis given to the use of the evaluation guidelines of the National Career Development Association on literature, media, and software.

Part Four, "Using Career Resources and Information," puts theory and information together by describing how such information is used in individual and structured group counseling. Chapter Twelve offers a discussion of using career information with populations with special needs: women, racial and ethnic minorities, and individuals with disabilities. Then, in Chapter Thirteen, we present the details of the organization and management of multimedia career development centers. Chapter Fourteen focuses on individual counseling. Chapter Fifteen emphasizes using information with structured groups.

Finally, the Resource at the back of the book presents the 1991 editions of two of the guidelines for evaluating career information prepared by the National Career Development Association. The first one is "Guidelines for the Preparation and Evaluation of Career and Occupational Information Literature." The second is "Career Software Review Guidelines." Their uses are described in detail in Chapter Eleven.

Who Should Read This Book

This book is designed for several groups of readers. First, practicing counselors in many and varied settings who do counseling for career development will find this book to be an excellent review of contemporary career concepts, techniques, methods, and resources. But it is more than just a review for practitioners.

With its four carefully crafted and connected parts—which follow a logical progression from career theory and the counseling process, to the development of sound foundation knowledge concerning work, education and training, leisure, and the family, to the gathering, organizing, and evaluating of such information, and to the use of this information in counseling with clients of all ages and circumstances—this book can be a source of renewal for practitioners. It represents a much more holistic approach to the topic than most similar books. Second, this also is a book for counselors in training because it provides them with the necessary knowledge and skills to do counseling for career development. It offers a framework for integrating theoretical concepts and information into the counseling process naturally and comfortably, something that many beginning counselors find difficult to do. It also provides beginning counselors with a perspective on the importance of counseling for career development in the many and varied settings in which they will be working across the life span.

Acknowledgments

Since the early 1900s the conceptualizations of career development and counseling for career development have continued to evolve. This evolutionary process will continue into the foreseeable future. Thus, the field of career development and career counseling has both a rich heritage and a bright future. This book is another step in the evolutionary process of refining and extending our field. The ideas in the book are a product of our rich heritage, and we trust they will contribute to our bright future. As a result, we wish to acknowledge the work of the early pioneers in the field such as Frank Parsons. In responding to the needs of individuals and society, they developed the basic outlines of the field as it exists today. We also wish to acknowledge those individuals who followed, who took those rudiments and enhanced them with new concepts and ideas derived from their research and development work. Finally, we wish to acknowledge ahead of time those whose work will further improve and expand the field in the future.

This section is not complete unless we acknowledge the support, encouragement, and tangible contributions of many colleagues. Discussions with our colleagues were invaluable in sharpening our thinking about the concepts in the book. We wish to acknowledge helpful comments of Paul Bloland, Reece Chancey, Rich Feller, Martin Gerstein, Fredrick Harper, Tom Krieshok, Larry Loesch, Johnnie Miles, Marge Neely, Robert Reardon, and Howard Splete, who reviewed the initial outline for the book. We especially appreciate the insightful and useful suggestions of manuscript reviewers who commented on the first draft of the book. In addition, this book could not have been completed without the effective and efficient work of the secretarial staffs at our institutions: Vicki Meadows at Virginia Tech and Brenda Baker, Kristi Leslie, Jon Oetting, and Barbara Thornton at the University of Missouri–Columbia. We also express our appreciation and thanks to Robert Hansen and Mary Heppner, who wrote the case studies presented in Chapter Fourteen. Finally, we wish to express our appreciation and thanks to our wives, Ann and Mary Lou, whose understanding and support made this book possible.

November 1991   Carl McDaniels
                                                    Blacksburg, Virginia

                                                    Norman C. Gysbers
                                                    Columbia, Missouri

The Authors

Carl McDaniels is professor and program area leader of counselor education at Virginia Polytechnic Institute and State University (Virginia Tech) in Blacksburg, Virginia. Since 1979 he also has been project director for the Virginia Career Information Delivery System (Virginia VIEW). He received his B.A. degree (1951) from Bridgewater College, Virginia, in psychology and history and his M.Ed. (1957) and Ed.D. (1964) degrees in counseling from the University of Virginia, Charlottesville. He is a Nationally Certified Counselor (NCC) and a Nationally Certified Career Counselor (NCCC).

McDaniels's main research interests are in career information systems and their use in a wide variety of settings for people of all ages. In addition, he has written extensively on the interrelationship of work and leisure in career development over the life span. In 1988 McDaniels was recognized by the National Career Development Association with its highest honor, the Eminent Career Award. He is on the editorial board of the *Journal of Career Development* and has served as guest editor of special issues entitled "Leisure and Career Development Through the Life Span" and "A Decade of Career Information Delivery Systems: 1977 to 1987." He has published articles in professional journals such as the *Occu-*

pational Outlook Quarterly, Vocational Guidance Quarterly, Personnel and Guidance Journal, and *Counselor Education and Supervision.* He is the author of *Developing a Professional Vita and Resume* (1978), *Finding Your First Job* (1981), *Leisure: Integrating a Neglected Component in Life Planning* (1982b), *Unlocking Your Child's Potential* (1982d, with D. Hummel), and *The Changing Workplace: Career Counseling Strategies for the 1990s and Beyond* (1989). He is also the editor of *Vocational Aspects of Counselor Education* (1965).

His professional experience includes the following positions: teacher and counselor in the public schools of Virginia; personnel specialist in the U.S. Navy; staff member of the American Association for Counseling and Development; and, for the past twenty-five years, counselor educator at George Washington University and Virginia Tech. He has been a visiting professor and lecturer at more than a dozen other colleges and universities. He was president of the National Career Development Association (formerly the National Vocational Guidance Association) in 1973–1974 and has also served as president of the following organizations: the National Capitol Personnel and Guidance Association, the North Atlantic Association of Counselor Educators and Supervisors, and the Virginia Vocational Guidance Association. In addition, McDaniels has served as a consultant to a wide variety of organizations, associations, government agencies, local school systems, and community colleges, primarily in the mid-Atlantic and Southern states.

Norman C. Gysbers is professor in the Department of Educational and Counseling Psychology at the University of Missouri–Columbia. He received his B.A. degree (1954) from Hope College in science education and his M.A. (1959) and Ph.D. (1963) degrees in counseling from the University of Michigan, Ann Arbor. He is a licensed psychologist in Missouri, a Nationally Certified Counselor (NCC), and a Nationally Certified Career Counselor (NCCC).

Gysbers's research interests are in career development, career counseling, and school guidance and counseling program development, management, and evaluation. In 1978

Gysbers received the American Vocational Association's Division Merit Award and the Missouri Guidance Association's Outstanding Service Award. In 1981 he was awarded the National Vocational Guidance Association's National Merit Award and in 1983 the American Professional Service Award. He was awarded a Franqui Professorship from the Université Libre de Bruxelles, Belgium, and lectured there in 1984. In 1987 he was awarded the United States Air Force Recruiting Service's Spirit of America Award and the Distinguished Service Award of the Association of Computer-Based Systems for Career Information. In 1989 he received the National Career Development Association's Eminent Career Award. Gysbers was editor of the *Vocational Guidance Quarterly* from 1962 to 1970. Currently, he is editor of the *Journal of Career Development.* He is author of forty-four articles in seventeen different professional journals, seventeen chapters in published books, twelve monographs, and seven books, including *Career Counseling: Skills and Techniques for Practitioners* (1987, with E. J. Moore) and *Developing and Managing Your School Guidance Program* (1988, with P. Henderson).

Gysbers has been a teacher and school counselor in the public schools and has served in the U.S. Army. He has been a visiting professor at the University of Nevada, Reno, and Virginia Tech. Since 1967 he has served as director of numerous national and state projects on career development and career counseling as well as on school guidance program development, implementation, and evaluation. He was president of the National Career Development Association (formerly the National Vocational Guidance Association) from 1972 to 1973; president of the American Association of Counseling and Development (formerly the American Personnel and Guidance Association) from 1977 to 1978; and vice president of the American Vocational Association from 1979 to 1982.

Counseling
for Career
Development

PART 1

The Important Role of Career Theory in Counseling

1

▟▟▟▟▟▟▟▟▟▟▟▟▟▟▟▟▟▟▟▟▟▟▟▟▟▟▟▟▟▟▟▟▟

Careers
and Career Development

▟▟▟▟▟▟▟▟▟▟▟▟▟▟▟▟▟▟▟▟▟▟▟▟▟▟▟▟▟▟▟▟▟

In the United States and many other countries, the concepts of career and career development are undergoing changes. Instead of being defined as job or occupation, career is increasingly being defined as the combinations and sequences of life roles, the settings in which life roles unfold, and the planned and unplanned events that occur in people's lives. Career development is being seen more and more as the unfolding and interaction of roles, settings, and events all through the life span.

What is causing this shift in perspective? First, far-reaching changes are taking place in the nature and structure of our social and economic systems. Second, the values and beliefs individuals hold about themselves, about others, and about the world are changing. Third, more and more people are seeking meaning and coherence in their life roles.

These trends are changing the way we define and use the concepts of career and career development in theory building, research, and counseling. This chapter reviews the evolution of these concepts since the early twentieth century. It first traces the changing definitions and applications of the concepts of vocation, occupation, career, vocational development, and career development. Then it identifies the implications of these changes for counseling. Finally, the chapter presents a framework for counseling for career development that uses the definitions of career and career development that have evolved over the past eighty years as a vehicle for understanding client information and behavior.

The Evolution of the Concepts of Career and Career Development

The development of these concepts in the twentieth century can conveniently be subdivided into four periods.

From 1900 to 1950: The Formative Years

By the beginning of the twentieth century, the United States was deeply involved in the Industrial Revolution. The early years of the century were a period of rapid industrial growth, social protest, social reform, and utopian idealism. Social protest and social reform were being carried out under the banner of the Progressive Movement, a movement that sought to change negative social conditions associated with industrial growth. Vocational guidance, the precursor of counseling for career development, was born during the height of the Progressive Movement as "but one manifestation of the broader movement of progressive reform which occurred in this country in the late nineteenth and early twentieth centuries" (Stephens, 1970, p. 5).

The implementation of one of the first systematic conceptions of vocational guidance in this century took place in the Civic Service House in Boston, when the Boston Vocation Bureau was established in January 1908 by Mrs. Quincy Agassiz Shaw based on plans drawn up by Frank Parsons. According to Davis (1969, p. 113), Parsons issued the bureau's first report on May 1, 1908; Davis says that "this was an important report because the term 'vocational guidance' apparently appeared for the first time in print as the designation of an organized service."

During this period of change in the United States, Parsons stressed the importance of assisting young people in making the transition from school to work. He explained his reasoning as follows:

> There is no part of life where the need for guidance is more empathic than in the transition from school to work—the choice of a vocation, adequate preparation for it, and the attainment of efficiency and success. The building of a career is quite as difficult a problem as the building of a house, yet few ever sit down with pencil and paper, with expert information and counsel, to plan a working career and deal with the life problem scientifically, as they would deal with the problem of building a house, taking the advice of an architect to help them [Parsons, 1909, p. 4].

This is an interesting statement because the terms *vocation* and *career* occur in the same paragraph. Later in the same book, Parsons used the phrases "working career" (p. 98), "scientific choice of occupation" (p. 99), "building up a successful career" (p. 100), and "building a career" (p. 101). It is unclear what meanings he attached to the words *vocation, career,* and *occupation* in these contexts. It appears that he used them synonymously. Whatever his intentions, however, one could read into his use of the terms a glimmer of the broader meaning of career and career development that was to unfold beginning in the 1950s and 1960s.

Following Parsons's lead, others seemed to favor the terms *vocation* and *occupation* over the next few decades. Occasional use of the term *career* occurred—for example, in "the life-career motive," a phrase used by Charles Eliot (Bloomfield, 1915), and in "life career classes" in schools that focused on the study of occupational opportunities and problems (Brewer, 1922). Even here, however, Brewer (1922, p. 290) defined the term *life career* as "the occupation of a person; that which offers him opportunity for progress and satisfaction in his work."

Under Parsons's influence, vocational guidance during the 1920s, 1930s, and 1940s came to be understood as the process of helping people select an occupation, prepare for it, enter it, and advance in it. The following definition of *vocational guidance* was first issued by the National Vocational Guidance Association in 1921 and revised in 1924, 1930, and 1937: "Vocational guidance is the process of assisting the individual to choose an occupation, prepare for it, enter upon, and progress in it. It is concerned primarily with helping individuals make decisions and choices involved in planning a future and building a career—decisions and choices necessary in effecting satisfactory vocational adjustment" (Myers, 1941, p. 3).

This was the normative conception of vocational guidance that persisted between the 1920s and 1940s. Note in the body of the definition the reference to "building a career," the same phrase used by Parsons in his book *Choosing a Vocation* (1909). Another interesting glimmer of things to come?

From 1950 to 1980: The Transitional Years

Current conceptions of career and career development began appearing in the literature during the early 1950s, although, as we have seen, the precursors of these conceptions seemed to have been present in the work of Parsons and other early professionals. During the 1950s, theorists began to emphasize a broader and more developmental view of occupation (vocation) and occupational (vocational) choice. This broader, more developmental view was exemplified by the work of Ginzberg and his associates (1951) and by the work of Roe (1956). For example, Roe (1956, p. 3) defined an occupation

> to mean whatever an adult spends most of his time doing. That may be what he does to earn a living or it may not. It may be a hobby, or it may refer to duties of one sort or another, paid or unpaid. Being a housewife, in this sense, is an occupation; so is being a mother. Being a father is not an occupation in this sense, because it almost never happens that it occupies the major part of a man's time, or that it is the central focus of his activities.

Stamp-collecting can be an occupation, and so can following the races. The occupation, then, is the major focus of a person's activities, and usually of his thoughts.

It was during this period that the term *vocational development* became popular as a way of describing the broadened view of occupational (vocational) choice and the many factors that influenced it (Super, 1957). At the same time, the word *career* was being used with increasing frequency. Relying on an interesting combination of concepts, a monograph titled *Vocational Development: A Framework for Research* (Super and others, 1957) described the framework for the Career Pattern Study, the longitudinal research project in vocational development. In an article in an issue of the *Personnel and Guidance Journal* presenting a symposium on vocational development, Super (1961, p. 11) used the terms *vocational development* and *career development*. He defined *career* as "the sequence of occupations, jobs, and positions in the life of an individual" (p. 11).

During the 1960s and 1970s, work in this field increased dramatically. The term *career* was used in place of *vocation* more and more often. In 1966, the National Vocational Guidance Association undertook a study called Project Reconceptualization, which examined the nature and status of vocational guidance. Papers were prepared by Field (1966), Katz (1966), and Super (1966). One of the questions the project addressed was "Should the term be vocational guidance or career guidance?" While these papers and the discussions that followed did not provide a definitive answer, the fact that Project Reconceptualization was initiated and the question about terminology was asked shows that a rethinking of concepts and terms was underway.

In 1965, McDaniels suggested that the career concept should be broadened to include leisure. He expressed this idea in the following formula: Career = Work + Leisure. He felt that in this way, the three concepts of career, work, and leisure could be combined in a holistic framework (McDaniels, 1965). McDaniels reiterated this concept in a special issue of the *Journal of Career Development* (1984a) and in his book *The Changing Workplace: Career Counseling Strategies for the 1990s and Beyond* (1989).

In 1973, the National Vocational Guidance Association (NVGA) published a joint position paper with the American Vocational Association that defined *career* and *career development*. The position paper defined *career* as "a time-extended working out of a purposeful life pattern through work undertaken by the individual" (National Vocational Guidance Association, 1973, p. 7). *Career development* was defined as "the total constellation of psychological, sociological, educational, physical, economic, and chance factors that combine to shape the career of any given individual."

Even as the NVGA position statement was being published in this document, the debate over definitions of *career* and *career development* continued. At one extreme, some people equated occupation with career, while at the other extreme, career was described as a general life pattern that included virtually all activities. Some writers delimited this broad definition somewhat by focusing on the major life domains that engage the individual in multiple roles—for example, worker, family member, community participant, and leisure-time participant. As we will see, this is the focus that most current definitions have come to embrace.

The expanded view of the career concept of the 1960s and 1970s, as embodied in the NVGA position statement, was more appropriate than the traditional narrower view of career as occupation. It was more appropriate because it broke the time barrier that previously restricted the vision of career to only a cross-sectional view of an individual's life. As Super and Bohn (1970, p. 115) pointed out, "It is well . . . to keep clear the distinction between occupation (what one does) and career (the course pursued over a period of time)." It was more appropriate, too, because the career concept had now become the basis for organizing and interpreting the impact that the role of work had on people over their lifetimes. Past, present, and possible future work and related behaviors could now be understood in the context of an individual's overall development. This expanded view of career placed emphasis on "vocational histories rather than on status at a single point in time, on career criteria rather than occupational criteria" (Jordaan, 1974, p. 264).

From 1980 to 1990: Broader Definitions Emerge

Although the definitions of *career* and *career development* that evolved between the 1950s and 1970s were broader than the traditional definitions, many still separated the work roles, settings, and events of people's lives from their other life roles, settings, and events. Because of the increasing complexity and interrelatedness of all aspects of society, today, and into the foreseeable future, it does not seem possible to clearly separate one role from another, if it ever was possible. Just as the time barrier was broken in our understanding of career development during the early 1950s, the work-oriented barrier that was inherent in some of the expanded definitions that emerged during the 1950s was broken beginning in the 1970s. Work roles, work settings, and work-related events were beginning to be seen in relation to other life roles, settings, and events. Jones and others (1972) suggested that the concept of career encompasses a variety of possible patterns of personal choice related to each individual's total life-style; its components are occupation, education, personal and social behavior, learning how to learn, and social responsibility (for example, citizenship and leisure-time activities). Building on the work of Cole (1972, 1973), Goldhammer and Taylor (1972), and Goldhammer (1975), Bailey (1976) identified four general life roles that he felt gave operational meaning to Cole's (1973) concept of the educated person. They included the work, family, learning and self-development, and social-citizenship roles.

During the same period, Gysbers and Moore (1974, 1975, 1981) proposed the concept of life-career development in an effort to extend career development from the traditional occupational perspective to a life perspective in which occupation (and work) has meaning. They defined life-career development as self-development over the life span through the interaction and integration of the roles, settings, and events of a person's life. The word *life* in the term *life-career development* meant that the focus was on the total person—the human career. The word *career* identified and related the roles in which individuals were involved (worker, participant in leisure, learner, family member, and citizen), the settings where they found themselves (home, school, community, and workplace), and the events, planned and unplanned, that occurred over their lifetimes (entry job, marriage, more advanced positions, divorce, and retirement). Finally, the expression *life-career development* brought these separate meanings together, but at the same time a greater meaning emerged. *Life-career development* described people with a diversity of life-styles.

In the mid 1970s, Super (1976, p. 20) defined *career* as "the sequence of major positions occupied by a person throughout his preoccupational, occupational, and post-occupational life; includes work-related roles such as those of student, employee, and pensioner, together with complementary vocational, familial, and civic roles. Careers exist only as people pursue them; they are person-centered." He made the elements of this definition clear by using the concept of the life-career rainbow to describe the various aspects of a career throughout the life span. In 1980, he elaborated on his original idea of the life-career rainbow in an article titled "A Life-Span, Life-Space Approach to Career Development."

Minor (1986, p. 36) reasoned along the same lines when she wrote that "the individual's occupational career is very much a part of the individual's life career. The interactions of occupational and life cycles, lifestyle, leisure, and other issues cannot be separated." Carlsen (1988, p. 186), focusing on the French and Latin meanings of *career,* suggested that the concept of career can become a path that provides meaning and direction to life: "It is obvious . . . that when I use the term 'career' I am not thinking of just a job—I am thinking of a guiding image or a concept of a personal path, a personal significance, a personal continuity and meaning in the order of things."

By the 1980s, the broader, more encompassing conceptualizations of career and career development were in place. The terms career, career development, and career guidance and counseling had almost completely replaced vocation, vocational development, and vocational guidance and counseling in the literature and in practice. An important event that underscored this change occurred on July 1, 1985, when NVGA changed its name and became the National Career Development Association (NCDA). Another important event that underscored the change occurred in September 1986, when the *Vocational Guidance Quarterly* became the *Career Development Quarterly*.

From 1990 Forward: The Broader Definitions Become a Reality

As the 1990s began, the broader definitions of career and career development were being used with increasing frequency. Super (1990) continued to refine and clarify his life-span, life-space approach to career development. And in this book, we endorse and use the broader definitions because they provide a more fruitful basis for viewing, understanding, and describing clients' career development over the life span. We prefer them because they provide clients with useful ways to perceive and order their past, present, and possible future life roles, life settings, and life events. This in turn helps further the achievement of their career goals or the resolution of their career problems.

Figure 1.1 depicts these broader definitions of career and career development in graphic form. Note the headings *life roles, life settings,* and *life events* across the top of Figure 1.1. The words circled underneath are examples of various life roles (parent, spouse, and so on), life settings (such as home, school, and work), and life events (marriage, retirement, entry job, divorce). They are interspersed throughout Figure 1.1 to indicate the dynamic interaction that occurs among them over the life span. Near the bottom of the figure, the words *gender, ethnic origin, religion,* and *race* appear.

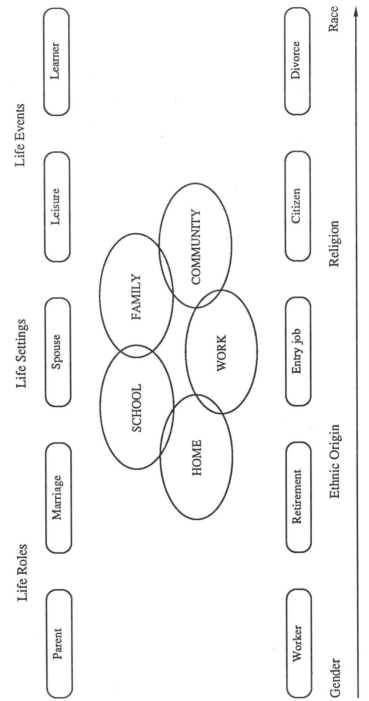

Figure 1.1. Life-Career Development.

They are there to remind us and our clients about the influence these factors have on their life-career development. Finally, the term *life span* is highlighted to clearly show that life-career development is a life-span phenomenon.

Wolfe and Kolb (1980, pp. 1–2) summed up this dynamic life-centered view of career when they described career development as involving one's entire life:

> Career development involves one's whole life, not just occupation. As such, it concerns the whole person, needs, and wants, capacities and potentials, excitements and anxieties, insights and blind spots, warts and all. More than that, it concerns him/her in the ever-changing contexts of his/her life. The environmental pressures and constraints, the bonds that tie him/her to significant others, responsibilities to children and aging parents, the total structure of one's circumstances are also factors that must be understood and reckoned with. In these terms, career development and personal development converge. Self and circumstances—evolving, changing, unfolding in mutual interaction—constitute the focus and the drama of career development.

The fact that Wolfe and Kolb closed their definition of career development with the words "the drama of career development" is worth noting. We call this drama the drama of the ordinary because it is unfolding each and every day. And because it is so mundane, it is not often seen or appreciated by clients. It is veiled by ordinariness. As a result, clients may fail to understand its dynamic nature and the substantial impact it has throughout their lives. By using the broader concept of life-career development as a way to understand human growth and development—the human career—we propose to make the drama of career development the drama of the extraordinary.

Implications for Counseling Practice

What are the implications of these changes in the definitions of career and career development? Are these changes of interest only to semanticists? Or do they have implications for the practice of counseling for career development? To answer our own questions, we will see that they definitely have a bearing on the perspective professionals bring to the counseling process and on their work with clients.

One implication of these changes revolves around the words *prediction* and *development.* Traditional practices in counseling for career development have often emphasized the assessment of individuals' abilities, aptitudes, interests, and values for the purpose of selecting an appropriate educational program or making an occupational choice. This approach focuses on prediction, trying to establish, through the use of various assessment devices and procedures, the chances of success clients may have in an education or training program or how closely their abilities, aptitudes, interests, and values relate to those of individuals already in an occupational field. Prediction offers an important perspective for our work, and efforts to improve the instrumentation and methodology involved must continue.

From a life-career development perspective, however, prediction alone is not sufficient. What is required are opportunities for clients to explore and develop their abilities and interests. Tennyson (1970, p. 262) underscored this point when he stated that "by concentrating upon assessment of abilities presumed to be related to choice outcomes, counselors have neglected to concern themselves with the development of abilities and aptitudes. While it is generally recognized that what a person is able to do depends to a considerable extent upon what he has learned or practiced, guidance personnel have been inclined to capitalize upon aptitudes already developed rather than cultivating new talents." Gordon (1974, p. 469) made the same point by saying that "overemphasis has . . . been placed upon selection and placement (both educational and vocational) rather than on the nurturing of interests and aptitudes and the development and training of capacities and skills."

A second implication of these changes revolves around the words *treatment* and *stimulus*. Herr and Cramer (1988) suggested that counseling techniques can be used as a treatment response to problems already present. They also suggested that counseling practices can stimulate clients to acquire needed knowledge and skills to become more effective in many areas of life.

A third implication centers on the words *deficiencies* and *competencies*. It is clear that a major focus of counseling for career development is on helping people deal effectively with their deficiencies and problems. Personal crises, a lack of information about training opportunities and the job market, and ineffective relationships with spouses, children, fellow employees, or supervisors are examples of goals or problems that counselors frequently are asked to deal with. This focus must continue, and better ways of helping people address their deficiencies must be found. But in addition, a preventive focus is needed to help people develop and use their talents and competencies to create a better world for themselves and for society.

The preventive focus is not new. It has been a part of the counseling language and literature since the turn of the century. What is new, however, is a sense of urgency about the importance of helping people focus on their competencies rather than only on their deficiencies. Bolles (1981) developed an assessment technique to identify the skills people have. Although many people do not think of themselves as having any skills (competencies), everyone possesses a substantial number of skills, and their identification in counseling can be an important part of positive growth and development. Tyler (1978, pp. 104-105) suggested that our perceptions of people will change if they can develop as many competencies as possible: "Competencies represent a completely different way of structuring our perception of others. The more competencies other people have the better for each of us, and it is essential for the functioning of a complex society that individuals develop different repertoires of competencies. The absolute limits of each person's living time make all-around competence for one individual impossible. We need one another."

A Framework for Counseling for Career Development

The purpose of the preceding discussion was not to artificially establish these six perspectives (prediction, development, and so on) as either/or categories from which to counsel. Rather, the purpose was to underscore the need to expand one's view of counseling for career development so that all of these perspectives are included in the counseling repertoire. At the same time, however, we also wanted to establish the importance of beginning work with clients with an overall development, stimulus, and competence vision of them and their goals and problems. Then, the use of the concepts of prediction, treatment, and deficiencies will follow naturally as the counseling process unfolds.

Before we describe a framework for counseling for career development that attempts to integrate these perspectives, it is first necessary to establish that there is a process involved in counseling for career development. In an article that reviewed the issues and problems of research in career counseling, Osipow (1982, p. 33) suggested that "the absence of process emphasis in career counseling has made career counseling very different from other kinds of counseling modalities. It has caused career counselors to focus on outcomes and on methods rather than interactions between client and counselor." The question is, do counselors who do counseling for career development neglect the process involved in counseling and concentrate instead on outcomes and methods? Or do they assume that "the same dynamics and concepts applied to other types of counseling relationships would seem to hold true"? (Osipow, 1982, p. 32). We assume that the same dynamics and concepts applied to other types of counseling relationships also hold true for counseling for career development.

Beginning with Parsons (1909) and Williamson (1939, 1965), a number of writers have described what is involved in the process of counseling for career development (recent examples include Brooks, 1984a, 1984b; Brown and Brooks, 1991; Crites, 1981; Gysbers and Moore, 1987; Kinnier and Krumboltz, 1984; Raskin, 1987; Reardon, 1984; Seligman, 1980; Super, 1983, 1984; Walsh and Osipow, 1990; Yost and Corbishley, 1987). Crites, Kinnier and Krumboltz, Super, and Yost and Corbishley in particular provided useful descriptions of this process.

Crites (1981) described the process of career counseling as involving diagnoses, problem clarification, problem specification, and problem resolution. He suggested that making a career choice, the acquisition of decisional skills, and enhanced general adjustment are often seen as the goals of career counseling. He pointed out that to reach these goals, interview techniques, test interpretation, and occupational information are the methods generally used as the career counseling process unfolds.

Kinnier and Krumboltz (1984) focused on three basic phases in their model of career counseling: assessment, intervention, and evaluation. During the assessment phase the counselor and client work on relationship development, agreement about the structure of the counseling sessions, and agreement about the goals of counseling. Exploration and identification of problems are part of the assessment phase. Part of the counseling sessions involves identifying obstacles that clients need to overcome. The intervention phase consists of activities that counselors and clients think will help alleviate clients' concerns or reach clients' goals. Finally, during the evaluation phase, clients and counselors evaluate how well the interventions worked.

In an article published in 1983, Super made the point that traditional approaches to career assessment were useful but not sufficient to encourage, support, and help people become active career planners and decision makers. To counteract the inadequacies of traditional models, he recommended that we consider a new model he called the *developmental assessment model.* In it, Super encompassed traditional methodology but also brought into focus the ideas of work salience and career maturity. In addition, he clarified the need to assist individuals in the assimilation of self and environmental information. Descriptions of this model were published in expanded versions later (Super, 1984, 1990).

Yost and Corbishley (1987) identified eight stages in the process of counseling for career development. These stages begin with the initial assessment phase, where responsibilities and goals are established and information gathered. This is followed by phases involving exploration of the self and interpretation of the resulting data. Generating alternatives is next; this stage is followed by obtaining occupational information, making the choice, making plans, and implementing plans.

For the purposes of this book, we envision the process of counseling for career development as having a number of phases and subphases. Building on the work of Gysbers and Moore (1987), we offer a framework for the process that addresses the six perspectives but does so from a developmental perspective:

I.   Client Goal or Problem Identification, Clarification, and Specification
     A. Opening
         1.   Identify the goal or problem.
         2.   Clarify the client-counselor relationship.
         3.   Define the client-counselor responsibilities.
     B. Gathering Client Information
         1.   Who is the client?
              a.   How does the client view self, others, and his or her world?
              b.   What language does the client use to represent these views?
              c.   What themes does the client use to organize and direct his or her behavior?
              d.   How does the client make sense out of and order in his or her world?

   2. What are the client's current status and environment like?
      a. How does the client view and make sense out of his or her life roles, settings, and events, past, present, and future?
      b. What personal and environmental barriers or constraints are operating?
      c. What decision (personal) styles are in place? Being used?
   C. Testing
   D. Understanding Client Information and Behavior
      1. Utilize the appropriate career behavior and developmental theories.
      2. Make use of counseling theories.
      3. Apply the relevant classification systems.
   E. Drawing Conclusions (Making Diagnoses)

II. Client Goal or Problem Resolution
   A. Taking Action
      1. Engage in the counseling process.
      2. Do the appropriate testing.
      3. Provide career information.
   B. Developing Individual Career Plans
   C. Evaluating the Results and Closing the Relationship
      1. If the goal or problem is not resolved, recycle
      2. If the goal or problem is resolved, close the relationship.

Keep in mind that these phases and subphases may take place during one interview or may unfold over two or more interviews with clients. Also, keep in mind that while these phases and subphases logically follow one another on paper, in actual practice they may not. There often is a back-and-forth flow to the process. Finally, understand that not everyone who seeks help wants or needs to go through the full process of career counseling. Some may want only selected amounts of assistance.

Goal or Problem Identification, Clarification, and Specification

This phase of the career counseling process has five subphases: opening, gathering client information, testing, understanding client information and behavior, and drawing conclusions (making diagnoses). Before we discuss these subphases in detail, however, we need to touch on the issue of the clients' goal or problem. Some clients seek help to improve the quality of their lives. No problems are present, but a goal of self-improvement is. Other clients may have problems and want help in solving them. The point is that counselors have to start where their clients are. Counselors should not assume there is a problem when none may exist. Some clients want information only, not counseling. On the other hand, other clients may ask for information initially but later may talk about a problem that is troubling them. There may be an initial testing time to see if it is safe to discuss a problem.

Sometimes goal or problem identification is straightforward. A client wants information about jobs in the local labor market because he or she wants to find a job that pays more. No feelings of anxiety, insecurity, or frustration are evident. At other times, goal or problem identification is more complex. The need for information about jobs may be mixed with emotional issues, issues relating to family pressures, and personal concerns about self-worth. The focus is on both emotional or personal concerns and career concerns.

Opening. Three tasks are usually undertaken in the opening subphase of the counseling process. First, the presenting goal or problem is identified and the process of clarification and specification is begun. Kinnier and Krumboltz (1984) pointed out that although the ways this is done vary according to counselor style and theoretical orientation, the opening questions are similar. "Who are you?, What is troubling you?, Why have you decided to seek counseling now?, Tell me more about yourself and what you want, and What do you want to gain from counseling?" (p. 308) are typical opening questions that all counselors ask in one form or another.

Second, during this subphase, the client-counselor relationship begins to unfold. If there is anything that is generally agreed on in counseling literature, it is that a positive, productive relationship between client and counselor is a basic and necessary condition if counseling is to be effective. Much has been written about the characteristics of such a relationship and the skills counselors need to bring it about, and so we will not spend time here discussing these characteristics and skills. It is important to remember, however, that listening and empathizing skills are especially important, as is the need to show clients that counselors are interested in them. It also is essential to remember that once positive, productive relationships have been established, they must be nurtured throughout the duration of the counseling process.

Third, this is the time when the nature, structure, and possible results of counseling are discussed with clients. What are the client's expectations? What time frame does the client have in mind? What can be expected realistically? What responsibility does the client have in the relationship? These and similar questions need to be addressed so that counselors and their clients can reach a mutual understanding about the nature of the counseling process and its expected results.

Gathering Client Information. As the counseling relationship is being established, the task of gathering client self and environmental information begins. This is necessary to help understand the goal or problem the client wants to work on or for which the client is being referred. In working with a client, the counselor should focus on the questions "Who is the client?" and "What are the client's current status and environment like?"

Gathering client information can be accomplished in many ways. Regardless of the process used, however, it is important to identify, discuss, and begin to understand as soon as possible the clients' life-career themes—their values, attitudes, and beliefs about themselves, others, and the world. This is important because such information provides ways to understand thought processes or representational systems that clients use to direct their behavior.

Testing. One way to gather client information is to ask them directly about their goals and concerns. Another way is to use standardized tests. As Herr and Cramer (1988, p. 453) pointed out, "We have come to accept the premise that assessment procedures help individuals to understand themselves not only in terms of their talents but also in terms of their interests, values, and personality characteristics." If testing is done during this phase of the counseling process, it is essential to involve clients in all phases, including orientation, test selection and administration, and test interpretation. Briggs and Keller (1982, p. 531) put it this way: "To use test information effectively in counseling, clients need to have a rationale for using tests and a high degree of involvement in the decision making regarding the use and the interpretation of the tests. They must also be taught to use test information to make observations, inferences, and hypotheses about themselves and their future courses of action."

Understanding Client Information and Behavior. The key counseling skills used to accomplish this phase of the counseling process are listening, understanding, and interpreting. These skills are important because the ability to systematically gather and interpret information clients share and the behavior they exhibit is basic to the entire process. Listening skills are important, but more is involved. Listening must be done with understanding so that the information clients present and the behavior they exhibit during goal or problem identification, clarification, and specification can be analyzed, interpreted, and understood.

How is listening with understanding achieved? It is achieved through an in-depth knowledge of theories of human behavior and human growth and development. Theories provide the language, the constructs, that help counselors explain client information and behavior. In this book, career theories are featured. Chapter Two presents selected theories and shows how specific constructs aid us in understanding and interpreting client behavior and information.

Drawing Conclusions or Making Diagnoses. As counselors are gathering and interpreting client information and behavior using career theories, they begin to draw tentative conclusions about the meaning of such information and behavior. These tentative conclusions are sometimes called *diagnoses.* Conclusions or diagnoses made initially are not one-time labels applied for all time. They are, instead, hypotheses that counselors substantiate, modify, or discard as the counseling process unfolds.

Crites (1981) suggested that there are three types of diagnoses that may be helpful: differential, dynamic, and decisional. Differential diagnosis is the identification and categorization of client goals or problems. Categories such as *undecided, indecisive,* and *incongruent* are often used. Differential diagnosis answers the question of what the client's problem or goal is. Dynamic diagnosis focuses on why—on determining the causes or reasons for the client's problem or goal. For example, a client who has been differentially diagnosed as undecided may lack information, whereas someone diagnosed as indecisive may suffer from self-doubt and hold a number of irrational beliefs. In the latter case, the use of information alone as an intervention strategy may be insufficient. In decisional diagnosis, attention turns to clients' approaches to decision making. It focuses on understanding the processes they go through to arrive at choices. In this type of diagnosis, clients' use of (or failure to use) decision-making strategies is assessed.

Client Goal or Problem Resolution

The reason for identifying, clarifying, and specifying clients' goals or problems is to find ways to resolve them through appropriate interventions.

Taking Action. Once clients become aware of the nature of their goals or problems, the focus of counseling turns to the counselor, and clients becoming actively involved in goal or problem solutions (Crites, 1981). Here the keys are the diagnoses or tentative conclusions reached as to the nature of the clients' goals or problems, because the diagnoses made determine the choices of interventions to be used. Test data, personal information, career and labor market information, and a variety of counseling techniques all play a part in how and when problem or goal resolution occurs. For example, tests and their use in counseling are an integral part of the process, not something separate. They aid in the process of self-understanding and assist people in comparing themselves with others in various occupations. As Crites (1981, p. 189) suggested, test interpretation "provides the client with relevant information for making a specific career choice; it models decision skills and how they can be used in problem solving; and it contributes to better adjustment through greater self-understanding and resultant self-confidence in coping effectively."

In addition, providing career information can serve to inform individuals about the realities of the work world and about themselves. Exposure to career information also can motivate people to explore new options, because such information may open up new possibilities. Finally, career information can help individuals adjust by helping them develop a balance between their needs and wants and occupational supply and demand in the labor market.

Developing Individual Career Plans. Wilhelm (1983, p. 12) recommended that counselors teach clients the skills to manage their careers: "That doesn't mean telling people what occupations they ought to pursue; nor does it mean we tell them what education they should get. . . . What it does mean is that we give them data—data about themselves, data about technology, data about the economy, data about demographic trends, data about employers—all the data we can gather that in any way impacts upon their vocational lives and choices—

and we teach them how to use those data to manage their own careers."

Individual career plans can be thought of as both instruments and processes that people can use alone or with the help of others to monitor and carry forward their career development. As instruments, plans can provide places to organize and record the abilities, interests, and values identified during career assessment and counseling. They can become organizers for personal, education, and career and labor market information, which then can be updated periodically. As processes, plans can become pathways or guides through which individuals can use the past and present to look forward to the future. They can become vehicles for planning.

Evaluating the Results and Closing the Relationship. During the goal or problem identification, clarification, and specification stage, counselors and clients determine the clients' goal or problem. Then, during goal or problem resolution, decisions are made about appropriate interventions to attain the goal or resolve the problem. The final phase of goal or problem resolution is assessing changes that may have occurred and evaluating the results of the interventions used. One way to accomplish this is to have clients review and summarize what has taken place during the counseling process. Then counselors can add their own review and summary.

During the summary, counselors and clients may find that there is some unfinished business. Clients may need more career information or more time to consider and reflect on the career information already available. As a result, counselors may recycle to the same interventions to allow more time for consideration and reflection, or they may try other interventions.

Also, it may turn out that clients are unsure about whether or not they are ready to close the counseling relationship. Counselors might want to open up this topic by saying, "It seems as if we have achieved what we wanted to achieve during our time together. Sometimes when people reach this point, having made some of the changes you have made, they wonder if they are ready to handle new situations. Could it be that you feel this way?" If counselors sense this is the case with their clients, then these feelings need to be addressed directly as a part of closing the counseling process. Part of closing this process is working through any emotional investment associated with the counseling relationship.

A Closing Note

The framework for the process of counseling for career development just presented is designed to provide a structure to review and examine the selected career theories that follow in the next chapter for possible use with clients. It also provides a structure that suggests where career information and career information systems fit into the counseling process. Finally, the framework clearly identifies the importance of assisting clients in the development of individual career plans as vehicles to help them solve their goals or problems.

2

░░░░░░░░░░░░░░░░░░░░░░░░░

Understanding
Career Theories

░░░░░░░░░░░░░░░░░░░░░░░░░

"Why study theory?" "What does theory have to do with practice?" "Most of the courses I took in college were too theoretical!" "Theory gets in my way when I am trying to listen to and respond to my clients!" These and similar questions and comments are heard frequently when counselors get together and discuss their current work and previous training. Why do they express these attitudes? Partly because there is, in fact, a gap between theory and practice. Many books and articles describe theory. Fewer books and articles explain how theoretical language is used in counseling.

Theory has been defined as a statement of general principles—supported by data—that is offered as an explanation of a phenomenon (Shertzer and Stone, 1980). A useful theory in counseling for career development summarizes and generalizes a body of information. It facilitates our understanding of and provides an explanation for the phenomena described by that body of information. It acts as a predictor of future developments, and it also stimulates further research.

Thus career theories provide the foundation knowledge from which counselors draw useful concepts to explain client behavior. They offer a framework within which client behavior can be examined and hypotheses formed about the possi-

ble meanings of that behavior. In turn, this knowledge helps
counselors to identify, understand, and respond to clients'
career goals or problems.

Chapter Two presents brief descriptions of selected
career theories that explain the nature, structure, and process
of career development. We have chosen these theories because
they offer a variety of constructs that facilitate our understanding of client behavior. These theories are (1) trait-and-
factor theory; (2) Holland's theory of vocational personalities
and work environments; (3) socioeconomic systems theory;
(4) Super's life-span, life-space approach to career development; (5) Schlossberg's adult career development transitions
model; (6) decision-making theory; and (7) cognitive theory.
The presentation of each theory begins with a brief description of its basic tenets. Then we identify their implications
for clients, counselors, and the counseling process.

Trait-and-Factor Theory

Trait-and-factor theory describes individuals as having measurable traits (for example, interests and abilities). It also describes
occupations in terms of the amounts and types of individual
traits required. It further suggests that the traits individuals
have can be compared with the amounts required by occupations. The goal of this comparison process is to provide individuals with a basis for making occupational choices.

The professional contributions of Parsons (1909),
along with those of Paterson (Paterson and Darley, 1936) and
Williamson (1939, 1965), provided the early conceptual base
for trait-and-factor theory (Rounds and Tracey, 1990). Parsons (1909, p. 5) described the process of helping individuals
select an occupation and make the transition from school to
work—a process he called vocational guidance—as follows:
"In the wise choice of a vocation there are three broad factors: (1) a clear understanding of yourself, your aptitudes,
abilities, interests, ambitions, resources, limitations, and their
causes; (2) a knowledge of the requirements and conditions
of success, advantages and disadvantages, compensation,

opportunities, and prospects in different lines of work; (3) true reasoning on the relations of these two groups of facts."

Following is Parsons's outline (1909, pp. 45–46) of the process of vocational guidance:

I.   Personal Data. A careful statement, *on paper*, of the principal facts about the person, bringing out particularly every fact that has a bearing on the vocational problem.

II. Self-Analysis. A self-examination, *on paper*, done in private, under instructions of the counselor, developing specially every tendency and interest that should affect the choice of a life work.

III. The Person's Own Choice and Decision. In a great majority of cases this will show itself in a marked degree before the work under I and II is finished. It must always be borne in mind that the choice of a vocation should be made by each person for himself rather than by any one else for him. The counselor can only guide, correct, advise, assist the candidate in making his own final choice.

IV. Counselor's Analysis. On the basis of the information obtained under I and II, so far as possible the counselor should test III by making an analysis under each of the following heads, seeking in every line for significance in the line of the main quest:
  1. Heredity and circumstance
  2. Temperament and natural equipment
  3. Face and character
  4. Education and experience
  5. Dominant interests

V.   Outlook on the Vocational Field. One who would be a vocational counselor should familiarize himself in a high degree with industrial knowledge, and he will need some

knowledge, as we have indicated in Part III
of this book, that is not at present easily
obtained. Investigations to be undertaken at
once are:

1. Lists and classifications of industries
    and vocations
2. The conditions of success in the various
    vocations
3. General information about industries,
    up-to-date, the kind that is found in cur-
    rent magazines and papers rather than
    in books
4. Apprenticeship systems now in practice
5. Vocational schools and courses available
    in your city and state
6. Employment agencies and opportunities

VI. Induction and Advice. This calls for clear
thinking, logical reasoning, a careful, pains-
taking weighing of all the evidence, a broad-
minded attitude toward the whole problem,
tact, sympathy, wisdom.

VII. General Helpfulness in Fitting into the Chosen Work.

The emergence of the psychometric movement in the
early 1900s, with its emphasis on the measurement of individual differences as well as on the identification of the traits
individuals possess required for successful job performance,
helped to enlarge Parsons's ideas and those of the other early
pioneers of vocational guidance. During the first few decades
of the century, researchers developed tests of abilities and aptitudes and inventories of interests, and these were increasingly
utilized in the counseling process. Specialists also paid more
and more attention to improving occupational information.
In the 1920s and 1930s, the National Vocational Guidance
Association (now the National Career Development Association) worked to improve occupational information by establishing standards for its development and use.

The impact of these developments can be seen in Williamson's (1939) conceptualization of counseling in which he divided the process into six steps. "These steps are analysis, synthesis, diagnosis, prognosis, counseling (treatment), and follow-up" (p. 57). The analysis step involved collecting data from many sources to obtain an understanding of the person. Synthesis referred to the collecting and summarizing of data to highlight the person's uniqueness and individuality. Diagnosis described the process of drawing conclusions concerning the characteristics and causes of the concerns exhibited by the person. Prognosis, the next step, referred to judging the probable consequences of the person's problem, the probabilities for adjustment. As Williamson pointed out, "Prognosis is a statement of the implications of the diagnosis" (p. 57). The next-to-the-last step, counseling, focused on the steps taken by the person and the counselor to reach adjustment or readjustment. Finally, follow-up included assisting people with new problems and with recurrences of the original problem and evaluating the effectiveness of counseling.

The similarities between Parsons's and Williamson's outlines are obvious. At the same time, however, there are some important differences. These changes reveal the evolution of trait-and-factor theory over a period of several decades.

New Approaches

As theorists were elaborating on the trait-and-factor foundation established by Parsons and Williamson, other approaches to counseling in general were emerging. In particular, the client-centered approach (sometimes called the *nondirective approach*) of Carl Rogers was becoming popular in the 1950s and 1960s. This innovation, coupled with what several writers viewed as the rigidity of trait-and-factor theory and with what they saw as an overemphasis on matching people and jobs, led them to suggest that trait-and-factor theory, as a basis for counseling for career development, was no longer viable (Brown, 1990).

To understand this criticism, let us look at some basic assumptions underlying trait-and-factor theory. Frederickson (1982, p. 18) presented four such assumptions:

- Each individual has a unique pattern of traits that can be accurately and reliably measured.
- Each occupation has a unique pattern of measurable trait requirements that are necessary in order to perform that occupation successfully in a number of settings.
- It is possible to match the individual traits with the job traits.
- The closer the match between individual traits and job requirement traits, the more productivity and satisfaction the person will have in that particular occupation.

Taken literally, these assumptions could (and perhaps did, in some instances) lead to a rigid interpretation of counseling for career development as matching people to jobs at specific times in their lives. Today, however, these assumptions are understood in looser terms. People and occupations are seen as more heterogeneous than a strict interpretation of these assumptions dictates. As Brown (1990, p. 20) pointed out, "No theory or approach yet developed has satisfactorily replaced trait-oriented thinking, whether the concern is work adjustment, career counseling, or personnel selection."

As a result of new understandings about human growth and development and the development of new counseling techniques and instruments (Kapes and Mastie, 1988), trait-and-factor theory, as it is understood today, continues to undergird counseling for career development. It has also been incorporated in varying degrees in many other approaches to counseling for career development. This is evident, for example, in Crites's (1981) synthesis of different counseling approaches, including the trait-and-factor approach, in a comprehensive model for career counseling. It also is evident in Super's (1990) developmental model for career assessment and counseling.

Rounds and Tracey (1990, p. 3) felt that as a result of the evolution of trait-and-factor theory from the turn of the century until today, it is time to reframe this approach as person-environment fit thinking. They put it this way: "It is our contention that the label *trait-and-factor theory* when applied to career counseling is best thought of as a problem-solving approach that emphasizes diagnosis, assessment, and actuarial methods guided by one or more person-environment fit models of occupational choice and work adjustment."

Implications for Practice

Trait-and-factor theory has a number of implications for counselors. First, because clients possess measurable traits that can be related to occupational choice, counselors should help them understand themselves: their interests, aptitudes, values, and skills. Second, because occupations can be described in terms of tasks, counselors also need to become familiar with occupational tasks and help clients become familiar with them so that they are aware of the features of different occupations. It is important to help clients learn about external and internal labor markets and the mix of occupations and industries that constitute different types of labor markets— local, state, regional, nation, and international. Third, because learning how to gather, understand, and apply information about self and the work world is an important skill and is basic to making informed and considered decisions, counselors should help clients learn these skills.

Holland's Theory of Vocational Personalities and Work Environments

Holland's theory of vocational personalities and work environments is based on seven assumptions (Holland, 1985b, pp. 3–5) that describe various vocational personalities and work environments and how they interact. These assumptions are as follows:

1. Most people can be categorized as one of six types: realistic, investigative, artistic, social, enterprising, or conventional.
2. There are six kinds of environments: realistic, investigative, artistic, social, enterprising, and conventional.
3. People search for environments that will let them exercise their skills and abilities, express their attitudes and values, and take on agreeable problems and roles.
4. A person's behavior is determined by an interaction between his or her personality and the characteristics of the environment.
5. The degree of congruence between a person and an occupation (environment) can be estimated by a hexagonal model.
6. The degree of consistency within a person or an environment is also defined by using the hexagonal model.
7. The degree of differentiation of a person or an environment modifies predictions made from a person's SDS [Self-Directed Search] profile, from an occupational code, or from their interaction.

Personality Types

As stated in assumption 1, Holland assumes that people can be categorized by personality type. While no individual is all one type, people tend to affiliate with, enjoy being around, and be most like one, two, or sometimes three of the types. People are categorized by the first, second, and third types that they are most like. The six personality types are described in the following paragraphs.

Realistic Personality. Typically, these are individuals who prefer to deal more with things than with ideas or people, are more oriented toward the present than toward the past or future, and have structured patterns of thought. They perceive themselves as having mechanical and athletic ability. They are apt to value concrete things or tangible personal characteristics like money, power, and status; they will try to avoid goals, values, and tasks that require subjectivity, intellectualism, or social skills. They tend to be more conventional in attitudes and values because the conventional has been tested and is reliable. They possess the qualities of persistence, maturity, and simplicity. Realistic types are found in occupations related to engineering, skilled trades, agriculture, and technical fields.

Investigative Personality. These persons are analytical and abstract and cope with life and its problems through the use of intelligence. They perceive themselves as scholarly, intellectually self-confident, and often as having mathematical and scientific ability. They hold less conventional attitudes and values, tend to avoid interpersonal relationships with groups or new individuals, and achieve primarily in academic and scientific areas. They are likely to possess a high degree of originality as well as strong verbal and mathematical skills. Investigative types are often found in occupations related to science, mathematics, and other technical careers.

Artistic Personality. This type tends to rely more on feelings and the imagination. They perceive themselves as expressive, intuitive, introspective, original, nonconforming, independent, and as having artistic and musical ability. They value aesthetic qualities and tend to place less emphasis on political or material matters. They have artistic rather than mathematical aptitude, avoid direct relationships, and learn to relate by indirect means through their medium. Artistic types are found in occupations related to music, literature, the dramatic arts, and other creative fields.

Social Personality. These are people who have a strong interest in other people and are sensitive to the needs of others. They perceive themselves as liking to help others, understanding others, having teaching ability, and lacking mechanical and scientific aptitude. They emphasize social activities, social problems, and interpersonal relationships. They use their verbal and social skills to change other people's behavior. They usually are cheerful and impulsive, scholarly, and verbally oriented. Social types are found in occupations related to teaching, social welfare positions, and the helping vocations.

Enterprising Personality. People who are adventurous, dominant, and persuasive conform to this personality type. They attach great value to political and economic matters and are drawn to power and leadership roles. They perceive themselves as aggressive, popular, self-confident, social, possessing leadership and speaking abilities, and lacking scientific ability. They use their social and verbal skills to achieve their political or economic goals. Enterprising types are found in occupations related to sales, supervision of others, and leadership vocations.

Conventional Personality. This type tends to be practical, neat, and organized, and to work well in structured situations. They feel most comfortable with precise language and situations where accurate accounting is valued. They perceive themselves as conforming and orderly, and as having clerical and numerical ability. They value business and economic achievement, material possessions, and status. They are happy as and make good subordinates, and they identify with people who are strong leaders. Conventional types are found in occupations related to the accounting, business, computational, secretarial, and clerical vocations.

Environments

According to Holland's second assumption, environments can be classified according to their demands and in terms of the types of people who work in them. Thus, the characteristics of the environments closely resemble the traits of the people dominating each environment. The following descriptions provide brief summaries of the six environments.

Realistic Environment. As the term suggests, the realistic environment is largely dominated by realistic personalities. These personalities are involved in technical and mechanical fields where there are demands and opportunities to use objects, tools, and machines. This environment stimulates people to perform realistic activities; encourages technical competencies and achievements; encourages people to see themselves as having mechanical ability; and rewards them for displaying conventional values and goals: an emphasis on money, possessions, and power.

Investigative Environment. The investigative environment is largely dominated by investigative personalities. These personalities are involved in the observation and creative investigation of physical, biological, and cultural phenomena. This environment stimulates people to perform investigative activities, encourages scholarly and scientific competencies and achievements, and encourages people to see themselves as scholarly or scientific.

Artistic Environment. The artistic environment is of course dominated by artistic personalities. These personalities are involved in unstructured, free, and creative acts producing art forms and products. This artistic atmosphere stimulates people to engage in artistic activities, encourages artistic competencies and achievements, encourages people to see themselves as expressive, original, intuitive, nonconforming, independent, and artistic, and rewards them for displaying artistic values.

Social Environment. As the term implies, the social environment is largely dominated by social personalities. These personalities are involved in social activities to inform, train, and improve the lot of others. This environment stimulates people to engage in social activities; encourages social competencies; encourages people to see themselves as liking to help others, understanding others, and being cooperative and social; and rewards people for displaying social values.

Enterprising Environment. As we would expect, the enterprising environment is mostly dominated by enterprising personalities. These personalities are involved in the manipulation of others to achieve organization or personal goals. This environment stimulates people to engage in enterprising activities, such as leadership or sales activities; encourages enterprising competencies and achievements; encourages people to see themselves as aggressive, popular, self-confident, and social, and as possessing leadership and speaking abilities; and rewards people displaying enterprising values and goals: those of money, power, and status.

Conventional Environment. The conventional environment is naturally dominated by conventional personalities. These personalities are involved in conventional activities such as keeping data ordered, keeping records, filing and reproducing materials, and operating business and data processing machines. This environment stimulates people to engage in conventional activities such as recording and organizing data or records; encourages conventional competencies and achievements; encourages people to see themselves as conforming and orderly and as having clerical competencies; and rewards people for displaying conventional values: an emphasis on money, dependability, and conformity.

Individual Behavior

According to Holland's third assumption, people search for work environments that will allow them to utilize their skills, express their attitudes and values, and take on suitable roles. Individuals also seek out others similar to themselves, and where similar people congregate, they create environments that reflect their personality types. Behavior is determined by the interaction between personality characteristics and the characteristics of the work environment (assumption 4).

Personality-Environment Interrelationships: The Hexagon

The last three assumptions in Holland's theory focus on person-environment interrelationships. To explain these assumptions, Holland (1985a) used the hexagon shown in Figure 2.1.

Congruence. Different types require different environments. For instance, realistic types flourish in realistic environments because such an environment provides the opportunities and rewards a realistic type needs. Incongruence occurs when a type lives in an environment that provides opportunities and rewards foreign to the person's preferences and abilities—for instance, a realistic type in a social environment (Holland, 1985a, p. 5).

Figure 2.1. A Hexagonal Model for Defining the Psychological Resemblances Among Types and Environments and Their Interactions.

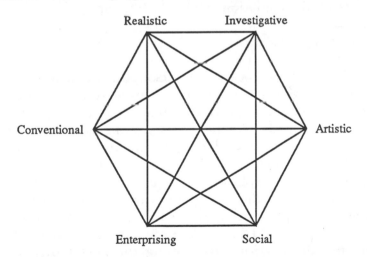

Source: From John L. Holland, *Making Vocational Choices: A Theory of Vocational Personalities & Work Environments,* Second Edition, p. 29. Copyright © 1985 by Allyn & Bacon. Reprinted with permission.

Consistency. In a person or an environment, some pairs of types are more closely related than others. For example, realistic and investigative types have more in common than conventional and artistic types do. Consistency is the degree of relatedness between personality types or between environmental models. Degrees of consistency or relatedness are assumed to affect vocational preference. For instance, a person who resembles the realistic type most strongly and next most closely resembles the investigative type (a realistic-investigative person) should be more predictable than a realistic-social person (Holland, 1985a, pp. 4–5).

Differentiation. Some persons or environments are more clearly defined than others. For example, a person may closely resemble a single type and show little resemblance to other types, or an environment may be dominated largely by a single type. In contrast, a person who resembles many types or an environment that is characterized by about equal numbers of the six types is undifferentiated or poorly defined. The degree to which a person or an environment is well defined is its degree of differentiation (Holland, 1985a, p. 5).

Implications for Practice

Holland's theory of vocational personalities and work environments suggests a number of implications for counselors. First, because career information is an important tool in counseling, Holland's codes are an excellent vehicle for career exploration and decision making. Second, because client knowledge of Holland's classification system is helpful in career exploration and decision making, counselors should teach the system to clients so they can rely on it as they explore occupations and use career information. Third, because Holland's hexagon is a useful way to understand the relationships among the personality and environment types, counselors can use the concepts of congruence and consistency to help clients analyze their career behavior.

Socioeconomic Systems Theory

Herr and Cramer (1988, p. 115) emphasized that "the social structure represents the context in which each person negotiates his or her identity, belief systems, and life course. The environments, the situational circumstances, in which people develop as human beings and as workers are significant influences in shaping the possibilities for choice, the knowledge available to people about their opportunities, and the reinforcement of specific career-related behaviors." This approach reflects the belief that socioeconomic factors have a major impact on career development.

The Role of Socioeconomic Variables

Theorists who focus on socioeconomic variables in career development deal with the processes by which occupations are passed on from generation to generation, the impact of environmental factors on options and decisions, the influence of the economy, and the meaning of work in our society. Theorists in this group assume that one's socioeconomic background has a great deal to do with the occupational choices one considers and makes. Influences on occupational choices include such variables as occupation and income of parents, education of parents, gender, race, ethnic group, religion, place and type of residence, family stability, size of family, birth order, values of peers, school environment, and community (Hotchkiss and Borow, 1990). Along with the variables of gender, race, and socioeconomic background, recent literature identifies as being important in occupational choices such economic factors as labor supply, labor demand, public knowledge of various opportunities and future job opportunity trends, one's ability to secure the necessary training and education as determined by individual resources as well as number of openings available for such experiences, and relative monetary return for services rendered.

Related to the question about the kind of influences that have an impact on career development is the question of how these influences do or do not shape career choices. Some researchers and writers tend to emphasize the role chance plays in this process. Two occupational sociologists, Miller and Form (1951, p. 660), analyzed the occupational backgrounds of a large group of people and came to the conclusion that "chance experiences undoubtedly explain the process by which most occupational choices are made." Osipow (1969, p. 15) commented on the role of chance: "The view may be summarized in a single sentence. People follow the course of least resistance in their educational and vocational lives. It may be a moot point as to whether the least resistance theory is more valid than one of the more self-conscious views of career development. The fact remains that in many cases people do react to their environments and follow those avenues educationally and vocationally which they perceive to be open to them with a minimum of difficulty."

The chance or least-resistance approach has some interesting implications for career development. The theory assumes that individuals have a tendency to pursue alternatives that they are already familiar with and that they think will be easy for them. People are likely to delay making decisions and then grasp opportunities that arise without considering how they fit into a career plan. In other words, this approach ascribes a major role to factors that are not within the control of the individual and occur accidentally but that have a major effect on one's career development.

Implications for Practice

Some implications arising from socioeconomic systems theory include the following. First, because clients' environments have an impact on the occupational options open or at least perceived to be open to them, counselors should provide opportunities to broaden their horizons through structured career exploration groups and career and labor market information. It is important to expose clients to alternatives and give them the skills to relate those alternatives to the career exploration and choice process. Second, because clients' cultural backgrounds, experiences, and values have an impact on the meaning they may attach to work, it is desirable to use these backgrounds, experiences, and values as a springboard for discussion. Third, because some clients may follow the path of least resistance, or the path with which they are already familiar in their career exploration, counselors should help them to appreciate career exploration as a quest rather than a track to follow routinely. Fourth, because labor markets change, counselors need to assist clients in developing adaptive skills to deal with shifting occupational demands and economic conditions.

Super's Life-Span, Life-Space Approach to Career Development

Super (1990, p. 199) described his theory as "a 'segmental theory'. . . . a loosely unified set of theories dealing with specific aspects of career development, taken from developmental, differential, social, personality, and phenomenological psychology and held together by self-concept and learning theory." His segmental model is illustrated in Figure 2.2. On the left is the person and on the right is society. The arch represents a career. The factors identified on each column are dynamic in that they interact with each other. In a similar manner, the totality of factors represented in the columns also interact.

The Fourteen Propositions

In the early 1950s, together with a number of colleagues, Super began to formulate the propositions that undergird his theory. He published a set of ten propositions concerning the nature of career development in 1953. There are now fourteen propositions. These fourteen propositions are presented here as modified and updated by Super in 1990 (pp. 206–208).

1. People differ in their abilities and personalities, needs, values, interests, traits, and self-concepts.

Figure 2.2. A Segmental Model of Career Development.

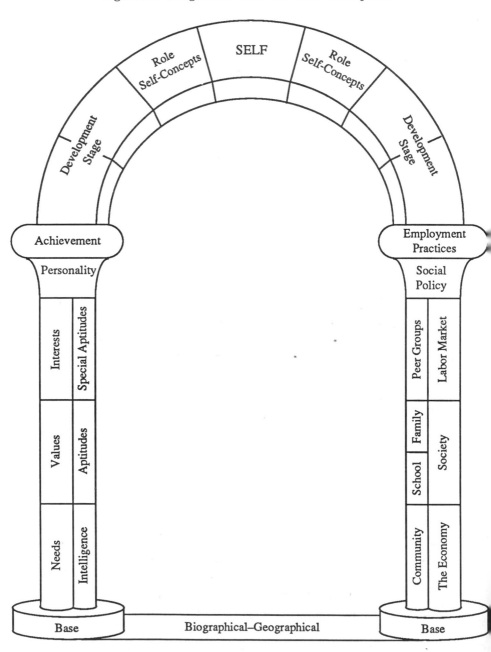

Source: Super, 1990, p. 200. Reprinted with permission.

2. People are qualified, by virtue of these characteristics, each for a number of occupations.

3. Each of these occupations requires a characteristics pattern of abilities and personality traits, with tolerances wide enough to allow both some variety of occupations for each individual and some variety of individuals in each occupation.

4. Vocational preferences and competencies, the situations in which people live and work, and, hence, their self-concepts change with time and experience, although self-concepts, as products of social learning, are increasingly stable from late adolescence until late maturity, providing some continuity in choice and adjustment.

5. This process of change may be summed up in a series of life stages (a "maxicycle") characterized as a sequence of growth, exploration, establishment, maintenance, and decline, and these stages may in turn be subdivided into (a) the fantasy, tentative, and realistic phases of the exploratory stage and (b) the trial and stable phases of the establishment stage. A small (mini) cycle takes place in transitions from one stage to the next or each time an individual is destabilized by a reduction in force, changes in type of manpower needs, illness or injury, or other socioeconomic or personal events. Such unstable or multiple-trial careers involve new growth, reexploration, and reestablishment (recycling).

6. The nature of the career pattern—that is, the occupational level attained and the sequence, frequency, and duration of trial and stable jobs—is determined by the indi-

vidual's parental socioeconomic level, mental ability, education, skills, personality characteristics (needs, values, interests, traits, and self-concepts), and career maturity and by the opportunities to which he or she is exposed.

7. Success in coping with the demands of the environment and of the organism in that context at any given life-career stage depends on the readiness of the individual to cope with these demands (that is, on his or her career maturity). *Career maturity* is a constellation of physical, psychological, and social characteristics; psychologically, it is both cognitive and affective. It includes the degree of success in coping with the demands of earlier stages and substages of career development, and especially with the most recent.

8. Career maturity is a hypothetical construct. Its operational definition is perhaps as difficult to formulate as is that of intelligence, but its history is much briefer and its achievements even less definitive. Contrary to the impressions created by some writers, it does not increase monotonically, and it is not a unitary trait.

9. Development through the life stages can be guided, partly by facilitating the maturing of abilities and interests and partly by aiding in reality testing and in the development of self-concepts.

10. The process of career development is essentially that of developing and implementing occupational self-concepts. It is a synthesizing and compromising process in which the self-concept is a product of the interaction of inherited aptitudes, physical makeup,

opportunity to observe and play various roles, and evaluations of the extent to which the results of role playing meet with the approval of superiors and fellows (interactive learning).

11. The process of synthesis of or compromise between individual and social factors, between self-concepts and reality, is one of role playing and of learning from feedback, whether the role is played in fantasy, in the counseling interview, or in such real-life activities as classes, clubs, part-time work, and entry jobs.

12. Work satisfactions and life satisfactions depend on the extent to which the individual finds adequate outlets for abilities, needs, values, interests, personality traits, and self-concepts. They depend on establishment in a type of work, a work situation, and a way of life in which one can play the kind of role that growth and exploratory experiences have led one to consider congenial and appropriate.

13. The degree of satisfaction people attain from work is proportional to the degree to which they have been able to implement self-concepts.

14. Work and occupation provide a focus for personality organization for most men and women, although for some persons this focus is peripheral, incidental, or even non-existent. Then other foci, such as leisure activities and homemaking, may be central. (Social traditions, such as sex-role stereotyping and modeling, racial and ethnic biases, and the opportunity structure, as well as individual differences, are important determinants of preferences for such

roles as worker, student, leisurite, homemaker, and citizen.)

In 1951, a major research program called the Career
Pattern Study (CPS) was undertaken in Middletown, New
York, to test some of the hypotheses of Super and his colleagues. The CPS began following the lives of 138 eighth-
grade boys and 142 ninth-grade boys. Super and his colleagues
theorized that the movement of individuals through life stages
was a typical process that could be loosely tracked according
to an age-referenced time line. (See proposition 5.) The subjects were followed up briefly at age twenty-one, more inten-
sively at age twenty-five, and then again at about age thirty-
six. The findings from the CPS have been made available
periodically in a series of monographs (Jordaan and Heyde,
1979; Super and Overstreet, 1960), in an article by Super
(1985), and in a recent dissertation (Fisher, 1989).

An important concept in Super's formulation of career
development is that of career maturity. While there are differences of opinion about the definition of *career maturity*, there
is general agreement that this term denotes a readiness to
engage in the developmental tasks appropriate to the age and
level at which one finds oneself. Maturity, however, is not
something that is ever reached, but instead is the goal relative
to where one is at any given time. This formulation of the
concept helps to promote a life-span notion rather than a
static, irreversible pattern of career development. In 1983,
Super refined his notion of career maturity. He suggested that
the term for adults should be *career adaptability*. Included in
his formulation of career maturity (adaptability) are the constructs of planfulness (including autonomy, self-esteem, and
reliance on a time perspective), exploration, information, decision making, and reality orientation.

One way to view Super's life-span, life-space model is
to use his life-career rainbow. (See Figure 2.3.) Note how the
life roles fluctuate, depending on age and other circumstances
across the life span.

Figure 2.3. The Life-Career Rainbow: Six Life Roles in Schematic Life Space.

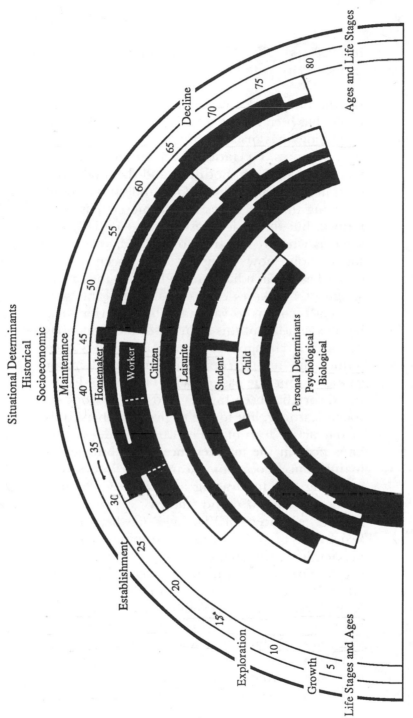

Situational Determinants
Historical
Socioeconomic

Maintenance
Decline

Homemaker
Worker
Citizen
Leisurite
Student
Child

Personal Determinants
Psychological
Biological

Establishment

Exploration
Growth

Life Stages and Ages

Ages and Life Stages

Source: Super, 1990, p. 212. Reprinted with permission.

In 1990 (pp. 236–237), Super summarized the current status of his theory as follows:

> During the past decades, this career development model has been refined and extended. Differential psychology has made technical, but not substantive, advances. Operational definitions of career maturity have been modified, and the model has been modified with them. Our understanding of recycling through stages in a minicycle has been refined, but the basic construct is essentially the same as when it was first formulated, years ago. Ideas about how to assess self-concepts have evolved as research has thrown light on their measurement, and knowledge of how applicable self-concept theory is to various subpopulations has been extended, but this segment of the model has not greatly changed. Life-stage theory has been refined but mostly confirmed by several major studies during the past decade. The role of learning theory has been highlighted by the work on social learning, but to the neglect of other kinds of interactive learning. The career model is perhaps now in the maintenance stage, but health maintenance does not mean stasis but rather updating and innovating as midcareer changes are better recognized and studied.
>
> The concept of life stages has been modified in recent years, from envisioning mainly a maxicycle to involving minicycles of growth, exploration, establishment, maintenance, and decline, linked in a series within the maxicycle. Reexploration and reestablishment have thus attracted a great deal of attention, and the term *transition* has come to denote these processes. . . . Important, too, is the greater emphasis on the fact that the typical impetus for any specific transition is not necessarily age itself, for the timing

of transitions (stage) is a function of the individual's personality and abilities, as well as of his or
her situation.

Implications for Practice

Here are some obvious implications of Super's theory of
career development. First, because one's life career includes
more than an occupation—it includes other life roles as
well—counseling for career development should not be
restricted to occupational choice only. Second, because occupational decisions are similar to other life decisions and continue to be made throughout the life span, counseling for
career development should focus on decision making over the
life span. Third, because career development can be described
as a stage process with developmental tasks at each stage and
since the nature of these stages is not linear but cyclical—
meaning that individuals in middle or later life may return to
earlier stages of development—counselors need to help clients
understand that they are not venturing outside of normalcy
when they do. Fourth, because people who are at different
stages of development may need to be counseled in different
ways, and since people at similar stages but with different levels
of career maturity also need to be counseled in different ways,
it is important to learn how to use life stages and tasks to make
diagnoses and select appropriate intervention strategies.

Schlossberg's Adult Career Development Transitions Model

In a review of adult development theories, Schlossberg (1984)
grouped them into three broad categories, which focused
on age and life stage, life event and transition, and individual timing and variability, respectively. All of the theories
grouped in these categories, she pointed out, said something
about transitions. As a result, Schlossberg (1984, p. 42) stated
that "we need a framework for examining what we know
about adults in transition, and then we need to connect this
framework to what we know about helping roles so that we

can best help adults in transition explore, understand, and cope." For her, a transition is not so much a matter of the actual change as it is a matter of the individual's perception of change. Adult lives are marked by the continuous adaptation to transitions that result from the general absence of change or new life events, the failure of an expected event or change to occur, or the mitigation of events or circumstances formerly considered stressful.

Schlossberg's transitions model has three parts. The first part describes transitions in terms of type, context, and impact. The second part describes the transition process. The third part identifies the coping resources available, including the variables that characterize transitions, the individuals involved in transitions, and the environment.

The Transition

To appreciate what transitions mean to clients, Schlossberg (1984) stressed that it is necessary to understand what type they are. She pointed out that "it is not the transition itself that determines its meaning for the individual; rather it is whether the transition is expected, unexpected, never occurring, or chronic" (p. 54). An expected or anticipated transition has somewhat predictable consequences because it is under the control of clients. Examples may include marriage, first job, and retirement. Unexpected or unanticipated transitions are not under clients' control and hence they may not be predictable. Examples include divorce, premature death, and illness. Finally, there is the transition that was counted on but never occurred, such as a marriage that was planned but did not take place, the expected promotion that was denied, and a planned-for family made impossible by illness.

Schlossberg (1984) also pointed out that it is important to understand the context of the transition and the relationship of clients to their transitions. In addition, the nature of the settings in which transitions take place needs to be understood and appreciated. Finally, to understand transitions, it is necessary to be aware of the impact they have on clients' relationships with others, on their routines, on the assumptions they make about themselves and others, and on the life roles in which they are involved. Clients involved in one transition often are involved in other transitions as well. As Schlossberg (1984, p. 55) stated, for some clients "it never rains but it pours."

The Transition Process

Transitions can be viewed "as a process of continuing and changing reactions over time—for better or for worse—which are linked to the individual's continuous and changing appraisal of self-in-situation" (Schlossberg, 1984, p. 56). While in transition, clients pass through a series of identifiable phases. At first transitions are pervasive. There is often total preoccupation with the transitions and complete disruption in clients' lives. There is disbelief ("This can't be happening"), then a sense of betrayal ("I worked for this organization for thirty years"), confusion ("What do I do now?"), anger ("I'll sue somebody!"), and finally, after a period of time, resolution ("I have many skills and I can get another job!").

It is tempting to oversimplify these phases and what is involved in them. Schlossberg stressed that transitions often contain many complex dynamics and that their satisfactory resolution depends on the characteristics of the clients and the nature of the contexts in which the transitions take place. Sometimes, for some clients, transitions end in deterioration. There is no satisfactory resolution.

How do counselors assess where clients are in the transition process? Schlossberg advised starting with clients' perceptions, because some clients view where they are in transitions differently from other clients who are involved in the same transitions. Another means of appraisal is to assess how preoccupied clients are with their transitions. Schlossberg (1984, p. 56) suggested that the continuum counselors are assessing begins with "pervasiveness," (transitions completely permeate clients' attitudes and behaviors) and ends with "boundedness" (transitions are contained and integrated into clients' self-concepts). Finally, measures of life satisfaction can be used to assess where clients are in their transitions, the assumption being that clients will express more satisfaction with their lives as they move toward transition resolution.

Coping Resources

The last dimension of Schlossberg's transition model emphasizes the coping resources clients have available. How can counselors help clients assess and balance their assets and liabilities? To accomplish this task it is necessary to understand the variables characterizing the transition, those characterizing the client, and those characterizing the environment.

Variables Characterizing the Transition. What are the variables characterizing the transition that counselors need to understand? Some of these variables are: the trigger (what triggered the transition?), timing (does the transition relate to the social clock?), the source (where does control lie?), role change (does the transition involve role change?), duration (permanent or temporary?), previous experience with similar transitions, and concurrent stress.

Variables Characterizing the Client. To understand the coping resources clients have available, it also is necessary to identify their personal situation, psychological resources, and coping responses. Personal and demographic variables that need to be considered include socioeconomic status, gender role, age and stage of life, and state of health. Psychological resources encompass variables related to ego development, personality, outlook, and commitment and values. Coping responses can be subdivided into functions (controlling the situation, its meaning, and the associated stress) and strategies (information seeking, direct action, and the inhibition of action).

Variables Characterizing the Environment. The last category of variables that Schlossberg recommended be considered are those that focus on clients' environments. As counselors work with clients in transition, it is important to consider the social support they have (intimate relationships, family, friendship network, and institutions), functions of the support available to them (affect, affirmation, aid, and feedback), and their options—actual, perceived, used, and created.

Implications for Practice

Some implications of Schlossberg's transitions model for counseling practice are as follows. First, because more people are changing occupations at later stages of career development, counselors should be open to clients who want to change and should understand and empathize with the frustration, pain, and joy involved in the transition process. Second, because clients who are going through transitions are often experiencing anxiety and emotional upheaval, it is essential to provide a safe environment—a counseling relationship that focuses on the use of listening and responding skills and attending and focusing skills. Third, because clients involved in transitions often have difficulty reframing and refocusing their situations, counselors need to provide new perspectives to them through interpretation, theme identification, and the presentation of internal and external information. Fourth, because clients involved in transitions usually need assistance in moving on, it is important to help them develop problem-solving, decision-making, and coping skills. Fifth, because social support is a key to successfully coping with transitions, counselors should provide clients with skills that aid them in developing social support systems and networks.

Decision-Making Theory

Decision-making theory suggests that although career development is a continuous process, there are critical decision points that occur when people face the selection of an entry job, a change in jobs, or a change in educational plans. We will present two approaches to describing career decision making: the work of Tiedeman and O'Hara (1963), then the work of Gelatt (1989).

Tiedeman and O'Hara's Model

Tiedeman and O'Hara (1963) maintained that career identities are formed by decision-making processes that are subject to people's comprehension and control. Their decision-making model is an attempt to help individuals bring to conscious awareness all of the factors inherent in making decisions so that they will be able to make choices based on full knowledge of themselves and on appropriate external information. This model divides the process of decision making into two phases, anticipation and accommodation. The anticipation period consists of individuals' preoccupation with the steps and details from which decisions are fashioned. The accommodation period involves the change from deliberation and choice to the implementation and reality-based adjustments that occur between self and external reality, once a choice is made and put into practice (Dudley and Tiedeman, 1977). Each of these phases is divided into the following stages.

Anticipation Phase. In the *Exploration Stage* of the anticipation phase, clients explore possible educational, occupational, and personal alternatives. It is a time and an opportunity for people to imagine various alternatives in a supportive atmosphere, to identify their interests and capabilities, and to consider the possible relationships among their interests and capabilities and the alternatives they are exploring. To help clients with these tasks during this stage, counselors provide a supportive atmosphere. It also may be necessary for counselors to teach some clients how to explore. Finally, counselors provide career information to facilitate the career exploration process—to expand the alternatives clients are considering.

The *Crystallization Stage* is a time for people to begin the process of organizing, evaluating, synthesizing, and ordering self information and information gained from exploring possible career alternatives. Stabilization of thought begins to occur. Distinctions among explored alternatives emerge. Counselors assist clients with these tasks by showing them how to organize, evaluate, synthesize, and order the results of their self-analysis and their exploration of alternatives using the language of personality and occupational classification systems. By sharing these systems counselors provide clients with "hooks" on which to hang/organize self and environmental information. Counselors also assist clients during this stage by continuing to provide a supportive atmosphere so that free discussion of issues and options can take place.

Next is the *Choice Stage* in which clients make a choice based on the results of the crystallization process. The consequences of making a choice are considered. Counselors assist in this stage by continuing the supportive atmosphere and by providing feedback concerning choice consequences.

The last stage in this phase of decision making is the *Clarification Stage.* Here clients form and carry out a plan to implement their choice. During this stage, counselors provide information as well as continued support and feedback about choice implementation issues that may arise during the clarification process. Counselors serve as sounding boards for the implementation plans developed during this stage.

Accommodation Phase. The first stage in this phase of decision making is called the *Induction Stage.* During this stage, generally occurring during the first months as the choices clients have made are being implemented, clients come in contact with the reality of the settings in which the choices unfold. They look to people in these settings for cues as to the correctness of their behavior. As this occurs, they begin to learn about what is expected of them—what is required of them.

In the second stage of this phase, the *Reformation Stage,* clients have worked through the tasks of induction. They are no longer responsive; they are more assertive. Clients' identities and the identities of the people in the settings of choice become congruent.

Finally, during the last stage, or *Integration Stage*, of the decision process, clients experience an integration of their identities with those of the people in their settings of choice. Equilibrium is established. There is a synthesis of purpose.

During all three stages of the accommodation phase, counselors help clarify and interpret the experiences clients are having in light of theory and reality. Counselors continue to provide a supportive atmosphere. And, counselors continue to serve as sounding boards for new insights and ideas clients may have as a result of their experiences negotiating the three stages of accommodation.

Gelatt's Model

In 1962, Gelatt presented an approach to decision making that emphasized defining objectives clearly, analyzing information rationally, predicting consequences, and being consistent—in his words, this involved "a totally rational approach to making decisions" (Gelatt, 1989, p. 252). Since then, he has changed his mind. In sharp contrast to traditional, more systematically based, rational approaches to decision making, Gelatt has presented a view of decision making in which being flexible, keeping one's mind open, and using the intuitive, irrational side of decision making are emphasized. Heppner (1989) pointed out that Gelatt's new way of defining decision making is comparable to the broader idea of problem solving or coping, particularly as Heppner and Krauskopf (1987) conceptualized problem solving. According to Heppner (1989, p. 258), the key message of Gelatt's model of decision making is that decision making (problem solving) is "a highly complex, intermittent, rational, irrational, logical, and intuitive process."

Gelatt (1989, p. 253) now defines *decision making* as "the process of arranging and rearranging information into a course of action." He has also proposed a new decision strategy called *positive uncertainty* (p. 252). The three parts of decision making, according to Gelatt, include obtaining the information that forms the basis of the decision, arranging and rearranging this information, and making the choice.

Information. According to Gelatt, information rapidly becomes obsolete. What is true today may not be tomorrow. Also, more information equals more uncertainty. While more information is available today, it is often beyond an individual's ability to process it all. In addition, there is no innocent information. It is always changed by the fact it is sent and received by people. Gelatt captures this point by using the metaphor of the mind's eye: what is sent and received depends on what is in the mind's eye.

The Process of Arranging and Rearranging. "Know what you want and believe but do not be sure," Gelatt (1989, p. 254) urges. Decision making focuses on discovering goals as much as it does on achieving them. He says that the process of arranging and rearranging in the mind's eye consists of contemplating various alternatives. Reflection, imagination, and creativity are the new decision-making skills.

The Choice. The new decision-making framework mandates the use of both rational and intuitive thinking, flexibility, and reflection. As Gelatt (1989, p. 255) puts it, "Be rational, unless there is good reason not to be." Using the decision-making skills just mentioned means that it is not always necessary to be consistent. Positive uncertainty helps clients to change old habits and invent their own futures.

Implications for Practice

Some implications stemming from these career decision-making models are as follows. First, because decision making is related to personality and the development of values, an important objective is to provide experiences to people that contribute to their emotional maturity, self-concept, and values orientation. Second, because one of the first steps in decision making is gathering information, counselors should provide information resources to clients as well as the know-how to use them. Third, because people habitually employ different decision-making strategies, counselors should try to facilitate learners' discovery of what their strategies are and how they might be improved. Fourth, because decision making is a learned process, counselors need to teach clients the specific skills of decision making. Fifth, because making choices is the responsibility of the chooser, after giving clients the necessary tools, counselors should encourage them to make their own decisions.

Cognitive Theory

The application of theoretical constructs from cognitive psychology to career behavior and career development is relatively recent. Wolleat (1989, p. 98) pointed out that "cognitive psychology is . . . a piece of the emerging multidisciplinary paradigm provided by what is being called 'cognitive science,' the study of the biophysiological, linguistic, and psychological processes underlying human cognitive functioning." Theorists such as Bandura, Beck, and Meichenbaum laid much of the groundwork for the application of cognitive psychology to therapy. Others have modified and extended their work and applied cognitive theory to counseling for career development (Keller, Biggs, and Gysbers, 1982).

Three Basic Organizers

According to Rest (1974), cognitive theories are built around structural organization, developmental sequence, and interactionism.

Structural Organization. Information processing is of central importance in cognitive models. These models regard people as active interpreters of their environment. They hold that individuals selectively attend to certain stimuli, arrange these stimuli in some meaningful pattern, and develop principles to guide behavior and solve problems. The way people process information is determined by relatively fixed patterns called *cognitive schemas.* According to Neimeyer (1989, p. 85), "A schema is regarded as an organized framework of knowledge about a particular domain of experience or events." These schemas (thought processes) define how individuals view themselves, others, and the environment. The way people think will determine how they behave. Changes in individuals' cognitive schemas must take place before changes in behavior can occur.

Developmental Sequence. Individual development is seen as progressing through a fixed sequence of hierarchical stages. Each stage involves a different way of thinking. Greater cognitive differentiation and integration is required as people advance to higher levels. As they pass through different stages, their views of themselves and the world are expanded and become more complex. For instance, "individuals with higher levels of vocational differentiation and integration have been found to show higher levels of career decision making self-efficacy" (Neimeyer, 1989, p. 90).

Perry (1970) was one of the first to use a cognitive model to describe the stages a person goes through in the career development process. Knefelkamp and Slepitza (1976) revised and extended his model. Their revised model contains four categories and nine stages. The categories include dualism, multiplicity, relativism, and commitment within relativism and are described as follows:

Dualism is characterized by simplistic thinking and reliance on external factors to control decisions. Individuals lack the ability to analyze and synthesize information. Occupations are seen as being either right or wrong for them, with little understanding of the complexity that is actually involved.

Multiplicity occurs when individuals accept a decision-making process provided by a counselor. The locus of control is still outside individuals but they are beginning to analyze occupational factors in more detail. An awareness of the relationship between consideration of multiple factors and occupational decisions begins to develop.

Relativism occurs when the locus of control is shifted from an external reference point to an internal one. Individuals see themselves as being primarily responsible for the decision-making process and begin to use higher levels of processing to analyze occupations. Individuals are able to deal with the positive and negative aspects of many occupations and can see themselves in a variety of life roles, including the worker role.

Commitment within relativism occurs when individuals begin to realize that commitment to an occupation is not simply a narrowing of the old world, but also is an expansion into a new world. The self becomes more integrated with the environment. Career identity and self-identity become more closely related. Values, thoughts, and behaviors become more consistent with one another. Individuals can now deal with more challenges and changes.

Interactionism. In cognitive theory, development is seen as the result of an interaction between people and their environment. Individual maturity or readiness must be matched with environmental opportunity in order for growth to occur. Growth takes place when people are confronted with stimuli from the environment that their cognitive constructs cannot handle. This creates dissonance or disequilibrium. To reduce this tension, people must change their cognitive structures to accommodate greater complexity. Too much dissonance can be overwhelming, however, and can prevent growth.

The following is a list of five cognitive intervention strategies that have been found to be effective in counseling for career development.

1. *Guided career fantasy exploration.* Clients are asked to imagine a typical workday in different professions, what they would like to be doing at different periods in the future, what benefits they would enjoy in different jobs, and so forth.
2. *Rational emotive therapy.* This strategy is aimed at eliminating the irrational ideas that prevent people from thinking and acting productively. As they develop more rational belief systems about themselves and their envi-

ronment they become better able to make appropriate career decisions.

3. *Elimination of dysfunctional cognitive schemas.* Effort is directed toward identifying and eliminating the following: drawing conclusions where evidence is lacking, making decisions on the basis of a single incident, exaggerating the negative or ignoring the positive aspects of a career event, blaming oneself too much for negative occupational occurrences, and perceiving career events only in extreme terms.

4. *Self-instruction techniques.* Clients are taught to talk to themselves about the processes that promote goal attainment. This may include such things as identification of goals, potential steps necessary to achieve goals, potential problems blocking progress, alternate solutions, and self-praise for each step that is accomplished.

5. *Cognitive self-control.* Individuals are taught to promote career development by seeking relevant information, monitoring their own behavior, using self-reinforcement and self-punishment to develop appropriate behavior, and engaging in alternative activities that interfere with or eliminate undesired behavior.

Implications for Practice

Cognitive theory has many implications for counseling. Here are a few of them. First, because counseling strategies are based on clients' current abilities, identifying where they are in their developmental sequence is the first step in helping them advance to the next level. Second, because people cannot skip stages but must instead advance one step at a time, a counseling strategy that is aimed at a level beyond clients' next stage of development will be ineffective and may even be detrimental. If individuals do not have the cognitive complexity to understand and integrate the information that is presented, they will become frustrated and may become temporarily stalled at their current level. Counselors need to design strategies that will guide people through the developmental stages with as few disruptions as possible. Third, because the emphasis is on process and content, it is important to help clients think in increasingly complex ways about themselves and their environment. Counselors should interact with individuals at their level and then provide enough cognitive dissonance to stimulate the expansion of their thought processes. That is, they should help clients move from one stage to the next in a deliberate manner. This process is called *plus-one staging.* Support and challenge are used to stimulate growth, and support is used to prevent overloading and to stimulate self-confidence. Fourth, because the cognitive approach to career development is based on the broader cognitive theories of counseling and therapy, counselors should apply techniques to counseling that have proved useful in cognitive therapy (Keller, Biggs, and Gysbers, 1982).

One More Time: Why Study Theory?

Why study theory? What does theory have to do with practice? A number of writers, including Jepsen (1984), Savickas (1989), and Stark and Zytowski (1988) answered these questions by saying that theory provides counselors and clients with possible explanations for client behavior not available ordinarily. They also pointed out that theory provides counselors with ideas about possible intervention strategies to use, when to use them, and how to use them. The use of theory in practice, then, provides counselors and clients with direction and focus for the counseling for career development process, assisting clients to reach their goals or resolve their problems.

3

█████████████████████████████

Using Theory
to Counsel Clients

█████████████████████████████

Chapter Three builds on the two previous chapters by showing how the theoretical approaches outlined in those chapters can be applied to work with clients. More specifically, this chapter reveals how the theoretical constructs provide a framework for eliciting clients' thoughts and feelings as well as a lens through which these thoughts and feelings can be interpreted. We begin with a general discussion of the interaction between clients, the counseling process framework, and career theory. We then present the counseling process framework in more detail, showing the relevance of career theory to this framework.

Client-Framework-Theory Interaction

How do clients, the counseling process framework, and career theory interact? Keeping the graphic representation of this interaction as presented in Figure 3.1 in mind, let us look more closely at the variables involved.

Clients

Clients often become involved in counseling for career development because they are in some sort of transition, either by

Figure 3.1. The Interaction of Clients, the Counseling
Process Framework, and Career Theory

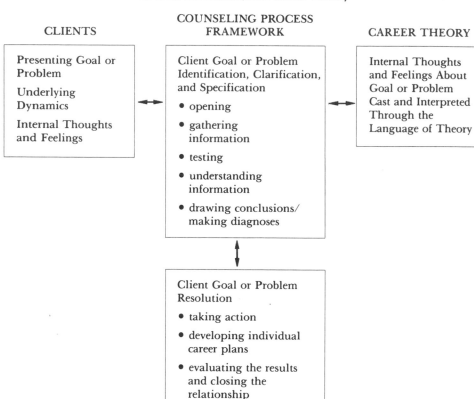

their own choice or because of conditions over which they have
only limited control or no control at all. Internal thoughts and
feelings concerning these transitions abound often without
shape or form. What should I do? Which direction should I go
in? How should I respond to and resolve my problem or achieve
my goal? These are the kinds of questions clients may be struggling with. Sometimes the questions—let alone any possible
answers—are not clearly formed in their minds.

The Counseling Process Framework

The counseling process framework consists of two major phases: client goal or problem identification, clarification, and specification and client goal or problem resolution. It provides a systematic way of eliciting clients' thoughts and feelings about their career goals and problems. It also provides a way of making explicit the life-career themes present in clients' responses while these themes may still be meaningless to them. A major goal "is to elicit inside information (from clients) so that it can be taught back to them or learned directly by them" (Field, 1966, p. 24). As counseling progresses, such a framework makes it possible to teach clients about the connections between these themes on the one hand and problem resolution or goal attainment on the other hand. As Field (1966, p. 9) emphasized, "The essential point is that persons who consciously recognize more of their behavioral patterns and emotional reactions possess greater freedom of choice; they can evaluate more alternatives and they can evaluate them more effectively." Carlsen (1988, p. 4) made the same point in describing a type of therapy titled *developmental meaning-making*. She stated that "clients who may never have explored themselves—and thus, never really known themselves—begin to understand the patterning and programs which have shaped their lives. Ordering and synthesizing this new information, they open their eyes to new possibilities and are often able to stand back with a new perspective on themselves. And, parallel to their cognitive understandings comes new awareness and recognition of the influence and meaning of their effective experience—not one without the other, but intertwining and developing in a dialectical synergy of life development."

Career Theory

Career theory helps us identify and interpret client behavior and information. Theory provides us with ways to give meaning to the internal thoughts and feelings of clients that often appear jumbled and confused, at least on the surface. These meanings can provide connections to practical strategies for assisting clients in pursuing career goals or resolving problems. For example, Holland's personality types and environments can be used to analyze clients' responses so that a direct connection with career information, arranged by Holland's codes, can be made. In listening to clients describe their thoughts and feelings, counselors may recognize Holland's social personality and environment categories. By casting clients' thoughts and feelings in Holland's language, counselors can provide them with a way to express their thoughts and feelings so they can directly link to career information organized by social personality and environment types.

While career theory helps us understand and respond to clients' problems and goals, it also provides us with insights into the possible outcomes of counseling for career development. Super (1990, p. 254) made this point as follows: "Career development theory makes clear what is to be fostered—occupational self-concept clarification and implementation and handling of the developmental tasks. It is growth in autonomy, time perspective, and self-esteem; exploration in breadth and then in depth for the crystallization, specification, and implementation of occupational self-concepts, interests, and a vocational preference; establishment with trial, stabilization, consolidation, and perhaps advancement; maintenance with adaptability, which means at least holding but better still keeping up, innovating, and in some cases transferring; and decline, or disengagement, and the shift of role emphases."

Using Career Theory in Combination with the Counseling Process Framework

With this brief review of the client-framework-theory interaction in mind, let us look more closely at the details of this interaction, paying particular attention to the use of career theory. The purpose of this section is to emphasize how the language of theory is used in counseling for career development.

The counseling process framework that was presented in Chapter One is repeated here because it is the structure used to elicit clients' career goals or problems and to help them achieve these goals or resolve their problems. The sections of the framework where career theory plays the strongest role are emphasized.

I. Client Goal or Problem Identification, Clarification, and Specification
  A. Opening
    1. Identify the goal or problem.
    2. Clarify the client-counselor relationship.
    3. Define the client-counselor responsibilities.
  B. Gathering Client Information
    1. Who is the client?
      a. How does the client view self, others, and his or her world?
      b. What language does the client use to represent these views?
      c. What themes does the client use to organize and direct his or her behavior?
      d. How does the client make sense out of and order in his or her world?
    2. What are the client's current status and environment like?
      a. How does the client view and make sense out of his or her life roles, settings, and events, past, present, and future?
      b. What personal and environmental barriers or constraints are operating?
      c. What decision (personal) styles are in place? Being used?
  C. Testing
  D. Understanding Client Information and Behavior
    1. Utilize the appropriate career behavior and development theories.

      2.   Make use of counseling theories.

      3.   Apply the relevant classification systems.

  E. Drawing Conclusions or Making Diagnoses

II. Client Goal or Problem Resolution

  A. Taking Action

      1.   Engage in the counseling process.

      2.   Do the appropriate testing.

      3.   Provide career information.

  B. Developing Individual Career Plans

  C. Evaluating the Results and Closing the Relationship

      1.   If the goal or problem is not resolved, recycle.

      2.   If the goal or problem is resolved, close the relationship.

Opening

Understanding the goals or problems clients want to work on begins with understanding the opening or presenting statements they make. Isaacson (1985, pp. 104–105) suggested that there are three types of presenting statements.

Type 1 Presenting Statement
(uncertain, indefinite)

1.   I saw a notice (on the bulletin board, in the newspaper) about counseling.
2.   Someone said I could take a test here.
3.   My (principal, teacher, friend) sent me for counseling.
4.   My spouse and I have split up.

Type 2 Presenting Statement
(suggests other problem may be present)

1.   My major doesn't seem right for me.
2.   I like _____ but I'm not doing well in it.
3.   I don't like the (school, major, job) I'm in.
4.   There seems to be no job in my field.
5.   I think I'm ready to make a change.

6. Every time they fire me they tell me to get some counseling.
7. I don't want to work, but it looks like I'll have to.
8. My job requires more (time, effort, travel, etc.) than I want to give.

Type 3 Presenting Statement
(probably needs career counseling)

1. I want to be sure I'm going into the right field.
2. I can't decide on a (college, major, job).
3. The only jobs I know are _____ and _____, but I (don't want either, like both) of them.
4. I want a job that involves (interest, activity, value, opportunity), what is there?
5. I don't want to be in the same rut as my (parents, sibling, friend).
6. My children are now in school so I'd like to do something outside of the home.

How do we respond to such presenting statements? There are many ways to do so, and most involve asking for more information. A typical counselor lead might be, "Can you tell me more about your concern?" As more information is forthcoming, the task is to understand what this information may mean in the context of who the clients are and what their environments are like.

Gathering Client Information

Gathering client self and environmental information is the next step in the process. It can be done in many ways, using a variety of perspectives. The Life-Career Assessment (LCA) (Gysbers and Moore, 1987) provides a useful perspective and structure to use to explore who clients are and what their current status and environments are like. The LCA offers a way of viewing clients' levels of functioning in their various life roles and also yields information about how they interact with their environment.

The LCA is based on the work of Adler (Dinkmeyer, Pew, and Dinkmeyer, 1979). Adler divided an individual's relation to the world into three life tasks: (1) work, (2) social relations, and (3) love (friendship). According to Adler, the three tasks cannot be dealt with separately, since they are intertwined. A change in one involves the others as well. Difficulty in one part of life implies comparable difficulties in the rest of life. Although it may appear otherwise, a person's life is usually quite integrated.

People tend to solve problems and attempt to obtain rewards or satisfaction in a similar manner in all three arenas. The phrase *life-career themes* is used by counselors and clients to describe these consistent ways of negotiating with the world. Themes are defined as the ways people express ideas, beliefs, attitudes, and values about themselves, others, and the world in general. There are many different themes by which people operate, and each individual will tend to use a number of themes. The themes people use can be considered to constitute a life-style. They are not always aware of their approach to life or the themes by which they operate, and they may not recognize the underlying consistencies that exist (Mosak, 1971). They may choose, rather, to dwell on specific, superficial feelings that serve to further obscure the way in which they are developing.

The LCA is presented below in outline form with brief descriptions of each section. There are four sections, which are titled *career assessment, typical day, strengths and obstacles,* and *summary.* By following this outline counselors can obtain several types of information. One type is relatively objective and factual regarding client work experiences and educational achievements. Another type involves estimates of the skills and competencies clients possess.

Career Assessment. The career assessment section of the interview is divided into three parts: (1) work experience, (2) education or training progress and concerns, and (3) leisure. Here is a bit more detail.

Work experience (part or full time, paid or unpaid)
  Last job
    Liked best about
    Disliked most about
  Supervision
    Liked best about
    Disliked most about
  Same procedure with another job

To assess clients' work experience, counselors should ask them to describe their last or current job. The jobs can be part or full time, paid or unpaid. Clients should be asked to describe the tasks performed and then to relate what they liked best and least about the jobs. As they discuss likes and dislikes, counselors can use the language of career theory to reframe clients' responses in a form suitable for career planning and exploration.

Education or training progress and concerns
  General appraisal
    Liked best about school/learning
    Disliked most about school/learning
  Subject preference
    Liked
    Disliked
  Teacher or instructor characteristics (for example, closeness, authority)
    Liked
    Disliked
  Classroom or training condition preferences
    Independent versus dependent only
    Contact with other students or trainees
    Learning mode
  Repeat for levels

To begin this section of the interview, counselors should ask clients for a general appraisal of their educational or training experiences. Usually themes begin to appear that can be translated into the language of career theory. Sometimes themes identified previously in the career assessment section of the LCA reappear. These themes should be repeated and clarified.

> Leisure
>> Social life (within leisure context)
>> Friends (within leisure context)
>> Weekends/weekdays, evenings

In this section of the career assessment, counselors should ask clients about their leisure time. It is important to note whether or not the leisure themes identified are consistent with their work and educational themes or are in contrast with them. This also is a good time to explore love and friendship relations. Exploring clients' social lives within the context of leisure is a relatively nonthreatening way of exploring this sometimes-sensitive area. Counselors should again be ready to interpret these themes with the aid of career theory language.

Typical Day. The purpose of the typical-day section of the LCA is to discover how clients organize and live their lives. Counselors can carry out this assessment by asking clients to describe a typical day in a step-by-step fashion. An understanding of the patterns that emerge can be very helpful, for it is these patterns that may cause problems in school, training, on the job, or at home. These patterns also provide rich data to interpret using the language of career theories.

Strengths and Obstacles. The strengths-and-obstacles section of the LCA consists of asking clients what they believe are their three main strengths and what they believe are the three main obstacles they may have to overcome.

Three Main Strengths
   Resources at own disposal
   What resources do for them
Three Main Obstacles
   Relate to strengths
   Relate to client themes

During the strength-and-obstacles section of the LCA, clients may not be able to respond to the request to list three strengths or three obstacles. In such cases, counselors should break the task down into smaller parts by asking clients to list just one strength or obstacle. After one has been discussed, they can ask for another. This approach takes the pressure off to come up with a quick list of things and allows time to add more details.

Counselors also may encounter clients who give short answers or answers that contain little information in response to the strengths-and-obstacles portion of the interview. For example, a client may give as a strength "I'm a good worker." This response does not reveal much information. To gain more information, the counselor can ask, "What does being a good worker mean to you?" or "What do you believe are the best things about the way you work?" Vague answers also may be encountered in other sections of the LCA. In describing a typical day a client may state "I get up, go to work, come home, eat, and go to bed." The counselor's response is to become more specific with such leads as "How do you wake up? Does an alarm clock wake you or does someone else get you up? How do you get breakfast?" and so on throughout the client's day.

Another situation that counselors should be ready to respond to is where a client cannot think of any strengths. One strategy is to simply move on to the obstacles section and then be especially sensitive to strengths that may be hidden. For example, a client who lists as an obstacle "I work too slow" may reveal on further probing, "I pay a lot of attention to detail and want to be sure everything is right." Another strategy is to recall and reflect on some of the themes expressed in other parts of the LCA. The counselor might say to the client, "When you were talking about your typical day, you explained that your schedule was different each day depending on the schedule of other people in your family. Yet you seem to be able to get done what you need to each day. It seems to me that you are very flexible and adaptable." Such statements may help clients discover strengths they can bring to a job, may result in higher self-esteem, and may stimulate clients to think of other strengths.

One final strategy that counselors should consider whenever clients seem unwilling to talk freely is to examine their counseling style. Although even the most skillful counselors encounter clients who do not open up to them, all counselors need to examine their use of human relationship skills when their interaction with clients seems to be unproductive. Are they using good attending and listening skills? Good perceiving skills? Are helpful response styles present?

Summary. The summary section is the last portion of the LCA. There are two primary purposes for conducting a summary. One purpose is to emphasize the information that has been gained during the interview. During the summary, it is not necessary to review every bit of information obtained, but prominent life themes, strengths, and obstacles should be repeated. It is helpful to ask clients to summarize what they have learned from the session. Having them take the lead in expressing what has been learned increases the impact of the information, thus increasing self-awareness. It also lets counselors know what clients have gained and, in some cases, missed. When clients have finished, counselors can add any points that seem to have been omitted. It is important that counselors and clients reach agreement about their life themes. This agreement is effective particularly when it can be reached using the clients' own words and meanings.

The second major purpose of the summary is to relate the information gained to goals that counselors and their clients may work toward during the taking-action phase that will enhance the clients' possible job choices, career exploration, or career planning. The life-career themes that have been revealed and given meaning through the language of career theory may suggest possible choices that require further exploration, may rule out certain other choices, and may suggest barriers that may need to be overcome. From the strengths and obstacles discovered on the part of clients, positive traits and skills may have been revealed that can be developed further. Then, too, weaknesses that need to be overcome also may be apparent, in which case counselors and clients can decide to establish goals and form plans of action to reach these goals.

Testing

Concurrent with or subsequent to the use of the LCA, other assessment procedures such as standardized tests of interests, work values, aptitudes, and career maturity may be used. The advantage of utilizing the LCA first is that it provides a basis for understanding clients' goals or problems as well as for making decisions about what types of standardized tests to rely on, if any. It also provides the opportunity to assess clients' maturity and readiness to benefit from the use of standardized tests. It does so by helping counselors understand the nature, amount, and quality of the information and knowledge clients have about themselves and their environment.

When the outline of the LCA is followed, counselors gain a sense of whether or not clients are well informed— that is, of how well they have integrated self- and environmental information. It will also become clear whether clients lack or are distorting such information. In addition, counselors find out about clients' decision skills and strategies. In effect, they gain a sense of people's career maturity through the use of the LCA. This helps remedy, at least in part, the criticism of a major assumption of the traditional matching model of career counseling. The assumption is that clients "who are assessed are all sufficiently mature vocationally to have mature and stable traits" (Super, 1983, p. 557).

The use of the LCA or a similar structured interview also helps respond to the problem of testing with older clients. Sinick (1984, pp. 550–551) pointed out that in working with older clients, greater reliance should be placed on work history and life history, interests and activities outside of work, and functional abilities: "Interviews can elicit most of this information and can surpass interest inventories, for example, in tapping duration, intensity, and underlying values. Longitudinal information is, in general, more useful with older persons than cross-sectional test data."

Understanding Client Information and Behavior

As clients' internal thoughts and feelings about their career goals and problems are being elicited through the use of the LCA and through standardized or nonstandardized testing, counselors' work of understanding this information is already underway. The LCA provides a way for the key counseling processes of listening, understanding, and interpreting to unfold in counseling for career development. This is important, because whatever techniques counselors use in client goal or problem identification, clarification, and specification, the ability to systematically gather, understand, and interpret the information clients share and the behavior they exhibit is basic to the entire process. Listening skills are important, but more is involved. Listening must be done with understanding so that the information clients present and the behavior they exhibit during client goal or problem identification, clarification, and specification can be analyzed and interpreted.

How is understanding achieved? It is achieved through the use of theories that describe human behavior, growth, and development. Such theories provide language to help explain the behavior exhibited by clients. As stated previously, these theories become the lenses through which client behavior is examined to help form hypotheses about the meanings of that behavior. In short, career theory helps counselors to better identify, understand, and respond to clients' career goals or problems.

For example, the broadened views of career and career development that have evolved in recent decades, and that were described in Chapter One, provide an invaluable prism through which to view and understand client information and behavior that surfaces during the use of the LCA. (See Figure 1.1.) The concept of clients' career development as an unfolding interaction of life roles, settings, and events (Gysbers and Moore, 1975, 1981; Super, 1975, 1984, 1990) is directly relatable to Adler's three-part system of work, social relations, and love. The notions of life roles, settings, and events can be used as a template to lay over the LCA structure, allowing counselors to listen for and extract information about how clients think and feel about their current and future life roles, life settings, and life events and the life-career themes that guide their behavior. Gathering information through the structure of the LCA and the prism of the broadened views of career and career development not only helps counselors understand clients better, but also helps clients better understand themselves.

Thus, a technique such as the LCA supports and reinforces a holistic approach to counseling for career development. It helps begin a discussion of such life roles as worker, learner, and family member, and the relationships among them. It also helps focus on the settings in which people live and work and the planned and unplanned events that happen to them over their lifetimes. As Berman and Munson (1981, p. 96) pointed out, "Significant career involvements do not exist in isolation of, nor can they be understood apart from, other life ventures. People can be helped to identify areas of meaningful individual-environmental dialogue and to examine their worklife experiences in conjunction with family, community, school, and other important roles." Career development theories are important, but so are other theories of human behavior. For example, other specialties within counseling—such as marriage and family counseling—have a great deal to say about clients' career goal and problem identification and the counseling techniques used to achieve or resolve them (Kinnier, Brigman, and Noble, 1990).

Drawing Conclusions or Making Diagnoses

Career theory constructs also play a role in drawing conclusions or making diagnoses. As information is being gathered, analyzed, and interpreted using the language of career theory, the process of drawing conclusions begins. Rounds and Tinsley (1984, p. 157) highlighted the importance of this phase of the counseling process: "Failure to identify, define, and categorize vocational problems adversely affects the practice of and research on career interventions by promoting poor communication among practitioners, precluding meaningful comparisons of career interventions, failing to obtain basic descriptive data about the prevalence of and prognosis for specific vocational problems, and generally encouraging uncritical thinking about career interventions."

The trait-oriented and cognitive theories are especially helpful in the diagnosis of career problems and concerns individuals may have. Trait-oriented theory is based on differential psychology. In fact, the concept of diagnosis as the differential classification of the characteristics of people's career concerns and problems, which was touched on in Chapter One, arises from differential psychology. Diagnostic evaluations of client goals or problems such as *unrealistic* (trait-and-factor) and *incongruent* (Holland's theory) are examples of differential diagnostic categories.

Cognitive theory has added to our diagnostic language an emphasis on the ways we process information and on the progressive development of reflective judgment. For example, a person might be differentially diagnosed as being at the dualistic stage. This is substantially different from being at, say, the commitment-within-relativism stage. The process of counseling for career development, the outcomes sought, and the methods used would be quite different in the two cases.

Cognitive theory is also helpful with dynamic diagnoses. It helps us understand, from a cognitive perspective, underlying reasons for behavior. Lewis and Gilhousen (1981) illustrated this by suggesting that some career problems may be rooted in irrational beliefs. For example, clients who are differentially diagnosed as indecisive may be indecisive because of the irrational belief that they must be perfect. Because this is not possible, no action can be taken; thus such clients may appear to be indecisive.

Decision-making theory and socioeconomic systems theory also are helpful in making diagnoses. Decision-making theory suggests possible frameworks by which to judge clients' decision-making skills. Socioeconomic systems theory provides ideas concerning what to look for in clients' growth and environment that will help in understanding the behavior they use to discover their identity. For instance, an understanding of a client's family and its values helps us grasp the value structure that underlies the client's choices. This is particularly important as it relates to gender-role stereotyping and occupational selection for males and females.

Another useful tool in arriving at possible diagnoses, whatever the types, are classification systems of possible client goals or problems. Campbell and Cellini (1981) developed such a system based on an extensive review of the literature. It contains four major career problem categories: decision making, implementation of plans, organizational/institutional performance, and organizational/institutional adaptation. Within each category are listings of specific career development problems. The authors pointed out that a career development problem can arise when a client experiences difficulty in completing tasks in any of the categories or does not even try to complete them.

Taking Action

The reason for identifying, clarifying, and specifying clients' career goals or problems is to find ways to resolve them through appropriate interventions. Once clients become aware of the nature of their goals or problems, the focus of counseling for career development turns to the active involvement of counselors and clients in finding goal or problem solutions. Crites (1981) suggested that there are at least three major general outcomes of counseling for career development—making a choice, acquiring decision-making skills, and enhancing general adjustment. The foundation knowledge counselors gain from career theory is useful in working with clients to help them achieve these outcomes.

Making a Choice. To enable counselors to help clients make a career choice, trait-and-factor theory offers the assessment of interest, aptitude, values, and career maturity. Socioeconomic systems theory provides insight into possible environmental pressures (from parents, spouses, peers). One example of this is the impact of clients' socialization on their career behavior (Harmon, 1989a). And finally, cognitive theory offers insight into how clients process and use information in making choices (Stone, 1983).

Acquiring Decision-Making Skills. The ability of counselors to assist clients in acquiring decision-making skills can be increased through the use of the foundation knowledge provided by career theory. For example, some clients may need to learn how to go about making decisions. Others may need to examine how they process information as they make decisions. In such cases, cognitive theory provides some answers (Krumboltz, 1983).

Enhancing General Adjustment. Since work roles, work settings, and work-linked events play a substantial part in our lives, job adjustment is critical to overall general adjustment. A number of career theories provide good insights here. Holland's theory helps us understand the relationship between personality and work environments. His concept of congruence is an important one. Developmental theories—particularly the concept of developmental tasks—can be very useful. An understanding of the tasks performed and of how the client has performed them sheds some light on the nature of the client's adjustment. The concept of career maturity—or, for adults, career adaptability (Super, 1990)—is also fruitful. Instruments are now available to help counselors obtain measures of career maturity and hence a notion of general adjustment of clients. Finally, there is decision-making theory. Tiedeman and O'Hara's model examines the processes that lead up to a choice as well as what happens once a person is on the job. They use such terms as *induction, reformation,* and *integration* to describe the phases workers may go through as they deal with job adjustment and advancement. The concept of role conflict is a useful construct to help explain and remedy job adjustment problems and issues.

Developing Individual Career Plans

At this point in counseling for career development, clients may need a way to organize the information about self and environment and to relate it to the career information they have gathered. Using the broadened concept of career, one approach may be to use a life-career plan centered around the following roles of worker, consumer/citizen, learner, leisure participant, and family member. Clients may find that by putting career information together in certain ways, they detect relationships that were not apparent before. Self-appraisal information and experience in auditing and cataloguing often can be translated directly into job-related knowledge, attitudes, and skills. When clients perceive these relationships, their self-confidence and sense of self-worth may be increased.

Worker Role. In this section, clients record information about the work-related competencies they possess. A listing of interest and aptitude data also can be included. In addition, tasks performed around home or school and the jobs clients have had can be recorded.

Consumer/Citizen Role. This section of a plan includes clients' competencies related to the role of consumer or citizen. Special attention is given to listings of community resources used or those that are available. Depending on the age of the clients involved, information is recorded concerning the purchase and maintenance of housing, the investment of money, and legal transitions, including the establishment of funds and wills.

Learner Role. In this section a complete record of clients' educational experiences and achievements is entered and maintained. Official transcripts, listings of learner competencies acquired, listings of informal learning experiences, and extracurricular activities are just a few of the types of learner-role information that can be included.

Leisure Role. This section can be used by clients to record and maintain information about themselves in such areas as friendships and leisure-time pursuits. In addition, this is the place to record and maintain complete health records. This section can also include hobbies and other avocational interests.

Family-Member Role. The family-member-role section is used to record and maintain such information as family background, data about relatives, and possible family crises and what was done to handle them. Other information that can be recorded and maintained includes data about family milestones or important family-related occurrences such as marriages, divorces, illness, and birthdays. Short anecdotes about such occurrences also can be included.

Evaluating the Results and Closing the Relationship

The final phase of the counseling process is assessing changes that may have occurred, evaluating the impact of the interventions used, and—when it is time—closing the relationship. Brown and Brooks (1991), in an excellent chapter on the topic, suggested that there are three overlapping tasks that require attention. The first task is to review client goals and consolidate client learning. One way to accomplish this is to have clients review and summarize what has taken place during the process of counseling for career development. Then counselors can add their own review and summary.

During the summary, some unfinished business may be discovered. Clients may need more information or more time to consider and reflect on the information already available. As a result, counselors may recycle back to the same interventions to allow more time for consideration and reflection, or they may try other interventions.

A second task suggested by Brown and Brooks is the need to deal with affect issues. Counselors should openly explore with clients any feelings there may be about closing the relationship. Brown and Brooks (1991, p. 346) suggested that a lead such as "I'm wondering how you're feeling about not coming here any longer?" might be useful to elicit such feelings if they were present.

The third task Brown and Brooks suggested was preparation for postcounseling and transfer of learning. Teaching clients how to develop and implement individual career plans is crucial. That is why the "Developing Individual Career Plans" section of the counseling process framework is there. Developing the plan underscores for clients the need to follow through on what they learned during counseling.

A final point Brown and Brooks (1991, p. 350) made in their discussion of the closing of counseling was the issue of termination when counseling may be incomplete. Premature termination can occur, they pointed out, when in "clients' judgment . . . they have achieved their goals, although the counselor may not agree, clients' fear of what might be uncovered in counseling, failure of counseling to meet clients' expectations, and/or lack of clients' commitment to counseling in the beginning." Sometimes premature closure may be avoided by dealing directly with client expectations about what counseling for career development is and, perhaps more important, what it is not. This is done during the opening phase of the counseling process. Brown and Brooks (1991, pp. 352–353) offered seven suggestions that may be useful to prepare counselors for a number of possibilities in closing counseling relationships:

1. Complete additional readings on termination: this is particularly relevant when coun-

seling has involved a mixture of personal and career counseling and has extended over a period of time.

2. Counselors who have difficulty with good-byes in general might profit from readings on loss. Supervision or personal counseling should be sought if the problem continues.

3. Many writers and supervisors have noted that it is not uncommon for counselors to experience difficulty in effectively terminating clients due, for example, to their own anxiety about loss. Martin and Schurtman (1985) discuss the sources of termination anxiety for counselors and therapists and the various defense maneuvers they might use to deal with the anxiety. Their article is recommended for counselors who find termination a persistent problem.

4. If you are in a supervised field experience, ask your supervisor to set aside some time for discussion of termination issues.

5. Talk to other experienced counselors regarding the various ways they handle termination.

6. Remember, sometimes it is in the client's best interest to terminate, even if you don't think he or she is ready.

7. Examine your own method of conducting career counseling to identify ways that you may "prematurely terminate" career counseling.

A Look Ahead

So far we have established that counseling for career development requires understanding of the thoughts and feelings of clients as expressed in their presenting problems and the subsequent concerns that may emerge. We have pointed out that these thoughts and feelings can be elicited and made explicit in systematic ways using the counseling process framework. And we have established that the language of career theory helps us explain client behavior, develop diagnoses, and suggest strategies to assist them in achieving their career goals and resolving their career problems.

But there is more to counseling for career development, much more. Counselors first need to understand the client-framework-theory interaction. Helping clients achieve their career goals and resolve their career problems also presupposes substantial foundation knowledge about the nature, structure, and dynamics of the worlds of work, education, leisure, and the family as well as the counseling skills to use this information with them. Parts Two and Three of this book are designed to provide the necessary foundation knowledge in each of these arenas, while Part Four is designed to help counselors develop the skills (or polish those they already have) to use this foundation knowledge with clients of all ages and circumstances in individual counseling or structured group work.

PART 2

Building
the Foundations
for Career Development

4

‣‣‣‣‣‣‣‣‣‣‣‣‣

The World
of Work

‣‣‣‣‣‣‣‣‣‣‣‣‣

To attempt to provide an in-depth treatment of the world of work in a short chapter is a difficult task. Everyone already has considerable knowledge of this sphere—knowledge gained from family, friends, education, travel, media information and, of course, direct employment experience. Thus this is not an unfamiliar subject for most people; it is just that it has become so much more complex over the last half of the twentieth century. The developments that have led to this increasing complexity include the growth of a global economy; the emergence of multinational corporations; leveraged buyouts and corporate takeovers; downscaling and downsizing by employers; the rise and fall of labor unions; the increasing role of women, people of color, and those with disabilities in the workplace; shifting work values; the changing occupational and industrial structure; the changing skills mix; and widening regional, state, and in-state economic differences. Each of these topics is the subject of full-length books. But each represents a factor that needs to be at least partially understood by counselors and other helping professionals concerned about career development, so that they can assist others more effectively in dealing with the world of work.

In this chapter, we provide an overview of work-related issues by focusing on six main questions:

1. *Who* is in the world of work?
2. *Where* do people work?
3. *What* are the educational requirements of various occupations?
4. *Why* do people work?
5. *When* have long-term changes taken place?
6. *Where* is the future workplace headed?

This discussion rests on the life-career development framework presented in Chapter One (see especially Figure 1.1). Major sources of information on the U.S. employment scene are discussed in detail in Chapter Eight. The topics covered in the present chapter are complex, but this six-part approach will establish a *foundation knowledge and structure* and a way of separating key factors in the past, present, and future world of work into convenient segments.

Who Is in the World of Work

The growth of the U.S. labor force is expected to slow perceptibly between 1988 and 2000, according to *Outlook 2000* projections by the Bureau of Labor Statistics (1990c). Under the most moderate of three alternative projections, the labor force is estimated to grow 1.2 percent annually, compared with the 1976–1988 growth rate of 2.0 percent. (Note: Much of this chapter is based on the *Outlook 2000* report. See Bureau of Labor Statistics, 1990c, for more detailed analysis.)

The labor force is projected to total 141 million persons in 2000, a net addition of 19 million over the decade of the 1990s. In contrast, the workforce grew by 25 million between 1976 and 1988. Under the alternative projections, the workforce in 2000 varies between a possible low of 137.5 million and a high of 144.0 million.

Women were only 40 percent of the labor force as recently as 1976; by the year 2000, women are projected to be 47 to 50 percent. The proportion of youth (those sixteen to twenty-four years old) is expected to drop from 24 to 16 percent by 2000. The decline during the 1976–1988 period reflected the end of the entry of the baby boomers, while the projected decrease between 1988 and 2000 reflects fewer births in the 1970s. The proportion of workers in the broad age span from twenty-four to fifty-four is projected to increase by 2 percent by the year 2000. The older population (fifty-five and over), which is growing, is projected to account for the same share of the labor force in 2000 as in 1988.

The proportion of African Americans in the labor force is projected to rise to 12 percent by 2000, compared with 10 percent in 1976 and 11 percent in 1988. The increase stems from population growth. Hispanics are projected to increase their share of the labor force from 7 percent in 1988 to 10 percent by 2000, reflecting increases in population and labor force participation. The proportion of the Asian-and-other group is expected to rise from 3 percent in 1988 to 4 percent in 2000, also the result of rapid population increase.

Population Changes, 1988–2000

The overall U.S. population, which increased by 1 percent annually between 1976 and 1988, is projected to grow 0.7 percent annually to 2000. This slowing reflects an anticipated drop in births as well as the slight decline in net migration. The increase will not occur uniformly across age, racial, or ethnic groups.

As a consequence of the end of the baby boom in 1965, the numbers of youth in the population—and thus in the labor force—will drop. However, the children of the baby boom generation will enter the labor force during the 1990s, but not before the number of youth continues to drop. Table 4.1 gives the year when the numbers of various groups of youth is expected to reach their trough or low point, with an accompanying drop in the population until then. The number of sixteen-year-olds will begin rising soon, following a 4 percent annual drop in numbers between 1988 and 1990. The age group from twenty-two to twenty-four will not reach a low for almost a decade. By the turn of the century, the entire youth population will be increasing. Those hiring teenagers

Table 4.1. Proportion of Youth in the Labor Force.

Age	Year of Trough	Annual Rate of Decline, 1988 to Trough (%)	Annual Rate of Increase, from Trough to 2000 (%)
16	1990	-3.9	1.4
16 and 17	1991	-3.6	1.5
16 to 19	1992	-2.7	1.7
18 and 19	1993	-2.3	1.9
20 and 21	1995	-1.4	1.9
16 to 24	1996	-1.2	1.3
18 to 24	1996	-1.5	1.3
20 to 24	1997	-1.5	1.5
22 to 24	1998	-1.8	1.4

Source: Bureau of Labor Statistics, 1990c, p. 3.

should anticipate only a short period before the numbers begin turning up; those hiring college graduates may expect a decline in numbers lasting until the end of the century. Nationwide, the segment of the population at the usual age to enter college will start increasing in 1993.

Increases in the Older Population

The population over age fifty-five is projected to grow rapidly. This reflects past immigration as well as the aging of those born between the birth dearth of the early 1930s and the baby boom. The population eighty-five and over is projected to grow most rapidly. Among the older age groups, only the sixty-five to seventy-four age group is projected to increase at a rate less than the overall population, a consequence of the low birth rates of the early 1930s.

Shifting Gender Patterns

The number of women in the labor force is projected to grow by 12.0 million from 1988, totaling 67 million in 2000. This represents an annual rate of growth of 1.7 percent, compared with the 2.9 percent of the 1976–1988 period, when the young women of the baby boom generation were entering the labor force. With the growth shown in these projections, women would account for 47 to 50 percent of the labor force in 2000, up from 41 percent in 1976 and 45 in 1988.

Men are nevertheless projected to remain a majority of the labor force, even though the number is not changing as dynamically as that of women. The male labor force is projected to grow by 7.4 million, or 11 percent, over the 1988–2000 period. (This compares with 22 percent for women during the same period.) Different components of the male labor force are growing at different rates; the younger male labor force is projected to decrease in size between 1988 and 1995, but actually to increase between 1995 and 2000.

Changes in the Representation of Racial Groups

People of color are generally expected to increase their share of the workforce, while that of whites will decline.

African Americans. There are projected to be 16.5 million African Americans in the labor force in 2000, up 3.2 million from 1988. This represents a higher growth rate—1.9 percent—than is projected for the overall labor force and is the result of faster population growth among African Americans. *By the year 2000, African Americans are expected to make up 12 percent of the labor force, up 1 percentage point from 1988.*

Asians and Others. The workforce participation of the Asian-and-other group (which includes American Indians, Alaskan Natives, Asians, and Pacific Islanders) is expected to be 5.6 million in 2000, an increase of 2 million from 1988. Their growth rate is projected to be 3.6 percent annually, higher than either the African American or white rate of increase but below that of Hispanics. Like Hispanics, their growth rate is influenced by immigration as well as by higher past fertility. *This group's share of the labor force would increase by 1 percentage point to 4 percent.* The participation rate of Asians and others is projected to remain virtually the same, comparable to the change over the 1976–1988 period.

Hispanics. There are expected to be 14.3 million Hispanics in the labor force in 2000, up 5.3 million from 1988, according to the Bureau of Labor Statistics projections. This represents a much higher growth rate, 4.0 percent, than is projected for the overall labor force. Hispanics may be of any race; their population and labor force numbers are also included in those for African Americans, Asians and others, and whites. Hispanic labor force participation is projected to grow 0.3 percent annually, similar to the overall labor force increase of 0.4 percent annually. *By 2000, Hispanics are projected to constitute 10 percent of the labor force, up 3 percentage points from 1988.* Workers of Hispanic origin are the youngest group in the workforce (as measured by the median age of 35.2) and are projected to remain by far the youngest group.

Whites. As in the past, most of the labor force is still projected to be white. In the year 2000, there would be 119 million whites (including Hispanics) in the labor force, up 124 percent from 1988. However, their share of the workforce is projected to drop from 86 to 84 percent. (If Hispanics are excluded, more than 95 percent of whom also are counted as white, the shares for whites would be 79 percent in 1988 and 74 percent in 2000.) White participation is expected to grow at the same rate as the overall labor force but more slowly than the participation of African Americans, Asians and others, and Hispanics, reflecting slower rates of population growth and older age structure.

Where People Work: The Major Occupational Groups

Each of the three major occupational groups requiring the highest levels of educational attainment—executive, administrative, and managerial occupations; professional specialty occupations; and technicians and related support occupations—is projected to continue to grow more rapidly than the average for total employment over the 1988-2000 period. Employment in executive, administrative, and managerial occupations is expected to increase by 22 percent, which represents an increase of 2.7 million jobs from 1988 to 2000 (see Table 4.2). Much of the growth of this occupational group is expected to be in retail trade and in the services industry, especially business services. The numbers of managers and administrators are expected to continue to expand through the year 2000 because of the increasing complexity of corporate activities and because of the start-up of many small firms. However, the growth rate for this occupational group is projected to be significantly less than it was from 1976 to 1988, when executive, administrative, and managerial workers grew faster than any other major group and more than twice as fast as total employment.

The number of workers in professional specialty occupations is projected to grow by 3.5 million, an increase of 24 percent. Much of this growth is due to the expected increase in demand for engineers, computer specialists; lawyers; health diagnosing and treating occupations; and teachers, except college and university. The professional specialty occupations group is expected to continue grow faster than total employment and to increase its share of total employment from 12.4 percent in 1988 to 13.3 percent in 2000.

Employment of the technicians and related support occupations group is projected to grow by 32 percent, more rapidly than any other major occupational group. Over the 1976–1988 period, this group also was among the fastest-growing major occupational groups. Jobs for health technologists and technicians are expected to account for nearly half of the 1.2 million new technician jobs that will be added from 1988 to 2000. In addition, more than a quarter of a million new jobs are expected for engineering and science technicians and computer programmers.

Marketing and sales occupations, which expanded much more rapidly than total employment from 1976 to 1988, are expected to increase only slightly faster than average through 2000. The employment increase is projected to be about 2.6 million workers. Occupations in this group are concentrated in industries expected to have average growth—wholesale and retail trade (excluding eating and drinking places).

Table 4.2. Employment by Major Occupational Group, 1988 and
Projected to 2000, Moderate Alternative Projection, and Percent Change
1976-88 and 1988-2000 (numbers in thousands).

Occupational Title	1988		2000		Percent Change	
	Number	Percent	Number	Percent	1976-1988	1988-2000
Total, all occupations	118,104	100.0	136,211	100.0	29.5	15.3
Executive, administrative, and managerial occupations	12,104	10.2	14,762	10.8	66.4	22.0
Professional specialty occupations	14,628	12.4	18,137	13.3	44.6	24.0
Technicians and related support occupations	3,867	3.3	5,089	3.7	53.9	31.6
Marketing and sales occupations	13,316	11.3	15,924	11.7	46.1	19.6
Administrative support occupations, including clerical	21,066	17.8	23,553	17.3	27.8	11.8
Service occupations	18,479	15.6	22,651	16.6	28.2	22.6
Agricultural, forestry, fishing, and related occupations	3,503	3.0	3,334	2.4	-7.7	-4.8
Precision production, craft, and repair occupations	14,159	12.0	15,563	11.4	25.3	9.9
Operators, fabricators, and laborers	16,983	14.4	17,198	12.6	2.9	1.3

Note: The 1988 and 2000 employment data, and the projected change 1988-2000, are derived from data from the industry-occupation matrixes for each year. The data on 1976-1988 percent change were derived from the Current Population Survey data because a comparable industry-occupation matrix for 1976 is not available. The resulting comparison of change between 1976-1988 and 1988-2000 consequently is only broadly indicative of trends.

Source: Bureau of Labor Statistics, 1990c, p. 42.

Employment in administrative support occupations, including clerical, is expected to grow more slowly than average from 1988 to 2000. However, this group is expected to add 2.5 million jobs over the period and to remain the largest major occupational group. The group grew about as fast as total employment in the previous twelve-year period, but technological innovations and greater utilization of office automation are expected to slow the future rate of growth. Some occupations in this group, such as computer operators, however, are expected to benefit from continued technological change requiring their skills, and, as a result, to grow rapidly. Other occupations in this broad group that involve a great deal of contact with people, and therefore are not affected significantly by automation, also are expected to have average or higher-than-average rates of growth. Among these are hotel desk clerks, interview clerks, and receptionists. Typists and word processors, stenographers, and statistical clerks are among the declining occupations in this group.

Employment in the service occupations group is expected to increase by 23 percent from 1988 to 2000. With an increase of more than four million jobs, it will add more jobs than any other major occupational group. Food preparation and service, health service, and cleaning and building service occupations are expected to account for nearly three-fourths of the total employment increase in service occupations. Service jobs are expected to increase from 15.6 percent of total employment in 1988 to 16.6 percent in 2000.

The number of agricultural, forestry, fishing, and related workers is projected to decrease by 5 percent between 1988 and 2000. Although continuing a long-term trend, this projected rate of decline is slightly less than the 8 percent drop that occurred between 1976 and 1988.

The number of precision production, craft, and repair jobs is projected to grow more slowly than the average for total employment from 1988 to 2000, just as it did from 1976 to 1988. Nearly all of the 1.4 million total increase in jobs is expected to be in the construction and services industry divisions. In manufacturing, about 100,000 fewer workers in this major group are projected to be employed in 2000 than in 1988.

Employment in the operators, fabricators, and laborers group, which grew by only 3 percent from 1976 to 1988, is projected to grow by about 1 percent through the year 2000. Although a large decline of nearly three-fourths of a million jobs is projected in manufacturing, job gains in services; wholesale and retail trade; construction; and transportation, communications, and public utilities should result in a net gain of 215,000 jobs by 2000. This major group is expected to have the largest change in the share of total employment, declining from 14.4 percent in 1988 to 12.6 percent by 2000.

The Fastest-Growing Occupations

Reflecting the very rapid growth of the health services industries, half of the twenty occupations with the fastest projected growth rates are health services occupations (see Table 4.3). The health-related occupation projected to grow most rapidly over the 1988–2000 period is medical assistants (70 percent). The next-fastest-growing occupation, home health aides, will be in great demand to serve the needs of the increasing population who are aged and ill but live at home. Other health occupations with rapid projected growth include radiologic technicians and technologists, medical record technicians, medical secretaries, physical therapists, surgical technologists, physical and corrective therapy assistants and aides, and occupational therapists.

Rapid growth also is projected for occupations related to computer technology. The number of data processing equipment repairers should increase rapidly to maintain the growing stock of computer and related equipment. Rapid growth of operations research analysts also is expected. These workers perform data analyses of the operations of manufacturing and other business organizations to improve efficiency. Their work often leads to changes in an organization's data processing methods. Computer systems analysts and computer programmers will be needed to improve methods of satisfying the expanding data processing needs of organizations.

Table 4.3. Fastest Growing Occupations, 1988–2000,
Moderate Alternative Projection (numbers in thousands).

Occupation	Employment		Numerical Change	Percent Change
	1988	*2000*		
Paralegals	83	145	62	75.3
Medical assistants	149	253	104	70.0
Home health aides	236	397	160	67.9
Radiologic technologists and technicians	132	218	87	66.0
Data processing equipment repairers	71	115	44	61.2
Medical records technicians	47	75	28	59.9
Medical secretaries	207	327	120	58.0
Physical therapists	68	107	39	57.0
Surgical technologists	35	55	20	56.4
Operations research analysts	55	85	30	55.4
Securities and financial services sales workers	200	309	109	54.8
Travel agents	142	219	77	54.1
Computer systems analysts	403	617	214	53.3
Physical and corrective therapy assistants	39	60	21	52.5
Social welfare service aides	91	138	47	51.5
Occupational therapists	33	48	16	48.8
Computer programmers	519	769	250	48.1
Human services workers	118	171	53	44.9
Respiratory therapists	56	79	23	41.3
Correction officers and jailers	186	262	76	40.8

Source: Bureau of Labor Statistics, 1990c, p. 59.

Among other occupations with rapid employment growth, paralegals—the occupation with the fastest projected increase—is expected to benefit from the rapid growth of the legal services industry as well as increasing use of paralegals within the industry. Other growth occupations include securities and financial services sales representatives, travel agents, and social welfare service aides.

Occupations with the Largest Job Growth

In addition to rapidly growing occupations, occupations having the largest numerical increases are important in identifying careers that will provide favorable job opportunities. As can be seen in Table 4.4, the rates of growth of some of the occupations expected to have the largest numerical increases are less than for the economy as a whole. Size of employment, however, has a major impact on numerical growth. All of the occupations in Table 4.4 are among the largest in employment size. In addition to numerical growth, employment size also is a major factor in the number of openings that will

Table 4.4. Occupations with the Largest Job Growth, 1988-2000, Moderate Alternative Projection (numbers in thousands).

Occupation	Employment		Numerical Change	Percent Change
	1988	*2000*		
Salespersons, retail	3,834	4,564	730	19.0
Registered nurses	1,577	2,190	613	38.8
Janitors and cleaners, including maids and housekeeping cleaners	2,895	3,450	556	19.2
Waiters and waitresses	1,786	2,337	551	30.9
General managers and top executives	3,030	3,509	479	15.8
General office clerks	2,519	2,974	455	18.1
Secretaries, except legal and medical	2,903	3,288	385	13.2
Nursing aides, orderlies, and attendants	1,184	1,562	378	31.9
Truck drivers, light and heavy	2,399	2,768	369	15.4
Receptionists and information clerks	833	1,164	331	39.8
Cashiers	2,310	2,614	304	13.2
Guards	795	1,050	256	32.2
Computer programmers	519	769	250	48.1
Food counter, fountain, and related	1,626	1,866	240	14.7
Food preparation workers	1,027	1,260	234	22.8
Licensed practical nurses	626	855	229	36.6
Teachers, secondary school	1,164	1,388	224	19.2
Computer systems analysts	403	617	214	53.3
Accountants and auditors	963	1,174	211	22.0
Teachers, kindergarten and elementary	1,359	1,567	208	15.3

Source: Bureau of Labor Statistics, 1990c, p. 59.

occur, because of the need to replace workers who leave the labor force or transfer to other occupations.

Some of the occupations with the largest job growth are closely associated with an individual industry group. For the occupations in Table 4.4, the industry groups are retail trade, health services, and educational services. These industries currently have high employment levels, and all are projected to continue to grow.

The category of retail trade contains the occupation with the largest expected job growth of all occupations—salespersons, retail, which is found in all retail trade industries. Within retail trade, the rapidly growing eating and drinking places industry has three of the top twenty occupations with the largest growth: waiters and waitresses; food counter, fountain, and related workers; and food preparation workers. Another retail trade occupation with a projected large increase is cashiers. Health services has the occupation with the second-highest expected increase— registered nurses. Nursing aides and licensed practical nurses are two other occupations among the top twenty growth occupations that are found in health services. Educational services has two occupations in the top twenty—secondary school teachers and kindergarten and elementary school teachers.

Other occupations that are expected to have large job gains are not as identifiable with an industry group and exhibit a wide range of skills and earnings levels. Janitors and cleaners, including maids and housekeeping cleaners, lead this group. Following closely behind in terms of employment gains are general managers and top executives, whose numbers are projected to grow because of the increasing complexity of industrial and commercial organizations. General office clerks are projected to increase as a result of record-keeping needs and other office procedures for which no computer programs can be economically devised.

What Are the Educational Requirements

An analysis of the occupational employment projections for 1988–2000 indicates that, in general, employment is expected to increase faster in occupational groups requiring the most education than in those requiring less education. Executive, administrative, and managerial occupations and professional specialty occupations have the smallest proportions of workers with less than high school education and the highest proportions completing at least four years of college; these categories are projected to grow more rapidly than average. There are some exceptions to this general pattern, however. Service workers—a major group having relatively few workers with a college degree and a high proportion with less than a high school education—is projected to grow faster than average. Also, among the professional specialty occupations, the number of college and university faculty is projected to grow slowly (3 percent) because college enrollments are not expected to increase between 1988 and 2000. Within the major occupational groups increasing more slowly than average, only computer operators and peripheral equipment operators will deviate from this trend and show unusual growth.

In spite of projected growth rates that are higher for the best-educated workers and lower for the least-educated workers, the structure of employment at the major-occupational-group level is not expected to change substantially from 1988 to 2000 (see Table 4.2). The ranking of occupations by employment size in 2000 should be similar to that in 1988. For example, the administrative support occupations category is expected to continue to have the largest number of workers, followed by service occupations. Professional specialty occupations, however, is expected to move up from the fourth- to the third-largest group, ahead of operators, fabricators, and laborers. All other major occupational groups should maintain the rank they had in 1988.

The projections show the structure of employment by major occupational group changing only slowly over time. Most of the major groups are projected to change their share of total employment by less than 1 percentage point from 1988 to 2000. The only exception is the major group consisting of operators, fabricators, and laborers; it is expected to decline by 1.8 percentage points.

The stability of the overall occupational structure between 1988 and 2000 implies that workers will continue to be required across a broad spectrum of educational requirements. Jobs will be available in 2000 for the less educated as well as for those who earn college degrees. Among each of the major occupational groups, however, workers with four-year college degrees earn more on average than workers without such degrees. Furthermore, within each occupational group, workers with more education are expected to earn more than workers with less education.

Despite this overall pattern, the inference should not be made that good jobs will be available in 2000 only for people with college degrees and only in those fields that are projected to grow faster than average. Many occupations that do not require a four-year college degree have above-average earnings and are expected to offer favorable employment prospects through the year 2000. This is because they have projected growth rates that are at least average and because many job openings will be created as workers who leave the labor force or transfer to other occupations are replaced. Several of these occupations are found in the construction trades, including bricklayers and stonemasons; electricians; plumbers, pipefitters, and steamfitters; and structural and reinforcing metal workers. Other skilled occupations with favorable employment opportunities are mechanics, installers, and repairers—including data processing equipment repairers; electronic repairers of commercial and industrial equipment; industrial machinery mechanics; heating, air conditioning, and refrigeration mechanics and installers; and mobile heavy equipment mechanics.

Why People Work

This section draws attention to the fact that people work for a variety of reasons. The conventional wisdom is that individuals work exclusively or mainly to earn money. While that may be the case for the majority of people, there are psychological, sociological, religious, and other reasons, too. These reasons have a bearing on why people select certain lines of work. Further, the issue may have to do as well with just how much job satisfaction they experience. Other factors that also enter into the issue of why people work have to do with family, gender, race and ethnicity, age, and the geographical location of their college or university. In addition, motives for working are influenced by a host of very personal values, beliefs, attitudes, and impressions and outlooks. In short, the matter of why people work (or do not work) is a very complicated one that defies pat answers or explanations.

There are some excellent chapters on motivation toward work in each of the National Career Development Association Decennial Volumes: *Man in a World at Work* (Borow, 1964), *Vocational Guidance & Human Development* (Herr, 1974), and *Designing Career* (Gysbers, 1984). Periodically the Gallup organization does opinion polling on the topic, and it conducted two polls in connection with National Career Development Association conferences in 1988 and 1990. (For further detail, see Brown and Minor, 1989.) The results of these and similar polls all seem to show that

- Most people are satisfied with their job.
- Most people have a fairly strong desire to work (rather than not work).
- Ten to twenty percent of adults at any one time are thinking about a major career change.
- Older workers experience more job satisfaction than younger workers.

Neal Rosenthal (1989) analyzed the issues involved in why people work and what they consider to be important in a quality job. He pointed out that while wages may be their most important concern, other factors also play a major role:

1. *Job Duties and Working Conditions.* The actual tasks performed on the job and the environment in which the tasks are performed—both the physical workplace and relationships with others—are important in evaluating

the desirability of jobs. The kinds of factors that are worthy of note include the presence or absence of repetitive and hazardous conditions, the amount of physical stamina required, the openness of the work space, the degree of stress and autonomy on the job, the amount of working with detail, and the opportunity (or lack of it) to be part of a team.

2. *Job Satisfaction.* Many job characteristics result in intrinsic satisfaction. Although all the characteristics that follow are positive, the lack of a characteristic is not necessarily negative. These characteristics include the chance to fully utilize one's skills and to learn new skills, opportunities to engage in problem solving and other forms of creative activity, the experience of seeing the results of one's work, receiving recognition for accomplishments, being able to influence others, and having advancement opportunities.

3. *Period of Work.* Working hours differ among jobs in terms of total hours worked per week and the hours when workers must be on the job. Some periods of work are generally viewed as negative aspects of a job and others are considered positive. Some concerns are: weekend and shift work, overtime, flexible work hours, and part-time work.

4. *Job Status.* The perceived importance of a job has an effect on an individual's view of the quality of his or her job. And socioeconomic background has a great impact on how an individual views a specific job in terms of social status and status within the organization.

5. *Job Security.* The possibility of keeping a job despite bad economic conditions or other factors can be a significant, positive aspect of a job. The amount of security associated with a job is more commonly determined by the employer or activity than by the occupation. Positions in government are generally more secure than such jobs as construction jobs, which have a high risk of layoff because of seasonal and cyclical factors that affect the construction industry.

A final factor influencing job satisfaction is size of employer. A number of small-business advocates report that employees of small- to mid-sized private companies are much more satisfied than those of larger companies—even though pay and benefits may lag behind the larger employers'. Small companies often place a premium on individual initiative and innovative thinking and thus may offer workers more challenge and a greater sense of accomplishment. In many cases, they also treat employees with more respect.

So what does all this mean to a counselor or other human services professional? Simply that people are motivated to work for a wide variety of reasons. And these vary considerably from one person to another. The counselor's job is to recognize and respect these differences. (See Chapter Twelve for a discussion of working with special populations.)

When Long-Term Changes Have Taken Place

In any consideration of the world of work, pains must be taken to see the larger picture, which is more than a snapshot of what is happening today—it is a moving picture over time of major trends. Three trends, illustrated here in graphic form, will demonstrate the importance of looking at the bigger picture. These are the steady growth of the civilian labor force, women's increasing participation in the workforce, and the increase in services-producing jobs.

Figure 4.1 depicts the long-term growth of the civilian workforce. There was rapid growth from 1972 to 1979, about a 2.7 million rate of change as opposed to 1.7 million per year from 1979 to 1986 and projected to slow even further to 1.2 million new workers per year. So, this long-term trend shows a continuing growth in civilian labor force, but at a slower rate of growth in the 1980s and 1990s.

Turning to a different trend, Figure 4.2 illustrates women's participation in the workforce between 1972 and 2000. The dramatic nature of this trend shows why many have hailed the increasing participation of women as the most significant labor force event of the twentieth century.

Figure 4.1. Civilian Labor Force, 1972–2000.

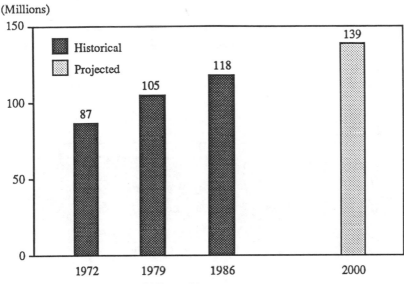

Source: Fullerton, 1987, p. 20.

What this means to counselors and other helping professionals is that if this trend continues as it has for the past fifty years, then nearly every young woman can expect to be in the labor force in an active role for some or all of her life, and career development considerations need to be as central for women as they have been for men. The question about women and work is no longer, "Will women work?" but "At what occupations and for how long?"

Finally, Figure 4.3 portrays the continuing growth in services-producing employment over the past thirty years (this continues a trend that started in the 1950s) as well as the stable situation with respect to goods-producing jobs. What this means to counselors and others in the helping professions is that the real increase in job opportunities will continue to occur in the services-producing area of the employment scene. The job growth in goods-producing employment will continue to provide about the same number of jobs in 2000 as it did in 1972. The significant point here is that replacement

Figure 4.2. Women as a Percent of the U.S. Labor Force, 1972–2000.

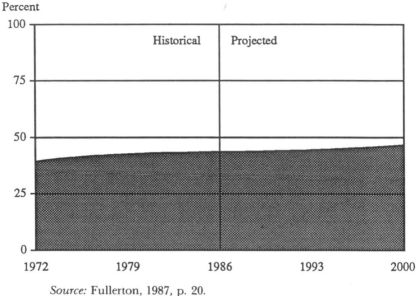

Source: Fullerton, 1987, p. 20.

Figure 4.3. Goods- and Services-Producing Employment, 1972–2000.

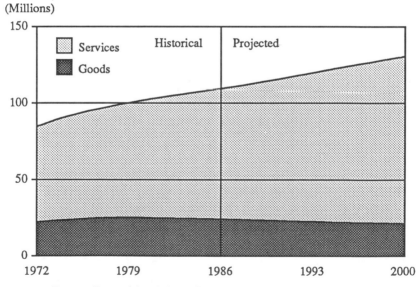

Source: Personick, 1987, p. 32.

needs will most likely be larger than those due to growth in the goods-producing sector.

Where Is the Future Workplace Headed?

This final section offers a brief look at the workplace of the future. It draws on material from a book titled *The Changing Workplace: Career Counseling Strategies for the 1990s and Beyond* (McDaniels, 1989).

Predictions regarding the future of the world of work abound—some forecasters anticipating that advances in technology will bring about a flourishing high-tech society, others expecting the decline in American industry to result in limited opportunities and high unemployment. This approach explores the workplace of tomorrow, offering counselors and others the practical guidance they need to confidently make recommendations based on three of many possible occupational scenarios: the high-tech visions of futurists like Alvin Toffler and John Naisbitt, the moderate forecasts of the Bureau of Labor Statistics, and the gloomier predictions of labor organizations. Then we will mention several "wild cards"—new career possibilities that could alter the picture significantly.

Three Scenarios for the Future of Work

Predictions about the future employment scene range from optimistic technologically based scenarios to pessimistic scenarios emphasizing a stagnant economy and limited worker opportunity.

The Green or Go Scenario: Fast Track and High Tech. This interpretation emphasizes the changes in career opportunities and working conditions predicted by futurist writers such as Alvin Toffler and John Naisbitt. According to this scenario, the use of computers will create new career options, and the expansion of robotics will dramatically affect jobs in manufacturing.

The Yellow or Caution Scenario: Evolution, Not Revolution. This moderate approach is supported by the projections of the Bureau of Labor Statistics for growth in occupations and industries based on a comprehensive, long-term study of employment in America. The Bureau of Labor Statistics report (1990c) contends that the occupations and industries that have the most potential for growth are already in existence; it maintains that changes in the future world of work will come slowly, with jobs available as much by replacement as by growth and change.

The Red or Stop Scenario: Unemployment or Underemployment. This scenario reflects the forecasts of labor organizations, economists, and others who predict continuing high unemployment, a dwindling middle class, and diminished opportunities as a result of a further decline in manufacturing as well as in other goods-producing industries. Those who subscribe to the red scenario see the growth of an underclass of bypassed workers who are underpaid, with limited or no worker benefits.

Three Wild Cards in the Changing Workplace

Three trends could generate many new career possibilities.

The Lure of Entrepreneurship. The growth of entrepreneurship in the United States may result in many new job opportunities. These opportunities will mainly be found in creative and innovative employment places both in small towns and large cities. Those who foresee this development sense a new vision that captures the spirit of an entrepreneurial economy in a venturesome society.

The Growth of Small Business. Most new jobs are now being created by businesses with under 250 employees. Many workers, especially including women and minorities, find it advantageous to work outside the often-rigid organizational structures of big business. The small-business world also offers expanding opportunities through the fast-growing area of franchising for those who own the business or work there.

The Work-at-Home Trend. There is a growing potential for people to work out of their homes—for instance, via computer links with employers in a telecommuting setup. In action, traditional arts and crafts produced at home now have expanded markets that are open through thousands of craft fairs and flea markets. Finally, there are the new career possibilities opening up through the area of direct retail sales, which in 1988 totaled nearly *$10 billion.*

5

〓〓〓〓〓〓〓〓〓〓〓〓〓〓〓〓〓〓〓〓〓〓〓〓〓〓〓〓〓〓〓〓〓〓〓〓〓〓

The World
of Education and Training

〓〓〓〓〓〓〓〓〓〓〓〓〓〓〓〓〓〓〓〓〓〓〓〓〓〓〓〓〓〓〓〓〓〓〓〓〓〓

Like all of the other chapters in Parts One and Two, Chapter Five deals with *foundation knowledge.* Gaining an understanding of the current status of education and training in the United States means also gaining some appreciation of the past, at least the scope of education in the United States in the twentieth century. For example, in the early 1900s only 10 percent of the youth sixteen to eighteen years old completed high school. During the rest of the twentieth century that figure has been reversed in some (not all) areas to the point that 90 percent of the local youth from sixteen to eighteen years old complete high school requirements and only 10 percent leave school before graduation. Nationally there is alarm about the dropout rate, but over the past fifty to seventy-five years, great strides have been made in education in some of the following areas:

1. The comprehensive inclusion, by secondary schools, of programs in vocational education, special education, and gifted education.
2. The rapid growth and development of a wide array of training opportunities for people of all ages, from eighteen to eighty.

3. The creation and expansion of a comprehensive community college system in nearly every state that puts the first two years of postsecondary education within driving distance of most citizens.

4. The diversification of four-year institutions, from small specialized colleges to comprehensive regional universities. The best example of this would be the many small state teachers' colleges/normal schools (sometimes for women only in the South) that have become midsized universities offering bachelor's and master's degrees.

5. The attendance of a growing number of adults over twenty-two years of age sometimes referred to as "nontraditional students." From the standpoint of its impact, this "greying" of the college student population is viewed by many as the most important trend in higher education in the past fifty years.

In view of these trends, this chapter will focus on the following five foundation knowledge aspects of the changing face of education and training in the United States:

1. Twenty options other than a bachelor's degree
2. Major shifts in graduate and undergraduate education
3. Financial aid for the 1990s
4. Accreditation/approval, or How do you know what are you getting?
5. Licensure and certification requirements—new pressures on our education structure

To set the stage for all of this is a *life-span tree of learning* (Figure 5.1). This provides a basic way of viewing education as a lifelong process with many options and branches. There should be no thought of "terminal degrees"—only opportunities for further study in formal and informal settings over the life span. This tree, like most trees, should continue to grow as you add additional choices open in your area.

Figure 5.1. Life-Span Tree of Learning.

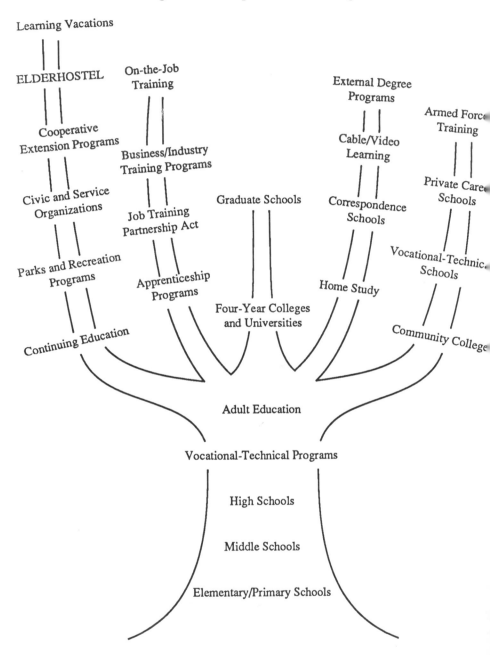

Options Other Than a Bachelor's Degree

Many parents and others assume that the *only choice* for high school graduates is to go on to obtain a bachelor's degree. But as this section will show through twenty illustrations, nothing could be further from the truth, since many other education and training alternatives exist. The following survey of options is not meant to be the final word; new groups form and delivery systems emerge all the time that may offer additional resources. For example, there is increased talk of distance learning and laser disk technology playing a more important role. The point is to be open to new possibilities.

1. Vocational Education

Vocational education is normally offered through a public school or regional/area vocational skills center in daytime, evening, or weekend classes. The opportunities here are enormous. They range from basic skills classes in carpentry, electricity, or plumbing to advanced training in computers, photography, or horticulture. In addition, many courses related to word processing, marketing, and home and business topics are offered. Typically the cost is low and classes are held at times and places convenient for full-time employees; they include not only traditional day and evening classes but also weekend workshops. Vocational education is available just about everywhere in the United States. It has something of value for everyone across the life span. For example, these programs may be of interest to the midlife or retired person who is looking for a chance to retool old skills or develop new ones. The *American Trade Schools Directory* (1990) is an excellent national source of information on vocational education programs.

2. Community Colleges, Junior Colleges, and Vocational-Technical Colleges

The growth and expansion of these institutions has been phenomenal. For the past fifty years, most of these institutions have had an open-door policy, which means that they will admit and give a chance to almost anyone without regard to prior academic achievement if they can do the required work. Students may need to go into some form of remedial program to show what they can accomplish—but it is a start. Costs for these courses/programs are kept to the lowest level possible. Financial aid is usually available. Courses are often arranged at a time and place convenient not only for regular day students but also for people holding down full-time jobs. Three types of programs are usually available: (1) *associate (two-year) degree programs in arts or sciences (AA/AS)*, which can be a basis for transferring to a four-year institution or may be used as a stepping-stone to professions such as nursing, surveying, or secretarial science; (2) *certificate programs*, which are at a lower level than the associate degree programs and emphasize certain skills or competencies needed for occupations in fields like heating and air condition repair or auto mechanics; and (3) *personal/professional growth programs*, which may be connected with work or leisure but normally do not lead to either an associate degree or a certificate (often they are in the form of short courses and may deal with almost any subject of interest to a group in the community—foreign languages, art, gardening, and so on).

3. Adult Education

Adult education is usually available in most communities at a variety of educational levels. A well-known program in this category is basic literacy preparation at the fundamental reading and writing skills level, often offered in cooperation with a group of local volunteers. These courses lead all the way to high school–level subjects and can culminate in the General Education Development (GED) certificate or the High School Equivalency diploma. Often these programs are attractive to non–English-speaking people seeking basic adult education as well as to those who have dropped out of school at any age.

4. Private Career/Proprietary Schools

These represent a wide variety of private, for-profit institutions that offer preparation in specific skill areas such as word processing, computer programming, fashion design, food preparation, or travel agency management. Programs of study available in these institutions usually lead to a certificate indicating a certain level of skill. The cost of attending these schools is normally higher than it is at a community college, but financial aid is usually available. Accreditation is typically granted by a state agency, like the state department of education, as well as by national groups, such as the National Association of Trade and Technical Schools, which helped to publish Myers and Scott's *Getting Skilled, Getting Ahead* (1989), a first-rate guide to choosing a private career school.

5. Health-Related Training

This type of training is customarily available in hospitals or health centers. Programs in this setting are often occupation specific; examples include medical records secretary or licensed practical nurse (LPN). There are also hospital-based registered nurse (RN) programs, which take three years, around the country. Programs in these settings are attractive to those who are interested in a helping occupation where there is full opportunity for clinical or field study while taking formal instruction.

6. Apprenticeship Programs

Apprenticeship programs represent one of the oldest forms of continuing education. They are typically administered through a joint labor union–industry council. Classroom and applied work is available in forty to fifty occupations in most states; apprenticeship frequently involves a one-to-one learning situation. Completion time ranges from two to six years, with most participants taking four years to finish an apprenticeship program. Contact can usually be made through the local office of the state employment (public) service, a local apprenticeship information center (AIC), or a regional apprenticeship office.

7. On-the-Job Training

On-the-Job Training (OJT) programs are normally available through large employers and closely resemble apprenticeship training except they are usually shorter in duration and are conducted by employers. In smaller work settings, the term may be used to describe informal procedures whereby a senior worker trains a new worker for an extended period of time— or until the new employee is competent to work independently.

8. The Job Training Partnership Act

The Job Training Partnership Act (JTPA) is the third in a series of mainly adult training or retraining programs dating back to the 1960s. Predecessors included the Manpower Defense Training Act (MDTA) and the Comprehensive Employment and Training Act (CETA). The main emphasis is on organized programs at little or no cost to the participants that are made available in communities where there appears to be a need for the training and prospective employment. The preparation is extensive, running from several weeks to a year or more. There is usually a stipend available to participants and a required period of classroom and applied study. Programs are usually run by a local or regional private industry council (PIC).

9. Military Service

Counselors have long recognized the military as a major source of education and training opportunity. This is true today more than ever before. Opportunities include everything from basic training (lasting twelve to sixteen weeks) to specialized training in areas such as medicine, computer technology, auto and aircraft mechanics, and construction technology. In addition, several branches of the military run their own two-year community colleges, such as The Community College of the Air Force. Military service also offers opportunities to put money aside for postmilitary education.

10. Correspondence Study: General

There are an amazing array of correspondence courses, from advertising and art to yacht design and zookeeping, with just about everything in between. Home study courses vary in scope, level, and length. Some have a few lessons that take only a couple of weeks to complete, while others have hundreds of assignments requiring several years of study. Correspondence courses are an ideal option for those who are homebound or in remote locations or who strongly prefer independent study. An accreditation list is available annually from the National Home Study Council.

11. Correspondence Study: Undergraduate and Graduate Level

These courses are available through the National University Continuing Education Association (NUCEA) and are listed in Peterson's *Independent Study Catalog* (Wells & Ready, 1989). Over seventy colleges and universities offer some 12,000 correspondence courses. These institutions include Auburn, Pennsylvania State University, the University of Missouri, the University of Colorado, and Washington State University, to name a few. Formal courses are organized and graded by regular college faculty.

12. Cooperative Extension Service

This operates under the provisions of the land-grant college mission and provides a wide variety of programs in every state. Normally information is readily available through the local extension office. In past years, these offerings were mainly focused on agriculture and home economics—but that is no longer the case. Courses and programs are available in fields related to business, engineering, and other areas of technology as well as in more traditional areas. The well known 4-H program for youth between six and nineteen provides a wide range of solid learning experiences for both urban and rural youth. There is also more and more assistance available for small businesses and work-at-home activities.

13. ELDERHOSTELS

This program is an effort to help meet the growing demand for educational opportunities for those over sixty. It was started by innovative educators in Boston in the 1970s and originally centered around summer offerings. Now the offerings are year round and around the world on just about any subject. Attendees usually stay in campus housing and choose from hundreds of short courses (usually lasting one or two weeks) on topics from "The Big Band Era" to "Medical Ethics" to "The Literature of Appalachia." The costs are kept far below normal institutional fees.

14. Learning Vacations

Learning vacations have been open to children and youth in the past, but in recent years they have grown in popularity for all age groups. The best source on this option is Eisenberg's (1989) *Learning Vacations*. Some of the topics this guide covers include learning cruises, camps, international tours, and U.S. tours.

15. Cable Television and Video Courses

While television may not have turned out to be the educational cutting edge it was once heralded to be, it is still a source of significant educational opportunity. The advent of cable television has spurred many advances in educational television. Some cable channels are dedicated to regular course offerings (both short courses and full-length ones). The availability of video instruction has taken off with the increasing popularity of VCRs. The education area represents one of the largest sections of some video stores. Bookstores are also expanding their services in this area as well.

16. Association-Sponsored Training

This form of training has grown by leaps and bounds in recent years. For example, the American Management Association puts out a semiannual fifty-page catalogue listing both short courses and longer, more intensive training in locations across the country. Almost every major professional association has preconvention or one- to three-day continuing education unit (CEU) offerings on contemporary topics at various locations.

17. National and Local Club Groups

Such groups provide education and training activities at levels from beginning to advanced. Often these programs are built around local, state, regional, or national meetings. There are over 3,000 groups in the United States, ranging from the Academy of Model Aeronautics to the Appalachian Mountain Club to the National Gardening Association. For an up-to-date listing of all the current groups and their addresses, see *National Avocational Organizations* (Germain, 1987) published by Columbia Books.

18. Civic and Service Organizations

These organizations provide training opportunities to people of all ages. For example, the local Jaycees or chamber of commerce may offer everything from small-business seminars to in-depth study of purchasing practices. Groups like the local Red Cross chapter or the rescue squad may provide instruction in CPR, water safety, advanced medical emergency training, and so on. The Rotary, Lions, League of Women Voters, YMCA, YWCA, and other organizations often conduct leadership development seminars or organize volunteer groups to provide community service.

19. Parks and Recreation Departments

In addition to offering the traditional physical activities and team sports, these departments now can be expected to provide all kinds of arts-and-crafts instruction for every age group. Classes are also held on an array of topics ranging from astronomy and foreign languages to dog training and grooming. Through a course in basic upholstery, a person may learn about a rewarding leisure activity as well as a skill for a possible part- or full-time job. Other options include educational tours and events.

20. Staff-Sponsored Programs

Well-known examples of staff-sponsored programs include the offerings of the American Institute of Banking (AIB), which is open to employees of all member banking firms. Other alternatives include company-sponsored courses provided during working hours or after hours. In many cases, tuition reimbursement or tuition waiver programs encourage employees to earn college credit or CEUs for formal classwork during or after working hours.

The twenty options just reviewed by no means exhaust all of the possibilities in each locality. For example, "free-university" programs are available in many communities on a regular basis. These emphasize short-term courses on everything from current stock market trends to the ancient art of calligraphy. Many programs are also available to specialized groups such as those through state departments of rehabilitative services for people with disabling conditions. In short, the preceding summary is just a starting point for those who want to take advantage of the rich variety of education and training options available in the United States. The life-span tree of learning should continue to grow as new possibilities are added to it.

Major Shifts in Undergraduate and Graduate Education

Since the end of World War II, higher education in the United States has undergone a series of major transformations. These have had the effect of greatly expanding the educational system. One significant development was the impact of the "GI Bill," which allowed millions of World War II veterans to enroll (or reenroll) in universities. Subsequently, large numbers of women and people of color have entered the system. Many new colleges and universities and new types of programs have arisen to meet their needs.

A natural outgrowth of the dramatic increase in bachelor's degrees has been an increase in master's and doctoral degrees. From the 1940s on, there have been competing demands for more technical education versus more liberal arts; following the GI Bill veterans came the inevitable "baby boom generation" to be followed by what was heralded as a major decline in enrollments in the seventies—which never really came about due in part to the unexpected growth of "nontraditional" students usually thought of as those older than twenty-two to twenty-four years. The details on information summarized in this section can be found in two publications of the National Center for Education Statistics: *The Condition of Education, 1989, Volume 2: Postsecondary Education* (1989a) or the *Digest of Education Statistics, 1988* (1989b), which has more detailed reporting.

One example of the changes sweeping higher education will be used to represent many others that could be noted if space permitted. This one pertains to external degrees at both bachelor's and master's degree levels. In 1980 the American Council on Education published the *Guide to Undergraduate External Degree Programs in the United States,* listing 150 undergraduate external programs. In 1987 the Regents College of the State University of New York issued the *Directory of External Graduate Programs 1987–1988* (Kahl, 1987) noting 200 such opportunities provided by colleges and universities already accredited by a regional accreditation unit. All this shows that innovative programs such as the Empire State College in New York and NOVA University in Florida have not gone away but have grown and flourished because of the appetite of adults who, once they have a taste of higher education, want to continue their degree pursuits. In short, the world of education and training in the United States is dramatically changed by the advent of these external degree programs.

The Changing Size and Scope of Institutions

As noted earlier, this process of expansion has been underway for many years. Only three of the many dimensions of these changes will be cited here. First, "megauniversities" have emerged. While any institution of 30,000 to 50,000 students may fit this description, an especially good example is Ohio State University in Columbus, Ohio, with 50,000+ enrollment. Institutions of this size typically have high-rise resident halls, large classes, heavy faculty emphasis on research and service, and comprehensive program and degree offerings. Second, the small state teachers college or normal schools have developed into mid-sized (5,000–10,000 enrollment) universities. Two examples in the South illustrate the point. East Carolina Teacher's College in Greenville, North Carolina, has changed its name to East Carolina University and grown from several thousand to 8,000–10,000 students. Likewise, Madison College (formerly all female) in Harrisonburg, Virginia, is now James Madison University, with an enrollment of 8,000–10,000. Third, large, diverse urban public universities have appeared. The University of Missouri, St. Louis, or the University of Missouri, Kansas City, stand out as Midwestern illustrations. (This type of educational growth in urban centers has coincided with the growth of metropolitan areas in the past fifty years.)

The Changing Gender Mix in Higher Education

This shift gained momentum in the 1940s and has not altered its course since then. Women represent a growing number and percent of those attending higher education institutions. The proportion of associate and bachelor's degrees earned by women increased from 43 percent at each level in 1971 to 56 percent of the associate degrees and 51 percent of the bachelor's degrees in 1986. The proportion of advanced and professional degrees earned by women also increased between 1971 and 1986. Now women earn nearly one-third of all advanced graduate degrees—up from around 10 percent in 1971. If the impact of women was the big story of the twentieth-century labor market, then women in higher education is the next big story, second only to the impact of veterans in the 1940s. See Table 5.1 for details of the trends of the 1970s and 1980s.

Age of Students Attending Higher Education Institutions

The number of older students has been growing more rapidly than the number of younger students. Between 1970 and 1985

Table 5.1. Percent of Degrees Earned by Women, by Degree Level: Academic Years Ending 1971–1986.

Academic Year Ending	Associate Degrees	Bachelor's Degrees	Master's Degrees	Doctoral Degrees	First-Professional Degrees[a]
1971	42.8	43.4	40.1	14.3	6.3
1972	43.1	43.6	40.6	15.8	6.2
1973	44.5	43.8	41.3	17.8	7.1
1974	45.2	44.2	43.0	19.1	9.8
1975	47.0	45.3	44.8	21.3	12.4
1976	46.4	45.5	46.4	22.9	15.6
1977	48.1	46.1	47.1	24.3	18.6
1978	50.3	47.1	48.3	26.4	21.5
1979	52.3	48.2	49.1	28.1	23.5
1980	54.2	49.0	49.4	29.7	24.8
1981	54.7	49.8	50.3	31.1	26.6
1982	54.7	50.3	50.8	32.1	27.5
1983	54.6	50.6	50.1	33.2	29.8
1984	55.2	50.5	49.5	33.6	31.0
1985	55.4	50.7	49.9	34.1	32.8
1986	56.0	50.8	50.3	35.2	33.4

[a]The National Center for Education Statistics recognizes ten first-professional degree fields: chiropractic, dentistry, law, medicine, optometry, osteopathy, pharmacy, podiatry, theology, and veterinary medicine.

Source: National Center for Education Statistics, 1989b (based on the HEGIS survey "Degrees and Other Formal Awards Conferred," various years).

the enrollment of students under age twenty-five increased by 15 percent. During the same period the enrollment of students twenty-five and over rose by 114 percent. In the later part of the period from 1980 to 1985, the enrollment of students under twenty-five decreased by 5 percent, while the enrollment of those twenty-five and over increased by 12 percent.

Minorities Enrolled in Higher Education

The proportion of college students who were minorities rose between 1976 and 1986. In 1976, 15.4 percent were minorities, compared to 17.9 percent in 1986. Much of the change can be attributed to sharply rising numbers of Asian students. However, the proportion of students who were African American fell from 9.4 percent in 1976 to 8.6 percent in 1986 and has continued to fall annually since then. The drop in the proportion of African American students is reflected mainly in the declining enrollment of black males.

Degrees Earned by Foreign Students

From 1977 to 1985, foreign students earned an increasing proportion of the bachelor's and graduate degrees awarded by American colleges and universities. The presence of foreign students is most pronounced at the master's and doctoral degree levels, particularly in the natural sciences and engineering, where they earned about one out of every four degrees in 1985.

Financial Aid for the 1990s

Changes in the financial aid picture have their modern roots in the National Defense Education Act (NDEA) of 1958. The NDEA created a large pool of federal funds both for specialized loan programs (like those encouraging students to go into science, mathematics, and foreign language teaching and then have their loans forgiven) and for general and guaranteed loans. Since then, a broad expansion of loans, scholarships, work-study, and other forms of financial aid has occurred. The amount of aid available in the early 1990s is around $6.4 billion annually from federal, state, local, and institutional sources. This is in addition to the millions of dollars in specialized aid available each year through national, state, and local private sources funded by religious, social, and civic groups. Many of these sources are obscure and take considerable effort to discover. The starting point for most of this aid is the College Scholarship Financial Aid form, the most widely used need-analysis form, with nearly three million forms filed each year at both the undergraduate and graduate levels. Current estimates are that among those receiving financial aid, about 49 percent receive direct grants or scholarships, 48 percent receive loans, and 3 percent are on work-study.

These are the best-known forms of financial aid:

Scholarships and Grants

Scholarships and grants are based on merit (academic, athletic, and specialized) or economic need and normally do not require recipients to pay back the money. There are growing specialized sources of aid for women and minority students and many other groups.

Loans

Since the passage of the NDEA in the late 1950s, loans for higher education have become respectable. There are three major federal programs: Perkins Loans, Guaranteed Student Loans (GSL), and PLUS loans. Of the three, the GSL loans are the most popular. In addition, a variety of state and institutional loan programs exist. In Virginia, for example, the Advantage Program makes loan funding available for up to $15,000 per year.

Work-Study

In work-study programs, students work up to twenty hours per week in institutionally related jobs in libraries, academic departments, administrative offices, and other locations. Cooperative education programs also exist at a hundred or so institutions. These programs alternate periods of full-time study and full-time work. Some feel this is the best form of aid because students gain valuable work experience while earning money to pay educational expenses. Often they can earn upwards of $8,000 to $10,000 for a semester of work.

The financial aid office is clearly the place to work with on the college campus, along with national and state career information delivery systems (see Chapter Ten for details on these delivery systems). Counselors also need up-to-date resources, including print sources like the guide published by the American Legion (1991), which is available in revised form each year.

Accreditation/Approval

Probably the question counselors most often hear from students, parents, and others is "How good is Subnormal University?" or "How good is Fly-by-Night Career School?" The answer can be a very easy one—the institution is either accredited/approved or it is not. In the United States, this recognition is extended primarily through nongovernmental, voluntary institutional or professional associations. These groups establish criteria for accreditation, arrange site visits, evaluate those institutions and professional programs that desire accredited status, and publicly designate those that meet their criteria.

Institutional accreditation is granted by the regional and national accrediting commissions of schools and colleges, which collectively serve most of the institutions chartered or licensed in the United States and its possessions. These commissions and associations accredit total operating units only.

Specialized accreditation of professional or occupational schools and programs is granted by national professional organizations in fields such as vocational education, correspondence study, business, dentistry, engineering, and law, among others. Each of these groups has its distinctive definitions of eligibility, criteria for accreditation, and operating procedures, but all have undertaken accreditation activities primarily to provide quality assurances concerning educational preparation of members of the profession or occupation. Many of the specialized accrediting bodies will consider requests for accreditation reviews only from programs affiliated with institutions holding comprehensive accreditation. Some specialized agencies, however, accredit professional programs at institutions not otherwise accredited. These are generally independent institutions that offer only the particular discipline or course of study in question.

The Council on Postsecondary Accreditation (COPA) is a nongovernmental organization that works to foster the role of accrediting bodies in promoting and ensuring the quality and diversity of American postsecondary education. The accrediting bodies, while established and supported by their membership, are intended to serve the broader interests of society as well. To promote these ends, COPA recognizes, coordinates, and periodically reviews the work of its member accrediting bodies and the appropriateness of existing or proposed accrediting bodies and their activities by granting recognition and performing other related functions.

In brief, there are five *national* institutional accrediting bodies. There are six *regional* institutional accrediting bodies. There are thirty-five *specialized* accrediting bodies. In addition, each state usually has some governmental body that approves both postsecondary education at the undergraduate and graduate level and in nondegree programs in proprietary/career schools. This state level of approval is normally done by a state council of higher education for colleges and universities and the state department of education for proprietary/career schools. Probably the best source to consult on this subject is Harris (1991), which has an excellent section on the entire accreditation process and is updated annually.

In recent years, an increasing number of surveys have appeared in books or in *Money* magazine, *U.S. News & World Report,* and similar publications. These reports usually have titles like "Public Ivies," "Top 10 Colleges and Universities,"

"Top 50 Most Selective Colleges and Universities," "Top 100 Graduate Schools in the Nation, Region, and State," and so on. These command a good deal of popular attention, especially when promoted by the institutions singled out for special attention, but the less publicized basic accreditation/approval voluntary process is the backbone of the system in the United States.

Licensure/Certification Requirements

As professionalism and the emphasis on accreditation have increased over the past fifty years, so has the concern over licensure/certification. Licensure requirements have long existed for professions such as medical doctors, lawyers, and registered nurses. Other professions have been added to this group. As the field of counseling has grown over the past thirty years, for example, course and degree requirements for school counselor certification through the fifty state departments of public instruction have generally become more stringent. This has meant increased preservice course requirements as well as certification renewal courses, which are needed every two to four years. Certification requirements for public and private school personnel have gone up gradually over the years at both the preservice and the in-service level. These increased requirements for licensure/certification groups have had a direct impact on graduate education programs in higher education.

To carry the counseling illustration a step further, the full impact of licensure can be noted in the origin and growth of the National Board of Certified Counselors (NBCC) and the parallel movement in Licensed Professional Counselors (LPC), starting with Virginia in 1975. There are now thirty-five states with some type of licensure requirement for work in the private practice of counseling. The NBCC has a full examination and certification function. Some 17,000 counselors have met the requirements for Nationally Certified Counselor (NCC), and over 1,000 are Nationally Certified Career Counselors (NCCCs). As with most professional groups, graduate education in counseling is regulated by an accreditation organization. This is the Council for Accreditation in Counseling and Related Education Professionals (CACREP). This group was formed under the sponsorship of the American Association for Counseling and Development (AACD) and the Association for Counselor Education and Supervision (ACES). It now has a fully functioning board of directors and executive secretary as well as teams of counselor educators prepared to make site visits. There were fifty approved CACREP graduate counselor education programs in 1990, and the number is growing. Graduates of CACREP-approved institution programs do not have to take the NBCC licensure examination.

The counseling illustration is paralleled in most other professional fields. Licensure/certification is required for some fifty occupations in most states, often with national examinations. These occupations include:

Accountant (CPA)
Alcoholism/Substance Abuse
  Counselor
Animal (Veterinary)
  Technician
Architect
Asbestos Inspector
Attorney
Barber
Chiropractor
Cosmetologist
Counselor (Licensed
  Professional)
Dental Hygienist
Dentist
Embalmer/Funeral Director
Emergency Medical
  Technician
Engineer
Geologist

Occupational Therapist
Optician
Optometrist
Pharmacist
Physical Therapist/Physical
  Therapist's Assistant
Physician/Physician's
  Assistant
Podiatrist/Podiatrist's
  Assistant
Polygraph Examiner
Private Security Agent
Psychologist/School
  Psychologist
Public School Administrator
Real Estate Agent
Registered Nurse
School Counselor
School Social Worker
Soil Scientist

Hearing Aid Dealer and
  Fitter
Insurance Agent
Landscape Architect
Librarian
Licensed Practical Nurse
Nursing Home
  Administrator

Speech Pathologist and
  Audiologist
Surveyor, Land
Teacher
Veterinarian
Water and Wastewater
  Worker

The example of counselor licensure/certification and the increasing educational requirements in this field is closely paralleled by most of the thirty-five specialized accreditation bodies approved by COPA. They govern the highly complex medical/dental areas, architecture, librarianship, psychology, teacher education, and so on. The best general source of information on licensure/certification and related matters is Harris (1991).

6

██

The Importance of Leisure in Career Development

██

In 1984, for the first time in the series of three decennial volumes published by the National Vocational Guidance Association or NVGA (now the National Career Development Association or NCDA), the topic of leisure was elevated to the status of a chapter. There are evident changes in the United States and other Western industrial nations demonstrating that the topic of leisure deserved that level of attention in such an important book. These changes have a direct bearing on tomorrow's workplace. Some of them are:

- shorter workdays and workweeks
- longer and more frequent vacations
- earlier and better retirement from a financial standpoint for many people
- greater availability and acceptability of leisure options
- higher levels of interest in leisure
- more unemployment and underemployment

The argument of Chapter Six is that work and leisure are part of one's career and both merit the attention of career counseling professionals. This chapter is a key section of the four chapters devoted to foundation knowledge that make up

Part IV of this book. Clearly, the inclusion of the role of leisure is a major departure from other books representing a part of our holistic view of career development through the life span. Other indications of the growing importance of leisure include the creation of NCDA's Commission on Leisure and Career Development; an invited paper on work and leisure at NCDA's 75th Anniversary Conference; occasional convention programs; an increasing number of articles on leisure over the last decade in the *Career Development Quarterly,* the *Journal of Counseling and Development,* the *Journal of Career Development,* the *School Counselor,* and other professional counseling periodicals; and some new books focusing on leisure counseling. The larger body of knowledge in the area, though, is still coming from the traditional recreation field. In many universities or community agencies, this field has been renamed *leisure studies* or *services.* Publications such as *Leisure Sciences,* the *Journal of Leisure Research,* or the "Leisure Today" section of the *Journal of Health, Physical Education, and Recreation* report regularly on the topic. Many writers in the leisure field have established international reputations. Important American works include de Grazia's *Of Time, Work, and Leisure* (1962), Kelly's *Leisure* (1982b), Kaplan's *Leisure Theory and Practice* (1975), Neulinger's *Introduction to Leisure* (1981), and Murphy's *Concepts of Leisure* (1981). European examples are Parker's *The Future of Work and Leisure* 1971), Roberts's *Leisure* (1981), Dumazedier's *Toward A Society of Leisure* (1967), Veblen's *The Theory of the Leisure Class* ([1899] 1935), Anderson's *Man's Work and Leisure* (1974), and Pieper's *Leisure: The Basis of Culture* (1964). Examining the works just noted would provide a good background in the area of leisure studies. Another ten or so professionals in counseling (whose works are cited in the References) are also building a foundation for a more compatible relationship between work and leisure in the career development process.

The chapter presents some working definitions of important terms, establishes a framework for the interrelationship of work and leisure, addresses some unresolved issues related to leisure, and suggests a life-span approach to work and leisure for counselors.

Definitions of Terms

The terms *work* and *leisure* have a great deal of personal meaning for people. Academic definitions can be stated here, but the average person in the street already holds a rather firm idea of what both terms mean. Work is what you get paid for and leisure is what you do not get paid for—it is as simple as that. Several years ago a group of elementary school children gave these definitions of *leisure:* "free time or play time," "when there ain't nothing to do," "when school is out," "when studying is done," "when I get to do what I want to do," and "when the family does things together." Adults might define leisure in similar terms, adding elements such as time, free choice, family activity, and so on. In short, there is no one accepted or established theoretical or common definition of *leisure.*

For purposes of this chapter, definitions of *work, leisure, career,* and *career development* are essentially taken from a report by Sears (1982, p. 139), which was reviewed by a panel of career guidance experts, the NVGA (now NCDA) board of directors, and *Vocational Guidance Quarterly* editorial reviewers. The definitions are:

> WORK—a conscious effort, other than having as its primary purposes either coping or relaxation, aimed at producing benefits for oneself and/or for oneself and others.
>
> LEISURE—relatively self-determined activities and experiences that are available due to having discretionary income, time, and social behavior; the activity may be physical, social, intellectual, volunteer, creative, or some combination of all five.
>
> CAREER—the totality of work [*and leisure*] one does in a lifetime.

CAREER DEVELOPMENT—the total constellation of psychological, sociological, educational, physical, economic, and chance factors that combine to shape the career of any given individual over the life span.

If adequate attention is to be given to the concept of leisure, it is essential to add the words *and leisure* to Sears's definition of *career*. Expressed as an equation, Career = Work + Leisure (C = W + L), a formulation McDaniels (1965) first suggested over twenty-five years ago. The coupling of work and leisure as the basis for a career over the life span brings all three elements together in a holistic framework. Obviously, other roles can also be incorporated into the career concept. Super (1984) includes nine roles in his life-career rainbow: those of child, student, work, leisurite, citizen, spouse, parent, homemaker, or pensioner. Super makes a strong case for this broader concept, but in this book the focus is on C = W + L. (See Figure 1.1 for a representation of the basic framework.) Through this linkage, leisure can be placed in the proper perspective as an important component of career development over the life span. Counselors and teachers can recognize the importance of leisure in elementary school, middle/junior high school, and senior high school. Counselors and other service providers can assist people in dealing with both work and leisure in one relationship—a career.

The Status of Leisure

There are many reports on the status of work; there are far fewer reports on leisure. But, as noted earlier, a growing number of sources show that the role of leisure is increasing in importance. For example, the Department of Commerce's *Survey of Current Business* (Bureau of Economic Analysis, 1989) showed that spending in this area was the fifth biggest category of personal spending, reaching a total of $247 billion in 1988. The single most significant rise in spending in this area was in "commercial participants amusements," which includes swimming pools, amusement parks, golf courses, and other similar commercial establishments. This spending is up from $2.4 billion in 1970 to $18.9 billion in 1988. A bowling tournament, a three-day pass at a Disney theme park, a ski lift ticket, a day of golf, or a sightseeing tour of New Orleans are counted in this category. One dimension of this is the fact that there were over 41 million people who went to Disney theme parks in Florida and California in 1990. Between 1985 and 1988, spending in all fifteen leisure categories went up from a total of $186 billion to $247 billion, a gain of $61 billion in spending in just three years.

Another way of looking at the importance of leisure is to see the reported rise cited by Cutler (1990) in the amount of spare time available to adults from eighteen to sixty-four between 1965 and 1985. In 1965 this was 34.5 hours per week, in 1975 38.3 hours per week, and in 1985 40.1 hours per week. Of the roughly forty hours of leisure time per week, about fifteen hours are spent watching television (about 38 percent), while reading books and magazines accounts for only about 10 percent. Cutler also reported increases in recreation activities to between four and five hours per week. Time for sports and related activities has more than doubled between 1965 and 1985. A recent Gallup poll (Gallup and Newport, 1990) showed that the interest of Americans in certain physical activities has remained rather constant over the past three decades, with swimming, bicycling, fishing, and bowling continuing to be favorite pastimes. The Gallup organization reports trends in what are called "back-to-nature" activities such as bicycle touring, camping, hiking, and boating, but swimming has held steady as the favorite American participatory sport over the past thirty years. The point of these illustrations is that adults in the United States have an increasing amount of leisure time available. Much of it is spent watching television, but a large and growing number of people are engaged in regular physical activity.

Two studies by the New York–based Research and Forecasts group provide further insight into the scale of leisure in

America. The first, *Where Does the Time Go? The United Media Enterprises Report on Leisure in America* (1982), is probably the most comprehensive study on leisure conducted in recent years. Over 1,000 people were interviewed in a carefully drawn nationwide sample. Some of the highlights of this report are:

- Reading a newspaper and watching television head the list of leisure activities Americans choose to participate in every day.
- Children in families in which both parents are employed outside the home get more daily attention than children in traditional families in which only the father is employed.
- Fathers in dual-career families spend much more of their leisure time in child-rearing activities than fathers in traditional families do.
- Television is not a disruptive force in American families; it actually may help bind families together.
- While watching television takes up more of our free time than any other leisure-time pursuit, six out of ten Americans say they do not pay close attention to television programs and often do other things while the television set is on.
- Parents who watch a lot of television daily are as likely as parents who watch little television to participate in activities with their children, interact with their spouse, and participate in community affairs.
- Half of all couples in the United States watch television together every day or almost every day. About 35 percent watch it together at least once a week.
- The top objective of Americans during their leisure hours is to spend time with their families. Eight out of ten Americans (79 percent) report that spending time with their families is the most important use of their leisure time, followed by seeking companionship (68 percent), relaxing (67 percent), learning new things (60 percent), thinking and reflecting (57 percent), and keeping informed about local, national, and international events (52 percent).

- Nearly half of all Americans (46 percent) say they participate in community volunteer activities. Dual-career parents and the parents of older children are the most active volunteers.
- Americans with few responsibilities to other family members have the greatest amount of leisure time. On a weekly basis, senior citizens have the greatest amount of leisure time (forty-three hours), followed by teenagers (forty-one hours), single adults (thirty-eight hours), childless couples (thirty-seven hours), parents with adult children (thirty-one hours), single parents (twenty-five hours), parents in traditional families where only the father is employed (twenty-fours hours), and, finally, dual-career parents (twenty-three hours).
- Single parents, surprisingly, say they have more free time than other parents with young children in America.

The second Research and Forecasts study, *The Miller Lite Report on American Attitudes Toward Sports* (1983), reported the result of a random sample through 1,139 national telephone calls. The main finding was that 96.3 percent of the sample relate to sports in an active or passive way at least once a month. Of those in the sample, 42 percent participated in some form of sports activity on a daily basis, with swimming being the most popular. Other activities included jogging, running, tennis, bicycling, bowling, and so on. Daily calisthenics showed a substantial number of adherents on a regular basis. People gave the following reasons for participation: to improve health, enjoyment, release of tension, and improved mental attitude. Finally, three out of four American parents reported that they sometimes or frequently engage in some kind of athletic activity with their children, and 81 percent reported that they frequently watch their children compete.

The impact of these studies may be viewed in a number of ways. In light of the previous findings on work and its future, the results on both leisure and work take on a somewhat different cast. The problem is, for the most part, that the findings are viewed separately—not as part of a holistic approach to people. The findings are not interpreted in terms of career, which by the definition proposed here encompasses both work and leisure. A brief summary of the findings about leisure is difficult, but the following points are inescapable:

1. Leisure is a major American enterprise, growing rapidly every year in magnitude and importance.
2. The family is a major focus of leisure activities.
3. Television viewing as well as spectator and participant sports take up a great deal of Americans' time.
4. The American public is seriously involved in volunteer activities.
5. American workers view leisure as a necessity, not a luxury. They want more of it.

Viewed collectively, these summary findings on the work-leisure connection suggest some major changes for both aspects of one's career in the near future. Leisure time and activities have been quickly growing in importance. Work and workers are probably in the most fluid state they have been in for the past century. Changes in Americans' attitudes toward work and leisure will have a significant impact on career development. A growing segment of the population is seeking increased satisfaction from both work and leisure— from work if they can find it there, but if not, through leisure or, under the best of conditions, through both. In some cases, they may look for ways to turn their leisure activities into work in a small business, entrepreneurial opportunity, or more satisfying home-based employment setting. Individuals entering the labor force, employees looking for new direction in their lives, and preretirees are all seeking a balance between work and leisure in their careers. Until now, career counseling has not been of much assistance because leisure has not been viewed as related to work in the context of career development. New programs providing career development assistance are needed that combine an emphasis on both work and leisure.

Some Unresolved Issues

If all the present and future trends continue, a number of unresolved issues will remain. Presently, the shifts in the marketplace and the workplace are evolving into significant societal trends. National policy directives and solid research and development activity are not addressing the changes. Few universities have ongoing research programs investigating work or leisure. Occasionally an association such as the World Future Society, the Association for Higher Education, or the National Career Development Association will publish a book related to work, but such groups do not promote sustained research and development activities. The Work-in-America Institute, the Upjohn Institute for Employment Research, and the Center for Research in Vocational Technical Education are notable exceptions and have an ongoing interest in work.

Only a few centers for the study of leisure exist. The best known of these is the Leisure Behavior Research Laboratory, which is part of the department of leisure studies at the University of Illinois, Urbana–Champaign. This department is producing highly significant studies by both faculty and graduate students (see Department of Leisure Studies, 1990). The groups that study work seem to show little interest in leisure, and the leisure centers show no visible interest in work. Therefore, many issues relating to the work-leisure connection go mainly unattended in a never-never land of mutually exclusive areas of interest. It may be that career development professionals who have no proprietary interest in either area can best resolve the issues noted below.

Do We Live in a Work or Leisure Society?

A host of studies have appeared in the *Monthly Labor Review* attempting to answer this question. Moore and Hedges (1971) traced the history of the work-leisure trends over the past century and found a reduction in the workweek between the mid 1800s and the 1940s. Since then the workweek has remained at around thirty-five to thirty-nine hours. The downward trend clearly seems to have leveled off. Hedges and Taylor (1980) reported a number of workers still working over forty hours. They also reported an increasing effort on the part of employees to obtain more and longer periods of paid leave rather than a reduction of the workday or workweek. In addition, they found that 5 percent of all collective bargaining agreements in recent years include provisions for extended paid leaves—sabbaticals. Hedges (1980) found a slight increase in the percentage of the labor force that was employed on a five-day, forty-hour schedule. She did not report significant gains in the four-day, forty-hour option except in very special situations where energy conservation was a concern or difficult transportation problems existed. No current or immediate future trend suggests that the United States is headed for a nonworking society, even though some futurist forecasters continue to see this as a possible direction. Increases are occurring in holidays, paid vacations, retirement benefits, and money to spend on leisure, but clearly there is no move toward a leisure, nonwork society.

Is "Leisure" a Dirty Word?

Put another way, leisure gets no respect! Some people in the career education movement avoid the use of this word by substituting the term *nonwork*. Yet clearly most people explore vocational interests through leisure activities. The vocational education literature is almost devoid of any mention of the term *leisure*. Nevertheless, millions of people each year use skills learned in vocational education classes for such leisure pursuits as cooking, photography, home repair, animal breeding, sewing, gardening, furniture refinishing, and so on and on—the list is almost endless.

The conventional wisdom is that leisure is not supposed to lead to any other activity. Leisure is thought of as an end in itself. It is not a matter of serious concern or study at the university or at the elementary or secondary school level. To be sure, a number of colleges and universities have renamed their recreation program *leisure studies,* but their interest is in mostly traditional recreation activities, with very limited emphasis on the intellectual, creative, social, or volunteer aspects of leisure. But a few scholars have evidenced solid and sustained interest in leisure as more broadly defined here. They include sociologists such as John Kelly at the University of Illinois, psychologists such as John Neulinger at New York University, and economists such as John Owen at Wayne State University.

The connotation of words is important. For example, vocational development seems to be taken more seriously if it is labeled *career development.* Leisure may simply mean play, free time, laziness, idleness, and not be recognized as a $250-billion-a-year industry affecting the lives of every person in the United States. In short, *leisure* clearly seems to be an abused and misunderstood term.

Do Schools Prepare Students for Leisure?

Remember the Seven Cardinal Principles of Education—1918? Remember principle number six: "worthy use of leisure time"! This principle was reaffirmed by a 1946 National Education Association study as an important school objective. This objective has not been met very well. The notable exceptions are art, music, dance, drama, physical activities (for all students), crafts, and so on, which are respected for contributing to student development. A balanced leisure program is often the first thing to be axed in budget cuts in school divisions across the country. At best, a mediocre job was being done in the preparation of youth for "worthy use of leisure time"; now the nation's schools seem headed for a period of time targeted for something even less.

Clearer standards must be set for career guidance, including leisure counseling. As it has turned out, seventy-five years with a vague cardinal principle have not accomplished much. Goals and objectives need to be established and monitored. In their book *Leisure Education: Theory and Practice* (1979), Mundy and Odum proposed goals for leisure education. The National Recreation and Park Asso-

ciation (1981) also conducted an active program, Leisure
Education Advancement Project (LEAP for short), which
attempted to implement a good plan of well-developed goals
and objectives.

Again, intervention by career development professionals
may be necessary to implement leisure education in the
schools. Mundy and Odum suggested an alliance with career
education to make both programs stronger. To combine leisure education with career education, the broader definition
of career (Career = Work + Leisure) must be accepted.

Can Leisure Satisfaction Replace Job Satisfaction?

If the high level of job satisfaction—80 percent, as reported
by Kalleberg and others (1983)—holds true on a national
scale, there is still a substantial percentage of workers who
are dissatisfied. Of 110 million people in the workforce,
approximately 22 million workers are unhappy with their
jobs. This is a large enough number to merit considerable
attention in attempting to find suitable life/leisure satisfaction. Further, with an unemployment rate that has ranged
between 5 and 10 percent, another ten million workers do not
have any job with which to be satisfied or dissatisfied. So a
combination of unhappy and unemployed workers may reach
thirty to thirty-five million. Could more adequate leisure programs help to make their lot more attractive? As Schumacher
(1977) and others have suggested, could some of those with a
high level of leisure skills put these satisfying activities to
work in self-employment or small-business settings? In effect,
by putting their leisure to work a significant number of
Americans could become employed *and* satisfied.

While there is no documented body of knowledge
regarding the impact of leisure on career satisfaction, there
are some indicators that leisure can be highly satisfying. Both
studies by Research and Forecasts (1982, 1983) suggested a
high degree of leisure satisfaction. Kelly (1982b) advocated
leisure as the central source of intrinsic satisfaction as opposed to the extrinsic satisfaction from a product or service

rendered. He thought leisure was a key to life satisfaction and a place to grow and expand in both intimacy and identity. Further, Kelly reported that one's leisure identity grows and expands throughout the life span to accommodate changing family, social, and economic situations. Yankelovich and Lefkowitz (1982a), writing in a special issue of the *National Forum* on "Leisure in America," reported that surveys over the past quarter century showed a strong trend toward people seeking life satisfaction in activities that do not depend heavily on the acquisition of goods and services. They agreed with Kelly that for a growing number of Americans, satisfactions will emerge through self-fulfillment, self-actualization, and self-expression—mainly in leisure activities.

Another dimension of the satisfaction issue is addressed by Lefkowitz in *Breaktime* (1979). He defined breaktime as life without work. He followed 100 people who were out of work for various reasons and found that many of them were reasonably satisfied with their "breaktime." Lefkowitz described people as being in search of ease, that is, relief from the daily pressures. They were seeking personal well-being, variation in their lives, and additional support for family and friends. For the most part, they found what they wanted while on their breaktime and at ease. They stayed out of work for two years or more, after which 60 percent of them returned to some type of regular employment. Forty percent or so continued to live off the underground or hidden economy and still had not returned to work when his study was complete.

In short, some people can be quite satisfied with leisure even on a full-time basis. This finding was supported by studies conducted by Tinsley and Associates at Southern Illinois University. Tinsley and Teaff (1983) described a group of 1,649 adults fifty-five to seventy-five years of age who were highly satisfied with the psychological benefits of their leisure. Some of the satisfactions mentioned were: companionship, compensation security, service, and intellectual aesthetics. The issue is still unresolved, but there are strong indications that leisure satisfaction could replace or complement job satisfaction for some people.

What Is the Future of Leisure Counseling?

Until a few years ago, most of the writing in the field of leisure counseling was by people in the field of recreation/ leisure services. They seemed to know the leisure area quite well but had limited credentials in counseling. Interest in leisure by recreation professionals seems to be less evident at the present. No clear indication exists of the direction of future interest in the area.

An emerging specialty—leisure counseling—seems to be of some interest for a few counselors and psychologists. Publications on leisure counseling include Edwards (1980); Loesch (1980); Loesch and Wheeler (1982); Overs, Taylor, and Adkins (1977); and Tinsley and Tinsley (1982). The fall 1981 issue of the *Counseling Psychologist* was devoted entirely to the topic of leisure counseling. Many of the developments in the new field of leisure counseling were summarized by Peevy in *Leisure Counseling: A Life Cycle Approach* (1981). Peevy defined leisure counseling over the life cycle as "that approach through which a person professionally prepared in leisure aspects of counseling attempts to help a counselee to accomplish the developmental tasks of each life stage through the selection and use of appropriate leisure activities" (p. 134).

At present, it is difficult to see exactly which way leisure counseling will go—to recreation or counseling professionals, or perhaps in part to both. Bloland and Edwards (1981) speculated that leisure counseling will be a short-lived specialty and will be taken in and considered part of the larger arena of career counseling. If the formula advanced earlier in this chapter— Career = Work + Leisure (C = W + L)—could be expanded to mean Career Counseling = Leisure Counseling + Work Counseling (CC = LC + WC), the direction would be clear. Some counselees may seek help in either the leisure or the work area or both. A skilled career counselor of the future should be able to provide assistance in both areas separately or in a combined holistic approach. Unless the leaders in the field of career counseling are more open to leisure counseling than in the past, there may be no place for the specialty to go except to leisure/

recreation professionals or be left to float free without strong professional roots. People need a more holistic, not a compartmentalized, approach to find satisfaction in the work world of the twenty-first century.

A Life-Span Approach to Work and Leisure

This final section of the chapter will focus on the interaction of work and leisure at various points throughout the life span. Career development is assumed to be a part of the larger concept of human development. The well-known work of Erickson, Havinghurst, Levison, and other human developmentalists undergirds the ideas expressed here. McDaniels (1973, 1976a, 1977) has provided a basis for examining the role of leisure in career development. A more detailed discussion of a life-span approach to work and leisure can be found in McDaniels's book *Leisure: Integrating a Neglected Component in Life Planning* (1982b) and his chapter in *Designing Careers* (1984b).

Readers should note also the important ideas of Rapaport and Rapaport in *Leisure and the Family Life Cycle* (1985). They substantiated the significant influence of the family in the origin, development, and nurture of leisure interests, experiences, and activities. Barrett and Chick (1986) found more recently that parents' leisure attitudes, satisfaction, and participation greatly influenced their children's level of leisure involvement. Sociologist John Kelly has conducted extensive research related to the influence of the family on leisure in the United States. For a detailed discussion of his concept of leisure and the *life course* (his term for *life span)*, see Kelly (1982b, 1983). He emphasized a three-stage life-course approach to leisure: preparation, establishment, and culmination. He described each major stage in terms of distinct leisure identities, interactions, and roles.

In the remainder of this section, we identify six stages that could easily be combined into Kelly's three periods or modified to form four or five phases. Stages are not defined by hard-and-fast age barriers. They serve as guidelines for counselors, organizations, and agency planners and as broad frames of references for individuals. They are flexible time frames, not brick walls. Some individuals go back and pick up activities from earlier stages. Others, for unexpected reasons, jump stages and move toward retirement at an earlier-than-expected age.

Childhood: Birth to Twelve Years—The Awareness Stage

Childhood is an important stage in that it acquaints people with the leisure activities that are available and provides potential experiences to test their levels of interest and skills in these activities. The first stage of childhood is divided into preschool and elementary school years, because during the first five years the home is the major influence in children's development, while during the next seven years peers and the school also become major factors.

In brief, the preschool years are important building blocks in the establishment of both leisure and work awareness. During this stage, children can begin to learn about the wide range of leisure and work activities, as well as their likes and dislikes—what is fun and what is not and who they like to be with for leisure and who they do not. They will also have an opportunity to observe the values of the significant adults in their lives in relation to leisure and work roles.

The elementary school years, roughly ages five through twelve, are a time of expansive opportunities for leisure and work awareness. Basic human physical, psychological, intellectual, and social dimensions and capabilities grow at a rapid pace during this period, and new activities can be introduced easily and freely. Usually, eye-hand coordination improves; manual dexterity and small and large muscles come under control. Elementary school–age children need to develop an awareness of a wide range of leisure-related activities, events, and experiences. They need the encouragement and the freedom to try out as many things as possible. They need to understand that not being good at everything is normal. They can learn about their different abilities and interests through leisure. By encouraging the development of leisure awareness, counselors can help children recognize their multiple dimensions, including their intellectual, physical, creative, social, and volunteer characteristics and interests.

An example of this sponsored by a nearby elementary school is what is called a spring camping weekend. From Friday evening till the camp ends Saturday night, each child participates in thirteen activities, from chess to gun safety. There are team and individual leisure-learning situations. The camping experience is now in its third year and gaining more support every year.

If all of these dimensions are valued equally, then every child should enjoy some important, genuine success with leisure and work activities. The emergence, establishment, and continued development of the leisure self-concept is important during this time period. Ample opportunities to test and refine likes and dislikes contribute to better self-understanding and self-esteem.

Adolescence: Thirteen to Eighteen Years— the Exploration Years

Adolescence, from age thirteen to eighteen, is the time when most individuals mature physically, socially, economically, intellectually, and emotionally. All of these traits play a role in the development and expansion of the work and leisure activities in which people may engage later in life. Adolescence is a time for continued awareness and beginning exploration of leisure. Kleibert, Larson, and Csikszentmihalyi (1986) found the leisure experiences of adolescence an important developmental link in acquiring the necessary skills to handle the demands of adult leisure options.

The school should provide leisure exploration both through classroom activities and through extracurricular activities. Opportunities exist for exploration in obvious subjects such as home economics and technology education. Music, art, and drama classes are other obvious places to explore the work-leisure potential. In English classes, exploration through writing activities can result in far-reaching work or leisure possibilities. Some types of intersessions in high schools and colleges help to draw these connections out and provide an opportunity for educational institutions to invite students to explore lifetime leisure (and maybe work) skills at school. Through extracurricular activities such as intramural and interscholastic athletics as well as lifetime activities like bowling, skiing, jogging, swimming, hiking, and so on, both males and females can explore leisure interests. Equally important are competitive and noncompetitive activities in drama, public speaking, and art through which students can move from awareness to exploration to preparation, if the skill and interest are present. Finally, all sorts of games such as chess, backgammon, and bridge can be explored to test interests and skills.

The family continues to be the single most significant influence on the leisure exploration of the adolescent. In cooperation with school and nonschool agencies, the family can provide an extremely wide array of useful, exploratory leisure and work experiences. In large population centers, nonschool agencies such as YMCA or YWCA, Scouts, Youth Clubs, and 4-H offer leisure-exploration activities not provided by the schools.

The educational system is structured so that students are expected to make both educational and vocational decisions during adolescence. At this time, teachers and counselors should be helping students examine the relationship between work and leisure. Students can learn to relate leisure interests to an occupation. They can also relate an occupation to their preferred leisure activities. However, before making a choice, students must be aware of the available options. They need to obtain information about the worlds of work and leisure and learn how they may interact. Adolescence must be a time for exploring both areas of career development, work and leisure.

Young Adulthood: Nineteen to Twenty-Four Years— The Preparation Stage

As young adults, people usually reach the crest of their physical, intellectual, and social development. They have more freedom than they had earlier in making decisions about how to spend their time. They probably have fewer financial responsibilities and less commitment to or investment in jobs than older adults do, and so they have greater freedom to participate in leisure activities. In addition, education is a personal choice (leisure pursuit) for the first time; it is now an option, not a requirement. Adult education, higher education, vocational education, correspondence study, and the military are just some of the educational options open to young adults (see Chapter Five for further discussion of these options). The preparation stage is also a time for risk taking and exploration, a time for trying new things and testing new possibilities. Leisure activities can be a part of this exploration process. In the transition from school and parental influence to a life-style of personal choice, young adults will prepare for a lifetime of interrelated work and leisure activities. Young adults seeking employment may use the available time to prepare for productive work or to engage in leisure activities, or some combination of both.

In most communities, the number of young adults continuing their education or working is about equal. For those in postsecondary education, the leisure options are quite different than for those working full time; however, interesting leisure opportunities exist in both educational and work settings.

For young college students, occupational choices can emerge from leisure interests in areas such as student government; musical, art, and drama organizations; social groups; and intercollegiate athletics. Popular leisure programs have been reported by the Leisure Exploration Services (LES) at Southern Illinois University, the Leisure Resource Room at Texas Woman's University, and the Leisure Fair at the University of Oregon.

Young workers can continue leisure activities started in childhood or adolescence or start off in some new directions. This is a time of preparation for lifetime leisure activities by expanding on older interests or building on new ones available because of newly acquired money, time, or social approval. Also, young workers who are dissatisfied with their occupations can seek life satisfaction or develop new work skills through leisure.

Adulthood: Twenty-Five to Forty Years—
The Implementation Stage

The next life stage in this scheme of things is adulthood, which extends from about twenty-five to forty years of age. Most adults in this age range are working full or part time. Their jobs may be instrumental in determining leisure pursuits and the time available for leisure. Job expectations can influence leisure. For example, an executive may carry on business while playing golf, or co-workers may expect a machinist to bowl or play softball on the company team. The types of company benefits or opportunities provided for leisure are also important. Chosen leisure activities may depend on whether the individual works alone or in a group. Paid vacations also may be a source of expanded leisure activities. Adults have the freedom to choose among leisure activities that include archaeological digs, singles camps, family vacations, camping, fishing, and so on. The choice of leisure activities is now more than ever an individual decision.

A new potential for leisure comes to many adults through their families. Families can make leisure planning a part of their regular activities. Family-oriented leisure pursuits—for example, growing an expanded garden, planting a tree farm, or forming a family musical group—can also become a source of additional income. Men or women who remain at home caring for children may find useful opportunities for leisure activities through volunteering. Volunteer activities may help a person keep job skills current.

In this stage of life, some people quickly become disenchanted on the job, feeling that their work is dull, boring, or generally unfulfilling. For the most fortunate adults, work and leisure complement each other, with both yielding equal satisfaction. But for others, leisure may replace work as the major source of life satisfaction.

Midlife: Forty to Sixty Years—
The Involvement and Reassessment Stage

At midlife, age forty to sixty, most people are at the peak of development in many continuous leisure and work interests. Whatever people like to do, they probably do it with some degree of expertise and may become consultants or teachers to family and friends in leisure matters.

During the midlife stage, a number of different factors affect people's leisure activities. For example, they may experience deepening job dissatisfaction, perceiving that they have reached a career plateau and that further promotions are unlikely. They can use leisure activities to provide alternative forms of life satisfaction. At this time, individuals may have more time for leisure activities because children are leaving the home, parents are dying, or job responsibilities are being reduced. More money may be available for leisure pursuits if they have reached the peak of their earning power at the same time that family financial responsibilities have decreased. For out-of-work individuals, leisure may be the major or only source of life satisfaction.

Midlife is also the time when some people begin to prepare both psychologically and financially for retirement. Development of leisure interests during this stage that can be continued during retirement will provide continuity from a full-time work life to a full-time leisure life. Midlife is also a time to build possible income-producing skills related to leisure interests that can be used on a part-time basis.

Retirement: Sixty Years Plus—
The Reawareness and Reexploration Stage

The retirement stage involves total identification with and fulfillment of the desire for leisure. Full-time work is or soon will be only a memory for many. Time is now available—vast amounts of time! For some people, there is too much time. During retirement, leisure activities can now provide alternative uses of time. Although there is an increase in discretionary time, income may decrease. The retired person's leisure activities may change because of reduced income; an individual may no longer be able to afford the things previously enjoyed. The availability of community resources can also affect the leisure activities of retired people. Some communities have very few leisure activities for retirees. Others, especially retirement communities, provide a great many leisure activities and opportunities for the development and pursuit of leisure interests. Work-related volunteer activities such as civic or service clubs, unions, professional associations, or other groups may offer a new source of leisure satisfaction for retirees.

The best preparation for retirement is a carefully planned change over a period of years, eliminating the dramatic shock of a transition from full-time work one day to full-time leisure the next. If work has given the person satisfaction, then planned leisure could provide the same satisfaction. The transition from full-time employment to retirement can be made more easily by individuals who have developed leisure interests throughout their lives.

Leisure or Career Counseling over the Life Span?

There are many varieties of counseling. One way to measure these is to look at the generic and specialized certifications and licenses available through the National Board of Certified Counselors (NBCC) and in the states which have licensure. There is one universal: all have a general recognition of counselors. NBCC's certification is the Nationally Certified Counselor (NCC); in many states it is the Licensed Professional Counselor (LPC). NBCC also has available the Nationally Certified Career Counselor (NCCC). There does not appear to be any licensure available for one specializing in leisure counseling, though some people claim to provide such service and there are several books on the subject such as Loesch and Wheeler's *Principles of Leisure Counseling* (1982), McDowell's *Leisure Counseling: Selected Lifestyle Processes* (1976), Edwards's *Leisure Counseling Techniques* (1980), and a spate of journal articles, especially over the past ten to fifteen years. The point is, there are obviously various specialties under the generic term of counseling, but leisure counseling has not yet reached a level of recognition and respectability to warrant subspecialty status by the national general counseling organizations and state regulatory bodies.

Regardless of official recognition, counseling can be viewed as having a number of rather specific special purposes. One of those purposes can be leisure counseling. One of those purposes can be work or vocational counseling. Or, one of those purposes can be career counseling. Now, by definition in this book and in other places, career counseling is the broader and more all-encompassing term of counseling than the other two mentioned above. This, of course, is the point being stressed in this closing chapter—that counseling for the broadest and best prospects is what is most desirable: not a limited focus on work and occupation alone or leisure alone, but both in the context of one's career.

Conclusion

In conclusion, concentrating on the broadest possible objectives in the career development of individuals across the life span will serve the best purposes of society. Narrow preparation and experience may turn out to be of limited value in an uncertain world. People who have attended to both the work and leisure dimensions of their lives can face the future with a measure of assurance that there are satisfactions ahead that have been built on solid preparation for an evolving world of work and leisure throughout the life span.

7

▚▚▚▚▚▚▚▚▚▚▚▚▚▚▚▚▚▚▚▚▚▚▚▚▚

Integrating
Career and Family

▚▚▚▚▚▚▚▚▚▚▚▚▚▚▚▚▚▚▚▚▚▚▚▚▚

Work roles and family roles, the relationships between them, and their connection to career development are being rethought and reformulated. Why? Because "work-family linkages are so strong and pervasive that focusing on career development without simultaneously taking into consideration the family's developmental needs will produce an incomplete understanding of career dynamics" (Sekaran and Hall, 1989, p. 159). Why is this true? Because worldwide changes in work environments, social values, and family structures are taking place at a rapid pace, and these changes are likely to accelerate as we enter the twenty-first century:

> The U.S. work force traditionally has been composed of white men, but projections indicate that by the year 2000 this group will become a minority among those working. . . . As the composition of the work force changes in terms of race, age, and sex, there are accompanying changes in other realms of life. The traditional nuclear family accounts for less than 20% of households in the United States; the traditional picture of a male wage earner committed to the support of a

wife and several children makes up only about 11% of all families. . . . Perhaps the greatest change is in the dual-worker family and the single parent family; about 40% of the work force is comprised of dual-earner couples and another 6% are single parents. . . . For most women and men today, employing organizations and family are the two central institutions in life [Zedeck and Mosier, 1990, p. 240].

At the same time that family, economic, occupational, industrial, and social environments and structures worldwide have been changing, so have our conceptions of career development. As we saw in Chapter One, modern theories of career development began appearing in the literature during the 1950s and 1960s. By that time, the occupational-choice focus of the first forty years had given way to a broader, more comprehensive view of individuals and their career development over the life span. In addition to breaking the time barrier that had restricted our vision of career development to a cross-sectional, occupational-choice view, the broader definition of career development provided us with a holistic perspective on a person's life. It provided us with the idea of life roles, life settings, and life events interacting throughout the life span. As a result, it became possible to relate one role to another, one setting to another, and one event to another—that is, to see and understand them individually or as they interact with one another over the life span. In Chapter One, this conception of career development was called *life-career development* (Gysbers and Moore, 1975).

As our understandings of these major changes are becoming more complete, rapid changes in the work-family connection are taking place. At the same time, new counseling strategies are being created to respond to these changes. Chapter Seven briefly reviews major changes concerning the work-family connection. Then attention is given to working with clients to help them respond positively to changing work and family issues and relationships. Specific counseling techniques such as Life-Role Analysis, Typical-Day Assessment from the Life-Career Assessment, and the career genogram are presented that can be used with clients who are exploring and sometimes struggling with traditional and new work and family roles and relationships.

Work and Family: Current Issues and Trends

There is a substantial literature on the relationship between work and family (Miller, 1984; Love, Galinsky, and Hughes, 1987; Voydanoff, 1987; Zedeck and Mosier, 1990). Economists, sociologists, and psychologists have written extensively on this topic, each providing unique insights. What is the structure of the family today? What will it be like in the future? What are the tasks that families carry out to provide family continuity and growth? Will these tasks remain the tasks of the future for families? These are some of the questions we will touch on in this section.

Changing Family Structures

The traditional family of two parents and two or more children with only the father working has been displaced by a wide variety of new combinations: "Clearly the trend in family structure over the past decade or two has been toward increasing pluralism in the forms they take" (Herr, 1989, p. 96). The traditional family still remains, but it accounts for only about 20 percent of all families (Friedman, 1987). Based on the work of Macklin (1980), Herr (1989) identified such nontraditional family types as nonmarital cohabitation, voluntary childlessness, the binuclear family–joint custody, and coparenting, the step family, open marriage/open family, extramarital sex, same-sex intimate relationships, and multiadult households. Masnick and Bane (1980), in reviewing trends in the changing family structure, noted the continued increase of single-parent families and blended families.

Perhaps the greatest changes that have occurred, however, are in the rapid increase in the numbers of dual-career families and single-parent families. According to Friedman (1987), approximately 40 percent of the workforce is made up of dual-career couples; another 6 percent of the workforce is composed of single parents. And as these types of families increase, so too do the stresses and strains experienced by them and those around them.

Single-Parent Families. Burge (1987, p. 3) pointed out "that one of every four families with children under 18 years old in 1984 was a one-parent family, up from 1 of every 10 in 1970." The number of single-parent families is higher among African Americans; in 1984 approximately 60 percent of all African American families were headed by single mothers, compared with 20 percent for white single-mother families. In the literature three groups of single-parent families are often identified: displaced homemakers, teenage parents, and single fathers.

Displaced homemakers—women who have lost their spouses through death or divorce—represent a growing number of single-parent families. Their income has been drastically reduced. They are at an additional disadvantage because they often have little or no employment history, obsolete training or skills, low self-esteem, and external locus of control (Kerka, 1988).

Adolescent mothers, the second category of single-parent families, also face many obstacles to self-sufficiency. These obstacles include lack of education, lack of job skills, and emotional immaturity. They often have a need to complete their education and find a job. These goals may be blocked, however, because of needs for such basics as food, housing, child care, and emotional support (Kerka, 1988).

Single fathers, the third category, find themselves struggling to fill social roles that are difficult for them to handle. They often find that child-rearing roles conflict with work roles. Because men have tended to validate themselves by work, stress is often created for single fathers because they fear family roles and responsibilities will cause them to compromise their work roles. At the same time, the traditional work role for males is being challenged by new societal expectations to become more involved in family roles. Hellmich (1990, p. 2) stated that single fathers' stress is aggravated by the same things that concern women. These include:

- Feeling there's never enough time to be with their kids.
- Rushing to and from work to drop children off at day care or pick them up.
- Facing watchful eyes of bosses and colleagues when leaving work early to go to a kid's baseball game or ballet recital.
- Taking time off to stay home with a sick child.
- Having work-related travel cut into family time.

Dual-Career Families. Zedeck and Mosier (1990) noted that all dual-career families are not equal. They recommended that a distinction be made between dual-career and dual-earner or dual-worker families. Their reasoning was that work has different meanings for people. In dual-career families, wife and husband pursue their work because it has meaning, there is a developmental sequence in the nature of the work, and there is substantial commitment to work. On the other hand, in dual-earner or dual-worker families, husband and wife often work because work is an economic necessity. Other writers, such as Greenhaus (1988) and Sekaran and Hall (1989), however, felt that since the issues and concerns faced by all working couples are similar, it does not make sense to make any distinctions among types of dual-career families.

While the names given to this relationship may be important, of more importance are the attitudes and behaviors of the individuals in the relationship. How are the multiple roles, settings, and events of life handled by the two parties? Who does what and how do the individuals feel about it?

Four types of dual-career couples were identified by Hall and Hall (1980). They called them *accommodators, allies, adversaries,* and *acrobats.* Accommodator spouses are not directly involved in each others' roles, while ally spouses are involved in the same roles but are not competing with each other. Adversarial spouses are both highly involved in work and want the other spouses to do home tasks. Finally, acrobatic spouses are highly involved in both work and home tasks. According to Hall and Hall, the types with the highest degree of stress are the acrobats, followed by the adversarial spouses.

A major issue for dual-career families is the way work and family roles and responsibilities are arranged. The term *boundary differences* has been used by some authors, such as Sekaran and Hall (1989), to describe conflicts between roles at home and work. Role overload and role conflict are two problems that occur in dual-career families. Role overload comes from taking on multiple roles, while role conflict occurs when two or more roles require time or attention at the same time. Role overload and role conflict often cause feelings of guilt, frustration, and anxiety.

Sekaran (1986) described five dilemmas faced by dual-career families. The first is role overload caused by both spouses working and juggling all of the other life-role responsibilities in which they may be involved. The second is identity: "The gender-based roles and values internalized by them early in life conflict with the nontraditional roles they are now trying to establish and often create role and identity confusion" (p. 7). Sekaran called the third dilemma *role-cycling.* Which life role—work, parent, student—takes precedence when? The fourth dilemma is created by normative or environmental sanctions. Society's attitudes about nontraditional families have not caught up to reality: "The discrepancies that exist between the life-styles that nontraditional spouses would personally prefer and the normative behaviors that are prescribed by society cause dilemmas and psychological stresses for nontraditional families" (p. 10). The fifth dilemma, the social network dilemma, is created by a lack of time for socializing, and, as a result, having to make difficult decisions about whom to socialize with.

The Family Life Cycle and Family Tasks

In a comprehensive review of family development, Duvall (1988) discussed the evolution of the concept of the family life cycle. She traced the concept from the 1930s, when sociologists used it to study the American family, to the present. In 1957 she outlined stages of the family life cycle that serve as a standard in the field. Even with today's rapidly changing family patterns, including the trend toward more single-parent families, the stages remain generally the same. Hill (1986, p. 28) argued that "the differences in paths of development of single-parent and two-parent families are seen primarily, not in stages encountered, but in the number, timing, and length of the critical transitions experiences."

In her review, Duvall (1988, p. 131) also discussed the concept of family tasks. She listed the following ones as being basic for family continuity:

- providing physical care
- allocating resources
- determining who does what
- assuring members' socialization
- establishing interaction patterns
- incorporating and releasing members
- relating to society through its institutions
- maintaining morale and motivation

Families undertake completion of these tasks at each stage of the family life cycle. Since family interaction is not static, families address these tasks in their own unique ways.

The life roles that various family members are involved in, the settings in which these roles unfold, and the events—planned and unplanned—that occur in their lives influence the way tasks are completed at each stage of the family life cycle. *"Everyone* is concerned about juggling a work life, a personal life, a family life, a leisure life, a home, and other facets of living" (Sekaran and Hall, 1989, p. 161). This connectedness is important because there has been a tendency in the past to separate life roles, settings, and events as these interact to influence the completion of life tasks—the so-called "myth of separate worlds" (Mortimer, Lorence, and Kumka, 1986, p. 19). Work roles, work settings, and work-linked events in particular have been treated as separate worlds. It is the thesis of this book that work permeates the completion of family tasks consciously or unconsciously; it is a dominant theme that must be reckoned with.

Family Crises and Critical Transitions

"Family crises (e.g. unemployment, critical or chronic illness, death, divorce, and remarriage) shake a family out of its usual ways of functioning," according to Duvall (1988, p. 131). Even normal, to-be-expected transitions, such as school attendance and taking on a first job, cause a family to gear up to respond. Both crises and critical transitions call for a family to focus attention on the family tasks involved. Conflict and stress, both for the family and the individuals involved, may be present.

In the work-family connection, three forms of work-family conflict and stress were identified by Greenhaus (1988, p. 25):

a.   time-based conflict, in which the time demands of one role interfere with participation in the other role;

b.   strain-based conflict, where the stress symptoms (e.g. fatigue, irritability) produced in one role intrude into the other role; and

c.   behavior-based conflict, in which behaviors that are functional in one role are dysfunctional in the other role.

In summarizing the literature on the effects of work on the family, Voydanoff (1988, p. 5) found that the following job demands are related to work-family conflict and stress: "role ambiguity, role conflict, intellectual and physical effort, rapid change, pressures for quality work, pressure to work hard and fast, and a heavy work load." Conversely, the impact of family issues and tasks on work centered on "(1) the influence of family responsibilities on labor force participation and job performance and (2) the effects of family structure demands and supports on work role performance" (Voydanoff, 1988, p. 6). Family responsibilities motivate family members to participate in the labor force, while family structure and support determine, in part, how workers meet the demands of the workforce.

Understanding the Work-Family Relationship

What are some possible explanations for the stress and strain often associated with the demands and obligations of work and family? How do we understand this increasingly complex and dynamic relationship? Based on an extensive review of the literature, Zedeck and Mosier (1990) identified five major models that attempt to describe and explain the complexities and dynamics of the work-family relationship. These five models include spillover theory, compensation theory, segmentation theory, instrumental theory, and conflict theory. They focus more on individuals in the family than on the family as a unit.

Spillover Theory

According to spillover theory, there are no boundaries between work and family; what happens at work "spills over" into the family sphere and vice versa. Job satisfaction or dissatisfaction is seen as directly related to life satisfaction or dissatisfaction. Work is viewed as a socializing force providing workers with skills and views about self, others, and the world that carry over into family life (Zedeck and Mosier, 1990). There can be a negative side; for example, people may have to respond to the work conflicts and strain experienced by family members, thus diverting energy that could have been used more positively elsewhere.

Compensation Theory

Compensation theory hypothesizes that work and family roles are inversely related. Individuals invest differently in their work roles and family roles and may compensate in one for what is missing in the other. Zedeck and Mosier (1990, p. 241), building on the work of Crosby (1984), pointed out that "events at home provide 'shock absorbers' for disappointments at work and vice versa."

Segmentation Theory

This theory suggests that work and family roles can exist side by side without influencing one another. In other words, people can compartmentalize their lives. Zedeck and Mosier (1990, p. 241) stated that "the family is seen as the realm of effectivity, intimacy, and significant ascribed relations, whereas the work world is viewed as impersonal, competitive, and instrumental rather than expressive."

Instrumental Theory

According to instrumental theory, one role is used as a means of obtaining the necessities and luxuries that are deemed important for another role. Individuals work to obtain goods for family life. They also work to finance the purchase of goods and services for leisure activities—buying a boat, sports equipment, or media centers for the home, for example.

Conflict Theory

This theory postulates that success in one role may mean making sacrifices in another role. Or, even more directly, responding to family obligations may result in individuals being absent from their job, tardy, or not working efficiently on the job because they are thinking about their family obligations. In summing up this theory, Zedeck and Mosier (1990, p. 241) observed that "the two environments [work and family] are incompatible because they have distinct norms and requirements.

Responding to the Work-Family Relationship: Sample Counseling Techniques

Given the changing family structure and the family tasks and issues that have been identified, the question is, how can practitioners interested in counseling for career development respond to people caught up in the stresses and strains of the work-family relationship? The answer is to apply the same processes and procedures we use in other circumstances. We elicit clients' internal thoughts and feelings about those stresses and strains using the process framework, give meaning to these thoughts and feelings through the language of theory, and, based on our diagnoses, assist clients to take action to achieve their goals or resolve their problems.

A number of techniques are particularly useful in eliciting clients' internal thoughts and feelings concerning work-family relationship issues and problems. We present three of them in some detail: Life-Role Analysis, Typical-Day Assessment from the Life-Career Assessment, and the career genogram.

Life-Role Analysis

The Life-Role Analysis technique provides clients with a process and a structure that they can use to perceive and then analyze, with counselor assistance, the crises or critical transitions in which they may be involved. It also can be utilized by clients involved in goal setting as they plan their next educational and occupational steps.

Rationale. In counseling clients who are struggling with work and family issues and concerns, it is sometimes difficult to identify, sort out, and understand the dynamics involved. What is required is a way to conceptualize these dynamics and a structure on which to display them. Often the issues involved pertain to more than work and family. They involve other life roles, settings, and events. Hence the approach utilized needs to be broad enough and sensitive enough to pick up these related problems. As a result, the conceptualization of career development used in this book—life-career development—is the lens through which to view and understand clients' work and family concerns.

Administration. The Life-Role Analysis technique involves asking clients to analyze their life roles, life settings, and life events, the relationships among them, and their relative importance at three points in their lives: where they were five years ago, where they are today, and where they expect to be five years from now. Figure 7.1 presents the format for the technique.

To use the technique, begin by asking a client to choose from among the life roles appropriate for them—parent, spouse, worker, learner, leisure participant, citizen, child, and so on. Then, on a form such as the one in Figure 7.1, ask the client to go back five years and place, in the first large circle, smaller circles representing the life roles he or she was involved in at that time, arranging them so that they show how the roles touched each other, overlapped, or did not touch each other. The size of the circles representing the roles should reflect the relative importance of these roles for the client. The client performs the same task in the large circles marked "Today" and "Five Years from Now." Life roles can be added or removed, depending on the time period. Also, depending on the client and the client's concerns, the past, present, and future circles can all be used, or they can be used in any combination. For some clients, the use of the "Today" circle only may be sufficient.

Analysis. To assist clients in identifying, sorting out, and understanding specific work-family issues and concerns, theoretical explanations are needed so that working hypothesis can be developed that may explain the relevant work-family dynamics. All of the theoretical conceptions that were

Figure 7.1. Life-Role Analysis.

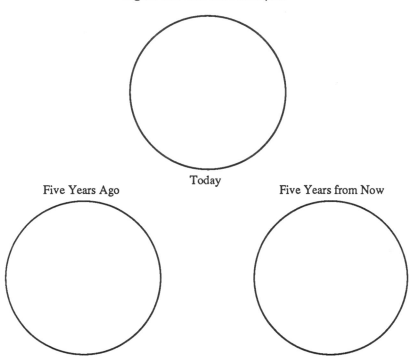

Five Years Ago   Today   Five Years from Now

Example Life Roles: Parent, Spouse, Learner, Leisure Participant, Citizen, Worker, Child

discussed in Chapter Two, as well as counseling theories in general, are available. In addition, Zedeck and Mosier's five models (discussed earlier in this chapter) provide useful language to help clients understand and derive meaning from the dynamics of their situations.

In characterizing these five models, Zedeck and Mosier pointed out that no one conception is usually sufficient to fully explain clients' behavior as they are involved in and experience work-family stresses and strains. Instead, combinations of these conceptions probably should be used to explain client behavior. But then the question is, "Do the theories function simultaneously or must they be sequential? That is, before one seeks to compensate for some factors, should there first be spillover for other factors?" (Zedeck and Mosier, 1990, p. 242). The answer varies.

To illustrate the use of these five models as well as other theoretical approaches to counseling for career development, suppose that a client filled out the "Today" circle as shown in Figure 7.2. Note that four roles overlap, one touches, and one does not. Given a presenting problem by the client of constant fighting at home and employer dissatisfaction with job performance, how does having the client complete this exercise help? First, it shows graphically how the client views life-role connections. It reveals the relative importance of each role in the client's mind. Second, it provides a visual way to assess the degree to which the five models can be used to explain the dynamics involved. Using leads such as "tell me about how this representation helps explain the problems with which you are dealing" and "tell me about how these roles—parent, spouse, learner, worker—overlap for you," the counselor can begin to help the client unravel the dynamics of the situation.

As these opening leads begin to generate client talk, hypothesis generation begins. In this situation, spillover theory may provide a useful framework within which the client can explore and gain insight into the situation. Conflict theory also might be fruitful.

Typical-Day Assessment

By focusing on a typical day in the life of a client, the counselor can obtain valuable information.

Rationale. The Typical-Day Assessment is part of the larger, longer assessment technique called the Life-Career Assessment (LCA) that was presented in Chapter Three. The Typical-Day Assessment is based on the work of Adler, as is the full-length LCA (Dinkmeyer, Pew, and Dinkmeyer, 1979). You will recall that Adler divided an individual's relation to the world into life tasks in three areas: (1) work, (2) society (social relations), and (3) love (friendship). According to

Figure 7.2. One Client's Version of the "Today" Circle.

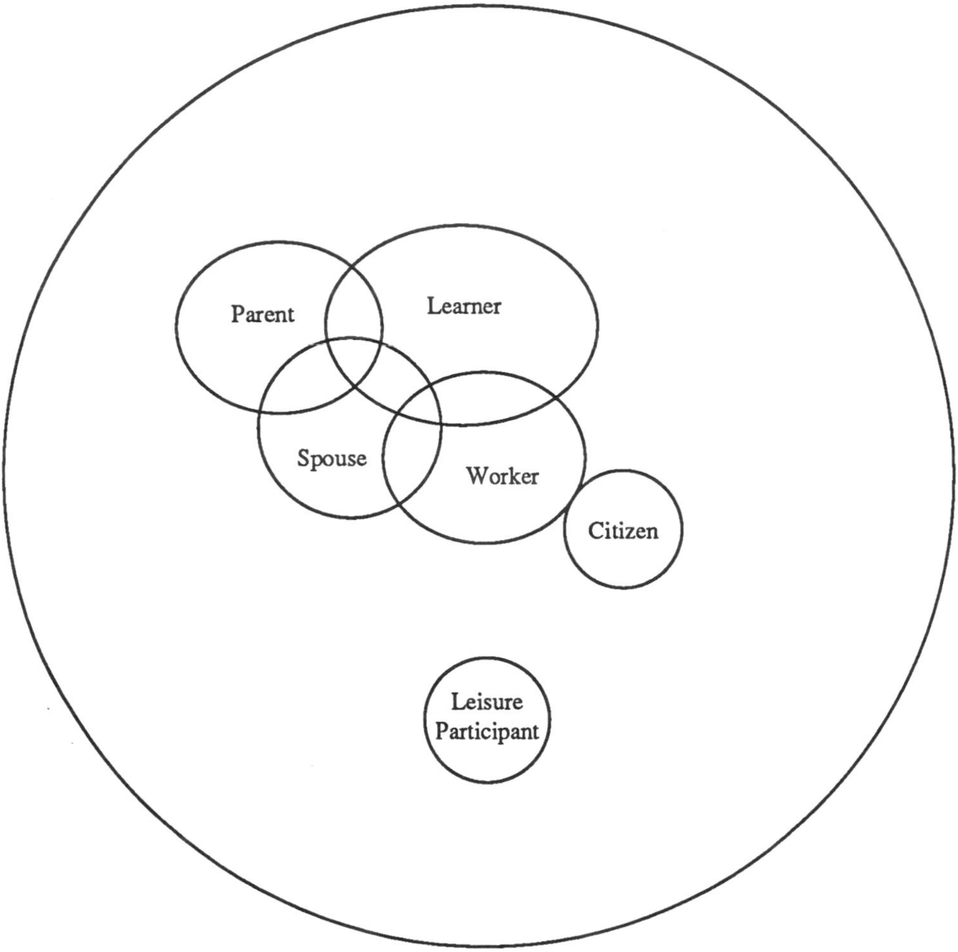

Adler, the three kinds of tasks cannot be dealt with separately since they are intertwined. A change in one involves the others as well. Difficulty in one part of life implies comparable difficulties in the rest of life. Although it may appear otherwise, a person's life is usually quite integrated. People tend to solve problems and attempt to obtain rewards or satisfaction in a similar manner as they strive to complete all three life tasks.

Administration. The purpose of the Typical-Day Assessment is to discover how individuals organize their lives. How do the life roles clients are involved in, the settings in which these roles unfold, and the events that occur in their lives come together during a typical day? Some clients may say that they do not have a typical day; in this case the word *yesterday* should be substituted for the phrase *typical day*.

This assessment is done by asking clients to describe a typical day in a step-by-step fashion:

- How do you get up in the morning?
- Do you eat breakfast? What do you have?
- Do you go to school? work? stay home?
- What is school, work, home like?
- With whom do you interact with at school? work? home?
- Do you eat lunch by yourself? With others?
- Do you eat dinner by yourself? With others?
- What is your evening like?
- Who does what family chores?
- Who decides who does what?

There is no one prescribed way to do the Typical-Day Assessment. You will need to discover your own personal style. It is important, however, to cover a full day, from the time clients arise to the time they go to sleep. It also is important to make it clear that the goal is not to invade their privacy. Rather, the intent is to provide them with a basis for talking about their levels of functioning in various life roles as well as how they negotiate the settings in which they live and work and the events that occur in their lives as typified during one day.

Analysis. A major goal of the Typical-Day Assessment is to understand how clients solve problems and obtain rewards and satisfaction as they negotiate all three life tasks. The phrase *life-career themes* is used to describe these ways of negotiating with the world. Life-career themes are reflected in the ways clients express ideas, beliefs, skills, attitudes, and values about themselves, others, and the world in general (Gysbers and Moore, 1987). There are many different themes by which clients operate, and each client will tend to operate using a number of themes. The themes clients use can be considered to constitute a life-style. Clients are not always aware of their approach toward life or the themes by which they operate, and they may not recognize the underlying consistencies that exist (Mosak, 1971). They may choose, rather, to dwell on specific, superficial feelings that serve to further obscure the way in which they are developing.

The framework of one day in the life of the client provides clients with the opportunity to talk about something they know—their day, their life. As they are describing their day, the counselor listens and begins to attach meaning through the development of working hypotheses. He or she shares these with clients on an ongoing basis by using such leads as "could it be that . . ." and "it seems as if . . . ," which are modified as needed. Zedeck and Mosier's five models are particularly useful for interpretive purposes. As clients share their day, one of the models—or, more likely, a combination of them plus other theoretical constructs—can help explain the dynamics involved in their situation. Thus, in conjunction with these five models or others, the Typical-Day Assessment technique can provide a straightforward, comfortable way to understand clients' work-family problems or goals.

Career Genogram

A genogram is a picture of a client's immediate and sometimes extended family drawn by the client using specific symbols to represent family members. The symbols that are used in constructing a career genogram are presented in Figure 7.3. It is used extensively in family counseling (Bowen, 1980; Heinl, 1985; McGoldrick and Gerson, 1985). Since this technique helps clients and counselors understand client career development issues and concerns from the perspective of family structure dynamics, it has been adapted for use in counsel-

Figure 7.3. Career Genogram Symbols.

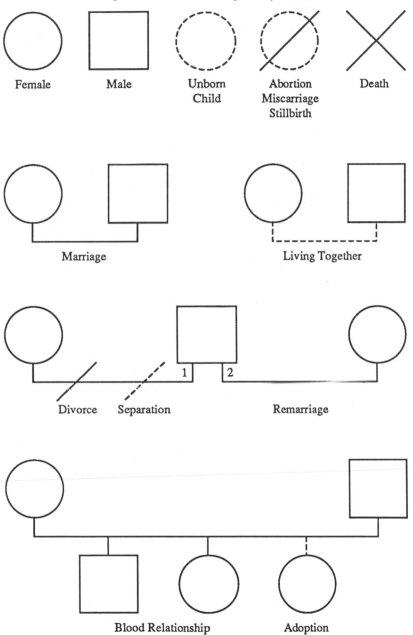

Female   Male   Unborn Child   Abortion Miscarriage Stillbirth   Death

Marriage   Living Together

Divorce   Separation   Remarriage

Blood Relationship   Adoption

Source: From Norman C. Gysbers and Earl J. Moore, *Career Counseling: Skills and Techniques for Practitioners,* p. 94. Copyright © 1987 by Allyn & Bacon. Reprinted with permission.

ing for career development (Brown and Brooks, 1991; Dagley, 1984; Gysbers and Moore, 1987; Okiishi, 1987). It is particularly useful for this purpose because it provides a direct and relevant framework for use with clients to shed light on work-family roles and responsibilities. It has substantial face validity for clients.

Rationale. Dagley (1984) summed up the rationale for the career genogram by suggesting that career issues (work-family issues) often can best be understood in the context of clients' sociological, psychological, and economic heritage: their family. Heinl (1985, p. 227) stated that a genogram "may provide pointers towards transgenerational and individual psychodynamic issues and may therefore contribute to fruitful therapeutic work." The career genogram can provide the client and counselor with a process to connect the client's understanding of the past to the present in order to better understand the work-family dynamics that the client may be facing in the present. Thus it is particularly useful to use with clients who are struggling with work-family issues and stresses. McGoldrick and Gerson (1985, p. 2) made the same point but from another perspective, as follows: "Genograms make it easier for a clinician to keep in mind family members, patterns, and events that may have recurring significance in a family's ongoing care. Just as language potentiates and organizes our thought processes, family diagrams which map relationships and patterns of functioning may help clinicians think systematically about how events and relationships in their clients' lives are related to patterns of health and illness."

Administration. The first step in the administration of the genogram is to tell clients what the purpose of the career genogram is. This can be done by explaining that the technique will provide them with insight into the dynamics of their current family and family of origin—that it will provide them with a picture of the career socialization they experienced while growing up.

The second step is to explain how clients can construct a career genogram. The following directions can be used verbatim or paraphrased to fit the client and the client's situation: "The career genogram can help us understand you and your current family and family of origin. Please draw a picture of your current family and family of origin using the symbols and format provided. Draw it on the sheet of newsprint on the table in front of you. (A chalkboard or other comparable writing surface also could be used.)"

A logical way of having clients begin the construction of a career genogram is with various stages of family life. They can begin with courtship, followed by marriage, children, and extended family examples. Have them write in the dates of birth, deaths, divorces, and remarriages, as well as the occupations of various family members to aid in the analysis process that follows. Sample questions to have clients respond to verbally or in writing are found under each of the stages of family life.

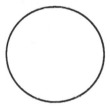 

Courtship Stage

- Length of courtship?
- What attracted you to each other?
- How much time did you spend together as a couple and how was this decided? (Probe into who pursued for more togetherness and time apart in the relationship.)
- When your relationship became exclusive, how did you handle your individual friendships?
- How did your parents view your relationship?
- Any previous marriages? Children from these marriages?
- Did you discuss how you would handle various work-family roles and responsibilities? What was decided?

Wife   Husband

Marriage Before Children

- What prompted you to get married at the time you did?
- How would you describe your relationship during this time?
- Amount and nature of individual time and time with friends?
- Life-style: social, financial, educational, time spent with in-laws?
- Work and family roles and responsibilities: Who does what? When?

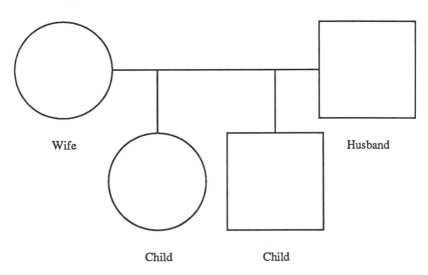

Family with Children

- What entered into your decision to have a child when you did?

- How did marital relationship change with birth of child?
- How did your individual roles change?
- Describe each child for me (oldest to youngest).
- Who is responsible for which family tasks? How were these decisions made?

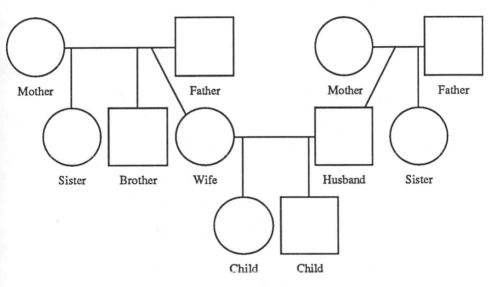

Extended Family

- How would you describe the family in which you grew up?
- What is your father's occupation? What is your mother's occupation? (Probe: other work experience? education or training? satisfaction with careers, unfulfilled dreams?)
- What is/was your mother like; father like; adjective to describe; nature of marital relationship (responsibilities).
- What are the occupations of your brothers and/or sisters? For younger siblings, what do they aspire to be? Where do your brothers and sisters live? Describe the life-style of each. Probe: If the family lives close by, explore cousin relationships (such as competitiveness for grandparents' approval).
- What is your role in the family (present and when growing up)?
- What is your relationship with your mother, father? Probe: career aspirations for you; cohesiveness.

- Who are you most like in your family? Probe: Who took care of whom? coalitions?
- What is your spouse's relationship with your family?

Dagley (1984) suggested another set of questions to be used in developing a career genogram:

- What are the dominant values in the family of origin?
- Vocationally, are certain "missions" valued?
- Are there any "ghosts or legends" that serve either as anchor points or "rightful roles" for the family?
- What myths or misconceptions seem to transcend generations?
- Are there any psychological pressures or expectations emanating from "unfinished business" of the family?
- How does the individual's description of economic values and preferences fit in with family's history?
- How has the family addressed the three boxes of life (learning, working, and playing)? Any imbalances?
- What family interaction rules and relationship boundaries have been passed along through generations?
- Are there any voids in the client's memory of family? What are the accrued debits and credits?
- Does the client have a sense of "owing" family traditions? What are the accrued debits and credits?
- How have the primary life tasks of love, work, and friendship been addressed by the family?
- What vocational patterns emerge, in terms of choice, as well as the choice and development process?

Analysis. "Since individuals carry the history of past experiences with them continually, in understanding psychological aspects of development it may be more important to understand the individual's interpretations of his/her experiences rather than to have objective information about these experiences" (de Vries, Birren, and Deutchman, 1990, p. 4). The career genogram provides a real-life structure on which the client can visually organize and map personal perceptions of work and family concerns and tasks into meaningful real-life representations in the context of overall family life. It is a stimulus device that provides a natural, direct, and comfortable way for clients to share family concerns and roles and responsibilities.

Family mapping using the career genogram can enhance counselors' in-depth understanding of clients by providing new perspectives. This is because work-family conflicts and the stresses and strains that result often can best be understood only in the context of a person's family life. The same is true with other conflicts, such as marital relationship difficulties and family interaction conflicts.

In the analysis specific attention should be given to the following points. First, note the occupations represented in a three-to-four-generation family tree. Second, pay attention to the status and value rankings typically assigned to occupations by various family members. Third, examine the career-choice patterns or ways in which family members have selected or changed occupations. Fourth, consider any economic expectations or pressures. Fifth, determine the peer-group context in which the client grew up (Dagley, 1984). Consideration of these points will help uncover possible pressure points or areas of concern that may be causing conflict in the client's life.

From Diagnosis to Taking Action

As counselors gain a more complete understanding of the work-family relationship and make diagnoses based on this understanding, the next step is to choose appropriate intervention strategies to help clients who are struggling with work-family issues to achieve their goals and resolve their problems. In choosing intervention strategies, Miller (1985) reminded counselors that such choices must be based on knowledge of career and family life developmental stages, especially family life stages where career roles may be the most demanding.

It is also clear that while work-family issues may be predominant as counseling for career development unfolds, other life roles may need consideration. Thus we recommend that counselors use a life career development perspective to understand, diagnose, and take action with clients dealing with work-family goals and problems. This broad view of human growth and development may provide clues and insights into client behavior not available using a work-family perspective only.

PART 3

Resources
for
Career Development

8

▚▚▚▚▚▚▚▚▚▚▚▚▚▚▚▚▚▚▚▚▚▚▚▚▚▚▚▚▚▚

Resources for
the World of Work

▚▚▚▚▚▚▚▚▚▚▚▚▚▚▚▚▚▚▚▚▚▚▚▚▚▚▚▚▚▚

There is a great deal of material in this chapter. There is much to learn about the main resources for understanding the world of work. Nevertheless, this is material which *can and should be* mastered by every counselor. You can learn about the resources included here and build on this beginning over the years as revisions come out and new material becomes available. This is a manageable task and can be accomplished with some organization, effort, and discipline. Do not be put off by the vast array of sources. You will soon learn that managing it boils down to a few key sources and simply having a good reference knowledge regarding how to find other world of work information you need. *Remember, nobody knows about all the occupational information available—but every counselor needs to know how to find what is needed quickly and easily.* A good reference knowledge will do very well.

A frequent concern that comes up in counselor conversations about the resources available for the world of work is "OK, if I know about all of this, what do I do with all my knowledge and understanding? In short, how do I use all of this stuff?" The answers presented in this book are quite direct. In Chapters Eight and Nine you will get information on counselor resources and in Chapter Ten you will learn how to combine the resources in a systems approach. In Chapter Eleven you will learn how to evaluate all types of career information—and in the process, you will develop a sense of appropriate application and use. In Chapter Thirteen you will discover how to organize and use career information materials in a multimedia career development center. Chapters Fourteen and Fifteen specifically show how to use career information resources and systems in both individual and group counseling through detailed illustrated case studies of clients across the life span. Chapter Twelve addresses acquiring and using career information materials for a wide variety of client populations with special needs—a necessity in the shifting client mix in almost every counseling setting. The starting point is that you acquire a good functioning understanding of the key sources for you in your employment setting. Then, using the five points noted above, you can answer the question "How do I use all of this stuff?"

Finally, do not relax and sit back on your laurels once you have mastered the content of the chapters in Parts Three and Four. *The timely nature of all you are acquiring is perishable.* It will not stand still and age well (like wine or cheese). It will instead grow old and out of date, and lack credibility for any client group. As important as gaining a solid grasp of the concepts and content at hand is a plan to keep up to date as long as you are an active counselor. Nothing will cause a faster loss of credibility than someone's walking into your office and seeing a ten-year-old *Occupational Outlook Handbook*. There are several reasons for this. One, the world of work is constantly changing. Unemployment rates rise and fall, occupations ebb and flow in terms of demand (elevator operator and key punch operator are examples of such occupations) and global economics, political, social, and environmental conditions are in a continual state of flux; therefore, sources and information cannot be taken for granted once they are understood. Two, there are new studies, reports, monographs, and books being published all the time. These new sources keep the counselor tapped into current research about demographic changes, workplace changes, and perceptions and attitudes about work. Three, there are constantly changing means of presenting world of work information to your clients. This means new or improved media as well as new opportunities to gain information on a firsthand basis. So, whatever is learned in this book is just a part of a long-term, continuing education process. This chapter presents sources in two sections: the first section introduces major government sources with some detailed description and the second section provides supplemental sources from the national, regional, state, and local areas, as well as commercial sources.

Major Government Sources

This section provides a brief summary of major government resources on the world of work. We have found, over the years, that these are the resources we use most; they are also the ones that keep showing up on surveys as the most commonly used sources of information. As government publications, they are more reliable than some others might be. And most of the commercial sources are based on these government publications.

We do not have enough space to fully describe all the details of the major or supplemental sources that follow. It is absolutely essential that counselors go to the original source documents to understand the scope and depth of each of these publications. They should try to acquire for professional use as many of the sources mentioned as possible or else should locate a convenient reference point where these sources are readily available.

Dictionary of Occupational Titles

This is one of the most valuable resources for counselors.

Scope of Coverage. The *Dictionary of Occupational Titles* (commonly known as the *DOT*) defines and classifies occupations and characteristics of workers. It is a comprehensive tool that describes the worker traits, methods, work requirements, and activities associated with various occupations. The concept of "occupations" in the *DOT* means a collective description of individual jobs performed with minor variations in many places of work. A single worker in a job does not necessarily perform all of the activities specified in a *DOT* definition. The current edition of the *DOT* contains 12,860 occupations listed by job titles most frequently used by employers. The term *DOT* collectively includes the *Dictionary of Occupational Titles* (4th ed., 1977), the 1986 supplement to the *Dictionary of Occupational Titles,* the *Selected Characteristics of Occupations Defined in the Dictionary of Occupational Titles,* and the *Dictionary of Occupational Titles Data Tape.*

Background and History of DOT. The first *DOT* was published in 1939. Its purpose and that of all subsequent editions was to furnish public employment service offices with occupational information and techniques for proper classification and placement of workers. Subsequent editions have been published in 1949, 1965, and 1977, and the supplements noted above have been issued.

The *DOT* has always been an integral part of labor market information systems. With each edition, the Employment and Training Administration (ETA) of the Department of Labor attempts to reflect the needs of the Employment Service, and where possible, the needs of users outside the Employment Service agencies.

The *DOT* was developed in order to have a system for describing and classifying workers for job placement in a labor market where workers were plentiful and jobs scarce. When this situation was reversed during World War II and a scarcity of workers emerged, a supplement to the *DOT* was published. The supplement described worker traits for specific jobs and was used to place inexperienced workers. With the third edition of the *DOT,* the idea that both job descriptions and worker traits were important to the *DOT* was firmly established. The third edition contained sweeping changes, including material for users outside the Employment Service.

The fourth edition further expanded the idea of using the *DOT* for purposes other than strictly matching a job with a worker. Over 350,000 copies have been sold through 1990.

Type of Information Presented. The *DOT* groups jobs into occupations based on their similarities. It also defines the job characteristics of all listed occupations. The definitions are the result of comprehensive analyses of how similar jobs are performed at work sites all over the country. The term *occupation*, as used in the *DOT,* refers to this collective description of a number of individual jobs performed at many work sites.

An occupational definition in the *DOT* normally has six basic parts. Each presents information about a job in a systematic fashion. The parts are: (1) the nine-digit occupational code number, (2) the occupational title, (3) the industry or industries in which the occupation is found, (4) alternate titles or other titles by which the occupation may also be known, (5) a description of the tasks performed, and (6) related occupations.

As indicated, each definition is assigned a unique nine-digit code. The first three digits identify a particular occupational group. All occupations are clustered into one of nine broad categories (first digit), such as professional, technical, and managerial, or clerical and sales occupations. These categories break up into eighty-two occupational divisions (first two digits), such as occupations in architecture and engineering within the professional category. Divisions, in turn, separate into smaller groups (first three digits); 559 such groups are identified in the *DOT.* The nine occupational categories (first digit) are as follows:

0/1   Professional, Technical, and Managerial Occupations

2   Clerical and Sales Occupations

3   Service Occupations

4   Agricultural, Fishery, Forestry, and Related Occupations

5   Processing Occupations

6 Machine Trades Occupations
7 Bench Work Occupations
8 Structural Work Occupations
9 Miscellaneous Occupations

In the following example for counselor (045.107-010), the first digit (0) indicates that this particular occupation is found in the category "Professional, Technical, and Managerial Occupations."

> 045.107-010   COUNSELOR (profess. & kin.) guidance counselor; vocational adviser; vocational counselor. Counsels individuals and provides group educational and vocational guidance services: Collects, organizes, and analyzes information about individuals through records, tests, interviews, and professional sources to appraise their interests, aptitudes, abilities, and personality characteristics, for vocational and educational planning. Compiles and studies occupational, educational, and economic information to aid counselors in making and carrying out vocational and educational objectives. Refers students to placement service. Assists individuals to understand and overcome social and emotional problems. May engage in research and follow-up activities to evaluate counseling techniques. May teach classes. May be designated according to area of activity as COUNSELOR, COLLEGE (education); COUNSELOR, EMPLOYMENT DEVELOPMENT DEPARTMENT (education); COUNSELOR, SCHOOL (education); COUNSELOR, VETERANS ADMINISTRATION (gov. ser.).

The second digit refers to a division. The divisions within "Professional, Technical, and Managerial Occupations" are:

00/01 Occupations in architecture, engineering, and surveying
  02   Occupations in mathematics and physical sciences
  04   Occupations in life sciences
  05   Occupations in social sciences

07 Occupations in medicine and health
09 Occupations in education

In the example, the second digit (4) thus locates the occupation in the "Occupations in life sciences" division.

The third digit defines the occupational group. The groups within the "Occupations in life sciences" division are:

040 Occupations in agricultural science
041 Occupations in biological sciences
045 Occupations in psychology
049 Occupations in life sciences, n.e.c. [not elsewhere classified]

The third digit (5) locates the occupation in the "Occupations in psychology" group. The middle three digits are the worker functions ratings of the tasks performed in the occupation. Every job requires a worker to function to some degree in relation to data, people, and things, as shown in the following example:

	Data (4th digit)	People (5th digit)	Things (6th digit)
Most Complex	0 Synthesizing	0 Mentoring	0 Setting up
	1 Coordinating	1 Negotiating	1 Precision working
↑	2 Analyzing	2 Instructing	2 Operating-controlling
↓	3 Compiling	3 Supervising	3 Driving-operating
Least Complex	4 Computing	4 Diverting	4 Manipulating
	5 Copying	5 Persuading	5 Tending
	6 Comparing	6 Speaking-signalling	6 Feeding-offbearing
		7 Serving	7 Handling
		8 Taking instructions-helping	

Definition of Worker Functions: Data—People—Things

Data: Information, knowledge, and conceptions, related to data, people, or things, obtained by observation, investigation, interpretation, visualization, and mental creation. Data are intangible and include numbers, word, symbols, ideas, concepts, and oral interpretation.

People: Human beings: also animals dealt with on an individual basis as if they were human.

Things: Inanimate objects as distinguished from human beings, substances, or materials; machines, tools, equipment, and products. A thing is tangible and has shape, form, and other physical characteristics.

Note: Detailed definitions of the terms *Data, People,* and *Things* are presented in the appendix of the *DOT,* 4th edition, pp. 1369–1371.

The levels are arranged in a descending scale of complexity. The lower numbers represent more complex levels of work performance. For example, with this numbering system, it may be inferred that an occupation having the middle three digits of .107 is of a higher level of complexity than a job coded .687. Although this type of inference is useful in comparing differing jobs, it should be applied mainly to jobs in the same occupational group (that is, a group that has the same first three digits). Finally, the last three digits indicate the alphabetical order of titles within six-digit code groups. They serve to differentiate a particular occupation from all others. A number of occupations may have the same first six digits; no two can have the same nine digits.

> **Reference:** Employment and Training Administration, Department of Labor. *Dictionary of Occupational Titles.* (4th ed.) Washington, D.C.: U.S. Government Printing Office, 1977, 1413 pages.

Special Note: As this book goes to press, a revised version of the fourth edition of the *Dictionary of Occupational Titles* (*DOT*) is expected to be published in two volumes in 1991. The basic organization and structure will remain the same, but some occupations will be added, some dropped, and some updated. It is expected that the *Selected Characteristics of Occu-*

pations Defined in the Dictionary of Occupational Titles and the *Guide to Occupational Exploration* will also be revised and published in 1992 or 1993. Further, an advisory panel has been appointed by the Secretary of Labor to study the entire scope of the *DOT* and make recommendations back to the Secretary of Labor on proposed changes by mid 1992. Major changes could be forthcoming by 1993–1995 in the fifth edition of the *DOT.*

Selected Characteristics of Occupations Defined in the Dictionary of Occupational Titles

The Department of Labor also published this document for use with the *DOT.*

Scope of Coverage. This publication provides an expanded interpretation of significant job characteristics for a wide range of occupations requiring similar capabilities. Supplementary information on training time (including mathematical and language development and specific vocational preparation), physical demands, and environmental (or working) conditions are listed for each job defined in the *DOT.* The previous (third) edition of the *DOT* included a volume that contained much of the same information included here. Some of this information also is presented in considerable detail in *Vocational Preparation and Occupations (VPO)*, mentioned later.

Type of Information Presented. As noted, this *DOT* supplement provides detailed information on physical demands, environmental conditions, and training time for each job defined in the *DOT.* The information is presented in two parts: Part A includes the titles arranged by the *Guide for Occupational Exploration (GOE)* work groups and physical demands; Part B is an index of titles by *DOT* code. The unique feature of Part A is the grouping of occupa-

tions according to similarity of physical demands requirements; that is, all jobs that are sedentary (within a work
group) are listed together, all light jobs are shown together,
and so forth.

Brief Description of Contents. Part A contains the following information on all *DOT* occupations: the strength
factor, physical demands, environmental conditions, levels of
mathematical and language development required to do the
work, and specific vocational preparation or training time. It
also clusters all *DOT* occupations by a coding structure outlined in the *GOE*. The *GOE* clusters all *DOT* occupations by
worker-interest factors. However, it is not necessary to be
familiar with the *GOE* to obtain this information. All of the
information contained in Part A is in a coded format. Keys
for interpreting the coded information are found in the following appendixes of *Selected Characteristics:* A (physical
demands), B (environmental conditions), C (mathematical
and language development), D (specific vocational preparation), and E (occupational aptitude patterns).

Part B is really an index organized numerically by *DOT*
code. This index provides the *GOE* code for each *DOT* code.
Because all information in Part A is listed by *GOE* code, this
is an invaluable index. For example, if you want to know the
specific vocational preparation for the occupation of counselor, you must first locate the nine-digit *DOT* code for counselor (045.107-010). In Part B, you will find 045.107-010 listed
on page 300 of the book. The number listed after the *DOT*
code is the *GOE* code, which you will use in Part A to find
the specific vocational preparation for counselor. The *GOE*
for counselor is 10.01.02; the needed information is located
on page 259.

Reference: Employment and Training Administration,
Department of Labor. *Selected Characteristics of Occu-
pations Defined in the Dictionary of Occupational
Titles.* Washington, D.C.: U.S. Government Printing
Office, 1981.

Guide for Occupational Exploration

This resource complements the other sources of information discussed earlier.

Scope of Coverage. The *Guide for Occupational Exploration (GOE)* is an Employment Service publication designed to provide job seekers with information about fields of work that match their own interests and abilities. The *GOE* organizes occupations into 12 interest areas, 66 work groups, and 348 subgroups. The interest areas are as follows:

01 Artistic
02 Scientific
03 Plants and animals
04 Protective
05 Mechanical
06 Industrial
07 Business detail
08 Selling
09 Accommodating (e.g., services)
10 Humanitarian
11 Leading-influencing
12 Physical-performing

The areas represent the broad interest requirements of occupations (for instance, 10–Humanitarian involves interest in helping others with their mental, spiritual, social, physical, or vocational needs). The work groups are the jobs suitable for exploration by those who have a particular interest (an example would be 10.01–Social Services). The subgroups are occupations organized to make it easier for the user to distinguish among the occupations (see, for example, 10.01.02–Counseling and Social Work).

Type of Information Presented. Descriptions are provided for each of the sixty-six work groups. Each description contains a general overview of the occupational area, followed by narratives regarding the following questions: What kind of work would you do? What skills and abilities do you need for this kind of work? How do you know if you would like or could learn to do this kind of work? How can you prepare for and enter this kind of work? What else should you consider about these jobs? The final section of each work group lists the *DOT* codes that are covered in the description. The sample below (from page 276) illustrates one type of question asked and a portion of the answer for Social Services (*GOE* 10.01):

> How do you know if you would like or could learn to do this kind of work?
> The following questions may give you clues about yourself as you consider this group of jobs.
>
> • Have you been active in church or civic groups? Do you like to work with other people toward a common goal?
> • Have your friends come to you for advice or help with their personal problems? Did you help them find solutions?

The final section of each description, as indicated, includes a listing of covered *DOT* codes. The following brief example (from page 277) is for Counseling and Social Work (*GOE* 10.01.02).

> Counselor (profess. & kin.) 045.107-010
> Dianetic Counselor (profess. & kin.) 199.207-010
> Director of Counseling (profess. & kin.)
>   045.107-018
> Parole Officer (profess. & kin.) 195.167-030
> Psychologist, Clinical (profess. & kin.)
>   045.107-022
> Psychologist, Counseling (profess. & kin.)
>   045.107-026
> Psychologist, School (profess. & kin.) 045.107-034

Social Worker, Medical (profess. & kin.)
195.107-030
Social Worker, Psychiatric (profess. & kin.)
195.107-034
Social Worker, School (profess. & kin.)
195.107-038

Brief Description of Contents. The *GOE* contains a brief introduction explaining the purpose and organization of the guide; a description of its use in career exploration; definitions of the interest areas; and a summary list of all the interest areas, work groups, and subgroups. This is followed by approximately 300 pages—"The Area and Work Group Arrangement"—devoted to the questions and answers and, in some cases, lengthy lists of relevant *DOT* titles and codes.

The second half of the document contains several valuable appendixes. For example, Appendix B discusses the related use of Employment Service interest and aptitude tests; Appendix C presents suggestions for using the guide in organizing occupational information; and Appendix D (380 pages) presents an alphabetical arrangement of the occupations, with related *DOT* and *GOE* code numbers.

> **Reference:** Employment and Training Administration, Department of Labor. *Guide for Occupational Exploration.* Washington, D.C.: U.S. Government Printing Office, 1979. (Stock no. 029-013-00080-2; cost: $14.00.)

Note: There are two versions of the *Guide for Occupational Exploration.* In addition to the government edition cited above, the private sector edition (1984) may be acquired from the American Guidance Service, Publishers' Building, Circle Pines, MN 55014-1796. (Publication no. EC 1140; cost: $24.95.)

Occupational Outlook Handbook

This handbook is an invaluable source of occupational information.

Scope of Coverage. The *Occupational Outlook Handbook (OOH)*, published by the Bureau of Labor Statistics of the Department of Labor, represents the most comprehensive information available on work today and job prospects for tomorrow. It is revised every two years; the 1990–91 edition covers about 250 occupations. For each occupation, the handbook provides information about job duties, working conditions, level and places of employment, education and training requirements, advancement possibilities, job outlook, earnings, and related occupations that require similar aptitudes, interests, or training. The occupations are grouped according to the *Standard Occupational Classification Manual* (1980). However, it also contains an index referenced to the most recent edition and supplement of the *DOT*. The 1990–91 edition includes information about the effect of the business cycle, defense spending, energy development, and other economic variables affecting employment. The handbook information is based on data from a variety of sources, including business firms, trade associations, labor unions, professional societies, educational institutions, and government agencies. Designed primarily for career guidance purposes, it is national in scope.

Type of Information Presented. Occupational "briefs" cover approximately 250 occupations clustered into twelve broader occupational groupings. For each occupation, detailed descriptive information is provided on the following topics: nature of the work; working conditions; employment; training, other qualifications, and advancement; job outlook and earnings; related occupations; and sources of related information. The descriptions also provide *DOT* code numbers for selected occupations for users who may wish to follow up with additional information from that source.

The twelve major occupational categories are as follows:

- Executive, administrative, and managerial occupations
- Professional specialty occupations
- Technical and related support occupations
- Marketing and sales occupations
- Administrative support (including clerical occupations)
- Service occupations
- Agriculture, forestry, fishing, and related occupations
- Mechanics, installers, and repairers occupations
- Construction trades and extractive occupations
- Production occupations
- Transportation and material moving occupations
- Handlers, equipment cleaners, helpers, and labor occupations

Brief Description of Contents. The *OOH* is divided into three parts. The first section, a guide to the handbook, contains valuable information for both the counselor and client. "How to Get the Most from the Handbook" is a short but useful section for the serious career planner and gives a solid foundation of information regarding all of the areas dealt with in the *OOH* (for example, nature of the work, working conditions, employment and so on). Another introductory section, "Where to Go for More Information," discusses in considerable detail various sources of career information, education and training information, financial aid information, counseling information for special groups, and information on finding a job. The section also furnishes addresses for each state occupational information coordinating committee and state employment security agency.

The introductory section on "Tomorrow's Jobs" describes the impact that population structure and regional differences will have on the labor force in the 1990s. It also contains future projections for occupations and industries. It is an especially valuable section for those beginning to plan for specific training programs. Finally, the introductory section includes a brief overview of the methods used in preparing the employment projections.

The bulk of the text contains the section on "Occupations," the detailed descriptions of the occupational groupings and the specific occupational areas. The text also contains sections on the nature of the work, working conditions, employment, training and other qualifications, job outlook, earnings, related occupations, and sources of additional information. Summary data for additional related occupations are presented in tables at the end of most chapters. Finally, there are two useful indexes: the first is organized numerically by *DOT* code, which also lists the *SOC* code and *DOT* title; the second is an alphabetical occupational title index.

> **Reference:** Bureau of Labor Statistics, Department of Labor. *Occupational Outlook Handbook. (1990–1991 ed.)* Washington, D.C.: U.S. Government Printing Office, 1990a. Also useful is: Bureau of Labor Statistics, Department of Labor. *Occupational Projections and Training Data.* Washington, D.C.: U.S. Government Printing Office, 1990 (Bulletin no. 2351, $5.00 paperback, 120 pages.)

Occupational Outlook Quarterly

This is a useful source of current information.

Scope of Coverage. The *Occupational Outlook Quarterly,* published by the Bureau of Labor Statistics of the Department of Labor, keeps readers abreast of current occupational developments between editions of the *Occupational Outlook Handbook.* It provides updated, timely information. It also organizes and synthesizes information printed elsewhere for use by counselors or clients. In addition, the *Quarterly* reviews new techniques and counseling aids.

Type of Information Presented. The *Quarterly* publishes a wide range of articles that are highly relevant to counselors. For example, a brief review of four issues reveals articles with projections for the next date, high-technology employment, the job outlook for college graduates through the mid 1990s, a follow-up survey on the occupations and continuing education of 1980 college graduates, working for the government, and how workers get their training. Also, a number of very specific topics are explored, such as managerial occupations; interpreting for the hearing impaired; three careers in new technologies—lasers, fiber optics, and biotechnology; and the occupation of a sailmaker! The first volume of the 1985 series includes more articles on high-technology fields—computer-aided design, numerical-control machine-tool operation, and office automation—as well as articles on general maintenance repairers, legal service personnel, and the occupation of prosthetist—a maker of artificial limbs.

Brief Description of Contents. For the most part, as noted, the articles cover employment outlook, new occupations, training opportunities, and salary trends. However, during the past several years the results of various Bureau of Labor Statistics studies have also been included. For example, a particularly valuable article appeared in the Winter 1982 issue: G. M. Martin and M. C. Fountain's "Matching Yourself with the World of Work." It contains a lengthy chart that does in fact attempt to match personal characteristics with the world of work. The *Quarterly* also periodically publishes articles called "The Job Outlook in Brief."

> **Reference:** Bureau of Labor Statistics, Department of Labor. *Occupational Outlook Quarterly.* Washington, D.C.: U.S. Government Printing Office. Also useful is the Bureau of Labor Statistics' *Monthly Labor Review,* which carries more in-depth technical articles.

Supplemental Sources

This section presents some of the supplemental sources that were not covered in the preceding section. These may be major sources of information for some counselors, depending on their employment setting. In any case, they represent reliable sources of information that can be used with confidence. Some, such as the census data, are updated on a regular basis; others, such as the Standard Industrial Classification (SIC) Manual, serve mainly as organization sources and therefore are not revised until there is sufficient reason to do so. Another such example is the *DOT*, which was last published in 1977 but has two supplements to update the content and is coming out in a 1991 revised fourth edition in two volumes, as noted earlier. Following are some useful supplemental sources of world of work information at the national, regional, state, and local levels.

Military Career Guide

The *Military Career Guide* (*MCG*) was developed by the Office of the Assistant Secretary of Defense for Manpower, Installations, and Logistics for the purpose of providing students with information about enlisted military and officer occupations.

The document clusters military occupational specialty information from the five military services (Army, Navy, Air Force, Marine Corps, and Coast Guard) by Standard Occupational Classification (SOC)–based groupings. The clusters represent occupational areas having common job tasks.

For each of the 134 enlisted clusters of occupations covered, the guide supplies information on topics such as typical work tasks, work environment, physical demands, training provided, helpful attributes, special qualifications, civilian counterparts, and opportunities. Generally, the publication demonstrates that for the military occupations that have civilian counterparts, technical and vocational training and work experience comparable to civilian occupations can be provided by the military services.

> **Reference:** Department of Defense. *Military Career Guide*. Chicago, IL.: U.S. Military Entrance Processing Command, 1988.

Note: Military Career Paths is available from the same source as above, free of charge. The publication shows career progression patterns for selected enlisted and officer occupations from the *Military Career Guide.*

Standard Occupational Classification Manual

The *Standard Occupational Classification Manual,* or *SOC Manual* as it is called, was first published in 1977 and revised in 1980. It was developed because Labor Markets Information (LMI) users and producers realized that they were all gathering and coding occupational data with the aid of a variety of different coding structures that usually were not "translatable" to other structures. Therefore, while vast amounts of occupational information were being collected, much of it was unusable because it had been collected according to a different structure. The *SOC Manual* was developed to provide a common structure, coding all occupations in which work is performed for pay or profit, including work performed in family-operated enterprises where direct remuneration may not be made to family members.

Twenty-two broad occupational divisions are covered. Within that broader classification, sixty-four major groups are presented. Further, within those subcategories, literally hundreds of specific occupations are listed in varying degrees of specificity.

> **Reference:** Office of Federal Statistical Policy and Standards, Department of Commerce. *Standard Occupational Classification Manual.* Washington, D.C.: U.S. Government Printing Office, 1980. (This document may be acquired from the U.S. Government Printing Office, Washington, D.C. 20402. Stock no. 0-332-946; cost: $9.00.)

Standard Industrial Classification Manual

Information on industries is important in career counseling because industries are where workers are employed and jobs are found. The *Standard Industrial Classification Manual* (or *SIC Manual*) was developed, among other reasons, for use in the classification of business establishments by the type of activity in which they are engaged, that is, according to the type of product or service. The classification is intended to cover the entire field of economic activities: agriculture, forestry, fishing, hunting, and trapping; mining; construction; manufacturing; transportation, communication, electric, gas, and sanitary service; wholesale and retail trade; finance, insurance, and real estate; personal, business, repair, and other services; and public administration.

For purposes of this classification, an establishment is considered an economic unit, generally at a single physical location where business is conducted or where services or industrial operations are performed—for example, a factory, mill, store, hotel, movie theater, mine, farm, ranch, bank, railroad depot, airline terminal, sales office, warehouse, or central administrative office, and the like.

The *SIC Manual* details the major industrial classification system used in this country; much data on industry growth are tabulated with the aid of SIC codes. Although the 1972 edition is the most recent, a brief 1977 supplement is available. The fifteen-page supplement includes new and deleted industries: for example, motor homes and real estate investment trusts are new; railway express services have been deleted. In addition, sixteen brief modifications have been made to industry descriptions and eighty-two brief modifications have been made to index items.

Reference: Office of Management and Budget, Executive Office of the President. *Standard Industrial Classification Manual.* Washington, D.C.: U.S. Government Printing Office, 1972. (GPO 041-001-00066-6; cost: $15.00.)

Reference: Office of Management and Budget, Executive Office of the President. *Standard Industrial Classification Manual: 1977 Supplement.* Washington, D.C.: U.S. Government Printing Office, 1977.

The following source, updated annually, is also useful: Bureau of Industrial Economics, Department of Commerce. *1990 U.S. Industrial Outlook: Prospects for Over 350 Industries.* Washington, D.C.: U.S. Government Printing Office, 1990.

A Classification of Instructional Programs

A Classification of Instructional Programs consists mainly of descriptions of instructional programs at the elementary, secondary, and—particularly—the postsecondary levels. A total of thirty-one programs are included, ranging alphabetically from programs in agriculture and architecture . . . to those in the life sciences and mathematics . . . to trade and industrial programs and programs in the visual and performing arts. Within these program categories, fifty specific subcategories are presented. For example, within the Agriculture area, three subcategories are noted: (01) Agribusiness and Agricultural Production, (02) Agricultural Sciences, and (03) Renewable Natural Resources. Within the Trade and Industrial program area, the following subcategories are noted: (46) Construction Trades, (47) Mechanics and Repairers, (48) Precision Production, and (49) Transportation and Material Moving.

> **Reference:** National Center for Education Statistics, Department of Education. *A Classification of Instructional Programs.* Washington, D.C.: U.S. Government Printing Office, 1981. (Stock no. 069-000-000-88-1; cost: $7.50.)

The following is also useful as a related source: National Occupational Information Coordinating Committee. *Vocational Preparation and Occupations.* Washington, D.C.: National Occupational Information Coordinating Committee, 1982.

Census of Population

The census is a complete count of the population of the United States and its territories. It has been taken every ten years since 1790. Recent censuses have collected such characteristics as age, gender, and race on a 100 percent basis and more detailed information from a sample of the population. Rather than going to employers, the census is directed to households to survey individuals.

Two important census documents are relevant to counselors: the *Alphabetical Index of Industries and Occupations* and the *Classified Index of Industries and Occupations.*

The basic content of both indexes is derived largely from previous editions. However, about 6,200 new occupation titles have been added. Many of these come from the *Dictionary of Occupational Titles.* The indexes list industry and occupation titles reported in earlier censuses and surveys, including titles used most often in the economy. However, some titles may not be listed because they are too new to be included. Some rarely used titles also are not included.

> **Reference:** Bureau of the Census, Department of Commerce. *U.S. Census of Population, 1980: Alphabetical Index of Occupations and Industries.* (Final ed.) Washington, D.C.: U.S. Government Printing Office, 1982a.
>
> **Reference:** Bureau of the Census, Department of Commerce. *U.S. Census of Population, 1980: Classified Index of Industries and Occupations.* (Final ed.) Washington, D.C.: U.S. Government Printing Office, 1982b.

Note: Also useful from the Bureau of the Census and updated each year is *Statistical Abstracts of the United States,* 1990 (paper $28.00, 984 pages).

Regional Sources

There are a variety of government and government-sponsored research and development centers that provide employment information. An example is the Southern Regional Education Board (SREB) in Atlanta, Georgia. A group like this performs a wide range of contract studies related to national, regional, and state work issues. Other sources—such as the Appalachian Educational Laboratory (AEL) in Charleston, West Virginia—carry out studies related to topics of regional interests. The Bureau of Labor Statistics also has regional centers that turn out state and multistate studies.

State Sources

The main source of relevant information in most states is the research and analysis branch (R&A) of the state public employment service unit. Normally it reports monthly or quarterly on employment and unemployment figures and trend data. In addition, among the state government sources would be an office of economic development or office of training and development as well as a higher education/ community college board and the state department of education. Private organizations such as the Virginia Association of Manufacturers, the Missouri State Chamber of Commerce, and the Virginia Health Careers Council are excellent sources of relevant career information. Finally, through various centers and study units, colleges and universities produce some very useful information for counselors. An example of this is the Center for Competitiveness and Employment Growth at the University of North Carolina, Chapel Hill. This particular center reported on a four-year study on job growth in North Carolina that showed a net gain of 398,000 new jobs in the mid 1980s, most of which were in small businesses that were independently owned and concentrated in the service sector. A study similar to this is probably available from every major state university or land-grant university in the United States. Of course, the state career information delivery system (CIDS) should be your best source for this type of information—see Chapter Ten for details.

Local Sources

Depending on the size of the local area, there are a variety of local information options on the world of work. These include the

- Local chamber of commerce
- Local employment service office
- Local rehabilitative service office
- Local education agency
- Local community college/four-year institution
- Local private industry council (PIC)
- Local civic or service organizations

Since each local area is so different, this list is just a starting point. There are, of course, plenty of other possibilities from which to choose—including local newspaper and magazine articles that focus on the world of work.

Commercial Sources

This section covers both print and nonprofit sources of a commercial nature.

Print Media

There was a time not too many years ago when print information on the world of work was just about all there was. Reasonably priced alternative media were not yet available. But print is still the medium of choice for much of the important information in this field. Surveys continue to show that the *Occupational Outlook Handbook (OOH)* is one of the top sellers in the entire U.S. Government Printing Office *Catalog of Publications*. A number of commercial firms have also reprinted the *OOH* (since it is in the public domain, that is legal); this has meant that many more copies have been sold. This section of the chapter will touch briefly on four print-type options available to counselors.

Serial Publications. Two firms—Careers and Chronicle Guidance Publications—continue to publish mainly print materials on the world of work on a regular basis. These materials are available on a monthly subscription basis and provide the bulk of what many counselors need.

Books and Monographs. Several firms provide continuing series of hardback and paperback books and monographs on a regular basis. These products offer in-depth coverage of particular topics; a typical example is "A Career as a Carpenter." Often the books are written by people in the occupation and thus provide firsthand accounts of what the work is like. Others are written by professional writers. At one time, there were many publishers specializing in this area; the following three now dominate the field:

- Vocational Guidance Manuals, 4255 West Touhy Avenue, Lincolnwood, IL 60646-1975
- Richard Rosen Press, 29 East 21st Street, New York, NY 10010
- Vocational Biographies, P.O. Box 31, Sauk Center, MN 56379-0031

Material from these three publishers meets the needs of counselors who want to make more detailed information available to their clients.

Smaller Publishers. Because of the consolidation of some of the larger publishers, the choices of providers narrowed for a time. Now some smaller publishers have emerged and filled in some of the gaps among the employment information providers. Three publishers are especially worthy of mention:

- Garrett Park Press, Garrett Park, MD 20896
- Ten Speed Press, Box 7123, Berkeley, CA 94707
- Impact Publications, 10655 Big Oak Circle, Manassas, VA 22111

For the most part, these are small businesses that have grown over the past twenty to twenty-five years essentially on the basis of their career information materials. Garrett Park Press also publishes *Career Opportunities News* six times a year, which has quickly established itself as a top newsletter in the field. The same publisher puts out a chart series on career-related topics. A development in recent years has been the distribution of career books and materials by a clearinghouse type of publisher such as the New Careers Center in Boulder, Colorado, which publishes *The Whole Work Catalog*. Firms like this often publish nothing themselves, but acquire titles from small publishers, pull them together on a topic like career information, and distribute the results to counselors for their use. In this era of emerging small businesses and entrepreneurships, counselors should be on the lookout for an increasing number of publishers and clearinghouse groups like those just cited.

Newspapers and Magazines. Daily and weekly newspapers are of course a constant source of information on the world of work. This may be the monthly employment/unemployment figures or an article about a plant opening or closing. This is the kind of information that makes excellent bulletin-board material, and it should not be overlooked as an important source. Counselors are fortunate to have access to a major national newspaper like *USA Today,* which has six million readers per day. This is a useful source of timely and accurate career information that is frequently put together in an attractive format. *USA Today* also provides occasional supplements on topics like opportunities in small business and work at home. In much the same way, magazines sometimes make valuable career information available. For example, in their occupational trends sections, some of the large-circulation regional magazines such as *Southern Living* or *Yankee* will carry first-person profiles of people at work in the region. Some quality magazine-type materials are also targeted at high school– and college-age youth and carry frequent items related to the world of work. Depending on your employment setting, be on the lookout for both newspapers and magazines that can provide you with bright and lively career information.

Nonprint Media

In recent years, the number of nonprint sources on the world of work has increased significantly. Though the impact of these sources is still limited and their cost often exceeds the reach of the average counseling setting, these sources still need to be mentioned and include:

- Videotapes
- Films
- Slide tapes
- Public and commercial radio
- Laser discs
- Computer software

There are several problems related to these nonprint sources. One of them—cost—has already been mentioned. Another is availability; they cannot always be obtained in sufficient numbers to make the material available to users in a convenient way. A third issue is that of evaluation and confidence in the product—especially in advance of preview (often inconvenient) or purchase (difficult to return once you have the product). These and other problems have seemed to stall the wider use of nonprint media related to the world of work. Established companies that provide career development videos, slide tapes, and software include:

- Career Development Software, Inc., The School Co., Box 5379, Vancouver, WA 98668

- Guidance Associates, Box 3000, Mount Kisco, NY 10549
- JIST Works, 720 North Park Avenue, Indianapolis, IN 46202
- Sunburst Communications, Box 40, Pleasantville, NY 10570

Twenty Key Resources on the World of Work

This following list brings together key sources of information on many of the major topics covered in the book. It is meant only as a general guide; other suggestions can easily be added. Also, many of the references cited here are updated on a regular basis (often every year), and so it is important to consult the latest materials available.

1. Employment and Training Administration, Department of Labor. *Dictionary of Occupational Titles.* (4th ed.) Washington, D.C.: U.S. Government Printing Office, 1977. (Watch for forthcoming two-volume revised 4th edition.)
2. Bureau of Labor Statistics, Department of Labor. *Occupational Outlook Handbook. (1990–1991.)* Washington, D.C.: U.S. Government Printing Office, 1990.
3. Bureau of Labor Statistics, Department of Labor. *Occupational Outlook Quarterly.* Washington, D.C.: U.S. Government Printing Office.
4. Employment and Training Administration, Department of Labor. *Guide for Occupational Exploration.* Washington, D.C.: U.S. Government Printing Office, 1979.
5. Department of Defense. *Military Career Guide.* Chicago, IL.: U.S. Military Entrance Processing Command, 1988.
6. Bureau of the Census, Department of Commerce. *U.S. Census of Population, 1980: Classified Index of Industries and Occupations.* (Final ed.) Washington, D.C.: U.S. Government Printing Office, 1982b.
7. National Center for Education Statistics, Department of Education. *A Classification of Instructional Programs.* Washington, D.C.: U.S. Government Printing Office, 1981.

8. Office of Management and Budget, Executive Office of the President. *Standard Industrial Classification Manual: 1977 Supplement.* Washington, D.C.: U.S. Government Printing Office, 1977.

9. Office of Federal Statistical Policy and Standards, Department of Commerce. *Standard Occupational Classification Manual.* Washington, D.C.: U.S. Government Printing Office, 1980.

10. Hopke, W. E. (ed.). *Encyclopedia of Careers.* (8th ed.) Chicago: Ferguson, 1990.

11. Careers. P.O. Box 135, Largo, FL 34649-0135.

12. Chronicle Guidance Publications. P.O. Box 1190, Moravia, NY 13118-1190.

13. Vocational Guidance Manual. 4255 West Touhy Avenue, Lincolnwood, IL 60646-1975.

14. Vocational Biographies. P.O. Box 31, Sauk Center, MN 56379-0031.

15. Garrett Park Press. Garrett Park, MD 20896.

16. Ten Speed Press. Box 7123, Berkeley, CA 94707.

17. Impact Publications. 10655 Big Oak Circle, Manassas, VA 22111.

18. New Careers Center. P.O. Box 297-K, Boulder, CO 80306.

19. Career Research and Testing. 2005 Hamilton Avenue, San Jose, CA 95125.

20. Military service toll-free recruitment numbers, Division of Vocations: Navy, (800) 327-NAVY; Army, (800) 872-2769; Marines, (800) 423-2600; Air Force (medical recruiting only), (800) 423-8723; Coast Guard, (800) 424-8883.

9

■■■■■■■■■■■■■■■■■■■■■■■■■■■■■■■■■■■■■■

Resources for
Education and Leisure

■■■■■■■■■■■■■■■■■■■■■■■■■■■■■■■■■■■■■■

This book, unlike any other in the field, emphasizes the concept of Career = Work + Leisure (C = W + L). Because of this basic difference, it is important to have a chapter that focuses on the education and leisure resources counselors should know about, be able to easily access, and use with people who need them across the life span.

A recent Roper Report (Roper Organization, 1990) spelled out some of the changes in American attitudes toward work and leisure that are having an impact on career development. In general, the changes have been evolutionary, not revolutionary, but they are still quite dramatic. Perhaps most important has been an apparent switch for some people from the traditional American work ethic to a new leisure ethic. For the first time in years, more Americans say that leisure, not work, is the primary objective in their personal lives than vice versa. Here is what the Roper Report (1990, pp. 2-3) found:

- Just 36 percent today—down from 48 percent in 1975— think "work is the important thing, and the purpose of leisure time is to recharge people's batteries so they can do a better job."

- A full 41 percent—up from 36 percent—believe "leisure time is the important thing, and the purpose of work is to make it possible to have the leisure time to enjoy life and pursue one's interests."
- Meanwhile, 20 percent—up from 13 percent—place equal emphasis on leisure *and* work.

Americans are much more likely now to complain about now having enough time for leisure. They are also more likely to spend the leisure time they *do* have on activities done strictly for pleasure, not for education or self-improvement.

What explains this decline of the work ethic and the rise of the leisure ethic? One key factor, no doubt, has been the steep drop in satisfaction that American workers now say they derive from their jobs. Compared to sentiments expressed in the early 1970s, employee satisfaction is down for every major aspect of employment. Salaries, benefits, number of hours worked, colleagues at work, opportunities for promotion, personal satisfaction derived from jobs, social importance of work—*all* of these are greater sources of disgruntlement today than they were in the past. Cutbacks in benefits provided by employers, along with less-than-spectacular salary increases during much of the 1980s, convinced many people (especially those on hourly wages) that they received few of the fruits of the "Reagan recovery." Instead, the rewards seemed to go to those who were already well paid: top management, sports and entertainment stars, elite professionals.

While Americans' commitment to the workplace seems to have faded for some people, their financial expectations have not. Quite the contrary. Refuting the notion of trade-offs, more than ever, people are dreaming of having the "lifestyle of the rich and famous." The evidence of widespread "aspiration inflation" is compelling. Lots of money, high-paying jobs, and the material goods that money can buy figure much more prominently in the hopes of average Americans now than was once the case.

The Roper Organization data provide support for our understanding of career development as Career = Work + Leisure (C = W + L). This is why we have included material on leisure resources in this chapter. This chapter on education and leisure resources will focus on what is needed for a balanced knowledge of work (Chapter Eight) and leisure. That division is rather arbitrary, because after the age of sixteen to eighteen, whenever compulsory education is no longer a factor, *education becomes a leisure option.* This means, according to the definition used in this book, that taking a course or pursuing a degree is really a leisure *option*—not something one has to do. Education for most adults is a matter of *discretionary time and money;* having both is usually a requirement in exercising the education option. This chapter is all about life options in the education and leisure world and knowing about the resources that can help people of all ages, all life stages, and all occupations to know about these options.

The chapter is divided into two main sections, which cover educational and leisure options, respectively. The first section will concentrate on two major life stages, the in-school stage and the much longer adult timespan. The second section will concentrate on leisure options over the life span in the five main areas of leisure—with a special focus on sources at the local, state, and national level. The chapter closes with several lists of basic references on education and leisure topics.

Sources of Information on Educational Options

In this section, we discuss three broad topics: first, in-school educational options, highlighting some of the most important choices that students (from kindergarten through high school) and their parents have; second, general sources for the adult user of education information; and third, financial aid information.

In-School Sources

Elementary School. With the increasing diversity of the school-age population, sources of in-school education options have expanded rapidly. In the elementary school years, it is important for counselors and teachers to know about all of the options available to students, regardless of their special needs. These types of programs vary from one local area to another, but examples include career awareness programs, special assistance for students with disabilities, bilingual program assistance, gifted education programs, special reading programs, after-school day care, special summer educational enrichment programs, plus a variety of other alternative education options.

Just as there is a need for counselors to have a thorough knowledge of these programs, it is equally important to make this information available to teachers, parents, and in some cases students through a variety of means. These include

- Career/development centers
- Career information advisory committee
- Planning/information guides to school and community educational resources
- Brochures
- Newsletters
- Slide-tape presentations
- Bulletin boards
- Community notices
- Parents' letters and conferences
- Tours

Middle School and High School. At this level, of course, the educational choices—and life in general—become much more complicated for students, parents, teachers *and the counselor.* Some of the programs necessary to know about at the elementary school level—such as summer programs, special education, and gifted education programs—apply at this level as well. Knowledge of these continues to be important on a sustained basis. The biggest change at the secondary school level is the vast array of choices in some local schools, as early as the eighth grade, among a variety of in-school educational options such as vocational education, music, art, drama, science, foreign languages, mathematics, and so on.

The need here is to make sure through school-based slide tapes, guidance handbooks, curriculum guides, and course listings and description, that students and their parents be made fully aware of all the options available to them. This can and should be done through a planned and organized effort to gather all of the proper information and get it out to all who need it, using all the suggestions in other chapters of this book.

Vocational Education. There is a rich and varied series of vocational education options starting as early as the eighth or ninth grade. Students can discover the many options available through vocational education programs in their local schools. These opportunities enable students to obtain a job while attending high school or following graduation. They may choose to continue their education by enrolling in an advanced program in a technical, community, or four-year college or university. Another option is to continue training in the military. The vocational education programs are listed below:

Agricultural education is designed to educate students in the production operations of an agricultural business and the services associated with them; the manufacturing and distribution of farm equipment, fertilizers, and supplies; the processing, storage, marketing, and distribution of agricultural commodities, including food and fiber; and the conservation, preservation, and use of our natural resources.

Business education provides education for and about business. It prepares people for employment in business or as owners and managers of business enterprises; it equips them with knowledge about business careers, personal money management, banking, and so on. Business education programs include a foundation in keyboarding, business and computer careers, and business management. The use of the computer, other automated office equipment, study of the global marketplace, and preparation for advanced study in business are integral parts of the instructional program. Cooperative Office Education, a strong school and business partnership, provides on-the-job instruction for business students. Future Business Leaders of America (FBLA) is a cocurricular organization of business students that develops leadership and civic responsibility and facilitates classroom learning.

Trade and industrial education prepares individuals for employment in the industrial and service sectors of the economy. Jobs range from those of operatives to semiskilled and skilled craftspersons and technicians. Trade and industrial education includes training for apprenticeable trades, technical occupations, and other industrial and services occupations. Some of these occupations are in layout, designing, producing, processing, assembling, testing, maintaining, servicing, or repairing. Trade and industrial education and training curriculums provide the hands-on development of job skills. Other complementary skills related to leadership and the responsibilities of citizenship are learned through active participation in the Vocational Industrial Clubs of America, Inc. (VICA). In addition, the curriculum includes mastery of complementary technology, appropriate areas of mathematics and science, communication skills, drawing and/or design, occupational safety and hygiene, labor and industrial relations and management, and other related experiences. Part- or full-time instruction may be provided in a formal institutional setting on the secondary and postsecondary level or cooperatively on the job. Over 80 percent of the graduates of trade and industrial programs are employed in their field of training or a related area.

Health occupations education attempts to meet present and predicted needs for health care workers. The competency-based curriculum for health occupations education encompasses both classroom and laboratory experience. Health Occupations Students of America (HOSA), a cocurricular student organization, provides the opportunity for students to share experiences with other people and to build confidence in their own ability to develop skills that will lead to successful employment in the health care field.

Home economics education provides training that enables young people to prepare for work related to the family enterprise. Students develop career skills, employability skills, skills pertaining to the work of the family, and basic education skills. Future Homemakers of America, Inc.—a vocational youth organization—is an integral part of the classroom program. Some of the jobs related to home economics education are full-time home manager and/or wage earner, child-care aide, fashion/fabric coordinator, food caterer, home decorator, and executive housekeeping manager.

Marketing education is designed to prepare students for full-time employment in a variety of marketing industries or for entry into advanced educational or training programs for marketing. Instructional programs assist students in performing marketing functions such as selling, buying, pricing, promoting, financing, transporting, storing, marketing research, and marketing management. In addition, instructional programs emphasize knowledge of products, ideas, or services; related communication and computational skills; and abilities associated with human relations and private enterprise. Cooperative programs in marketing education require the joint efforts of the school and the local business community. Participation in DECA, the marketing education students' organization, gives students a chance to develop leadership and other skills through social, civic, and professional activities. DECA also fosters students' respect for education in marketing, which will contribute to vocational competence and an appreciation for and understanding of the responsibilities of citizenship in a free competitive system.

Technology education helps students develop technical know-how and an understanding of how things work. Technology classes at the middle school level focus on exploring technological and educational choices. Students explore the wonders of a technological world by learning how and why technology works, working with technological tools, using new materials, inventing a new product, discovering technological communications systems, and learning about production and transportation of goods and services. The high school technology program focuses on the application of technology to student needs and on making intelligent judgments about problems associated with technology. In this program students apply design concepts to practical problems, use technological systems, apply engineering concepts and practices, evaluate technology's capabilities, and make connections between theory and practice. Because technology influences all careers, this program will provide a foundation that benefits each student.

Area vocational centers train students and adults for the world of work. These centers offer many advantages, mainly in making a variety of occupational training opportunities easily available to many youths and adults. These centers are centrally located, usually serving students from several high schools. They provide a maximum number of occupational courses at minimal cost. Students are transported from their "parent" high school and spend part of the day at the vocational center, training for employment in the occupation of their choice. The remainder of the day is spent in their own high schools, attending other classes and participating in school activities on the campus. Thus they still feel a part of their home schools while preparing for a career. The area vocational centers have classrooms and laboratory settings that simulate the work setting in the occupational field for which the student is training. The competency-based instruction is constantly modified to keep up with new developments and changes in the field. Courses offered in area vocational centers are selected to match student interests and employment opportunities. The centers are not only used in the daytime for high school students, but also are open at night for adult learning.

Postsecondary Educational Information. Postsecondary school information should stress educational opportunities across the life span, as illustrated by the Life-Span Tree of Learning in Chapter Five. The twenty choices other than a bachelor's degree that appear in Chapter Five are summarized in the next section of this chapter. First, counselors need a sound sense of career development theory. Second, counselors should have a solid knowledge of and ability to interpret educational options. Finally, they must engage in action-oriented efforts on behalf of clients.

Taking the first point first, several recent studies supplement basic career development theory by emphasizing precollege considerations. Two reports are especially noteworthy: *Keeping the Options Open: Recommendations*, by the College Board's Commission on Precollege Guidance and Counseling (1986), and *Frontiers of Possibility*, prepared by the National College Counseling Project (1986), which was sponsored by the National Association of College Admissions Counselors. These two panel findings call for stronger efforts at precollege counseling, especially for disabled and minority individuals.

Second, the publication of more numerous and more sophisticated commercial college guides and the growth of career information delivery systems at the state and national levels have made it much easier for counselors to keep up with the available educational options. Most states are also trying to do a better job of providing information on higher education and financial aid. College information fairs have grown as well, often in major civic centers and convention facilities on a local, state, or even regional basis. And there are always the time-honored firsthand institutional visits by counselors. (For further discussion of resources on higher education, see the listing of sources at the end of this chapter as well as Chapters Ten and Thirteen.)

The last of the three responsibilities of counselors that were cited earlier is a program of action targeted toward positive student outcomes. Probably the best single source of information available that can provide help in putting such an organizational plan into action is the National Association of College Admissions Counselors' *Statement on Precollege Guidance and Counseling and the Role of School Counselor* (1990). In essence, the statement emphasizes that precollege guidance and counseling are part of a larger developmental process that must be implemented no later than the middle or junior high school years to be effective. At the same time, it calls for full recognition of the special needs of women and multicultural and disabled individuals and for the provision of a wide range of services and activities for all students at each level. Among other things, it stresses the need for a written statement of philosophy; a written comprehensive plan of action; an evaluation process; and strong communications among a variety of constituencies, including students, parents, the general community, and educators. The strong school based effort is there to be fully and strongly implemented by the counselor at the middle or junior high school and senior high school levels. An especially good reference on the role of counselors is Hitchner and Hitchner's *Making a Difference in College Admission* (1989).

For K-12 school counselors, the first order of business is to be as knowledgeable on the subject of educational options as possible. This means a full understanding of what sources are available at the local, state, and national level. Much of this may be accomplished by using a strong state career information delivery system or a commercial system (see Chapter Ten for details on this), and second, by having all of the resources readily accessible through the best career development center possible (see Chapter Thirteen on this topic). The second order of business for school counselors, once the basic information sources are available, is to be sure there is a concern for all students and all school subjects on an equal basis. This means that every student with a disabling condition or a reading problem should know about all the educational options open and should have a sense of how to choose wisely among these options. The same is true for all other students. Third, school counselors must make every effort to gather current information on a regular basis and to distribute it in as many ways as possible to all the students, teachers, parents, and community sources (for example, by setting up career information booths in shopping malls, working with the scouting group and 4-H, and so on), so that students and their parents can make the best choices based on the best information available.

Educational Options for the Adult Years

As indicated earlier in this chapter, for people over sixteen or eighteen years old, education is basically a leisure option.

Thus, almost all the resources we discuss in this section are choices (not requirements) that counselors should make clients aware of. Information on most of these educational resources can be found in a state career information delivery system (see Chapter Ten for details on this source of information as well as on the commercial software systems that provide some of the same information). Again, counselors' first priority has to be to become familiar with the wide array of educational options available. As we saw in Chapter Five, the basic array of choices include

- *Postsecondary Vocational Education:* This may be in an area vocational center or in a local high school with offerings in all the traditional areas, plus some workshops on things like "Starting a Small Business."
- *Adult Education:* This may encompass basic literacy training in mathematics, reading, and so on, as well as bilingual classes or General Educational Development (GED) preparation.
- *Private Career/Proprietary Schools:* These schools can include everything from art school to zookeeper assistance, and everything in between. Be sure to check on state/national accreditation.
- *Apprenticeship:* This is run through local/state/regional boards that are made up of labor and management representatives for forty to fifty occupations in most states.
- *On-the-Job Training:* This is available mainly through large employers who want to train their own employees in the specifics of their workplace.
- *Community Colleges:* These provide occupational preparation, courses that make it possible to transfer to a four-year college or university, or classes of personal/professional interest.
- *Four-Year Bachelor's Degree Institutions:* These provide traditional course offerings plus some new options open to adults in the evening and at weekend colleges.
- *Graduate/Professional Degree Institutions:* This level of training is available at the larger universities and at some specialized professional institutions.

- *Military Service:* This is a useful educational option for young people who want to earn some money, serve the country, and get some good education plus postdischarge educational benefits.
- *Correspondence Study—Nondegree:* This is the training program "in your mailbox" for those who prefer to study on their own for personal reasons or because of geographical isolation.
- *Correspondence Study—Undergraduate and Graduate:* This is a great suggestion for individuals who have to withdraw from regular college and university study for health or economic reasons.
- *Job Corps:* This is still a viable option for young people in most areas. Contact the local public employment service office for details.
- *Job Training Partnership Act (JTPA) Programs:* This used to be CETA and before that MDTA. It still provides important skill development opportunities at the local level for people who need them.
- *Special Training Program Through Department of Rehabilitative Services (DRS):* This is the main option for those adults with disabling conditions. Information on these options is available through state DRS representatives.
- *Learning Vacations:* These are a growing option for those who have the money to take advantage of them. They include everything from "fantasy baseball camps" to art instruction to wildlife appreciation.
- *Alumni/Organization-Sponsored Tours:* These tours are also a growing option, since some people prefer touring with groups with which they have something in common.
- *Special Programs for Over-Sixty Adults (ELDERHOSTELS):* This segment of the population is increasingly taking advantage of work and leisure options. ELDERHOSTELS have grown at a fantastic rate.
- *Local Community/Business/Organization Training Programs:* These programs are growing in quality and quantity in most areas as the push for lifelong continuing education expands.

- *Specialized Health Training Programs:* These programs are usually at less than the community college associate degree level in areas such as licensed practical nursing (LPN) and the like.
- *Specialized Licensure Training Programs:* These have grown in importance as new licensure requirements— such as those for counselors—have emerged. Trade and professional publications are the best resource.

Counselors need to take several key points into account in regard to providing timely, accurate, and up-to-date educational resources. A few of these are discussed in the following paragraphs.

What materials should be available? Only those materials that counselors feel will best serve the interests of users should be on hand. For schools, this may mean having items that are of interest to teachers and parents *as well as students.* Likewise, counselors who work mainly with adults may want to have some items that are helpful for the children of these users. A full range of multimedia materials that meet professional standards of career information as established by the National Career Development Association are appropriate (see Chapter Thirteen).

Where should these resources be kept? Our suggestion is in a complete career development center (see Chapter Thirteen for details). If there is no possibility of a full-fledged center, counselors should do the best they can to have the materials out where people can see and use them easily.

How should these resources be made available? A computerized or microfiche information system is the most economical way to keep everything together, but the main thing is that the resources be used, and so setting up a station in the library or hallway may provide better access. Furthermore, different means of formatting may help; possibilities include an education newsletter, tabloid information, a college video, or vocational education information on a local cable-access channel.

When should these resources be available? They should be available whenever they can be used by the people that counselors want to reach. This may mean early in the morning, in the afternoon, or at night. It may also mean trying to reach people where they work or at home through radio or television announcements, as well as through various handouts for people to take along to discuss with family or friends.

Financial Aid

Again, the single best resource for financial aid information should be the state career information delivery system, or—if no system exists in your state—a commercial software package such as GIS, DISCOVER, CHOICES, SIGI-Plus, or COIN. The financial aid office at the postsecondary institution the person wants to attend is the second most important source of information. There are, of course, a host of print sources available that represent prime information. Many people feel the best source for the money is the annual update of the American Legion's *Need a Lift? Educational Opportunities, Careers, Loans, Scholarships, Employment*, which was expanded in 1990 but still costs only $2.00. (Many American Legion posts will make copies available at no charge to local high schools.) The two other principal sources of information at the national level are the College Board and Peterson's Guides. Both of these publishers specialize in higher education and financial aid information. Their annual catalogues are a must to keep up to date on the latest information on both higher education and financial aid. Since most of the funding is available through the federal government, good national sources on the changing U.S. Department of Education programs, updated on an annual basis, are also a must. See the listing at the end of the chapter for some specific resource suggestions and addresses.

State Financial Aid Information. There are a host of state programs, both public (government) and private (associations and organizations). Often these are overlooked in the race for large amounts of money from national sources. For example, each state has some kind of higher education authority—such as the Pennsylvania Higher Education Assistance Agency—that can help counselors get started. The names of state aid agencies should be available from the state career information delivery system or from a listing of state agencies for loans, tuition assistance (often to those attending in-state private colleges), and other sources in the annual update of the American Legion's guide (1991). A good ongoing project for counselors would be to add at least five to ten new *state* resources each year to their files.

Local Financial Aid Information. The local level runs a close second to the state level in terms of sources of information that are often overlooked. The local civic, service, or religious group frequently has some type of financial aid. In building a local file, counselors should be sure to check annually with sources such as the following:

SCHOOLS	CIVIC ORGANIZATIONS	OTHER
___ Counselors	___ Jaycees	___ Unions
___ Teachers	___ Rotary Club	___ Churches and
___ Principals	___ Lions Club	Synagogues
___ PTA	___ Women's Club	___ Physicians
	___ League of Women	___ Medical Research
	Voters	Organizations
	___ Scout Clubs	___ Businesses
	___ Historical Societies	___ Chamber of Com-
EDUCATIONAL	___ Sororities and	merce Offices
ORGANIZATIONS	Fraternities	___ Special Interest
___ Alumni Groups	___ Junior League	Groups
___ 4-H Groups	___ American Business	___ Ethnic Groups
___ Educational	Women's Association	___ Knights of
Association	___ Daughters of the	Columbus
___ Teachers Guilds	American Revolution	

In addition, numerous contests and other competitions make funds available to local students both for college and for various forms of postsecondary education that may be of special interest to vocational education students. Oftentimes local groups will offer loan assistance to a continuing group of local students in need. Finally, there are a number of focused sources such as a scholarship available for a student who is preparing to teach special education. The point is, *no book like this* can begin to list all of the local and state sources of financial aid. Finding sources at the state or local level is accomplished by constant searching and collecting for future use every reasonable source you can find. See the list of basic sources at the end of the chapter.

Sources of Information on Leisure Options

There are three important points to be stressed in connection with this section. First, as we use the term, *leisure* denotes "relatively self-determined activities and experiences that are available due to having discretionary income, time, and social behavior; the activities may be physical, intellectual, volunteer, creative, social, or some combination of all five" (McDaniels, 1984b, p. 560). In addition, of course, we view leisure, along with work, as a part of the totality of career; this is expressed in the formula mentioned earlier: Career = Work + Leisure (C = W + L).

Second, our conception of leisure stresses a life-span approach. Leisure should be given special attention in the elementary schools because that is an important developmental period (but not to the exclusion of attention to leisure for the rest of the life span). The interaction of work and leisure goes on throughout life—not just in grades K-12 or till the end of adolescence. This section will emphasize the need for counselors to know about sources of information on leisure for people across the life span—not just for one age period.

Third, in building leisure information resources, it is important to recognize the main types of leisure activities.

- *Physical:* These are the leisure activities many people think of first; they include jogging, swimming, biking, walking, team sports, and the like.
- *Intellectual:* Intellectual activities include games like chess, checkers, bridge, and hundreds of other card and table games, as well as reading and writing.

- *Volunteer:* Volunteer activities involve donating time and service for others. Examples include giving time to a Red Cross Bloodmobile, school tutoring, Little League coaching, and serving as a host in community hospitals or senior citizens centers.
- *Creative:* The creative activities that are most visible deal with all forms of art, music, dance, drama, writing, and photography.
- *Social:* These include clubs and activities that get individuals out into a social context, like tour groups, the American Association of Retired Persons, fraternities and sororities, and school extracurricular activities.
- *Combination of the Above:* Teaching photography to a scout troop is an example of a volunteer leisure activity that is both creative and intellectual. Thus, leisure pursuits may combine more than one type of activity. They should not be thought of in exclusive terms.

Where to Locate Leisure Resources?

To get people to think about some of their leisure options, try to use something like the McDaniels Leisure Development Inventory (MLDI) as an icebreaker (see Exhibit 9.1). This can be an easy, nonthreatening way to get all but the youngest children to think developmentally about their leisure activities and interests over a ten-year period. This makes it easy to spot trends, gaps, or interesting patterns that lend themselves to counseling for satisfying career development. For a more detailed workbook on drawing out leisure interests, see Kimildorf (1989).

Local Sources

The leisure resource system should start where most people get involved with leisure—at the *local level.* Counselors should have available a file index or computer program to serve as a ready reference of individual or group needs in this area. Where to start?

Exhibit 9.1. The McDaniels Leisure Development Inventory (MLDI).

FUTURE GOALS (3–5 years ahead)	List 3–5 Leisure pursuits in which you expect to be active in the future.

1. _____   4. _____

2. _____   5. _____

3. _____

List 3–5 Leisure pursuits in which you feel or think you might be interested in the future.

1. _____   4. _____

2. _____   5. _____

3. _____

(Note: Feel free to list others if you want to.)

PRESENT (Current)	List 3–5 Leisure pursuits in which you are currently active.

1. _____   4. _____

2. _____   5. _____

3. _____

List 3–5 Leisure pursuits in which you feel or think you are interested but in which you are *not currently active.*

1. _____   4. _____

2. _____   5. _____

3. _____

(Note: Feel free to list others if you want to.)

PAST (3–5 years back)	List 3–5 Leisure pursuits in which you were active in the past.

1. _____   4. _____

2. _____   5. _____

3. _____

Exhibit 9.1. The McDaniels Leisure Development Inventory, Cont'd.

List 3–5 Leisure pursuits in which you felt or thought you were interested in the past.

1. _____   4. _____

2. _____   5. _____

3. _____

(Note: Feel free to list others if you want to.)

Telephone yellow pages
Local club directories
Local newspapers
Local magazines
Local recreation groups

Local education agencies
Local community information and referral sources
Local religious groups
Local youth groups
Local senior citizens groups

These sources can serve as the basis also for an attractive bulletin-board display or looseleaf notebook arrangement to simply make people aware of the wide array of leisure resources available to them in their area. Cutting out newspaper, magazine, or newsletter stories also provides a concrete way of bringing some of these leisure opportunities to life for a person striving for career satisfaction. Another approach is to bring into the counseling process some models of people enjoying their leisure activities. Examples might include local craftspeople demonstrating weaving or a dance group putting on a performance for interested spectators.

State/Regional Sources

These leisure resources are also an important source of information to be aware of, since people with more advanced leisure skills may need to be referred to them. Often larger-scale classes, tournaments, tours, and the like are only available on a state or regional basis. Some of the same sources used locally can open up new vistas at the next level. In addition, counselors should keep these sources of information in mind:

1. Regional newspapers such as the *Washington Post,* the *St. Louis Post Dispatch,* and the *Charlotte Observer*
2. Regional magazines; examples include *Southern Living, Yankee,* and *Texas Monthly*
3. Regional/state tournaments and other competitions like the Southeastern Regional Iris Show, the Pacific New Car Show, and the Mid-America Quilt Exhibit
4. Regional/state television; this could include a series on home repairs or a series on regional recreational opportunities
5. Regional club and tour groups; typical examples would be New England Fall Foliage Tours, the New Orleans Jazz Club Meeting, and Wildlife of the Deserts of the Southwest United States

National Sources

Leisure resources abound for those who are looking for a cruise, a tournament, a film festival, a marathon, an exhibit, or a place to volunteer as an alternative to a traditional spring vacation. The challenge for counselors of all age groups is to begin to build a resource file (hard-copy or computer based) of national sources that can be called up as a means of making clients aware of the options, or to help them explore these options in additional depth, or for well-skilled people who are looking for broader challenges. The following would provide a good starting point for such a resource file:

1. National directories; the best is Germain (1987)
2. Newspapers, especially the section "USA at Play" in the Thursday *USA Today,* and also the *Wall Street Journal* and *Sporting News*
3. Newsletters—for example, *About Conventions, Reunions, Continuing Education,* and *ELDERHOSTELS*
4. Magazines; examples include *Travel & Leisure, Mechanics Illustrated,* and *Photography*

5. Cable Television—special networks like ESPN, A&E, and C-SPAN post their monthly schedules on bulletin boards
6. ELDERHOSTEL; counselors can contact the national headquarters at 80 Boylston Street, Suite 400, Boston, MA 092116 to get on the mailing list for regular listings of offerings

In brief, there is no shortage of leisure information resources! It is just a matter of taking the time to look around for some of the resources that are readily available. To help with this, counselors may want to get a group of co-workers to add to their collection, as well as getting themselves on mailing lists to receive information about regular sources of activities. It is a good idea to plan different ways to display this information to receive the maximum visibility through bulletin boards, reception areas, reading rooms, and library space, and by creating a separate section in the career development center.

Fifteen Key Resources for College Selection

1. Elfin, M., and Bauer, B. (eds.). *America's Best Colleges and Professional Schools.* Washington, D.C.: U.S. News & World Report, 1990.
2. Bear, J. *Bear's Guide to Non-Traditional College Degrees.* (10th ed.) Berkeley, Calif.: Ten Speed Press, 1988.
3. Cass, J., and Birnbaum, M. *Comparative Guide to American Colleges.* (13th ed.) New York: HarperCollins, 1987.
4. *College Blue Book: Degrees Offered by Colleges and Universities.* (21st ed.) New York: Macmillan, 1987.
5. Dilts, S. W. *Peterson's Guide to Two-Year Colleges—1991.* (21st ed.) Princeton, N.J.: Peterson's Guides, 1990.
6. Dilts, S. W. *Peterson's Guide to Four-Year Colleges—1991.* (21st ed.) Princeton, N.J.: Peterson's Guides, 1990.
7. Fiske, E. B. *Selective Guide to Colleges.* New York: Times Books, 1989.
8. Harris, S. (ed.). *1990–91 Accredited Institutions of Postsecondary Education.* New York: Macmillan, 1991. (A publication of the American Council on Education.)

9. Hayden, T. C. *Handbook for College Admission: A Family Guide.* (3rd ed.) Princeton, N.J.: Peterson's Guides, 1980.

10. Moll, R. *The Public Ivys: A Guide to America's Best Public Undergraduate Colleges and Universities.* New York: Viking, 1986.

11. *Peterson's Graduate Education Directory.* (22nd ed.) Princeton, N.J.: Peterson's Guides, 1987.

12. *Peterson's Guide to Graduate and Professional Programs: An Overview—1990.* (24th ed.) Princeton, N.J.: Peterson's Guides, 1990.

13. Straughn, C., and Straughn, B. L. *Lovejoy's College Guide.* New York: Monarch Press, 1988.

14. College Board. *The College Handbook—1991.* (50th ed.) New York: College Board, 1991.

15. Torregrosa, C. H. *1989 Higher Education Directory.* Falls Church, Va.: Higher Education Publications, 1989.

Eight Key Resources Available from the National Association of College Admission Counselors

1. *Getting into College.* An exciting new fifty-three-minute video that takes students step by step through the college exploration and admissions process.

2. *Parents in the Process.* A special video (sixty-five minutes) in which college admissions officers and school counselors interact with real parents who are helping their children with college choices, the admissions process, and financial aid.

3. *A Guide to the College Admission Process.* Written for the secondary student who is about to participate in the college admissions process, this forty-eight-page guide offers a step-by-step approach to college admissions.

4. *Selecting the Right College.* This very informative booklet addresses the college exploration, financial aid, and high school–to–college transition concerns of students.

5. *High School Planning for College-Bound Athletes.* This sixteen-page booklet, with a thought-provoking foreword

by Pennsylvania State University football coach Joe Paterno, provides student athletes with a year-by-year look at planning for college entrance.

6. *Map of Two- and Four-Year Colleges.* This top-quality counseling resource shows the location of more than 2,800 colleges and universities in the United States. If you wish to make a bulletin-board display, order two copies, since Eastern and Western states are presented front and back.

7. *NACAC Collegelines.* This resource contains the telephone numbers of the admissions offices of more than 1,200 NACAC member colleges and universities (including toll-free numbers where available).

8. NACAC Statements.
   Statement on Counseling Dimension of the Admission Process at the College/University Level—1990
   Statement on Precollege Guidance and Counseling and the Role of the School Counselor—1990
   Statement on Counselor Competencies, forthcoming.

For availability and current prices, contact NACAC Publications/Media, Suite 430, 1800 Diagonal Road, Alexandria, VA 22314; telephone (703) 836-2222.

Ten Key Resources on Financial Aid

1. American College Testing Program. *Applying for Financial Aid.* Iowa City, Iowa: American College Testing Publications, 1986.

2. American Legion. *Need a Lift? Educational Opportunities, Careers, Loans, Scholarships, Employment.* (40th ed.) Indianapolis, Ind.: American Legion, 1990.

3. Bailey, R. L. *How and Where to Get Scholarships and Financial Aid for College.* New York: Arco, 1986.

4. College Blue Book. *College Blue Book: Scholarships, Fellowships, Grants, and Loans.* (21st ed.) New York: Macmillan, 1987.

5. Fabish, V. *The A's and B's: Your Guide to Academic Scholarships.* (9th ed.) Alexandria, Va.: Octameron Press, 1985.

6. Leider, A. *College Grants from Uncle Sam.* (8th ed.) Alexandria, Va.: Octameron Press, 1989.
7. Leider, R., and Leider, A. *Don't Miss Out: The Ambitious Student's Guide to Scholarships and Loans.* Alexandria, Va.: Octameron Press, 1988.
8. Peterson's. *Peterson's College Money Handbook—1991.* (7th ed.) Princeton, N.J.: Peterson's Guides, 1990.
9. Schlacter, G. A. *Directory of Financial Aid for Women—1990-91.* Redwood City, Calif.: Reference Service Press, 1991. (Five other good publications are also available from this source.)
10. College Board. *The College Cost Book—1991.* (10th ed.) New York: College Board, 1990.

Fifteen Key Resources on Leisure

1. Edwards, P. *Leisure Counseling Techniques.* (3rd ed.) Los Angeles: Constructive Leisure, 1980.
2. Eisenberg, G. G. *Learning Vacations.* (6th ed.) Princeton, N.J.: Peterson's Guides, 1989.
3. Gault, J. *Free Time: Making Your Leisure Count.* New York: Wiley, 1983.
4. Germain, R. (ed.). *National Avocational Organizations.* (7th ed.) Washington, D.C.: Columbia Books, 1987.
5. Gillespie, G. A. *Leisure 2000: Scenarios for the Future.* Columbia: University of Missouri, 1983.
6. Kelly, J. R. *Leisure Identities and Interactions.* Winchester, Mass.: Allen and Unwin, 1983.
7. Kelly, J. R. *Leisure.* Englewood Cliffs, N.J.: Prentice-Hall, 1982.
8. Loesch, L. C., and Wheeler, P. T. *Principles of Leisure Counseling.* Minneapolis, Minn.: Educational Media Corporation, 1982.
9. McDaniels, C. *The Changing Workplace.* San Francisco: Jossey-Bass, 1989.
10. McDaniels, C. "The Work/Leisure Connection." *Vocational Guidance Quarterly,* 1984, *33,* 35-44.
11. McDaniels, C. "The Role of Leisure in Career Develop-

ment." *Journal of Career Development,* 1984, *11* (2), 64-71. The entire issue is on this subject.

12.   McDaniels, C. "Work and Leisure in the Career Span." In N. C. Gysbers and Associates, *Designing Careers: Counseling to Enhance Education, Work, and Leisure.* San Francisco: Jossey-Bass, 1984.

13.   McDaniels, C. *Leisure: Integrating a Neglected Component in Life Planning.* Columbus, Ohio: National Center for Research in Vocational Education, 1982.

14.   Peterson's *The Independent Study Catalog.* (4th ed.) Princeton, N.J.: Peterson's Guides, 1989.

15.   Sinetar, M. *Do What You Love, Money Will Follow.* Boulder, Colo.: New Career Center, 1987.

10

██

Working with Career
Information Delivery Systems

██

One of the most important developments in the area of career resources in recent years has been the emergence of the concept of the *career information delivery system (CIDS)*. What this means, first, is a broader, more comprehensive notion of career information, one that encompasses more than occupational or educational information alone and that can include information in any format (print, film, computer, and so on). Second, it emphasizes the importance of being able to deliver the information in an interesting and informative way to a wide range of users—including both genders, people of all ages, all disabling conditions, and all racial groups. And third, the term *system* suggests an all-encompassing approach that focuses on bringing together many differing elements— not a piecemeal one.

This concept is the outgrowth of earlier developments, as McDaniels (1982a) pointed out. The heavy reliance on print material as the main source of information on career resources gave way between 1950 and 1980 to a much more diversified approach. During this period, the Department of Labor funded some start-up state systems and enlarged and improved the biannual *Occupational Outlook Handbook*. Commercial publishers began to provide a wider range of choices

for various reading and interest levels, and in general the role
of the media was greatly expanded, as films, television, filmstrips, audiotape, radio, and video came into common use.
Technological innovations resulted in less expensive mainframe and personal computers, which provided a means of
storing large amounts of career information. Microfiche
equipment also aided in the process. Finally, the opportunity
to acquire information through firsthand experience in such
programs as work-study, cooperative education, career shadowing, Junior Achievement, volunteering, and the like was
greatly enhanced.

The trend toward more effective career information
resources received a boost in 1976, when Congress authorized
the National Occupational Information Coordinating Committee (NOICC) as a federal interagency committee that pro-
motes the development and use of educational, occupational,
and labor market information. NOICC's primary mission is
to improve coordination and communication among developers and users of career information and to help states meet
the occupational information needs of various groups and
individuals. These include vocational education and employment and training program managers as well as people making career decisions. (See Flanders, 1988, for more detail on
the formation of the NOICC and on its accomplishments
between 1977 and 1987.)

NOICC works with a network of state occupational
information coordinating committees (SOICCs), which were
also established by Congress in 1976. SOICC members represent state producers and users of occupational information,
including vocational education boards, vocational rehabilitation agencies, employment security agencies, job training
coordinating councils, and economic development agencies.
Many SOICCs also include state representatives from two-
and four-year higher education groups.

NOICC and the SOICCs encourage coordination and
communication among their respective member agencies at
the national and state levels, and they also work together in
larger federal and state networks. As a result, data producers

and users become more aware of each others' programs and services, requirements, and needs. Information on new products and research is exchanged. Projects of mutual interest are identified and carried out cooperatively at both state and federal levels.

NOICC and the SOICCs have developed data systems that are designed to help provide planners and program managers with up-to-date and locally relevant labor market information on which to base program decisions. Similarly, they have developed systems and programs to make useful information available to individuals facing career decisions. NOICC/SOICC systems include

1. *Occupational Information Systems.* These are computerized data bases that contain mechanisms for combining multiple-source occupational and educational data and integrating and formatting the data so that they can be understood and analyzed by a variety of audiences. NOICC, working with SOICCs, was responsible for the concept and design of the systems; SOICCs develop and implement them.

2. *Career Information Delivery Systems.* These are computer-based systems that provide information about occupations and training opportunities. The systems help individuals match personal characteristics with compatible occupations. CIDs are located at some 15,000 sites nationwide.

The importance of the NOICC/SOICC presence is that it has, at least in the short run, transformed the way career information is organized and delivered all across the country. To those who use the systems that emerged in the 1970s and 1980s, these may seem to be the only way to operate. They are not the most modern resources, but they are the product of the advances on the various fronts mentioned above. The organizational function of the NOICC/SOICC programs has been the most important of these advances.

NOICC provides Basic Assistance Grants (BAGs) to each state and territory in the United States. Each state, through its

SOICC, plans what that activity will be. For fiscal year 1988 most states received around $100,000 from NOICC in BAG support. The balance then had to come from state funding, other federal sources (such as vocational education funding), or fees charged to system users. In addition, NOICC awards ten to fifteen special grants each year for things like the National Crosswalk Service Center and an NOICC Training Support Center. For further information, see National Occupational Information Coordinating Committee (1990).

The Elements of a Comprehensive
Career Information Delivery System

Two key words in this heading, *comprehensive* and *system,* make the current situation in career counseling so different from that of the preceding seventy years. It is now possible to reach a far wider audience of users with a much greater mix of media in more locations than was the case earlier—a truly comprehensive effort has emerged. And all of these factors can now be put together in some type of orderly arrangement commonly called a "system approach." In the years ahead, even more exciting innovations will emerge.

As McDaniels (1982a) argued, efforts to establish comprehensive CIDSs need to rest on four foundations.

Foundation 1: Build on a Wide-Ranging
Multimedia Approach

The sophisticated media developed in recent years must all be included in this system. We now have a rich pool of resources to draw from. For example, a computer information approach is not the beginning and end of a system. Expanded personal experience opportunities and other firsthand means of acquiring information need to be included. Every effort should be made to make part-time, summer, and internship experiences available as a means of learning about an occupation. In the same way, a visit to a proprietary school or college for as long as possible—an overnight stay for example—is better than reading about it in a book. In short, all the means outlined above should be used in a comprehensive system. Drier (1980) has made some useful suggestions on how all of these approaches can be combined into a harmonious unit.

Foundation 2: Build on Wide-Ranging Locations of Systems

Although school and postsecondary institutions have traditionally served as prime locations for career information, many other locations must now be considered. Libraries, senior citizens centers, Job Training Partnership Act (JTPA) programs, employment agencies, correctional units, rehabilitative services offices, women's resource centers, and others should all be included. In statewide coordinated efforts, there must be an effort to reach agencies large and small in which career information would be useful. Large employers offering career development programs for employees should have a comprehensive career information system available as part of an overall plan.

Many suggestions on the proper locations for such a career information system have been made. In the *Occupational Outlook Quarterly,* Martin (1980) outlined a clear and concise approach to organizing and using a career resource center in a variety of locations. The center can be a focal point for central one-stop information distribution. A center can serve as a springboard for innovative approaches, such as a career information hotline providing local or statewide information.

Foundation 3: Build on a Wide-Ranging Appeal to Users

According to a user survey conducted by McDaniels, Snipes, and Peevy (1980), those between the ages of twelve and twenty-two, who are mainly in educational institutions, are already well-served users. Now is the time to reach out to much broader user groups, to all ages, to all reading levels, to all interests, and to all areas of a state or community. The rural or inner-city users must be as well served as any others. Innovative uses of existing media must be examined. It may take some close cooperation with a library or community center to serve certain groups. For some, a mobile career information center will be best. Newspapers, radio, or television may be the most effective way of reaching other user groups. For some learners, posters, charts, or other large visuals will serve best. The user groups who are most underserved are adults, the disabled, women, minorities, and rural and inner-city populations, and they must be adequately reached along with those users who are already well served.

Foundation 4: Build on a Wide Range of Sources of Career Information

The Bureau of Labor Statistics and the Bureau of the Census furnish helpful information that can be used in national program approaches. State and local information seems much less adequate in providing the same quality and quantity of information. Even though there have been some efforts to bring about improvements at the state level in recent years, much remains to be done in this area. In particular, a system of data collection that is equal to the level of the distribution system must be developed. The demand on the part of counseling professionals for these improved resources is growing all the time (McDaniels, 1976b). The long-term future of these systems will rest jointly on the ability of a state to provide creditable information in a variety of ways, in various accessible locations, to a full range of public users of all ages.

Given these basic fundamentals, how do these systems deliver career information? Various states utilize a wide array as the National Occupational Information Coordinating Committee (1990) has reported. These delivery modes include the following:

1. Mainframe computers. About twenty-one states use this mode.
2. Microcomputers. About forty-one states use this growing method of delivering career information.

3. Microfiche Readers. Ten states use this means of inex-
    pensive delivery.
4. Needlesort. About twenty-two states use this method.
5. Print. Twenty or so states use this method to publish
    career tabloids or directories.
6. Films/videos/film strips/slides. These media are used by
    most states to deliver various kinds of information on a
    rent or purchase basis.
7. Career information telephone hotlines. This method is
    being used by six states to reach a wide audience through
    toll-free 800 numbers.

According to the National Occupational Information
Coordinating Committee (1990) and the Association of Computer-Based Systems for Career Information (1990), there are
some fifty CIDSs operating in forty-six states; they serve
nearly five million people seeking general career information.
Millions also make use of career tabloids, videos, and career
information hotlines. These individuals are served in over
13,000 locations nationwide in public and private elementary,
middle, and senior high schools; postsecondary institutions;
vocational-technical schools; rehabilitation agencies; public
and private employment agencies; JTPA centers; libraries; and
extension offices; as well as in a variety of other public and
private agencies such as Veterans Administration hospitals,
women's resource centers, senior citizens centers, and military
bases. Of course, commercial systems (to be discussed later in
the chapter), which have been around for some twenty years,
are used in some high schools, postsecondary institutions,
and agencies with a lease/rent arrangement on a yearly basis.
But these systems are, for the most part, available for microcomputers only and do not serve the full range of media available. The state systems provide information on the following
topics:

*   *Occupations:* This is the heart and soul of these systems,
    with ten to fourteen pages of detailed information each
    on 250 to 500 occupations.

- *Higher Education:* This involves state/national data on approved postsecondary institutions, including career (proprietary) schools.
- *Financial Aid:* This is basic information on state/national sources for postsecondary education.
- *Military Service:* This involves complete information on enlisted and officer opportunities in all branches of the military service.
- *Apprenticeships:* Everything a person needs to know about the subject is covered.
- *Approved High School Subjects:* This relates high school subjects to particular occupations.
- *Miscellaneous Topics:* Examples include licensed occupations in the state, approved specialized training programs, adult education, and so on.

Examples of State Systems

The spring 1988 issue of the *Journal of Career Development*—edited by Flanders and McDaniels—was devoted to the topic of "A Decade of Career Information Delivery Systems—1977–1987." This is the most comprehensive survey of this subject. The following brief comments on state CIDSs draw on that source. Those who want more detailed information should consult the original publication.

Virginia

The Virginia Career Information Delivery System is now in its second decade. It is supported about equally by state and federal (vocational education) funding. It is a comprehensive CIDS with all of the components noted above, except mainframe computers. It serves Virginia in over 1,300 locations (second only in number of sites to Michigan) and has an especially active career information hotline, which has responded to over 33,000 callers from all over the commonwealth. Another widely used part of the system is the tabloid called *The Career Hunt,* which goes out to all 1,300 sites on a yearly basis. Over 150,000 copies are distributed annually. A user-services component of the system is a series of thirty to thirty-five fall workshops, where over 1,700 counselors, teachers, librarians, and other users and professionals meet in half-day regional sessions to receive updated materials on Virginia VIEW. Two settings that are targeted for expanded use of the system are all public libraries and cooperative extension centers. For more details, see McDaniels (1988).

Oregon

This state was one of the original group of states to receive start-up funding from the Department of Labor in the early 1970s. Oregon's Career Information System (CIS) led the way; this system was later extended to a consortium of states as well as to other states that would use this approach. There are now sixteen states in the national CIS network that work together to support the continuing development of CIS software materials and methods. The CIS system carries the basic educational, occupational, and military information available through a variety of microcomputers (hard and soft disk) as well as time-shared mainframe computers. An active fall workshop program is part of a dedication to user services. For more details on the Oregon CIS and the national network, see McKinlay (1988).

Florida

Florida has adapted the CHOICES commercial system to accommodate state data on occupations and education. This system is housed in the Bureau of Career Development in the Florida State Department of Education. It has a diverse delivery approach using microcomputers, microfiche, and print material and is known to be one of the most innovative and creative of the state systems. Special features available include listings of job openings in Florida as well as academic advising information. The budget for this CIDS is annually over $2 million in service fees and central funding (state and federal sources). For further discussion, see Wooley (1988).

Maine

One of the smallest states in terms of population, Maine has developed a system that makes available to users three adapted commercial software programs: CHOICES, GIS, and DIS-COVER. Its unique program offers something most other states do not—a choice of systems available from a central source. Maine calls this the *Grohering effort* and sponsors four regional workshops, at which time all three Maine-adapted, commercial systems are introduced. In addition, the Maine SOICC has created a number of products that can be used in the schools. These include *The ABC's of the World of Work in Maine,* The Maine Job Box, the CIDS career planners, and job cluster videos. An especially close collaboration exists between the Maine CIDS and the public schools. A considerable amount of ongoing research has also been a hallmark of this small system. For more information, see Thompson (1988).

The Commercial Software Systems

The most recent directory of the Association of Computer-Based Systems for Career Information (1990) listed thirteen supporting members that are commercial career information software producers. McCormac (1988) mentioned seven in a review of the history and services available from the group. If we include some of the smaller and more specialized firms, the total of those working at the national level comes to around twenty. These systems, some of which have been in the developmental stage since the late 1960s or 1970s, started out as time-sharing systems on mainframe computers. In recent years, as technology has changed and telephone-line costs for mainframe connections have increased, they have gone mainly to microcomputer hard-disk programs. There has also been a diversification of software from a primarily high school–age focus downward to middle school–age and upward to more diverse college-age users and adults. Most of the systems are available on either an individual site lease (a school or school division, college, or private agency) or to states for direct or adaptive use, as in the case of the Maine and Florida systems noted earlier.

Table 10.1 presents McCormac's (1988) summary of seven of the major systems along with basic discussion of the advantages and disadvantages of using commercial systems, new initiatives, and linkages with other software systems. A detailed description of one of those systems—the DISCOVER program—follows, as an example of the complete listing available in the Association of Computer-Based Systems for Career Information's directory (1990).

DISCOVER

DISCOVER is a comprehensive set of computer-based career guidance and information systems designed for multiple audiences. All current DISCOVER systems were developed by the American College Testing Program (ACT) under the leadership of JoAnn Bowlsbey.

DISCOVER Versions

Five versions of DISCOVER are designed to serve the career-planning needs of various client groups.

DISCOVER for Junior High and Middle Schools has been available since February 1987. This system helps students in middle schools do initial career exploration and plan for their transition to high school. The content of this system is parallel to that of other DISCOVER versions but with levels of sophistication and detail appropriate for students in grades six through nine. The education files in this version can be customized to include graduation requirements and course offerings of high schools the users will attend. This feature allows students to plan their high school studies by using DISCOVER, assuring that students select courses appropriate for their career aspirations. DISCOVER for Junior High and Middle Schools is available for Apple II and IBM PC and compatible computers.

Table 10.1. System Descriptions.

System	Developer	Setting[a]	Content of Basic System	Additional Modules/Versions
CAREER INFORMATION SYSTEM (CIS)	National CIS University of Oregon Eugene, OR 97403	Junior high and high school; vocational-technical and community colleges; vocational rehabilitation; 4-year colleges; corrections; JTPA; employment services	National, state, and local	National College Information, Micro-SCHOOL SORT, Micro-Micro-QUEST, Needle Sort, High School Planner, Time-Shared CIS
CHOICES	Canada Systems Group Federal Services Division 955 Green Valley Crescent Ottawa, Ontario, Canada K2C 3V4	Middle schools, high schools; community colleges; 4-year colleges; business and industry	National and state	CHOICES Jr. (6th–9th grade), CHOICES (9th grade and beyond with more extensive occupational data base), CHOICES Colleges
COORDINATE OCCUPATIONAL INFORMATION NETWORK (COIN)	Dr. Rodney Durgin COIN Career Guidance Products 3361 Executive Parkway Suite 302 Toledo, OH 43606	High schools; vocational-technical and community colleges; middle schools; 4-year colleges, corrections; JTPA; employment services; vocational rehabilitation	National (state available in South Carolina)	COIN; COIN PLUS (integration of basic academic skills with occupational file)
DISCOVER	DISCOVER Center Schilling Plaza South 230 Schilling Circle Hunt Valley, MD 21030	High schools; community colleges; 4-year colleges; universities; business and industry; junior high and middle schools	National (state available in Maine). Capability for customer sites to localize occupational information	DISCOVER for High Schools, DISCOVER for Colleges and Adults, DISCOVER in Junior High and Middle Schools, DISCOVER for Organizations

System	Company/Address	Setting[a]	Scope	Additional
GUIDANCE INFORMATION SYSTEM (GIS)	Houghton Mifflin Company Educational Software Division P.O. Box 683 Hanover, NH 03755	High schools; 2- and 4-year colleges; vocational rehabilitation; corrections; employment services; military; business and industry	National and state	
KANSAS CAREERS	KANSAS CAREERS College of Education Kansas State University Bluemont Hall Manhattan, KS 66506	Middle and high schools; vocational rehabilitation; 4-year colleges; counseling agencies	National and state	State Careers, U.S. Careers, Elementary Careers (4th–6th grades), Kaleidoscope of Careers (video–high school), Spanish Language
SYSTEM OF INTERACTIVE GUIDANCE AND INFORMATION (SIGI)	SIGI Office Educational Testing Service Princeton, NJ 08541	4-year colleges and universities; community colleges; business and industry; private counseling	National (local/state information may be added using local information option)	SIGI PLUS

[a] Setting indicates where systems are used in order of size; only settings that constitute more than 2 percent of user sites are listed.

Source: McCormac, 1988, pp. 200–201. Reprinted with permission.

DISCOVER for High Schools uses DISCOVER's standard guidance approach, with an added feature that makes it easy to retrieve information from all major files in the system by a quick "direct-access" approach. DISCOVER for High Schools has a unique introductory section that helps users review their career decision-making maturity. Based upon this inventory, the system recommends activities appropriate for completion by individual users.

DISCOVER for High Schools facilitates group implementation through the use of the *Career Planning Guidebook,* which can save substantial time on the system. Licensees are encouraged to produce a copy of this resource for each user.

DISCOVER includes files on military training programs and vocational/technical schools in addition to extensive files on two-year and four-year colleges. DISCOVER compiles numerous elements of user data and generates reports upon request for use by the professional staff. DISCOVER for High Schools operates on MS-DOS computers.

DISCOVER for Colleges and Adults has content parallel to that of Discover for High Schools, but it is presented at a higher reading level. It includes extensive activities for people in career transitions. These activities are based on Donald Super's *Life/Career Rainbow* and Nancy Schlossberg's work on effectively dealing with transitions. A special version of DISCOVER for Colleges and Adults designed for use in non-academic settings is also available. This special version is recommended for use in public libraries, on military bases, and in JTPA programs.

DISCOVER for Organizations serves clients who seek a career development experience within the context of their current employment. A major revision of this DISCOVER version was completed in 1988. The revised system offers greatly enhanced flexibility and ease of operation. It is typically used within the human resource development, training, or personnel branches of government, business, and industry. DISCOVER for Organizations permits extensive customization at the user site to meet the specific needs of the licensee. The system is available for MS-DOS microcomputers.

DISCOVER for Retirement Planning provides support for people preparing for their retirement and is intended for use by individuals between ages 45 and 65. This version of DISCOVER contains activities to help people effectively deal with four important aspects of the retirement transition. The areas of focus are life-style (changes in roles, relationships, and use of time), financial planning, physical well-being, and living arrangements.

DISCOVER Content

A strong emphasis on interactive guidance components makes DISCOVER a leader among computer-based systems for career planning. Though there are significant variations in the content of the four primary versions, each contains a major focus on interactive exercises that help users gain self-knowledge.

All versions of DISCOVER include exercises that help users identify their interests and abilities. In addition, some versions include exercises through which users rate their values and inventory their experiences. DISCOVER scores and interprets the results of each inventory or assessment immediately on its completion and provides users with a list of suggested occupations based on their personal profiles. Also, DISCOVER allows entry of users' results from many popular interest inventories and ability assessments taken off-line. The system relates users' results to ACT's World-of-Work Map, which is a model for organizing occupations into clusters, regions, and families.

Files and activities in each version help users plan for educational and training experiences that will prepare them for their selected occupational goals. In addition to the common items of content, each version has unique features that make it appropriate for the intended users.

More information about DISCOVER, including license fees and detailed hardware specifications, can be obtained through any of ACT's regional offices or at the national headquarters: American College Testing Program, Educational Services Division, P.O. Box 168, Iowa City, IA 52243; telephone

(319) 337-1000. For a detailed discussion of evaluating com-
puter-assisted career guidance systems, see the special theme
issue of the *Journal of Career Development* (Winter 1990).

Summary and Conclusion

Since the 1970s, the NOICC/SOICC network has been a
major force in making career information available to an
ever-increasing number of users. Even though year-to-year
changes occur because of funding cuts and other developments, CIDSs are available to the residents of about forty-five
states. The twenty or so commercial producers of career information software extend this coverage to hundreds of other
locations where funding is available to lease their programs.
Those who work with career development programs of any
kind should be skilled at fully utilizing the wide variety of
systems available.

Four Key Resources on Career Information Delivery Systems

1. Association of Computer-Based Systems for Career Infor-
    mation. *1991 Directory of State-Based Career Information
    Delivery Systems.* Eugene, Oreg.: Association of Com-
    puter-Based Systems for Career Information Clearing-
    house, 1990. This is an annual update on what is going
    on in each of the state systems as well as a description of
    the products and services available from the ACSCI sup-
    porting members. A key source for ACSCI members is a
    quarterly newsletter as well. Be sure to get the latest
    edition.
2. National Occupational Information Coordinating Com-
    mittee. *Status of the NOICC/SOICC Network—1989.*
    Administrative report no. 14. Washington, D.C.: National
    Occupational Information Coordinating Committee,
    1990. This annual update by NOICC provides an excel-
    lent statistical and narrative overview of NOICC/SOICC
    activities, including coverage of innovative programs.
    Again, look for the latest edition.

3. *Journal of Career Development,* 1988, *14* (3) (entire issue). This is a theme issue on a decade of career information delivery systems: 1977–1987. It includes an outstanding historical perspective by former NOICC Executive Director Russell Flanders, as well as a look into the future of the NOICC by Julietta Lester and Harvey Ollis of the NOICC staff. For those who want a viewpoint other than statistical reports and narrative of the current scene, this is the place to look.

4. *Journal of Career Development,* 1990, *17* (2) (entire issue). This is another theme issue; it is edited by James P. Sampson and Robert C. Reardon. It is based, in part, on their ongoing research through the Center for the Study of Technology in Counseling and Career Development at Florida State University. It is a top resource in the entire evaluation area.

11

▟▟▟▟▟▟▟▟▟▟▟▟▟▟▟▟▟▟▟▟▟▟▟▟▟▟▟▟▟▟▟▟▟▟▟▟

Renewing and Evaluating
Career Information

▟▟▟▟▟▟▟▟▟▟▟▟▟▟▟▟▟▟▟▟▟▟▟▟▟▟▟▟▟▟▟▟▟▟▟▟

At this point, the amount and types of career information available for client and counselor use may seem overwhelming. And, in the state of being overwhelmed, counselors are probably asking several questions: "How do I keep myself and my clients up-to-date, given the amount and types of career information available?" "How do I evaluate career information?" "Are there standards I can use?" Chapter Eleven provides answers to these and similar questions by focusing on career information renewal and evaluation procedures. The standards for evaluating career information established by the National Career Development Association are featured.

Developing a Career Information Renewal Plan

When it comes to the task of renewing career information, some counselors think of it as simple and clerical. While there are clerical functions involved, we contend that renewal requires substantial professional involvement, expertise, and energy, because information renewal is a professional task. Career information renewal is a component of overall professional work and responsibility. Thus, we maintain that a career information renewal plan is necessary.

What follows in this section of Chapter Eleven are guidelines on establishing a renewal plan. Counselors should not expect supervisors and co-workers to assume responsibility. While background, education, work experience, and work setting may suggest some modification, these guidelines are a point of departure. A workable plan can be built around these main areas:

- Professional development
- Information development
- Community development

Of course other areas can be added later, but these are a starting point. In practices all three may tend to blend together at times. For example, working with a group of civic club members may lead to community development, but ultimately it may lead to information development, and, in some cases, to the establishment of a relationship with a business-person who may serve as a mentor for counselors or clients. So the separation is made more for clarity of ideas than to suggest that they will be this distinct in day-to-day activities. The main point is that action is needed on all three fronts.

Professional Development

Four main professional development tasks need to be emphasized.

Task 1: Counselors Should Join and Become Active in Professional Associations at the Local, State, and National Level. The objective here is to establish and maintain a high degree of professional involvement and responsibility. Though most professional organizations make it easy to join, counselors should not wait for an invitation. It is best to show initiative by getting involved before being asked. For those who have been student members of national/state/local organizations, it should be relatively easy to shift to the status of regular members as full-time professionals.

There are a number of professional associations that counselors may wish to consider joining. We list three: the American Association for Counseling and Development (AACD), the American Vocational Association (AVA), and the American Psychological Association (APA). Each association has numerous divisions. For our purposes we list all sixteen for AACD, one for AVA, and one for APA. Readers interested in the other divisions of AVA and APA can write directly to those organizations:

American Association for Counseling and Development
5999 Stevenson Avenue
Alexandria, VA 22304-3303

American College Personnel Association (ACPA)
Association for Counselor Education and Supervision (ACES)
National Career Development Association (NCDA)
Association for Humanistic Education and Development (AHEAD)
American School Counselor Association (ASCA)
American Rehabilitation Counseling Association (ARCA)
Association for Measurement and Evaluation in Counseling and Development (AMECD)
National Employment Counselors Association (NECA)
American Mental Health Counselors Association (AMHCA)
Military Educators and Counselors Association (MECA)
Association for Multicultural Counseling and Development (AMCD)
Association for Religious and Value Issues in Counseling (ARVIC)
Association for Adult Development and Aging (AADA)
Public Offender Counselor Association (POCA)
Association for Specialists in Group Work (ASGW)
International Association of Marriage and Family Counselors (IAMFC)
American College Counseling Association (ACCA)

American Vocational Association
Guidance Division
1410 King Street
Alexandria, VA 22314

American Psychological Association
Division of Counseling Psychology
1200 Seventeenth Street, N.W.
Washington, DC 20036

Task 2: It Is Important to Get on Various Mailing Lists, Both Free and Subscription. The pace of change is moving so fast that counselors must keep up or find that they are dropping behind. One way to keep up is to sign up for relevant newsletters and news releases published by local, state, and national associations and organizations such as the National Alliance of Business and the Department of Labor. Another alternative is to subscribe to newsletters such as those published by Chronicle Guidance Publications, Moravia, New York, or Garrett Park Press, Garrett Park, Maryland.

Task 3: Counselors Should Establish a Network of Trusted Professional Colleagues. One of the advantages of joining professional organizations is to meet colleagues. Counseling professionals should find out which ones have similar interests and work settings to theirs. It is a good idea to set up a regular time for discussions, maybe a meal together before or after meetings. It is useful to collect directories of professional associates so that they can be reached as needed. Most professionals work most effectively through consultation and communication. Counselors should get their network started early and continue to expand it.

Task 4: One of the Most Valuable Things Can Be to Establish a Mentoring Relationship with One or More Respected People. This is a more selective form of networking. It means building an ongoing relationship with a professional person(s) who can help a counselor grow. This should be someone he or she respects and wishes to emulate. It should be someone who can be contacted whenever the need arises. Otherwise, a counselor may want to keep up with a mentor on a regular basis through professional or personal meetings, correspondence, and phone calls. A mentor may be a professor, a supervisor, or a veteran counselor. It should be a person willing to share his or her time and talent with a more junior colleague.

Information Development

The idea is to develop good information mainly for the people counselors serve—students, clients, and others. A secondary benefit may be for counselors themselves to gain more understanding about career information in the process. The goal is ultimately to become a career information expert and to learn about the local community from a career perspective. But not all of these things can be accomplished at the same time. Counselors need to find out what type of career information their clients need the most. They should decide which tasks are most important and add some ideas of their own— but it is essential to get started.

Task 1: A Place to Begin Is by Contacting Local Employers. Before contacting local employers at random, counseling professionals should first conceptualize their community and surrounding area as a local labor market. A local labor market can be thought of as a dynamic geographical area in which workers can change jobs without changing their residence. A labor market consists of industries, occupations, and people (the labor force).

The next step is to contact local employers in the major types of industries in the local labor market. This may include

- A major health care facility
- A major retail distribution facility
- A major food and lodging facility
- A major manufacturing facility

- A major banking facility
- A local and/or state government facility

There are numerous ways to organize the information that is gathered. The data should be collected in a standardized way so that they can be compiled easily in a local job guide. A suggested format for collecting information from each employer contacted is provided in Exhibit 11.1.

Contacting local employers is an excellent way to get an overview of the local employment situation. Once they have done this, counselors should have an idea of area job opportunities. Then it is a good idea to involve as many other counselors as possible, so that more employers can be contacted.

Exhibit 11.1. Local Job Survey Form.

Name of Facility and Address: _____ _____

_____ _____

Name of Contact Person: _____

Position and Title: _____

Total Number of Employees: _____

_____

General Types of Employees: _____

_____

Entry Jobs for High School Graduates and Numbers: _____

_____

Entry Jobs for Community College Graduates and Numbers: _____

_____

Entry Jobs for Four-Year College Graduates and Numbers: _____

_____

_____

Exhibit 11.1. Local Job Survey Form, Cont'd.

Employment Needs Over Next Twelve Months: _____

_____

_____

Employment Needs Over Next Five to Ten Years: _____

_____

_____

Jobs for Disabled Workers: _____

_____

_____

General Working Conditions: _____

_____

_____

_____

In-Service Training Programs: _____

_____

_____

_____

Opportunities for Advancement: _____

_____

_____

_____

Salary Ranges for Entry Workers: _____

_____

_____

Fringe Benefits: _____

_____

_____

Additional Comments: _____

_____

_____

_____

_____

Another potential source of assistance is a university business-industry practicum that might make it possible to earn graduate credit under appropriate supervision. If the contacts are comprehensive enough, the results may be worth putting together as a local guide to employers. Funding may be available through a local service or civic club. Organizations like this should be approached for some community support. It is important to remember that this series of contacts is only a supplement to existing local labor market information. Counselors should try to build on that base in an effort to personalize their contacts with local employers. This is an informal contact, and so it should not turn into a scientific survey. The idea is to build goodwill and gather information through area employer contacts.

Task 2: An Important Responsibility Is to Identify Local Leisure Activities. Some clients may explore work possibilities through leisure. Counselors who are working with this type of client need to know what local leisure opportunities are available so that their clients can explore both work and leisure options in their career development. Often a skill developed in a leisure activity can lead to part- or full-time employment. Consider the case of the factory worker who learned upholstery in her leisure time from the local recreation department and opened up a shop in her basement when her employer shut down the factory in which she was working, or a high school student who learns bicycle repair in a local adult education night class and opens up a small repair business following graduation. Clients need to know more about the work-leisure connection. Counselors can help by having a "Local Leisure File" that is timely and comprehensive. Many localities conduct leisure fairs, where they bring in area craftspeople and others to model ways people are putting their leisure to work.

Task 3: It May Sometimes Be Helpful to Develop Charts of Local Occupations. An outgrowth of the local job survey may be to develop one or more charts featuring local employers or local occupations. This also can be done with pictures and brief job descriptions to be posted in prominent local areas such as shopping centers. One possibility would be to feature young workers in entry positions and to name the series using the name of the community—for example, "Blacksburg at Work" or "Columbia at Work." This provides a visual way of highlighting local jobs and employers.

Task 4: Counselors Need to Gather Local Wage and Salary Information. Many clients simply do not know what workers make on the job. Counselors can help them by collecting and making information available on wages and salaries. A first step would be to try to obtain this information from state or local sources. If this is not possible, it might have to be obtained from a local job survey. Another way may be to turn to a business class to collect the data as a project. Local civic or service clubs may also be willing to help.

Task 5: It Can Be Very Useful to Establish Profiles of Recent Graduates or Vocational Biographies. This is an excellent way to bring out the "psychosocial" aspects of work. Counselors can make career information come alive through people activities. What is the secretary like? What is the data entry operator like? What is the truck driver like? Clients can be told the story through words, pictures, videotapes, or audiotapes of descriptions of what people are like and what they do on the job.

Task 6: Another Possibility Is to Publish a Newsletter Describing New or Expanded Jobs in a Particular Area. Regular communication can help colleagues and constituents learn about what counselors are doing and how they can use any information that has been collected. Local job survey data can provide copy for the newsletters. The content should be kept light and attractive to readers and suitable for photocopying to put on bulletin boards.

Task 7: Some Counselors May Want to Conduct an Apprenticeship Survey. This can be a spin-off of the local job survey and can lead to a more in-depth look at area apprenticeship opportunities. If a local apprenticeship information center or council exists, it may have the information already or may have people who can help gather data. Counselors can survey the major apprenticeships available locally by using a modification of the local job survey form. If apprenticeships are not available in a particular area, then local on-the-job training opportunities can be surveyed. Charts and pictures are an attractive way to communicate findings.

Task 8: It Is Helpful to Conduct a Survey of Part-Time and Moonlighting Jobs in the Local Area. For a variety of reasons, some people prefer to work part time. Sometimes they want to work full time but cannot locate such employment. Others have full-time jobs but want additional income or experience. In short, there are many people looking for part-time jobs. Good local surveys of this type are hard to find. This would be an excellent project for a retired citizens group to take on as a community contribution.

Task 9: An Interesting Project Would Be to Develop Charts on Jobs in a Particular Area in the Year 2000. This could be an outcome of a local conference on "Work in the Year 2000," which is suggested under the community development section of this chapter. It would give some concreteness to the conference. It also would provide a way of visually forecasting how the job outlook in a particular geographical region might be similar to or different from what it is now. Graphs and pictures are helpful in getting points across.

Task 10: Many Counselors Will Find It Desirable to Survey Small Businesses in Their Area—Those with Less Than Twenty-Five to Fifty Employees. Most surveys are of major or larger employers—those with fifty to a hundred employees or more. In today's economy, many small businesses are growing faster than large ones. Counselors should find out what is happening in their area with respect to jobs in these fast-growing businesses. One possible approach is to start out with a group of small businesses, such as automobile dealers, drug stores, plumbing shops, and electrical repairers. Local jobs survey forms can be used to get started.

Community Development

It is vital to get out of the office and get to know people and organizations in the community. Most counselors will have some ideas about this on their own, but here are some possible tasks to consider.

Task 1: It Is a Good Idea to Build a File of Contacts in Local Civic and Service Groups such as the AAUW, BPWC, YMCA, YWCA, Women's Network, Lions, Kiwanis, Civitan, Optimist, Rotary, and Jaycees. There may be a host of other organizations in a particular locality that quickly come to mind, but the above list is a starting point. An organization like Rotary International has well over one million members and has as one of its main objectives—vocational service. In addition to helping furnish contact people for arranging business-industry tours, Rotary members often volunteer to speak to those interested in their occupation. They may be willing to assist in setting up a speaker's bureau for the use of counselors.

Task 2: Counseling Professionals Must Establish Plans for Various Periods of Career Emphasis Throughout the Year. It is imperative that counselors keep the public informed about their work. It is also important for counselors to let clients know what they are doing and to give clients a feeling that these accomplishments are relevant to them. One way to do this is through various periods of career emphasis. Two examples of times to do this include (1) National Career Development Week—usually in early November—which is sponsored by the NCDA (a division of AACD), and (2) National Vocational Education Week—usually in February—which is sponsored by the AVA.

Task 3: Something That May Be Very Productive Is to Organize a Local Conference on "Work in the Year 2000." Many people are concerned about all aspects of the future. In many ways we live in a future-oriented society. One way to capture much of that interest is to organize a local conference on "Work in the Year 2000." Some counselors also may want to join the World Future Society or one of its local chapters. Some of the local civic, service, and government groups can be encouraged to become involved also. If the conference goes well, the proceedings could be published.

Task 4: Counselors Should Make Contact with Their State Occupational Information Coordinating Committee, State Employment Security Agency, and State Rehabilitative Services Agency. It is important to get in touch with at least these three state agencies. They probably publish newsletters and send out news releases that counselors should sign up to receive. Further, these agencies may have state/local conferences and meetings that would be informative to attend. All three of these agencies generate numerous kinds of useful career information. These contacts should extend to a variety of special-needs groups with whom counselors work.

Task 5: It Is a Good Idea for Counselors to Establish an Advisory Committee for Their Work Setting. One of the most effective ways of building local support for a program is to invite community people to serve on an advisory committee. Counselors can work with local groups such as the Jaycees, the chamber of commerce, and the local business-industry council to determine who some good candidates could be. The advisory group should be selected from a broad range of citizens who have an interest in counseling work and will strive to see that it gets better. Regular meetings should be planned, such as on a quarterly, bimonthly, or monthly basis. Some responsible tasks should be lined up for the council.

Evaluating Career Information

As career information is being gathered, the task of evaluation begins. What steps are involved in evaluating career information? What criteria should be applied in making judgments about career information? Are there specific criteria for evaluating career information for minority clients? What standards are available to assist counselors in making judgments about career information?

This section of Chapter Eleven presents steps in the evaluation process that counselors may wish to consider as well as criteria that they may wish to apply in making judgments about career information. Specific attention is given to making judgments about career information for minority clients. This section also briefly outlines the current NCDA guidelines and describes the availability of rated information through the *Career Development Quarterly*. The substantial work of the NCDA since the 1920s is highlighted.

Before we discuss some steps to follow in evaluating career information, however, criteria that guide the evaluation process need to be considered. Herr and Cramer (1988) suggested criteria such as the source of the information, currency, validity, and applicability. Isaacson (1986, p. 245) recommended that career information "should be measured against these criteria: accuracy, currency, usability, reader appeal, and comprehensiveness." We use a combination of these criteria in order to ensure coverage according to the NCDA guidelines. We focus on career information structure and organization, content, and applicability.

In addition to following these steps and using the suggested criteria, counselors should give special attention to the career information needs of minorities. Coelho and Wilkins (1980) stressed the need for counselors to take an active role in the evaluation of career information used with particular racial/ethnic groups. To do this, counselors need to evaluate information carefully themselves and sometimes in the presence of clients: "Although taking clients through the process will enable them to appraise similar literature for themselves, either option will eliminate many of the chance factors that often occur in career formation. Chance factors are forces outside the client's control that may lead to inappropriate occupational choices (i.e., finding and obtaining a job from a newspaper ad). These forces are far more prevalent among minority groups than among others. Vocational decision-making processes should, therefore, be the product of careful and critical evaluation of all choices and options available to minorities" (Coelho and Wilkins, 1980, p. 4).

Step 1: Counselors Should Begin by Reviewing Career Information Structure and Organization. For example, *currentness of information* needs to be considered. Career information does not become better with age. While this point has been stated several times in this book before, it is most critical now. Thus, in reviewing career information, it is a good idea to check the date first. The copyright date indicates when the information was originally published. If the copyright section says that the publication has been reprinted, that is exactly what it means. Nothing has been changed since the original copyright date. On the other hand, if it says that it has been revised, then at least some of the information has been changed since the original copyright date. If the information is not dated, counselors can date it with the date they receive it. This will provide a reference point when they go through the information later to throw out old material.

Accuracy of information is directly related to the sources used to generate the information. Are the authorship and the sources cited recognized as being professionally sound? How careful and comprehensive was the research that provided the facts and data? Career information should be free of promotional material.

Organization of information is another key point. The NCDA guidelines strongly recommend that career information publishers pay attention to graphics and format. Clear, readable formats and good graphics should be incorporated into all career information. As practitioners, counselors do not have much control over how career information publishers meet this criterion, but they can urge them to follow NCDA guidelines when they publish material.

Counselors should pay attention to the *language* used in the information sources. They should know their clientele and their reading levels so as to be able to select career information that they can use. It is important to be alert for biased and stereotyped language, glittering generalities, and inappropriate conclusions. Photographs and other illustrations should also be checked to make sure that they are free of bias and stereotyping.

Step 2: Counselors Must Also Review Career Information Content. What makes career information comprehensive? Coverage! NCDA recommended that adequate coverage include the following topics:

1. Duties and Nature of Work
2. Work Setting and Conditions
3. Preparation Required
4. Special Requirements or Considerations
5. Methods of Entry
6. Earnings and Other Benefits
7. Usual Advancement Possibilities
8. Employment Outlook
9. Opportunities for Experience and Exploration
10. Related Occupations
11. Sources of Additional Information

See the National Career Development Association "Guidelines" in the reference section at the back of the book, for a more detailed discussion of these topics.

Step 3: It Is Essential to Review Equal Opportunity Provisions. Coelho and Wilkins (1980, p. 6) stressed the need to review career information for statements about equal opportunity:

Occupational information should include precise statements of employer's commitment to the recruitment and hiring of minority persons (that is, racial groups, women, handicapped). Also, reference to special groups (such as the emotionally or intellectually handicapped) should be covered. If minority or special groups are mentioned, data should be presented as to the distribution of the group members within the field or occupation. The counselor should pay special attention to entry levels for minority and other special group members. If there is a specific minority recruitment person available, information should be provided as to how this person may be contacted for further information.

Step 4: Career Information Usability Needs to Be Reviewed. Evaluating usability of career information begins with a clear understanding of the needs of clients. Then career information is gathered based on those needs. Because of the diversity found in most clientele groups, combinations of printed career information, media, and software will be required.

Step 5: Counseling Professionals Should Clean House Periodically. Following the adage that old career information is bad career information, it is necessary to clean house periodically. Every collection of career information should be reviewed thoroughly once a year. If a decision is made to keep material older than five years, Hoppock (1963, p. 49) suggests placing the following label on it: "This document is more than five years old. Some of the information in it may now be out of date. Ask your counselor where to get more recent information."

A Note About Evaluating Educational Information

In 1989, the National Association of College Admission Counselors (NACAC) published a policy statement concerning college guides. While it was written for student use, the points made are relevant for counselors as well. Also, though the statement focuses on college guides, the points are relevant for guides for other types of education and training. As a result, we reprint the guideline questions concerning ratings of colleges here:

1. What institutions are being included in or excluded from the publication? If the book does not feature a comprehensive listing, what types of institutions are excluded?
2. What is the primary focus, point of view, or objective of the comparison or rating? Is the focus or objective clearly stated?
3. What special expertise qualifies the author or publisher for the guide? If the authors recommend one institution or another, are they qualified to make such recommendations?
4. When was the guide published? Does the author update the information regularly or are you reading old news? Numbers such as tuition costs and enrollment statistics are the publisher's worst enemy because they change every year. Make sure that you have the current edition (or at least not more than one year old) of the guide.
5. Does the publication use the same standards to measure all the institutions, or do some receive special treatment?
6. Is the publication a serious attempt to inform you and help in the college admission process—or was it written primarily to entertain or present offbeat or humorous aspects of various institutions? [National Association of College Admission Counselors, 1989, p. 22.]

The Work of Professional Organizations in Evaluating Career Information

As counseling and guidance activities and programs evolved from their beginnings in the early 1900s throughout the ensuing decades, the improvement of career information became a professional mission. Lane (1927) noted that between 1920 and 1926, definite progress in occupation research was taking place. She reported on the activities of seventeen agencies and cities engaged in collecting and organizing information. During the same period, Allen (1925) became concerned about the increasing amounts of occupational information and the difficulty counselors were having keeping up. He recommended the establishment of a clearinghouse for information.

One outgrowth of this concern was the organization of the Occupational Research Section of the National Vocational Guidance Association (NVGA) at its annual meeting in Chicago in 1924. Once organized, the section became active immediately. This is reflected in the fact that a complete issue of *Vocational Guidance Magazine,* the journal of NVGA, was devoted to the work of the section in 1926 (Corre, 1926).

Of particular interest to us is the fact that the contributors to this special issue began to define standards for preparing and evaluating career information. For example, an article by Lane (1927) was titled "The Content, Volume, and Uses of Occupational Studies." It later became known as the "Basic Outline." In 1931 it was reprinted under a new title, "Outlines Used in Preparing Occupational Studies" (Lane, 1931).

In February 1933, an organization that was to greatly influence the evaluation of career information opened its doors. The National Occupational Conference (NOC) was supported by a Carnegie Corporation grant. Franklin Keller was the first director, while Robert Hoppock served as his assistant. Some of NOC's accomplishments included the preparation of a comprehensive bibliography covering some 8,000 titles in the occupational literature of 1920 to 1935 and support for the publication of NVGA's official journal, *Occupations* (Keller, 1937).

By 1939 the Occupational Research Section of NVGA had established criteria for judging occupational monographs. These criteria were published as "Distinguishing Marks of a Good Occupational Monograph" (National Vocational Guidance Association, 1939). The following year, 1940, a revised form of the "Basic Outline" was published under the title "Content of a Good Occupational Monograph—The Basic Outline" (National Vocational Guidance Association, 1940). In the late 1940s, at a meeting celebrating the twenty-fifth anniversary of the Section of Occupational Research of NVGA, it was proposed that the occupational information standards published in 1939 and 1940 be revised. Out of this and subsequent meetings came a single document titled "Standards for Use in Preparing and Evaluating Occupational Literature" (National Vocational Guidance Association, 1950).

Encouraging developments in career information evaluation also took place later in the 1950s. In 1954, NVGA established the Guidance Information Review Service. This service was charged with the task of identifying occupational literature that met the standards acceptable to the profession and of encouraging the preparation of such information for use in counseling. The August 1956 issue of the *Vocational Guidance Quarterly* printed the first evaluations of the Guidance Information Review Service (Peterson, 1956).

The work of this committee continues today. The committee is now called the Career Information Review Service. Once a year, the results of the work of the Career Information Review Service are published in the *Career Development Quarterly*. The format and ratings used are as follows:

Type of Publication

   I. Vocational
       A.   Occupations
       B.   Trends and Outlook
       C.   Job Training
       D.   Employment
  II. Educational
       A.   Status and Trends
       B.   Schools, Colleges, and Universities
       C.   Scholarships, Fellowships, and Loans
 III. Personal
       A.   Planning (resume, job search, etc.)
       B.   Adjustment

Ratings

1. Highly recommended (maximum adherence to NCDA Guidelines)
2. Recommended (general adherence to NCDA Guidelines)
3. Useful (limited in scope, does not adhere to NCDA Guidelines but contains authentic, objective, timely, and helpful information) (Career Information Review Service Committee, 1991, p. 372).

The guidelines were revised again in 1964 with the publication of "Guidelines for Preparing and Evaluating Occupational Materials" (National Vocational Guidance Association, 1964). Also, in 1966, NVGA established standards for evaluating film (National Vocational Guidance Association, 1966). Then in 1971 (National Vocational Guidance Association, 1971) and again in 1980 (National Vocational Guidance Association, 1980), the guidelines were revised. In addition, the film version was retitled to include all types of media except software. Finally, guidelines for career information software were developed.

Then in 1991, the literature guidelines were revised and titled "Guidelines for the Preparation and Evaluation of Career and Occupational Information Literature." In the same year the software guidelines were revised and titled "Career Software Review Guidelines." The full texts of these 1991 revisions appear in the reference section at the back of the book. Work on revising the film guidelines continues, with publication of the revision scheduled for 1992.

A Final Word

The renewal of career information is not separate from our work with clients. It is part of it. It is part of it because, through the gathering of career information in its many forms, we learn about the worlds of work, education, leisure,

and the family. We develop the foundation knowledge necessary for our use and for use directly with clients. At the same
time, we develop important contacts with people in business,
industry, and labor as well as with many community agencies
to share with clients to aid them in their networking.

Just as the renewal of career information is not separate
from our work with clients, neither is career information evaluation. Clients expect timely, accurate, and up-to-date information they can count on. It is our obligation as professionals
to make sure that these clients' expectations become realities.
Thus, we have the professional responsibility to know how to
evaluate career information using the guidelines that have
been developed by the NCDA.

PART 4

Using Career Resources and Information

12

Focusing on Populations
with Special Needs

What do we mean by special populations and why do they deserve separate attention? Special populations as defined in this book comprise those individuals in our society whose career development needs are out of the mainstream (the standard for which has traditionally been set by white males) of opportunity in American life. Operationally, for us, this means mostly women, because women represent a majority of the population. Therefore, gender issues are treated first in this chapter. Second, this means those who are nonwhite, including African Americans, Hispanics, Asian and Pacific Islanders, and Native Americans. Third, this means individuals with any disabling condition. Obviously others could be treated in a chapter on special populations—for example, veterans, displaced workers, and older workers—but we have decided to focus on these three major groups. Members of these groups (or others not included) merit extra career development attention and support. People who are members of two or three groups, such as African American women who are disabled, call for unusual efforts.

Why the special attention is a legitimate question readers might ask. Our answer is based mostly on our social consciousness, but it is supported by some stark statistics concerning the lack of equitable representation across educational and occupational lines. A recent survey of African Americans in the accounting profession showed that 2,500 out of 400,000 accountants were African American, for just 0.6 percent of the total. Other estimates indicate that African Americans make up 0.2 percent of commercial pilots and navigators, 2 percent of attorneys, and 3.3 percent of the medical profession. Studies show that African Americans, Hispanics, and other people of color are at a distinct disadvantage with respect to employment opportunities (for example, see Arbona, 1989). These studies indicate that they are overrepresented in low-level jobs and underrepresented in all other types of work. It is important for counselors to serve as change agents in helping members of minority groups expand their educational and occupational knowledge and be broadly exposed to a wide variety of career options. At the summer 1990 meeting of the National Governors' Association, there was a call for extra efforts to attract more females and minorities into engineering fields—where they are also significantly underrepresented. The governors requested special programs to ensure that female and minority students are prepared for college-level mathematics and science and that they receive equitable financial aid at public colleges and universities. Finally, the passage of the Americans with Disabilities Act of 1990 (Public Law 101-336) rested on the assumption that millions of Americans have one or more physical or mental disabilities and deserve better civil rights than they have been getting. The bill was signed into law in 1990.

The professional literature has paid increasing attention to populations with special needs. This has been true for example of the last two National Career Development Association (NCDA) decennial volumes (Herr, 1974; Gysbers, 1984). Books on career development such as Brown and Brooks (1984, 1990) attest to the same interest. And an NCDA Luncheon Address by Kenneth B. Hoyt in Chicago in March 1988, which was subsequently published in the *Career Development Quarterly* (Hoyt, 1989), brought many of the career development special population issues squarely before professional career counselors again—in a twenty-year retrospective. In essence, this article said that there had been some good policy statements and some solid professional attention, but that change had been very slow in coming in the educational and occupational equity areas. Hoyt indicated that NCDA (and all career counselors) should know enough to be much more active in bringing equality of opportunity for career development *to everyone*. We agree completely, as did Linda Mezydlo Subich (1989) and Courtland Lee (1989), who wrote reactions to Hoyt's article.

A case can obviously be made for trying to integrate this special attention into the ongoing material in an article or book, but after carefully weighing the pros and cons, we feel that the need for educational and occupational equity is so compelling that only a separate chapter can properly call attention to the urgency of the situation. Thus this chapter focuses on special career issues related to gender, race/ethnicity, and disabling conditions. A final section touches on special things that can be done for special populations.

Special Issues Related to Gender and Career Development

Though women make up over half the U.S. population, they are still underrepresented in almost all areas of education and in almost all occupations. Women are expected to make up about half of the American workforce by the year 2000; thus the need to provide stronger career development support could not be more evident. This point has been brought home increasingly in the professional and popular press. While a number of classic books and articles were published in the 1960s and 1970s, a veritable explosion in the professional literature occurred in the 1980s. Progress toward gender equity seems to have been made in recent years, but as Hoyt (1989) pointed out, a great deal still needs to be done. A premium should be put on gender equity programs and practices that really get results. There are plenty of sources of material dealing with women's career development over the past thirty years. Some of the most widely cited authors and their works are reported here as key sources to form the basis for deeper study. Two lists present them in alphabetical order, first a list of the five most important sources and then a list of other important sources.

1. Linda Brooks coedited a special issue of the *Journal of Career Development* (1988) with M. Haring-Hidore and wrote a chapter titled "Counseling Special Groups" in Brown, Brooks, and Associates' *Career Choice and Development* (1984).

2. Nancy E. Betz and Louise F. Fitzgerald coauthored *The Career Psychology of Women* (1987), a rigorous review of the literature related to women's career development— probably the most comprehensive work of the books published in the 1980s. Earlier, Fitzgerald coauthored with John Crites two articles on career counseling for women (1979, 1980), which are often cited in the literature.

3. Barbara A. Gutek has edited and written several important works. *Enhancing Women's Career Development* (1979) is a collection of nine papers by an all-star group that led the way with some new directions for the 1980s. A more recent coedited book, *Women's Career Development* (Gutek and Larwood, 1987) takes more of an organizational psychology point of view with a narrow concept of what a career is but still contributes to the thinking in this area. Her book *Women and Work* (Nieva and Gutek, 1981) also is worthy of note.

4. L. Sunny Hansen was coeditor of a key 1970s book, *Career Development and Counseling of Women* (Hansen and Rapoza, eds., 1978) and her chapters in it are a landmark contribution. Hansen also has a significant chapter titled "The Interrelationship of Gender and Career" in the NVGA 70th anniversary volume *Designing Careers* (1984). In addition, she was the director of a major gender equity project called *Born Free*.

5. Lenore W. Harmon's article "Longitudinal Changes in Women's Career Aspirations: Development or Historical?" is one of the better studies examining changes in

women over time (Harmon, 1989b). She has a major chapter in the Hansen and Rapoza book *Career Development and Counseling of Women* (Harmon, 1978), as well as a long list of articles in major professional journals.

Several other works often cited in the literature are

- Astin, H. S. (1984) takes a major look at the meaning of work in women's lives from a sociopsychological approach. There are a number of interesting reactions to her article in the special issue of *The Counseling Psychologist* (volume 12:4, 1984) on women.
- Farmer, H. S. (1984) has a strong response to Astin's article in the special issue of *The Counseling Psychologist*, noted above as well as in numerous other sources.
- Matthews, E. wrote a chapter on women's career development in the NVGA 60th anniversary volume *Vocational Guidance and Human Development* (1974). She also wrote an entire section of four landmark chapters in *Counseling Girls and Women over the Life Span* (1972).
- Osipow, S. H. edited the often cited *Emerging Women: Career Analysis and Outlook* (1975).
- Zytowski, D. G. is known for his article "Toward a Theory of Career Development of Women" in the *Personnel and Guidance Journal* (1969).

In addition, there are frequent special issues and significant articles in journals such as *The Career Development Quarterly, The Journal of Career Development, The Journal of Employment Counseling, The Counseling Psychologist,* and *The Journal of Vocational Behavior.* There are also popular magazines such as *MS, Working Woman,* and *Women's Enterprise.* The National Vocational Guidance Association (NVGA), now the National Career Development Association (NCDA), has three very helpful monographs from the early 1970s and 1980s that should be studied if at all possible: (1) *Counseling Girls and Women over the Life Span* (Whitfield and Gustav, eds., 1972), (2) *Facilitating Career Development for Girls and*

Women (House and Katzell, eds., 1975), and (3) *Sex-Fair Career Counseling* (Hawley, 1980). The insights gleaned from these three gems are as relevant in the 1990s as they were ten to twenty years ago.

Proposed Solutions

Many of the numerous sources cited above have specific reports of action programs that provide plenty of ideas for creative efforts on behalf of optimal career development for girls and women over the life span. Some further selected sources are:

The importance of the parental family roles as a positive influence for girls in the six to twenty-four year age range and later for all adult years has been brought out by Lavine (1982), Lunnenberg (1982), and Auster and Auster (1981), among a number of writers. Their findings call for closer cooperation between counselors and parents or family in their approach to women's career development.

The significance of strong self-concept and self-esteem has been stressed by a number of writers such as Bartlett and Oldham (1978) and Hackett, Esposito, and O'Halloran (1989). These writers stress the need for ample opportunity to test one's "performance self-esteem" and to continue learning more about the self in relation to educational and occupational options. Among other writers, Cini and Baker (1987) call for more comprehensive and developmental approaches to furthering women's career development and for less emphasis on short-term interventions.

Career *modeling* and *mentoring* for women at all stages in the life span have been stressed by writers such as Nester (1983), Ableton (1984), Fort and Cordisco (1981), Bolton (1980), and many others. It has been pointed out that there is a special need to provide models and mentors for African American women in a wide range of occupational and educational settings.

Though most of the literature cited has to do with career development of girls and college-age women, there is a growing interest in better understanding the career development needs of adult women. Kahn (1983) stresses the importance of providing a special place for women seeking assistance with career development needs—such as a specialized women's career resource center.

Sullivan (1983) has pointed out the special effectiveness of group activities for adult women. Christian and Wilson (1985) have made a special appeal for attention and assistance to reentry women who may have left the workforce under one set of conditions but reentered it under another set of circumstances. Finally, Watts (1989) has found that the career anchors (needs) of adult women are often quite different from those of men, especially among women in administrative support occupations, which she studied. Finally, in 1973 at an NVGA-sponsored conference called "Facilitating Career Development for Girls and Women," McDaniels (1975) argued for a more adequate balancing of work and leisure in the career development of girls and women.

Special Issues Related to the Career Development of Racial/Ethnic Groups

American society is increasingly becoming a multicultural society. The highest density of ethnic diversity in the United States roughly starts in the New York City area, goes down the East Coast (including Florida), and spreads across the southern tier of states to California on the West Coast. The most diverse states are New York (mainly New York City), Florida, Texas, New Mexico, Arizona, and California. America's ethnic diversity is growing—not static or slowing down. The 1980 Census data showed African Americans at 11.7 percent of the population and Hispanics at 6.4 percent. The estimates for 1990 are 12.4 percent African American and 7.9 percent Hispanic. Demographers forecast that sometime around the year 2000 there will be more Hispanics than African Americans and roughly twenty-five to thirty percent of the total population of the United States will be made up of minorities. Obviously, these changes in the ethnic make-up of the nation over the next ten to twenty years will have an impact on the educational and occupational landscape. Certainly there will be more, not less, pressure to have career equality for all Americans—especially the growing ethnic minority. Thus the current emphasis on multicultural counseling will greatly intensify. In turn, this will have an increasing impact on the preservice and in-service preparation of counselors by making their training more responsive to the needs of various racial and ethnic groups. This was the focus of a special section of *Counselor Education and Supervision* (Bradley, 1987), which explored how to improve multicultural counseling through counselor education programs.

As these issues have received more attention, some differences of opinion have emerged. For some years now, for example, there have been calls for separate theories of ethnic career development, such as those articulated by Griffin (1980). However, most writers have felt that what is required instead is better understanding of the needs, values, and expectations of members of various racial/ethnic groups. White (1979) and Philip and Bradley (1980) made this appeal with respect to African Americans; Avasthi (1990), Kazalunas (1979), and Ayala-Vazquez (1979) did the same with regard to Hispanics. (The entire April 1979 special issue of the *Journal of Non-White Concerns in Guidance* was also devoted to Hispanics.) Leong (1985), Hartman and Askounis (1989), Sue (1975), and Leong (1991) called for a similar understanding of the career needs of Asian Americans, and Herring (1990) and Ayers (1977) did so with respect to Native Americans. In short, while the literature in this area is not voluminous—in contrast for example to the literature on women's career development—there is an ample core of strong materials available for counselor use. Some of the better general sources are the following: *Counseling American Minorities: A Cross Cultural Perspective* (Atkinson, Morten, and Sue, 1990) and *Career Behaviors of Special Groups: Theory, Research, and Practice* (Picou and Campbell, 1975); professional journals such as *Journal of Multicultural Counseling* (formerly *The Journal of Non-White Concerns*—see especially the January 1980 issue devoted to African American career development), *Journal of Negro Education, Social Issues, Career Development Quarterly, Journal of Career Development,* and association newsletters such as the AACD *Guidepost;* also popular periodicals such as *Black Enterprise, Black Collegian* (outstanding), *Jet, Ebony, American Demographics,* and *Black Issues in Higher Education.*

Among other things, the literature stresses the importance of role models. June and Fooks (1980) found that role models on the job and parents (especially mothers) had the greatest influence on African American youth's occupational choices. They called for extended use of African American occupational models to help serve as positive influences on the next generation. Newlon, Nye, and Hill (1985) determined in working with minority youth in a career awareness summer workshop at the University of Arizona that there was a high level of satisfaction with the special efforts and strong endorsement to continue. Of course, minority youth who have taken part in Talent Search, Upward Bound, and summer transitions programs have had similar positive program outcomes. In a large sample of African American and white youth enrolled in vocational education classes in Maryland, Richmond, Johnson, Downs, and Ellinghaus (1983) found that the African American students expressed a strong desire for more and better counseling regarding their educational and occupational choices.

Washington Post columnist William Raspberry (1990) called for a stronger place for African American adult role models in the lives of young African American males, who he felt need special encouragement. Leonard (1985) studied the career development needs of African American males and found that they wanted most to be understood for who they were and wanted more proactive counseling. McDavis and Parker (1981) called for five specific career development proactive strategies to assist ethnic minorities: (1) enhancement of the self-concept, (2) better information distribution, (3) better and more helpful assessment, (4) more direct help in decision making, and (5) development of culturally relevant career guidance materials. Smith (1980) recommended much earlier emphasis at the elementary school and middle school level on successful achievement in mathematics and science as a prerequisite for postsecondary school study in engineering and related occupations. Griffin (1980) called for more proactive school counseling and more continuing support for African Americans in their adult years. He also emphasized the need for a stronger proactive role on the part of counselors who are assisting African American men and argued in favor of many more outreach activities in the school, the home, and the community.

Finally, Lee (1989, p. 220) urged that all professional counselors be "career development *advocates,* who possess the awareness, knowledge, and skills to transcend boundaries of ethnicity or sex in his or her career development intervention." In a very strong blueprint for counselors to intervene and serve as change agents on behalf of special populations, Gordon (1974) called on counselors not to see all people as fully developed—but see them for what they *might* be. He challenged counselors to be futurists in seeing the career potential of persons from special populations. He saw counselors as growing and cultivating talent and potential rather than solely assessing and interpreting—in a sense, as being farmers, not miners. In response to Hoyt's (1989) call for more positive involvement in the career development of both women and minorities, Lee said that counselors must first build a knowledge base of career theory relevant to the needs and expectations of these groups. He also recommended that counselors sift through the various models and methods being used and establish a repertoire of things that work in promoting the career development of women and people of color. Above all else, he emphasized that counselors must be career development advocates for populations with special needs.

Some programs targeting minority youth have been very successful. Leatherman (1990) summarized a General Accounting Office (GAO) study that reported that nearly 43,000 high school students were taking part in over 100 private, nongovernmental programs to motivate ethnic minorities to stay in school and graduate. The whole effort had its most recent start when New York businessman Eugene Lang established his "I Have a Dream Foundation" in 1981 for a group of sixth graders in his old East Harlem elementary school. The best programs were those that used adults as mentors and offered tutoring to students as early as the fifth grade.

Collison (1990) reported on one such program in California called Young Black Scholars. The effort was started in 1985 and has worked with over 1,800 students. The program selected promising eighth graders and provided tutoring, college counseling, and close personal attention by African American adults not connected with school. Mentoring and modeling assistance was a key ingredient in the program. In essence it focused on African Americans helping African Americans, in terms of both time and money to support the five-year investment. Successful African Americans felt that it was an opportunity to give something back to the community in the form of aid to the next generation of promising youth.

Across the country in North Carolina, Tifft (1990) described a similar program called Love of Learning, a minority enrichment effort located at Davidson College. This is a student and parent program designed to motivate and enrich the lives of some thirty new students each year. It does so by creating an extended family that provides support during the critical precollege years, by teaching students good study habits, and by bolstering individual self-confidence. The keys to this endeavor are the parents' promise to participate in quarterly discussions on a wide range of topics with their children as well as the dedication of the program's staff members.

Special Issues Related to
the Career Development of the Disabled

On July 7, 1990, President Bush signed the Americans with Disabilities Act of 1990 (Public Law 101-336) into law. An estimated 2,000 people were present at the signing on the White House lawn—one of the largest groups ever to be present at the signing of an official bill. This symbolized the importance attached to the passage of this bipartisan landmark legislation. The general purpose of the act is to provide a clear and comprehensive national mandate for the elimination of discrimination against individuals with disabilities, which are defined as physical or mental impairment that substantially limits one or more of the major life activities. For purposes of opening up opportunities for career development, the major emphasis on nondiscrimination in employment is very significant. The new legislation calls for employers to make "reasonable accommodations" of existing facilities to permit hiring of qualified disabled job applicants. In sum, this means greatly expanded career horizons for individuals with disabilities.

The need to work more affirmatively with this special population is clear both for school-age youth and for adults. The President's Commission on Employment of People with Disabilities estimates that 43 million Americans have disabilities such as epilepsy, muscular disorders, blindness, deafness, accident-caused injuries, and the like. Of this number, the Department of Labor estimates that 13 million are of working age. But only 34 percent of these people are working full or part time, which leaves 66 percent or 8.6 million unemployed. The figures are worse for women—only 29 percent employed, as against 42 percent of the men employed. The picture for young graduates of special education programs also has not been bright. It is estimated that only 21 percent of young people will be fully employed, while 40 percent will be underemployed and will barely eke out a living. All this should now change with the passage of the Americans with Disabilities Act of 1990. A solid effort on the part of all counselors to assist disabled individuals with their optimum career development throughout the life span is called for.

Sources

Fortunately, there are some good sources available to inform counselors about disabling conditions and how to aid in the career development process. Here are some key suggestions. It should be clear that rehabilitation counselors with state or federal agencies such as the Veterans Administration are the ones who would provide specialized help for adults, but school and college counselors need to be well enough informed to work with disabled individuals *before* they are old enough to receive state rehabilitation services. Two helpful books in this regard are Schero-Geist's *Vocational Counseling for Special Populations,* 1990 (a new book that focuses on handicapped people) and Picou and Campbell's *Career Behavior in Special Groups: Theory, Research, and Practice* (mentioned in the previous section on minorities, but useful here as well). Several useful journals are: *Career Development for Exceptional Individuals,* published by the Division of Career Development of the Council for Exceptional Children (CEC)—the best source for ongoing career development activities with special education students, *Exceptional Children,* published by CEC, *Rehabilitation Counseling Bulletin,* published by the American Rehabilitation Counseling Association (ARCA), a division of the American Association for Counseling and Development (AACD), *Journal of Counseling and Development,* published by AACD (has several issues with special coverage of this population and good ongoing articles), *Journal of Rehabilitation* (published by the American Rehabilitation Association), *Journal of Applied Rehabilitation Counseling, Career Development Quarterly,* and *Journal of Career Development* (especially the special issue on exceptional individuals, Summer 1987).

Successful Programs At Work

A number of successful career-oriented programs for the disabled have been established. The Mesa (Arizona) public schools have a comprehensive career and vocational education program for disabled students (see D'Alonzo, Marino, and Kauss, 1984). The model program is developmental in nature, starting in the seventh grade and continuing with targeted activities each year. It culminates in a senior-level experience called Pre-Employment Preparation (PEP). This provides twelfth-grade students with classroom vocational instruction together with three or more hours per day of on-the-job training with wages. The key to the success of the Mesa coordinated effort is a school-based multidisciplinary team that monitors each student's progress every year and evaluates the results in a comprehensive six-year program of career opportunities for the disabled.

Various professional journals publish a continuing supply of reports dealing with career development for disabled individuals, especially school-based efforts. In a study done in Washington State, Kortering and Edgar (1988) pointed out that there is a serious need to have school counselors and special education teachers work more closely with state vocational rehabilitation officials to help in the transition from school to work for special education students. They found that 55 percent of the former students were employed (often at low wages and with limited benefits) but that many of these youth—as well as many of the remaining 45 percent—were not working with state rehabilitation staff and were feared to be "falling through the cracks."

Steinhauser (1983) reminded counselors that for disabled individuals, career development books and articles and the theories they purvey do not do the job that really needs to be done—namely, job development and placement. He reported on four successful approaches that seemed to have stood the test of time: (1) job-finding clubs, (2) project employability, (3) projects with industry, and (4) employer contact. Steinhauser pointed out that these are only four of many possible approaches, but that counselors need to keep in mind this all-important final step in the special education/rehabilitation process. They should follow the professional literature and meetings for information on newer and better programs.

Curnow (1989) considered the career development of people with disabilities and found that several writers saw a need for special application of conventional theory to the disabled, because of such factors as reduced mobility, sensory or mental impairment, and prolonged medical treatment. Also mentioned were limited early experience and problems in decision making and with self concept. Curnow called for a longer-term, more systematic approach with increased exposure to early vocational and social experiences, development of decision-making skills, and more supportive counseling with improved occupational information.

With respect to public and professional stereotypes, Dahl (1981) outlined some positive steps to take in overcoming two main misconceptions, namely, that (1) disabled people can succeed in only a limited range of careers, and (2) disabled people need to be protected. Dahl built a case for a series of actions that a school or agency can take in attacking stereotypes on the part of counselors to make sure that career information systems are used to inform disabled people about a wide range of career options.

Overs, Taylor, and Adkins (1977) have done extensive research on the relationship between work and leisure in various Milwaukee (Wisconsin) rehabilitation efforts. They came up with a strong avocational counseling design that could help in the career development of the disabled.

Finally, it is important to recognize Donn Brolin's work with a number of career development initiatives involving disabled young people. The Lifelong Career Development Project provides information and resources of interest to disabled people, their families, professionals, and others concerned with disability-related issues. Designed for implementation at the community college level, this model provides a competency-based approach to meeting the career development needs of disabled persons and provides for a greater effort at networking or linking together various service units. Brolin and Elliott (1984) urged counselors and special educators to increase their career education efforts in all classrooms (K-12) and programs. They also called on special educators to reach out to adults to be supportive beyond the high school into community colleges and into the adult years through adult education courses. Obviously Brolin and Elliott came to the same conclusions as did Kortering and

Edgar about how easy it seemed to be for special education students to get lost once they left school.

Brolin also served as editor of the special Summer 1987 issue of the *Journal of Career Development,* which focused on exceptional individuals. In his introduction (Brolin, 1987), he pointed out that the main objective of the issue was to underscore the importance of the parents' role in the career development of disabled youth. He also stressed the role of teachers and counselors in bringing a set of positive perceptions and attitudes about disabled individuals to bear. Finally, he pointed to the need to broaden the career potential for all persons with disabilities.

In the same issue of the *Journal of Career Development,* Tindall and Gugerty (1987) called for counselors to produce and promote occupational and educational role models for disabled youth. Izzo (1987) and other authors strongly endorsed the necessity of a smooth school-to-work transition and called for active parental involvement in this process. All in all, this special issue is probably the best single source of quality ideas in working with career development with young disabled students.

Another important source is the *Journal of Counseling and Development* (November-December 1989), which had a special feature on counseling people with disabilities. There Brolin and Gysbers (1989) outlined a strong program of action on behalf of career development for students with disabilities. They urged the creation of a program built around a life-centered career education curriculum, which includes specific skills and competencies for students with disabilities. In short, there is much innovative thinking about career development for the disabled.

Special Things to Do for Special Populations

In the preceding sections and in other chapters, a consensus seemed to emerge around some attitudes and practices that facilitate the optimal career development of people with special needs (these may also be good principles to apply to the rest of the population as well). They include the following concerns, interventions, and considerations:

Three Personal Concerns

Of the many possible personal concerns counselors might have, three stand out.

1. Counselors Should Consider Their Own Values and Prejudices as They May Apply to Special Populations. This may mean doing some real soul searching, carrying out some assessment of personal positions by standardized instruments, getting involved with some encounter groups, or maybe doing some serious reading and talking to get a clearer picture in this regard. Another way to approach this could be through professional conferences, workshops, and the like. Taking stock of personal attitudes and prejudices and finding out what to do about them if some changes are in order will allow counselors to function more effectively with *all* types of clients.

2. Counseling Professionals Should Strive to Seek a Deeper Level of Understanding of the Various Population Groups with Special Needs. Counselors should make this a comprehensive, ongoing effort at building a knowledge base about gender, racial/ethnic groups, and disabling conditions—that is, about the people involved and their cultural, sociological, psychological, and economic background.

3. It Is Important to Be in a Constant State of Growth. The completion of a class, degree, certificate, workshop, or whatever does not mean that a counselor has arrived! Instead this should set the stage for the next level of professional and personal advancement and should provide a basis for better service to others.

Four Professional Interventions

Four professional strategies in particular require emphasis.

1. Counselors Must Work Aggressively with Family Members in Promoting Better Career Development for Populations with Special Needs. It is increasingly evident that counselors cannot relate solely to a student/client in isolation. The family system must be considered as fully as possible in the total picture. Working with parents was a recurring theme in most of the successful efforts reviewed for this book. This is a *must* consideration.

2. Counselors Should Promote the Visibility of Career Models Wherever and Whenever Possible. While this may only seem important for youth from a special population, it is also important for a recent adult accident victim who has a new disability to deal with or for a recently displaced homemaker thrust into the job market for the first time in twenty years. Both are likely to need strong career (and personal) role models close to their own situation that they can believe in and relate to.

3. It Is Important to Find Career Mentors for Individuals from Special Populations. Career models can be people who are far away, but they must be available as a source of encouragement, support, and nurturance to the extent possible. Finding and promoting career models and mentors represent highly desirable interventions.

4. Counselors Should Try to Stand Out and Stand Up as Advocates of Career Development for Everyone in Special Population Groups. Action-oriented counselors—the ones who constantly go to bat for clients—are likely to produce the best results.

Three Theoretical Considerations

Finally, we will make three theoretical proposals.

1. It Is Desirable to Look at Career Development for Individuals with Special Needs in the Largest Possible Context of Life-Career Development Over the Age Span. (See Figure 1.1 for an illustration.) The main objective should be to get away from viewing things from a narrow perspective. People should be seen as they might be tomorrow, not necessarily as they are today.

2. Counselors Should Grasp the Full Meaning of the Career = Work + Leisure (C = W + L) Concept That Is Discussed Throughout This Book. If there is one major consideration that is overlooked in the literature reviewed for this chapter, it is the narrow idea of career/work/job/occupation all meaning about the same thing across the life span. We believe there is compelling evidence that clients tend to perceive the relevance of leisure to a person's career much faster than counselors do.

3. Counselors Should Take a Career Information Systems Approach to the Problems of Career Development for Populations with Special Needs. Firsthand career information from a career mentor is important, but so is accurate print, computer, microfiche, or telephone information. Counselors should think career information *systems*—not single sources.

Of special interest to readers of this chapter who want more detailed information on the subject are two new publications: One is a special issue of the *Career Development Quarterly* on career development of racial and ethnic minorities, March 1991. It has eight outstanding articles under the guest editorship of Frederick T. L. Leong. The second publication is a 1991 book from AACD edited by Courtland C. Lee and Bernard L. Richardson entitled *Multicultural Issues in Counseling: New Approaches to Diversity.* It has sixteen chapters of solid content. Both of these publications are major additions to the literature on populations with special needs.

13

Designing and Managing Career Development Centers

Many career development professionals feel that the career development center (CDC) is at the heart of their best efforts to serve a wide range of users. To be sure, the counseling aspect is important, but there also needs to be a sound commitment to having the most timely, accurate, and usable career information available. It really is not an either/or situation; both are important and need every counselor's full energy to provide the best career counseling *and* career information possible. How to organize, arrange, make attractive, use, and evaluate a CDC is the focus of this chapter. We will take the reader through four essential questions:

1. *What* general approach should the CDC take? A multimedia approach.
2. *How* should the CDC be organized? Whatever fits local needs best.
3. *Who* should use the CDC? A wide range of users should be attracted to it.
4. *Where* do you find sources of material for the CDC? Everywhere you can.

First, what about the name? Well, call it a

Career Center
Career Resource Center
Career Information Center
Career Education Center
Career Development Center
Educational/Occupational Informational Center

The term *career development center* emphasizes the needs of the user rather than the contents of the center. This is why we prefer this term. However, there are many other alternatives, including *career center, career resource center, career information center, career education center,* and so on. The name should not matter in the end; what is important is that it meet the needs of users.

Such a center does not require a lot of space or money. In the very best of situations, it is in the largest space available filled with multimedia materials that appeal to a wide range of users in individual and group settings. But a useful CDC may consist only of the state career information delivery system (CIDS) plus whatever additional resources counselors can afford in their setting. It can be limited to a corner in a school, church, or community library.

All CDCs share certain features. This does not mean that a CDC in an elementary school will be the same as a CDC in a senior citizens center; of course they will have some important differences. However, they should basically fulfill the same purposes. This chapter will focus on the similarities that can assist readers to establish CDCs in a variety of settings where some of the specific developmental needs of the users may require attention to age, ethnic, religious, or gender issues. Hopefully if the four key principles of the CDC— what, how, who, and where (mentioned earlier)—are mastered, they can be applied in any setting.

Everything cannot be covered in this chapter that relates to a CDC. Most of the essentials are covered, but other chapters in this book on sources (Chapters Nine and Ten) or on evaluation (Chapter Eleven) discuss how you build a fundamental knowledge of a CDC. We suggest that readers consider sources outside of this book as well. For the serious reader a collection of half-a-dozen related sources can form the basis for a good, strong, varied approach to what ought to be considered for a CDC that is starting up or being revitalized, especially sources that relate to specific location needs, such as library, college, or school settings.

Finally, the issue of placement is clearly important in regard to counseling for career development. A brief discussion of placement is included further on in this chapter. The importance of placement is borne out by the fact that most placement activities have a Career Development Center in connection with their operation and the typical CDC often has some type of placement function incorporated in its operation. At any rate, any book on this topic should give some attention to the concept of placement as a vital form of assistance for individuals looking for help in the next phase of career transition.

Taking a Strong Multimedia Approach—the *What*

The effective CDC in the 1990s and beyond, no matter where the setting, will be multimedia in nature. In times past it was not unusual to see a CDC with print material only, and it is not unusual now to see a mainframe computer terminal or a microcomputer that is referred to as "the CDC." Of course, each of these offers only one dimension of what a comprehensive center should be like. People of different ages and backgrounds have different learning styles, which means that it is necessary to provide a wide variety of learning approaches to help the users of a CDC take advantage of the assistance available to them. The media utilized in a CDC can roughly be categorized under seven major headings. For further details on the following groupings, see McDaniels and Puryear (1991).

One: Firsthand Observations

Firsthand observations are the best way to learn about any kind of career information—they are direct and personal. This may involve simple things like 3 × 5 card files (or computer lists) of contacts on various occupations, volunteer opportunities, summer learning camps on college campuses, local leisure resources, plus a host of other possibilities that provide clients with meaningful exposure to some useful career information. Among the options are the following:

- Part-time work opportunities—short and long term
- Summer full-time/part-time work
- Volunteer opportunities
- Shadowing experience
- Complete range of leisure activities and options
- Cooperative work and work-study programs
- Career visits—short and long term
- Summer school work/learning/vacation/leisure opportunities
- Role model/mentor contacts—on the job and/or in educational institutions
- Suggestions for planned visits to educational institutions

Two: Action Pictures and Sound

This has been called the video era, and certainly to make a CDC interesting and attractive, videos are a necessary dimension. Fortunately, the cost of local production of videotape, even with sound, has been reduced to the point that it is certainly within reach of most modern CDCs. The advent of VCRs also means that videos can be loaned out for showing at home for other family members to see and discuss. Possibilities include

- Videos—commercial or locally produced
- Commercial films (mostly 16mm)
- 16mm films—locally produced
- 8mm films—locally produced
- Television—film or tape from commercial or Public Broadcasting System (PBS) programs

Three: Still Pictures and Sound

For some users, slides, tapes, and transparencies in various forms can add an important dimension to the CDC. In most cases they can be locally produced or purchased at a reasonable cost—thus making this dimension an attractive alternative to more expensive video purchases. Some of the options here are

- Silent filmstrips
- Sound filmstrips
- Transparencies with script or audiotape
- Audiotapes or records available for loan
- Slides alone or with an accompanying audiotape
- Radio—commercial or National Public Radio (NPR) live and on audiotape

Four: Large Visual Displays

For many users, an attractive bulletin board or eye-catching poster or chart can be an introduction to more in-depth information available in the CDC. These need to be creative and current. They should capture viewers' attention quickly while presenting solid, accurate information. Clippings from local, state, and regional newspapers and magazines can be interesting and eye-catching if kept up to date. Here are several other possibilities:

- Posters—with strong content
- Posters—with mostly pictures
- Charts—with strong content
- Charts or posters with instructional tape
- Bulletin boards—changed weekly or biweekly
- Posters planned and created for various emphasis weeks such as National Career Guidance Week, American Education Week, Vocational Education Week, and so on

Five: Print Media

This is still the core of most CDCs. The *Occupational Outlook Handbook*—by all accounts the most widely used single piece of career information—is the heart of most CDCs and is only available in print form. There are a wide variety of other print options available for use in CDCs, and many are increasingly attractive and interesting. They include the following:

- Monographs and briefs
- Workbooks and brochures
- Books—paperback and hardcover
- Comic books on career topics
- College catalogues and other postsecondary guidebooks
- Complete and timely financial aid information
- Magazines—commercial or specialized by region or content
- Newspapers, newsletters, career tabloids, and clippings

Six: Automated and Semiautomated Systems

Since the early 1980s, these systems have been the fastest growing and in some cases the only dimension to a CDC. The resources available in this category are attractive, modern, timely, and usually *expensive*. They are perceived by many users as somehow better than the same information in other forms. Key elements of these systems (and of any up-to-date CDC) include

- State CIDSs on microcomputer such as Virginia VIEW and Missouri VIEW
- Microcomputer commercial systems and systems such as GIS, CHOICES, DISCOVER, SIGI, CIS, and others
- State CIDSs on microfiche
- McKee Sort, used by Chronicle Guidance Publications in their College VIEW

Seven: Miscellaneous Career Sources

It is obvious that technology is changing rapidly, so that new approaches to media in a modern CDC are continually emerging. Various combinations of current technology as well as new technological developments need to be watched via professional journals and meetings. Some of these include

- Career information telephone hotlines—local, state, or national
- Simulation activities and hands-on kits
- Complete career assessment resources—both paper and pencil and computer aided
- Games and puzzles
- Laser-disc technology

Organizing a Career Development Center—the *How*

There is no one way to organize a CDC. There are many factors to consider: money, space, time, support, user groups, and so on. What follow are some suggestions. The trouble with most of the organizational arrangements is that they relate only to occupational information. The modern CDC offers much more than that, although occupational information is still important. The *what* and *how* need to be carefully thought out, along with the *who* and *where*. Only then should the CDC be designed and developed.

Systems for Organizing Resources

There is a wide variety of systems for organizing resources. A partial list follows.

Bennet Occupations Filing Plan and Bibliography. The organizational scheme for this system is based on the field-of-work coding from the *Dictionary of Occupational Titles* (*DOT*). The plan includes a set of preprinted tabs for file folders and instructions for setting up the system. All types of career materials can be catalogued and filed under this system.

Ann Roe's Two-Dimensional Occupational Classification Scheme. Occupational titles are categorized on one level according to the kinds of activities workers engage in, and jobs that share common factors are clustered. A second dimension is job stratification according to the level of responsibility, skills, or capabilities required.

The basic two-dimensional system has been expanded to include two additional factors that further clarify the nature of contrasting occupational clusters. Factor I separates interpersonal relations, or working with people, and natural phenomena–oriented occupations. Factor II specifies orientation toward purposeful communication or resourceful utilization. With the field and level dimensions of the original system superimposed on the axes created by Factors I and II, the Roe system illustrates the degree to which various occupations involve contact with people and the natural sciences, and the type and degree of communication and organizational skills they require.

Academic Subject Classification. Occupational materials can be filed according to school subject areas to which they relate. The appropriate occupations related to each subject are organized alphabetically under the subject heading. Students can easily identify with the academic areas and see what occupations are associated with different areas. On the other hand, extensive cross-reference is needed since one occupation can pertain to more than one academic area.

Dewey Decimal System. A modification of the Dewey Decimal System can be used as a filing system. This type of system is one which most people are somewhat familiar with and can easily use. However, in order to implement the system, one needs to know how to set up the Dewey Decimal System.

Chronicle Guidance Publication Plan. This plan is based on the arrangement of titles of codes found in the *DOT*. Materials are arranged under ten major headings and subdivided into occupational fields.

Appalachian Educational Laboratory Career Information System. This system uses the main titles of the *DOT* and codes materials according to the appropriate Career Area/ Worker Trait Group numbers. All occupational information is either filed or indexed into the system by Worker Trait Group numbers. Omnibus materials are assigned to the appropriate Career Areas and filed or indexed by Career Area numbers.

DOT Occupational Titles Classification. The *DOT* coding system is a basis for a filing option. The occupational materials are filed according to the classifications used in the *Dictionary of Occupational Titles*. Through this system all related occupations are placed together.

Census Classification of Occupations and Industries. This provides an alphabetical and a classified index covering several thousand titles, which are grouped in occupational and industrial categories. It has been largely abandoned as a basis for occupational filing systems since the publication of the *DOT*.

Alphabetical. Information is filed alphabetically by the name of the occupation or the appropriate heading of the piece of educational information.

Field of Interest or Other Personal Traits. Materials are filed by categories of interests or traits as measured by various instruments or structures of the world of work used in publications.

Holland Occupational Organization System. This approach organizes occupations into Holland codes based on six interest areas and six work environments—Realistic, Investigative, Artistic, Social, Enterprising, and Conventional— with all the various combinations of these six.

School Subjects. This is the same as Academic Subject Classification.

Groupings by Categories. Numerical or alphabetical designations are used to denote each station. Following is a list of stations:

- *Self-Understanding Materials.* Information designed to assist individuals in gaining a better understanding of themselves is located at this station.
- *College and University Information.* Resources at this station provide descriptions of colleges and universities throughout the nation.
- *Career Games.* This station contains career games, kits, and so on that provide experiences in decision making, values clarification, occupational exploration, career planning, and career selection.
- *State CIDS.* Information from a state occupational information system in many instances is available on microfiche or computer.
- *Local Employment Opportunities.* Placement opportunities are enhanced by this station, which identifies up-to-date job opportunities in the local area.

A model CDC jointly created by Virginia Tech's Counselor Education Programs and the Appalachian Educational Laboratory, focused on secondary school use, consists of four color-coded stations: (1) Self-Awareness, (2) Educational-Occupational Information, (3) Taking Action, and (4) Life Management. All stations are designed so that individual users can work through them at their own pace, perhaps over several days or even several weeks. A brief description of that organizational plan follows.

Self-Awareness: This station consists of such self-awareness tools as a work-values inventory, an activities preference checklist, a skills-level checklist, an aptitude checklist, and a work-environment-preference checklist. Checklists and inventories are color-coded green. Books and pamphlets on career planning are also included at this station.

Educational-Occupational Information: Resource materials that provide a basis for informed career decisions are found in this section. A multimedia approach to the distribution of information ensures that it will appeal to a wide variety of students' abilities. For example, sources range from college guides, dictionaries, and encyclopedias of career information and a videotape career library to computerized career information systems. This section is color-coded blue.

Taking Action: The third station is designed to complete the career decision-making process through practical application. Strategies for setting career goals, hints on writing résumés, and tips on job interviewing are included. Handouts in this section are color-coded gold.

Life Management: The fourth and final station is color-coded yellow. It addresses life issues that students may face, such as effective time management, grief, building self-esteem, how to stop smoking, and coping with family violence.

The CDC at Virginia Tech presently serves as a model for school counselors and administrators who are able to visit the center. A slide-tape presentation describes the CDC and is available to schools on request.

Appealing to a Wide Range of Users—the *Who*

The challenge to make a CDC as useful as possible to a wide range of users will be with us for some time. In the past, a single-focus CDC may have been acceptable, but this is no longer true. It is essential to start with a needs assessment of what potential users want in a CDC. This should continue with an ongoing evaluation of the program by users, with annual summaries of activities and evaluation results. Another way to help determine if a CDC is reaching the focus population(s) is to form an advisory group made up of a variety of users, staff, and selected others—such as parents in the case of a school CDC or employers for a community-agency CDC. Make it diverse and do not staff it with friends, who will not give you good comments on how to improve the CDC. We strongly suggest that counselors plan a series of visits to nearby CDCs to see how they are set up and how they target various user groups as well as how they deal with needs assessments, evaluations, and advisory groups. In short, get out and make some professional visits over the course of a year to take a good look at some successful CDCs in operation.

Chapter Twelve focused on career development for populations with special needs. A place to implement those concerns is in the CDC. Special efforts should be made to create a CDC that is attractive and useful to *all client groups*. Create a career development center that is *proactive* for all users.

What are some of the various user groups to keep in mind? Any CDC should be

1. *Age Appropriate.* Keep in mind the age of your targeted user group and acquire content that fits their interests. Certain general sources like the *Occupational Outlook Handbook* and state CIDSs are available, and there is a growing base of age-specific materials to look out for as well.
2. *Gender Appropriate.* The CDC must be attractive to both gender groups. It can have sections for "women only" or "men only," but nothing that is gender offensive.
3. *Racially Appropriate.* Be especially attentive to the visual nature of certain materials and make sure that there are no racially offensive items in the CDC.
4. *Ethnically Appropriate.* There is increasing sensitivity to this issue, so guard against any items that could be misunderstood or considered offensive.
5. *Disabilities Appropriate.* Because of the growing need to provide equal access to the CDC and to make it responsive to the needs of the disabled, it should contain materials that will be of interest to an increasingly active group of disabled individuals across the life span.
6. *Learning-Level Appropriate.* People have different learning styles and preferences. Not everyone relates equally well to print material. Variety in style and content is what is called for here, based on the recognition that there are various modes of learning.
7. *Multilanguage Appropriate.* Be mindful of the multicultural, multilanguage needs of your users. Spanish and

Asian language versions of certain materials are increasingly appearing. Be conscious of various user groups in this regard.

8. *Visually/Auditorially Appropriate.* Make the place attractive! Use color and style to brighten the place up. Use background music that does not disturb. Make the CDC a place to be.

9. *Staff Appropriate.* The staff where you work may want to use some of the CDC materials also. Set aside a special shelf or have a special reading list that will be of interest to them. The staff can be a key support and user group, so treat them well. Make them feel welcome.

10. *Community Appropriate.* Keep in mind the needs of the community members who may be expected to use the CDC. All of the above points should relate to a variety of community members who may be users of the CDC or key supporters. Make sure they feel at home in your CDC.

This works out in simple ways, such as making sure that a CDC in a senior citizens' club has plenty of information about the ELDERHOSTEL Program, with brochures and catalogues displayed in abundance. By the same token a high school–based CDC should have plenty of materials that appeal to a wide range of teen-age users: information on how to get work permit and postsecondary school information, for instance. In addition, all centers should have ample information about vocational education opportunities for all age groups—not just materials focusing on high school, but those for community college students and adults visiting a local library CDC.

Take a good look at the population your CDC is trying to serve. Be sure it appeals to *all* user groups, rather than just the highly visible people. Make sure there is no "underserved" group in your setting. One way to reach out with career information is to use innovative approaches to get potentially underserved groups into the CDC. Reach out to them through charts and posters in gathering places that direct them to the

CDC for details. Get community service announcements on radio and television about the services and assistance available at the center. Create a short video that can be shown on a local cable access channel. Another idea is to open up evenings and weekends in order to attract people who may not find it convenient to come in during normal working hours. Hold an occasional open house. Set up booths in shopping malls and city and county fairs. Finally, get an advisory group to come up with innovative ways of attracting a full range of user groups to the CDC. For instance, here are some ideas for outreach.

- Local craft workers' week
- Local leisure opportunities week
- Photographic display of women at work
- Photographic display of workers with disabilities
- Special hours for staff use of CDC
- Special week on financial aid information
- Special displays during Vocational Education Week

Being Open to a Variety of Sources—the *Where*

This section suggests some answers to the question, "Where do we get all of the stuff to put in the CDC?" The most general answer is to be on the lookout *everywhere*. To build a strong CDC, counselors must constantly search for timely and relevant items for the appropriate user group. They must also be constantly concerned with *the quality* of what is available in the CDC. And finally, they must want their CDC to be the very best center for the users it serves.

Where does one start to look for material in developing or revitalizing a CDC? There are many obvious sources. These include formal sources such as

1. Commercial producers of the type of multimedia items appropriate for a particular CDC
2. Professional association sources, which offer journals, newsletters, catalogues, and conventions with relevant exhibits

3. Commercial newsletters, which feature new materials and often evaluations as well
4. Local, state, and federal government sources, including the Bureau of Labor Statistics in the Department of Labor, the Bureau of the Census, and related agencies such as the Small Business Administration
5. State CIDSs (see Chapter Ten for details)

Informal sources include

1. Newspapers of all types (national, state, local), which carry timely materials from clippings to full tabloid sections
2. Magazines, which publish regular series as well as special features
3. Radio, which often presents information on local jobs or training that may be worth taping to have in your CDC along with other relevant materials
4. Television, which may have regular or occasional broadcasts that can be videotaped for use in the center
5. Miscellaneous sources, such as reports on employment or educational outlook, as well as recreation sources that may be of interest to users

The main point of this section is to make you aware of the multitude of sources for all areas of work and leisure available to a quality CDC effort. It is important to be open to new sources as they become available and to try them out. The worst thing is probably to sit back and rely only on print material that is several years out of date. To have a broad-based CDC, you need to pay equal attention to the leisure, education, and occupation aspects of your center. Please refer back to Chapters Eight, Nine, Ten, and Eleven for further details on what to put in your CDC and how to evaluate it.

Placement

Often placement is a part of a CDC. Certainly it is a major function of most educational institutions and a very large part of a number of separate agencies and for-profit businesses serving adults. In some ways it may be viewed as the key or final stage in a career transition process. For example, for a student leaving a high school or college, placement assistance may well be the most positive thing the educational institution can provide in terms of tangible help. Likewise, for a newly disabled adult, the final and perhaps best service provided by the state rehabilitative service can be placement into suitable employment. The same can probably be said for the displaced worker who turns to the local community college for retooling courses, hopefully followed by successful placement in a new job. In short, a strong case can be made for a placement function as a part of the career development process at many age levels. Indeed, many career counselors work full time in placement activities in a wide variety of settings— mostly serving adults. This brief section will highlight some of the key placement functions that are carried out in three main areas: in-school placement for grades K-12; postschool placement, which takes many forms; and institutional, agency, and self-help placement.

In-School Placement

For the school counselor, there are a number of in-school placement functions that have to do with helping students improve their overall development through appropriate in-school placement. This takes on a variety of forms, and in most schools the counselor is involved in the process, if not at the actual core of the particular placement function. In the elementary school, this may involve assisting in placement in matters like the following:

- Special education placement
- Special tutoring placement
- Gifted and talented placement
- Special summer school placement
- Placement in community support programs
- Other leisure-related experiences

At the middle (junior high) school as well as the senior high school level, placement becomes more complex, with the counselor taking on a more central role. Various curriculum choices have to be made; for example, counselors might need to help students work out a four- or five- or six-year in-school career development plan that can be reviewed and revised each year in consultation with parents. This type of plan may include various leisure activities and part-time and summer work experience, in addition to any number of career development growth activities in and out of school. It is in fulfilling a practical role on behalf of students that counselors can help students become aware of all of the various options that are open to them as well as of the possible outcomes. Further, counselors can assist students in broadening the options open to them when there are apparent limitations on what they have to choose from. For example, this might include a limited variety of in-class or out-of-class options because of barriers imposed by gender, ethnicity, or disabilities. In other words, through the placement function, counselors become advocates for the students.

Postschool Placement

Both secondary and postsecondary institutions have provided varying degrees of placement assistance over the years. The public secondary school placement programs have experienced more ups and downs in terms of interest and support than those in higher education. The key point here, of course, is that postschool clients are in a clear career transitional period, and most are looking for some type of assistance in that process, whether the institutions provide it or not. Formalized job placement programs are much more common in higher education institutions than in high schools. Johnson and Figler (1984) provided a state-of-the-art profile of career development and placement services in postsecondary institutions. They argued that there has been a merging in recent years of (1) the separate, centralized career center that emphasizes career development and (2) the traditional placement function into a comprehensive CDC that includes placement on a comprehensive placement operation that includes a CDC.

In addition to Johnson and Figler's chapter, materials are available from the College Placement Council (CPC) and in its periodical, the *Journal of Career Planning and Employment*. Regional and state affiliates of the CPC also come together regularly in meetings and workshops. Thus, job placement at the higher education level is a viable enterprise. This is much less true in secondary schools.

Institutional, Agency, and Self-Help Placement

A wide variety of placement functions go on outside of educational settings. These may or may not occur in connection with a CDC, but often a small center may be available as part of a larger placement effort. In general, the settings and functions that follow are available in most areas, or from a resource within a particular state.

State Employment Services. Examples include the Virginia Employment Commission, which is supported mainly by federal government funding based on the level of unemployment in the state. There are usually offices in all major metropolitan areas that offer a wide range of services, including screening/assessment, job placement, veterans assistance, and follow-up. A state employment service normally has some type of CIDS and a small CDC. The *Journal of Employment Counseling* has plenty of good articles on this entire subject.

State Rehabilitative Service. This is often called a department of rehabilitative services; it serves adult disabled clients. Normally, individual rehabilitation counselors in local or regional offices provide screening/assessment referral to training programs, special medical restorative assistance, job placement, and follow-up. Job placement is considered a key part of the service. There are many useful books as well as articles in periodicals such as the *Bulletin of Rehabilitation Counseling*. A growing number of private agencies perform many of the same functions under a variety of contractual arrangements.

Job Training Partnership Act (JTPA). These programs tend to be more involved in "pure training" activities, but they often prepare graduates for placement by using staff counselors. In some instances, on-the-job training results in regular full-time employment. Usually this involves a close working relationship with the state employment service in locating clients and in helping to place them if assistance is needed.

Private Employment Agencies. These are fee-charging services (as opposed to the state employment services, which are free); they derive their support from employers (most often) or job-seeking employees (sometimes). Some handle all occupations, but often they are specialized in clerical, technical, manufacturing, sales, or other fields. Executive search outfits, outplacement services, temporary help firms, and contract/contingency workers' organizations are found among these private employment groups.

Self-Help Techniques. These are rooted in the do-it-yourself idea that is still popular in this country. A well-supplied CDC will usually have a good stock of self-help booklets, guides, films or filmstrips, videos, tapes, and so on. These treat job search, résumé writing, interviewing, and other topics. Also, CDCs often conduct regular job search, résumé writing, and interviewing workshops and seminars in structured groups. And most college and commercial bookstores have an ample supply of self-help books or will stock them at the request of local counselors who want to refer people to them as a resource. (See the listing at the end of this chapter for some ideas.)

Eight Key Resources on Career Development Centers and Placement

1. Brown, S. T., and Brown, D. *Designing and Implementing a Career Information Center.* Garrett Park, Md.: Garrett

Park Press, 1990. (A publication of the National Career Development Association.) A brand-new resource, which has just about everything counselors will want to know about a career information center in a secondary school setting. The senior author is a counselor at a Chapel Hill, North Carolina, high school and her coauthor-husband is a professor at the University of North Carolina. Extensive listing of sources.

2. Hubbard, M., and Hawkes, S. *Developing a Career Information Center.* (Rev. ed.) Montreal, Canada: Guidance Information Center, Concordia University, 1987. A first-rate book put out by the Canadian Career Information Resource Advisory Group. If you are only able to buy one book (other than this one!), then this is probably the best and most comprehensive source on the general topic of CDCs. Ten chapters cover all topics and possibilities. Useful for all career settings.

3. American Library Association. *Job and Career Information Centers for Public Libraries.* Chicago: American Library Association, 1985. Public Library Reporter no. 21. For any school or public library interested in setting up a CDC, this book is a must. Really shows how the modern library can reach out to its adult users through an effective CDC. Even has a chapter on writing a proposal to fund the program. If you are working with a librarian, this is the best resource to use.

4. Weiss, S. C. *Career Resource Centers.* Ann Arbor: ERIC Counseling and Personnel Services Clearinghouse, School of Education, University of Michigan, 1983. This book is the result of an ERIC computer search on career resource centers. A bit dated, but still provides a good state-of-the-art status report on the scope of the additional sources available.

5. Fine, S. (ed.). *Developing Career Information Centers: A Guide to Collection, Building, and Counseling.* New York: Neal-Schuman, 1980. Still a strong source, especially as it relates to the roles of librarians and counselors in working together to make the CDC a useful entity. A standard work from the early 1980s.

6. Heppner, M. J., and Johnson, J. A. (eds.). *Journal of Career Development,* 1986, *13* (1) (special issue on college career centers). Well-balanced state-of-the-art reports on the comprehensive role of a modern college career center, especially as the CCC relates to students as paraprofessionals and also in regard to various outreach programs.

7. Johnson, C. A., and Figler, H. E. "Career Development and Placement Services in Postsecondary Institutions." In N. C. Gysbers and Associates, *Designing Careers: Counseling to Enhance Education, Work, and Leisure.* San Francisco: Jossey-Bass, 1984. This is an excellent review of what the postsecondary CDC and placement services had developed into by the early 1980s. Also provides an extended listing of promising exemplary programs for the 1990s and beyond. A top resource for people in higher education.

8. Walz, G. R., and Bleuer, J. *Counseling Software Guide.* Alexandria, Va.: American Association for Counseling and Development, 1989. First effort at putting together a software review published for counselors. Good section on career counseling, academic advising, and so on. Provides special help in the form of an eight-point software evaluation checklist.

Here are some *specific types* of references to include in a Career Development Center. The primary sources are front line, basic, must-have materials. The secondary sources are nice to have if at all possible. Other useful sources should be included if funds are available. This list is state specific for Virginia, so local sources should be substituted. Of course, the most recent version of all materials is always called for.

Primary Sources

American College of Sports Medicine. *1990 ACSM Graduate Program Directory.* Indianapolis, Ind.: American College of Sports Medicine, 1990.

Bureau of Labor Statistics, Department of Labor. *Occupational Outlook Handbook (1990–91)*. Washington, D.C.: U.S. Government Printing Office, 1990.

Croner, U.H.E. *American Trade School Directory.* Queens Village, N.Y.: Croner Publications, 1990.

Dilts, S. W., and Kaye, K. R. (eds.). *Peterson's Guide to Southeast Colleges—1990.* Princeton, N.J.: Peterson's Guides, 1989.

Dilts, S. W., and Kaye, K. R. (eds.). *Peterson's Guide to Middle Atlantic Colleges—1990.* Princeton, N.J.: Peterson's Guides, 1989.

Dilts, S. W., Martin, D. L., and Zidzik, M. A. (eds.). *Peterson's Guide to Four-Year Colleges—1990.* (20th ed.) Princeton, N.J.: Peterson's Guides, 1989.

Dilts, S. W., Martin, D. L., and Zidzik, M. A. (eds.). *Peterson's Guide to Two-Year Colleges—1990.* (20th ed.) Princeton, N.J.: Peterson's Guides, 1989.

Employment and Training Administration, Department of Labor. *Dictionary of Occupational Titles.* (4th ed.) Washington, D.C.: U.S. Government Printing Office, 1977.

Harris, S. (ed.). *1989–90 Accredited Institutions of Postsecondary Education.* Washington, D.C.: American Council on Education, 1990.

VonVorys, B., Harrower, G., III, and Jacobs, J. E. (eds.). Princeton, N.J.: Peterson's Guides, 1989.

Peterson's Graduate and Professional Programs—1990. (24th ed.)

Peterson's Graduate Programs in Engineering and Applied Sciences. (24th ed.)

Peterson's Graduate Programs in Business Education, Health, and Law. (24th ed.)

Peterson's Graduate Programs in Physical Sciences and Mathematics—1990. (24th ed.)

Peterson's Graduate Programs in the Biological and Agricultural Sciences—1990. (24th ed.)

Peterson's Graduate Programs in the Humanities and Social Sciences—1990. (24th ed.)

Well, J. H., and Ready, B. C. (eds.). *The Independent Study Catalog.* Princeton, N.J.: Peterson's Guides, 1989.

Three-book set from the College Board, New York.
1. *College Handbook* (1990–91).
2. *Index of Majors* (1990–91).
3. *The College Cost Book* (1990–91).

Secondary Sources

Adams, J. P. (ed.). *College Check-Mate: Innovative Tuition Plans That Make You a Winner—1990–91.* (3rd ed.) Alexandria, Va.: Octameron Press, 1989.

American Legion Education Program. *Need a Lift? Educational Opportunities, Careers, Loans, Scholarships, Employment.* (39th ed.) Indianapolis, Ind.: American Legion Educational Assistance Program, 1989.

Berger, S. L. *College Planning for Gifted Students.* Reston, Va.: Council for Exceptional Children, 1989.

Butterworth, A. S., and Migliare, S. A. (eds.). *The National Directory of Internships.* (7th ed.) Raleigh, N.C.: National Society for Internships and Experiential Education, 1989.

Cass, J., and Birnbaum, M. *Comparative Guide to American Colleges.* (14th ed.) New York: HarperCollins, 1989.

College Placement Council. *CPC Annual.* (33rd ed.) 4 vols. Bethlehem, Pa.: College Placement Council, 1989.

College Research Group of Concord, Massachusetts. *Best Dollar Values in American Colleges.* (2nd ed.) New York: ARCO, 1990.

Department of Defense Dependent Schools. *Overseas Employment Opportunities for Educators.* Washington, D.C.: U.S. Government Printing Office, 1988.

Elfin, M., and Bauer, B. (eds.). *America's Best Colleges—1990.* Washington, D.C.: U.S. News & World Report, 1989.

Fiske, E. B. *The Fiske Guide to Colleges.* New York: New York Times Books, 1989.

Fiske, E. B., and Steinbrecher, P. *Get Organized! Fiske's Unbeatable System for Applying to College.* Princeton, N.J.: Peterson's Guides, 1990.

Gruber, G. R. *Gruber's Complete Preparation for the SAT.* (3rd ed.) Savage, Md.: Barnes & Noble, 1988.

Gupta, G. R., and Hedrick, H. L. (eds.). *Allied Health Education Directory.* (18th ed.) Chicago: American Medical Association, 1990.

Institute of International Education. *Financial Resources for International Study.* Princeton, N.J.: Peterson's Guides, 1989.

Leider, R., and Leider, A. *Don't Miss Out: The Ambitious Student's Guide to Financial Aid—1990-91.* (14th ed.) Alexandria, Va.: Octameron Press, 1989.

Mangrum, C. L., and Strichart, S. S. (eds.). *Peterson's Colleges with Programs for Learning Disabled Students.* (2nd ed.) Princeton, N.J.: Peterson's Guides, 1988.

National Association of Student Financial Aid Administrators. *The Advisor: A Counselor's Guide to Student Financial Assistance.* Washington, D.C.: National Association of Student Financial Aid Administrators, 1990.

Re, J. M. *Earn and Learn: Cooperative Education Opportunities Offered by the Federal Government—1990-91.* (11th ed.) Alexandria, Va.: Octameron Press, 1988.

Rosenblatt, R. (ed.). *U.S. News Guide to America's Best Colleges.* Washington, D.C.: U.S. News & World Report, 1989.

Rushing, B. C. (ed.). *1990 Internships.* Cincinnati, Ohio: Writer's Digest Books, 1989.

Russell, J. J., Downe, B. J., and Steele, J. V. (eds.). *National Trade and Professional Associations of the United States.* (25th ed.) Washington, D.C.: Columbia Books, 1990.

Schlachter, G. A. *Directory of Financial Aid for Women—1989-90.* San Carlos, Calif.: Reference Service Press, 1989.

Schlachter, G. A., and Goldstein, S. E. (eds.). *Directory of Financial Aid for Minorities—1989-1990.* San Carlos, Calif.: Reference Service Press, 1989.

Schlachter, G. A., and Weber, R. D. *Financial Aid for Veterans, Military Personnel, and Their Dependents.* San Carlos, Calif.: Reference Service Press, 1990.

Schneider, L. (ed.). *Independent Secondary Schools—1990-91.* (11th ed.) Princeton, N.J.: Peterson's Guides, 1990.

Schwartz, J. (ed.). *College Financial Aid Annual—1990.* New York: Arco, 1989.

The Student Guide for Federal Financial Aid Programs (1990–91). Washington, D.C.: U.S. Department of Education. For a copy of this free publication, call 1-800-333-4636.

Other Useful Sources

Basta, N. *Peterson's Top Professionals.* Princeton, N.J.: Peterson's Guides, 1989.

Bloch, D. P. *How to Make the Right Career Moves.* Lincolnwood, Ill.: VGM Career Horizons, 1990.

Bolles, R. H. *The 1990 What Color Is Your Parachute?* Berkeley, Calif.: Ten Speed Press, 1990.

Devon, C. S., and LaVeck, J. (eds.). *Great Careers.* Garrett Park, M.D.: Garrett Park Press, 1990.

Frankel, R. (ed.). *The National Parks Trade Journal.* (3rd ed.) Yosemite National Park, Calif.: Taverly-Churchill, 1989.

Kimeldorf, M. *Write into a Job.* Bloomington, Ind.: Meridian Education Corporation, 1990.

Krannich, R. L. *Careering and Re-Careering for the 1990's: The Complete Guide to Planning Your Future.* Manassas, Va.: Impact Publications, 1989.

Lindquist, C. L., and Feodaroff, P. L. (eds.). *Where to Start Career Planning—1989–1991.* (7th ed.) Ithaca, N.Y.: Career Center, Cornell University, 1989.

McDaniels, C. *The Changing Workplace: Career Counseling Strategies for the 1990s and Beyond.* San Francisco: Jossey-Bass, 1989.

McDaniels, C. *Developing a Professional Vita or Resume.* Garrett Park, Md.: Garrett Park Press, 1990.

Myers, J. R., and Scott, E. W. *Getting Skilled, Getting Ahead.* Princeton, N.J.: Peterson's Guides, 1989.

Petras, K., and Petras, R. *Jobs '90.* Englewood Cliffs, N.J.: Prentice-Hall, 1990.

Renetzky, A., Jacobsen, D. J., and Rudd, H. (eds.). *Directory of Career Resources for Women.* Santa Monica, Calif.: Ready Reference Press, 1990.

Sacharov, A. *Offbeat Careers*. Berkeley, Calif.: Ten Speed Press, 1988.

Schneider, L., and Wells, J. (eds.). *Summer Opportunities for Kids and Teenagers—1990*. (7th ed.) Princeton, N.J.: Peterson's Guides, 1989.

Ware, C. *Summer Options for Teenagers*. New York: Arco, 1990.

Wegmann, R., Chapman, R., and Johnson, M. *Work in the New Economy: Careers and Job Seeking into the 21st Century*. Indianapolis, Ind.: JIST Works, 1989.

14

Using Techniques
for Individual Counseling

"How can I use career information in individual counseling?" "Will the use of career information interfere with my relationships with clients?" "How does career information help my clients reach their goals or solve their problems?" These and similar questions are often asked by counselors and other helpers who are unsure about career information resources and systems and their place and use in individual counseling for career development.

This chapter addresses questions such as these by first discussing the place, purposes, and uses of career information in counseling. Then an occupational card sort technique is presented as an example of one way of helping counselors and clients access clients' views of self, others, and the world, thereby gaining an understanding of the depth and breadth of their career information knowledge and their career information needs. Finally, two cases are presented to illustrate the uses of career information in individual counseling.

The Place, Purposes, and Uses of
Career Information in Individual Counseling

This section provides a general picture of career information as it figures in individual counseling.

The Place of Career Information

Before we examine the purposes and uses of career information, it is first necessary to establish the place of career information in individual counseling. There are common misconceptions on the part of some counselors about the place of career information. We call these misconceptions variations of the "separate from and not a part of the counseling process" theme.

Variation 1: The Stand-Alone Variation. Variation 1 of the "separate from and not a part of the counseling process" theme is that career information stands alone—that it is not a part of counseling. As we stated previously, in some situations, under certain circumstances, some clients need and want career information only. They do not see themselves as needing or wanting to be involved in individual counseling. For many other clients, however, career information is the intervention of choice to be used in counseling to help them reach their goals or solve their problems. In these situations career information does not stand alone. It is a part of individual counseling because it is a counseling intervention.

Variation 2: The Over-There Variation. Variation 2 of the "separate from and not a part of the counseling process" theme holds that career information is not to be used directly in individual counseling. Career information is seen as "over there" and clients are sent "over there" to read or view something; then they are to come back to the counselor when they are finished "over there," so that counseling may proceed. Apparently the use of career information is regarded as an interruption of the individual counseling process, not as a part of it. Career information gained from resources may be important, but its use in counseling is awkward at best. Our point is that for most clients, career information is not "over there" but is "here" and is part of the individual counseling process because it is a counseling intervention.

Variation 3: The Hardware Variation. This variation of the "separate from and not a part of the counseling process" theme suggests that the problem some counselors may have with career information resides in the "hardware" of the books, media, or career information delivery systems. In the case of computer-based career systems, these counselors focus on the hardware (the computer) at least initially, not on the information. Somehow the hardware is seen as foreign—as a cold intrusion in the warm individual counseling relationship. Thus the systems are not used. But if we remember that it is the information that is important, not the "hardware," then the "hardware" can be seen simply as the vehicle that delivers information to be used in individual counseling.

Variation 4: The It-Takes-Too-Long Variation. Variation 4 goes something like this: "Yes, I would like to use career information with clients, but it takes too long to use it" or "There is too much career information and it is too confusing to use" or "It takes too long to complete the computer-based career system, and, as a result, the counseling process is disrupted." The skillful use of career information often does take time, but, as a part of the individual counseling process, it is an appropriate and necessary use of time.

The Purposes of Career Information

Many years ago, Brayfield (1948) suggested that the purposes of using career information with clients were informational, readjustive, and motivational. Around the same time, Christensen (1949) identified three purposes: instructional, instrumental, and therapeutic. Rusalem (1954) stressed two purposes: exploration and verification. Authors such as Hoppock (1976), Norris, Hatch, Engelkes, and Winborn (1979), and Herr and Cramer (1988) suggested other variations on these themes. We subsume all of these purposes under two: educational and motivational.

Educational Purposes. In the counseling process, it is apparent that some clients' needs can best be met by providing them with career information immediately. Career information is used *to inform* these clients of educational, occupational, or other life-role alternatives. They have a solid foundation of career knowledge without distortion and there is little in the way of emotions involved. In such situations, the appropriate counselor response would be to share the required career information, always checking to see how the clients are processing the information. What connections do they make to past foundation knowledge? How do the clients relate the information to the goal they are working on? Super (1990, p. 254) suggested that this purpose of career information places the counselor in the role of facilitating career development: "Fostering career development means, in some cases, facilitating it, for sometimes people are self-directing, and merely facilitating with information, a suggestion, or a question that leads to clarification by the counselee is enough."

For other clients, however, the use of career information in individual counseling is not a matter of straightforward information sharing. Some clients have not had sufficient life experience to develop an adequate knowledge base. Prediger and Swaney (1985, p. 5) found, for example, that clients' interest inventory scores are more likely to be "in line with their subsequent occupations when they have had experiences in line with their predominant interests." Super (1990) made the same point, suggesting that scores on interest inventories will be misleading if people have inadequate foundation knowledge about themselves and the work world.

Thus, another purpose of career information in counseling is *to expand* clients' foundation knowledge about self, work, education, leisure, and other life roles as they unfold and interact over the life span. While they are gathering client information, it is imperative that counselors listen closely for the amount and nature of information clients have about themselves and about work, education, leisure, and other life roles. As we will see later in this chapter, an occupational card sort is a particularly useful strategy, as is the Life-Career Assessment. Both provide ways to identify the breadth, depth, and possible distortions in clients' career information foundation knowledge.

In addition to a lack of knowledge (many young people and adults as well are occupationally illiterate), you may find that some clients lack the organizers or "hooks" on which to hang the knowledge they have. Having such organizers is important, because they improve the retention and thus the use of career information: "The only way we can remember things is by having some bucket in which to put them. And so you've got to give them some kind of structure. It may be a skimpy bucket to start with, but as you put more in it, the bits become attached; they become a sort of network. And then you can hang things on the network" (Glaser, 1986, p. 2).

If this is the case, then helping clients learn to incorporate occupational and interest classification systems into their thinking can be very useful. For example, sharing with clients at appropriate times the classification systems of the *Guide for Occupational Exploration* (Employment and Training Administration, 1979), the *Dictionary of Occupational Titles* (Employment and Training Administration, 1977), and the Holland code system in the *Dictionary of Holland Occupational Codes* (Gottfredson and Holland, 1989) can be an important individual counseling intervention.

Listening closely in counseling for the amount and nature of career information that clients have available for use is important. Equally important, however, is listening for possible distortions that may be present in the career information and the organizers possessed by clients. What lenses or filters have they been using that may have precluded learning appropriate career information or that may have distorted what was learned? What defense mechanisms are in place? Are the clients using irrational beliefs or distorted thinking to guide daily living at home, school, or on the job? Are they making excuses? Thus, another educational purpose of information is to *correct* the biases and beliefs individuals have about themselves and their environment.

One reason clients may be distorting career information is the fear of taking responsibility. Acceptance of responsibility for decisions is one of the most difficult things we face in our lives. The counselor's awareness of the potential burden and threat that taking responsibility represents to clients is a prerequisite to dealing with resistance in a positive manner. In his work with clients, Low (1966, p. 279) discovered that anything sounds more hopeful and more comforting than the bleak prospect of having to undergo training in self-discipline: "Even brain tumors, mental ailments, and hereditary 'taints' are preferable to that dreadful indictment as being a weak character and needing training in self-control." Some pain is only temporary; however, the fear of being unable to perform hits directly at a client's sense of self-worth. This presents the ominous prospect of continual, everlasting pain. Insulation from and manipulation of career information, for example, become necessary for survival.

Defense mechanisms and sabotaged communication serve as safeguards of self-esteem. This allows for an evasion of work and other life tasks. It is always possible to collect more or less plausible reasons to justify escape from facing the challenges of life. We often do not realize what we are doing. Some strategies are intended to ensure against failure, exposure, or other catastrophes. The strategy used may have the effect of making it impossible for a client to meet an onerous responsibility—or at least it may delay the "moment of truth." Clients may try to disqualify themselves from a race they do not wish to run. If the race must be run, can failure be justified?

In addition, we are educated at an early age not to risk statements that might eventually be proved wrong or described as foolish. We learn how to avoid "owning" statements. Very often during a discussion, statements of obvious beliefs are prefaced with, "Don't you think . . . ?" We frequently use the words *you* and *it* to direct ownership away from ourselves in conversations. Owning is threatening. There is an advantage to mystifying situations so that there is always room for doubt and, therefore, justified inactivity. If the situation gets too threatening, one can always justify gracious withdrawal. Keeping communication incomplete allows for the freedom to do what one pleases.

In working with clients, counselors may hear statements

that Lewis and Gilhousen (1981) referred to as *career myths*. According to these authors, career myths are statements that reflect clients' thoughts about the career development process that are based on underlying irrational beliefs. Here are some typical client statements that they cite:

> "I am not sure if I want to do this the rest of my life."
> "I want to be sure that I don't have to change majors at midyear and lose my credits."
> "I think I had better be sure since I am deciding for the rest of my life" [p. 297].

As Lewis and Gilhousen point out, the irrational belief underlying such statements is, "I must be absolutely certain before I can act (make a decision, gather information, do anything that requires risk)" (p. 297). Such thinking creates a paradox. Clients must be sure before action can take place, but there is no way they can be sure unless they act first. The task is to help them become aware of the irrational beliefs they hold. As they become aware of these beliefs and their effects, counselors can then begin to introduce alternative, more rational beliefs for consideration. In the case of the preceding example, a more rational alternative belief might be: "I may not be sure; however, that does not mean that I cannot do something now. If I act now, I will be gaining information that will be important to me in decisions I will make in the future" (p. 297).

Another way to listen to and understand clients during counseling for career development is to identify distorted thinking. Distorted thinking involves the use of partial career information from which to draw conclusions, faulty perceptions, and inadequate or partial generalizations of career information and ideas. A list of twelve types of distorted thinking and their definitions, as developed by McKay, Davis, and Fanning (1981, p. 26), follows:

1. *Filtering:* You take the negative details and magnify them while filtering out all positive aspects of a situation.

2. *Polarized Thinking:* Things are black or white, good or bad. You have to be perfect or you're a failure. There is no middle ground.

3. *Overgeneralization:* You come to a general conclusion based on a single incident or piece of evidence. If something bad happens once you expect it to happen over and over again.

4. *Mind Reading:* Without their saying so, you know what people are feeling and why they act the way they do. In particular, you are able to divine how people are feeling toward you.

5. *Catastrophizing:* You expect disaster. You notice or hear about a problem and start "what if's: What if tragedy strikes? What if it happens to you?"

6. *Personalization:* Thinking that everything people do or say is some kind of reaction to you. You also compare yourself to others, trying to determine who's smarter, better looking, etc.

7. *Control Fallacies:* If you feel externally controlled, you see yourself as helpless, a victim of fate. The fallacy of internal control has you responsible for the pain and happiness of everyone around you.

8. *Fallacy of Fairness:* You feel resentful because you think you know what's fair but other people won't agree with you.

9. *Blaming:* You hold other people responsible for your pain, or take the other tack and blame yourself for every problem or reversal.

10. *Shoulds:* You have a list of ironclad rules about how you and other people should act. People who break the rules anger you and you feel guilty if you violate the rules.

11. *Emotional Reasoning:* You believe that what you feel must be true—automatically. If you

feel stupid and boring, then you must be stupid and boring.

12. *Fallacy of Change:* You expect that other people will change to suit you if you just pressure or cajole them enough. You need to change people because your hopes for happiness seem to depend entirely on them.

Another way of understanding, interpreting, and working with client behavior exhibited during counseling for career development is to use the concept of excuses. Snyder, Higgins, and Stucky (1983, p. 4) defined excuses as "explanations or actions that lessen the negative implications of an actor's performance, thereby maintaining a positive image for yourself and others."

In the counseling process, it may become apparent that clients' behavior is different from what they or others expected. How are such discrepancies explained? Sometimes clients use excuses hoping that they will serve as logical and legitimate reasons for their behavior. Snyder, Higgins, and Stucky (1983) listed some common excuses as follows:

Lessening Apparent Responsibility
(I didn't do it.)

Denial
Alibis
Blaming

Reframing Performances
(It's really not so bad.)

Minimization
Justification
Derogation

Lessening Transformed Responsibility
(Yes, but . . .)
I couldn't help it.
I didn't mean it.
It wasn't really me.

Motivational Purposes. Career information can be used to *stimulate* some clients into action—that is, to develop in them a readiness to explore educational, occupational, and other life-career options. The goal is to extend hope to them about possibilities where no hope may have existed before. Counselors should try to create in them a vision of possible futures, to help them use the opportunity structure as it exists, not as they may distort it.

In other cases, career information can be used to *challenge* clients' current beliefs about themselves (self talk) and the work world (occupational talk). As understanding of clients unfolds during the information-gathering phase of counseling, counselors should listen for the schemas clients are using to represent their knowledge of self, others, and their worlds. It is important to do this, because as clients draw on their foundation knowledge, "Recall will be distorted to fit the schemas that a [client] has" (Anderson, 1990, p. 178). Career information can be utilized to help clients transform the schemas they are currently using into schemas that more adequately represent the reality of the work world.

Finally, in still other cases, career information can be used to *confirm* the direction that clients are taking. And career information gives them the language they need to communicate effectively during the job search. Their job-seeking skills are enhanced because they have appropriate real-world vocabulary.

The Use of Career Information

With the major purposes of using career information with clients in mind, the next task is to determine clients' knowledge of and need for career information. There are many ways to accomplish this task. One way is to confront clients directly: "What do you know and how and when did you learn it?"

Sometimes, however, it is useful to use an indirect approach that allows clients to have more personal control over the inquiry process. The occupational card sort is an example of a technique that provides clients with personal control but that at the same time mandates an active role for counselors. Pritchard (1962) reminded us of the need for personalizing the inquiry process several decades ago when he stated that we should "personalize" or "custom-tailor" the bridges of understanding between one's self and one's work life. To accomplish this, occupational titles can be used because they involve common, everyday terms, and even though clients may have stereotypical ideas about occupations, information can be obtained about how they look at themselves, others, and the world they live in. Occupational titles are stimuli from which we can gain understandings concerning their current knowledge of and possible needs for career information.

Occupational Card Sort Administration

There are many ways to have clients complete an occupational card sort. If counselors have purchased a commercially available one, they should read the manual and follow the directions given. For purposes of this chapter, we will illustrate one way to use an occupational card sort to help us and our clients gain information about their knowledge of and need for career information.

Before having clients sort the cards, however—whatever the procedure to be followed—counselors should be sure to explain the process and the reason they are using it. Then clients will know what to expect and will probably be more relaxed. It is important to emphasize that the major focus of the card sort is not to select the "right" occupation, but rather to help clients explore their foundation knowledge about self, others, and the world—including the work world. Based on the information that emerges, the appropriate types of career information and their use can then be determined.

The card sort should be administered in a location where counselor and client can work undisturbed. A table or desk is necessary. The card sort materials should be arranged so that the client sits next to the counselor. This arrangement will facilitate communication. It also will help if there are worksheets to fill out and discuss.

Step 1: Sorting the Cards

The first step in the process is to have the client sort the occupational cards. The counselor can read—or can have the client read—the following directions:

> In front of you is a pack of cards. On each card is an occupational title. Some of the occupations will be of interest to you and others will not be. Go through the cards and sort them into three piles: Like, Dislike, or Undecided. For all cards, assume that you have the ability for the occupation. The Like pile are occupations you might actually choose, that have some specific appeal to you, or that seem appropriate for you. The Dislike pile are occupations that you are not interested in, that you would not choose, or that do not seem appropriate for a person like you. The Undecided pile are those occupations that you have both Likes and Dislikes for, or ones that you are not sure if you would like or not.

Step 2: Identifying and Understanding Themes

After the client has sorted the appropriate grouping of cards, the next step is to talk about reasons behind choosing or not choosing a particular occupation. Clients often are not aware of the reasons for their choices or why they like or dislike an occupation. Becoming more conscious of their underlying reasoning will help them identify the themes that guide their life-styles. It also will assist the counselor in determining their career information knowledge and needs.

The counselor should help the client get started in theme identification by reading or paraphrasing the instructions. In the sample instructions that follow, there is an example of occupational choices and the possible reasons for these choices. It is useful to point out that often there is more than one reason for liking an occupation.

In order to better consider the reasons (themes) for choosing certain occupational titles, begin by thinking about the first occupational card in the Like pile. Explain the reason or reasons why you like it. Do this for each card in the Like pile. Make sure each reason is specific. For example, if working with people is a reason, what specifically do you like? Would you prefer working with people by instructing, persuading, leading, or being led by them? Another example might be working with objects or things. What kinds of things? Do you prefer office machines, tools, factory assembly, or heavy equipment? Some examples for liking certain occupations might be:

Occupational Titles	*Reasons*
Physician, psychologist, lawyer	Prestigious
	Pays well
Physician, engineer	Working with people,
Lawyer, insurance broker	persuading

Sometimes an occupational title will stimulate two or more reasons. For example, the reasons for choosing physician may be "prestige" and "pays well." Now, begin giving reasons for choices in the Like pile.

If the client has difficulty and cannot describe any reasons, the counselor should explore the reasons behind a particular choice. Questions such as the following may help elicit this information:

- What attracts you to this occupation?
- What parts of it would you like best?

- Would you enjoy the opportunity to work with numbers (people, heavy equipment, or whatever is appropriate)?
- Would you like it because you're indoors (or outdoors)?

Questions such as these usually will help a client get started. Or the counselor may be able to personalize the discussion by briefly sharing his or her reasons for liking a particular occupation.

As the client identifies reasons, the counselor should write the reasons in the Likes column on a worksheet divided into two columns as follows:

Finding Themes

Likes	*Dislikes*

The idea is to place a slash mark next to each reason mentioned. If it is mentioned again, another slash mark should be added. In this way, a running tally can be kept for every reason mentioned. For example, the Likes column on the "Finding Themes" worksheet might look like this:

Finding Themes

Likes	*Dislikes*
Prestigious **11**	
Pays well **1111**	
Working with people **1** (teaching)	

The next step is to have the client identify the reasons for placing occupational titles in the Dislikes pile.

Now, think about the cards in the Dislikes pile and explain the reasons for not choosing these occupations.

The reasons mentioned for placing the cards in that pile are recorded in the Dislikes column on the "Finding

Themes" worksheet in the same manner as before. The Dislikes column might look like this:

Finding Themes

Likes	*Dislikes*	
	Working with machines	1111
	Menial work	1111
	Too much structure	1

The next step in the process of determining reasons or
themes involves using the "Understanding Themes" worksheet. On this worksheet the reasons or themes that were identified on the "Finding Themes" worksheet are rank ordered.
To review quickly, the completed "Finding Themes" worksheet from our previous example was filled out as follows:

Finding Themes

Likes		*Dislikes*	
Prestigious	11	Working with machines	1111
Pays well	1111	Menial work	1111
Working with people (teaching)	1	Too much structure	1

On the "Understanding Themes" worksheet the reasons
or themes are rank ordered. By ranking these reasons, priori-
ties can be established. The first step is to rank order the
reasons in the Likes column. These should be in descending
order, from those with the greatest number of slash marks to
those with the fewest. This is how the "Understanding
Themes" worksheet will begin to look:

Understanding Themes

Likes	*Dislikes*
Pays well _____	_____
Prestigious _____	_____
Working with people (teaching) _____	_____

After the Likes have been rank ordered, counselor and client can fill in the Dislikes column. Of the reasons mentioned for the Dislikes column, some of them will be direct opposites of the reasons mentioned in the Likes column. The first reason in the example, "pays well," does not have an opposite; however, "prestigious" and "working with people (teaching)" do. The opposites for these, respectively, are "menial work" and "working with machines." This is how the worksheet should look now:

Understanding Themes

Likes	Dislikes
Pays well	
Prestigious	Menial work
Working with people (teaching)	Working with machines
	Too much structure
	Outdoor work

Readers will note that "too much structure" and "outdoor work" were also mentioned as Dislikes. Even though these reasons do not have direct opposites in the Likes column, they are still included, but on lines just below the other Dislikes.

To complete the worksheet, the counselor should fill in reasons for which direct opposites were not given. This can be done by asking the client what the opposites are. The purpose of filling in opposites is to find out more about the reasons behind the client's choices. In the preceding examples, "indoor work," "independent," and "doesn't pay well" were not mentioned as original reasons. However, this part of the step brings them into focus. A focus on opposites may result in insight for the client. The following is an example of what the worksheet might look like when it is completed:

Understanding Themes

Likes	*Dislikes*
Pays well	Doesn't pay well
Prestigious	Menial work
Working with people (teaching)	Working with machines
Independent	Too much structure
Indoor work	Outdoor work

In this example, the individual responded with "doesn't pay well" as an opposite of "pays well," "independent" was the opposite of "too much structure," and "indoor work" was the opposite of "outdoor work." Sometimes the client may not be able to come up with an opposite. It is not necessary to fill one in if he or she does not have one.

At this point, the counselor may wish to spend some time discussing the reasons or themes with the client. This is an optional step; however, if time permits, it can be beneficial. Here are some examples of some types of questions the counselor could ask:

1. Explain what meaning each of the reasons has for you.
2. If you could not have an ideal job with all the reasons listed, which two or three would you have to have?
3. Describe someone you know who has a job with some or all of the reasons listed.

Some individuals will be able to discuss their reasons spontaneously, while others will need more structure. Question 1 above may need more structure than the other two questions. Questions to facilitate that discussion might include the following:

1. Explain what meaning each of the reasons has for you.
    *   "Pays well" means one thing to one person and another to someone else. What would be considered

good pay and what would be considered poor pay
for you?

- Does "indoor work" mean never being outdoors?
- Who do you know who has a "prestigious" job?
  What about the job makes it important and valued?
- For the reason "working with people (teaching),"
  what kinds of subjects, with what age group, and
  with what sort of population?
- How "independent" would you like to be? Do you
  want to be your own boss or would you prefer to
  have a boss that likes some structure but not a lot?

What Can We Learn?

The use of an occupational card sort evokes the life-career
themes that clients use to guide their self and occupational
behavior. At the same time, this process reveals the career
information foundation knowledge clients have and the possible distortions that may be taking place. Occupational titles
are the common everyday terms that supply the stimuli, while
the card sort process supplies the setting for the process to
unfold. This process is similar to the one that was anticipated
by Pritchard (1962, p. 667) when he wrote: "Particular occupational stimuli should be selected and used, with the counselee's participation, for their apparent specific utilities (as in
the case of tests) in helping to elicit, explore, and clarify his
needs, values, attitudes, aspirations, expectations, and work-
role and self perceptions."

Two Cases

To shed more light on the use of career information in individual counseling, we present two cases. The flow of these
cases follows the framework for counseling for career development presented in Chapter One. Remember that that framework provides a systematic and comprehensive way to elicit
and make explicit clients' internal thoughts and feelings
about their goals and concerns. It provides an external struc-

ture on which to sort out, arrange, and display them. It also provides cues as to when to use career information with clients, because timing (the readiness of clients for information) is crucial. Finally, it offers cues as to what types of career information should be used.

The Case of Ted
by *Robert Hansen**

Ted, an eighteen-year-old high school senior, approached his guidance counselor and asked to be given a pass to see her later in the day. He wanted to talk with her about his dropping out of school and taking a full-time job. Ted comes from a family in which both parents work at the local electronics manufacturing plant. His only brother had graduated from high school two years ago and enlisted in the Navy.

Session 1

The *goals* were as follows:

- To listen to and understand Ted's concerns
- To begin generating, with Ted, some career alternatives
- To encourage Ted to continue his active thinking and planning

The major *elements* were as follows: relationship development and problem/goal identification.

Counselor preparation included reviewing Ted's student file prior to his visit, paying particular attention to notes from previous advisement sessions, previous grades, and any other relevant information.

The *interview session* unfolded as follows. Ted came to the guidance office during his morning study hour and went directly into his counselor's office. Ted told her that he was

*Robert Hansen is Director, Counseling Center, Westminster College, Fulton, Missouri.

very worried about his future. He said he was not sure if he wanted to stay in school and finish out the year or take a job recently offered to him by a local auto body shop owner. The counselor listened intently as Ted indicated his growing lack of motivation in school, his inability to complete homework assignments, and his family's financial trouble. He was wondering whether, by getting a job and making some money, most of his worries would be over.

Ted had spoken with his mother the previous evening but was afraid to say anything to his father because he knew exactly what his father would say. His father had always encouraged both his sons to finish school and, if possible, to go on to college. Ted's mother did not say no but encouraged him to stay in high school for the remaining eight months until graduation.

The job offered to Ted was one he had hoped to get the previous summer. He had worked for the same company during his junior year as part of a cooperative education program and had enjoyed it so much that he applied for a full-time job that became available at the beginning of last summer. Although a more experienced man was given the job, the owner, Mr. Peters, had told Ted he could use the shop's tools and other equipment to work on his own car. Auto body work was something Ted enjoyed doing, and he felt he had considerable skill in this area. More than once he had considered this as a full-time career field.

The counselor discussed with Ted the immediacy of the decision. Ted thought that Mr. Peters wanted somebody to start soon but said that he would ask Mr. Peters tomorrow. The counselor encouraged Ted not to make a hasty decision and to give himself some time to weigh the options and then make a well-thought-out plan.

Although disappointed by not being given a yes or no answer, Ted agreed to meet with the counselor a few times before making up his mind. The counselor told him that making a good decision was going to take patience and some hard work. Ted agreed to do his best. Together they made a list of things Ted would do before they met again: (1) talk

with Mr. Peters to find out how much time he had to make a
decision and (2) get a little more information about some of
the career fields he had been considering.

Before leaving, Ted expressed some concern as to his
father's feelings about his upcoming decision. He wondered
if he should tell him now or just go ahead and make the
decision without telling him in advance. They agreed that no
easy solution was possible and decided that telling his father
was the best thing to do, but when and how to do it would
still need to be determined. They decided to discuss it again
at their next meeting in two days.

As Ted left, the counselor showed him the career information library she had been developing next to her office.
She pointed out two books in particular that she wanted him
to use in getting more information about potential career
fields: the *Occupational Outlook Handbook* (*OOH*) and the
Guide for Occupational Exploration. To illustrate how helpful
these books could be, the counselor had Ted look up auto
body repair and skim the information in the *OOH.* He found
the occupational information for auto body repairers under
the major cluster called "mechanics, installers, and repairers."
The two-page description was next to descriptions of similar
kinds of occupations, automotive mechanics and aircraft
mechanics/engine specialists. He quickly skimmed the material and indicated that he was particularly interested in
reading the sections on "employment" and "training, other
qualifications, and advancement."

The counselor also had Ted take a quick look at the
Guide for Occupational Exploration. The format was quite
different from the *OOH,* and he needed a little help from the
counselor to understand its organization. Once he understood
it, Ted found a long list of auto body–related job titles clustered under the work group heading of "craft technology
05.05" and more specifically under the subgrouping called
"metal fabrication and repair 05.05.06." The counselor took
a minute to explain the six-digit coding system that would
help Ted use the book on his own. She also showed him that
in addition to the listing of occupationally related job titles,

this reference book provided information about interests, aptitudes, adaptabilities, and other characteristics for each occupational area.

Because Ted had taken the Armed Services Vocational Aptitude Battery (ASVAB) earlier in the year and had discussed the results with the counselor, she let him check out the *Military Career Guide*, which provides extensive information on what military occupational specializations are available to service personnel and to which civilian occupational areas these skills will transfer. Ted found that the military services also have some jobs related to auto body work. Although the various branches of the service call them by different titles, they generally have the same prerequisite academic background, physical requirements, and experience needed to enter that field. The counselor also showed Ted additional civilian training information relating to auto body repair contained in the state career information delivery system. Although some of the state information overlapped with other reference books, it included local and regional job vacancy projections along with a comprehensive list of training opportunities in the state. Ted checked out these materials and agreed to meet with the counselor in two days, after completing the necessary tasks.

Turning now to *case analysis and conceptualization,* Ted is typical of many students who are not feeling motivated or successful in school and who consider dropping out when something new or exciting becomes available. The fact that Ted came to the counselor was a sign that he knew it was a serious decision, one not to be taken lightly. Establishing a time frame with Ted allowed the counselor to do two things: (1) it promoted the idea that good planning takes time and (2) it removed some immediate pressure from Ted, who was thinking he had to decide that same day.

Having reviewed Ted's file in advance, the counselor knew that Ted's grades had been falling, yet his test scores were generally average or above average. Motivating Ted to take an active role in making this decision started by having him look up career information in the reference materials mentioned earlier. The OOH would provide a good overview of general career areas and specific occupational groupings, and the *Guide for Occupational Exploration* would help him see how his career interests, aptitudes, and temperament translate into potential career fields. This procedure would also let them use the General Aptitude Test Battery (GATB) scores that Ted had taken the previous year as a way of cross-referencing possible occupational clusters. Ted's continued interest in the military also led the counselor to provide basic information about military occupational specializations and the civilian jobs they might lead to on discharge from the service.

In general, the counselor hoped to show Ted that career planning was not an activity limited to the counselor's office but was something he could learn to do on his own once he understood the process and the availability of good career information.

Session 2

The *goals* were as follows:

- To review what Ted had accomplished on his own since his first visit
- To share with Ted his previous interest inventory and aptitude scores
- To discuss Ted's concern over telling his father and develop some strategy for Ted to implement

The major *elements* were as follows: problem/goal clarification and specification.

Counselor preparation included carefully reviewing Ted's student file and analyzing the results of various tests that he had taken as a high school student. The counselor also checked with his current instructors (with Ted's permission) as to his current progress and his ability to complete the covered work.

Ted came to the second *interview session* with a worried look and reported that Mr. Peters would be needing a replacement a week earlier than he had anticipated. Ted was concerned that he did not have enough time to make a good decision, but he was assured by the counselor that they would do everything possible to make the decision easier within the reduced time schedule. She reinforced the idea that the most important consideration at this time was to continue making progress by gathering good information on the alternatives available.

Ted indicated he had visited the career information section of the guidance office after school the previous day and had found the *OOH* and the *Guide for Occupational Exploration* to be quite helpful in providing basic information about the career areas he had been considering. From what he read, obtaining an initial job would be possible without additional education or training, but if he ever wanted to advance to a management position or own his own business, finishing his high school education and receiving some formal technical training would be extremely helpful.

He also found the *Military Career Guide* to be reassuring in that it provided job descriptions for the various branches of the military that were very similar to the kind of work he enjoyed doing. He was also quite pleased that basic material about the armed services at the beginning of the book informed him about the steps in the enlistment process, the training programs available, and other general characteristics of military life.

The counselor then discussed with Ted the importance of interests and abilities in making a sound career decision and shared with him his scores on tests taken earlier in the year. The interest inventory indicated strong interests in the "mechanical," "leading/influencing," and "business detail" areas. His aptitude scores were generally average except for the mechanical area, which was in the 90th percentile. The ASVAB results indicated Ted had a very high score on the Mechanical and Crafts composite. The counselor also described the Holland categories to Ted and together they agreed that the "Realistic" category described him best, with the "Enterprising" category being the next closest description.

Despite Ted's success in finding summer and part-time employment after school, he was worried about his ability to land a good long-term job. The counselor showed Ted some additional materials that described future job trends and general employment projections. These labor market publications provided Ted with a general view of what would be available in the future. In general, employment for auto body work would be steady in the future, with no predicted increase or decrease. Opportunities in the military for auto body workers would also be steady.

Ted was committed to telling his father soon, that same night if possible, but was frightened of what his father's response might be. With the counselor, Ted practiced different ways of bringing the subject up, and after using several different approaches decided on one specific way of communicating his present situation. They ended the session by setting up a time to meet the next day to discuss his father's reaction.

It is appropriate to offer *case analysis and conceptualization* at this point. Ted was using the resource material to good advantage, but had not researched the occupational areas in any depth. However, he did find useful information that led him to make the conclusion that advancement within occupational fields depended in part on the amount of training and/or education received.

It was obvious during the interview that Ted was continuing to question the advantages of going to work full time. He now saw the advantages of leaving school as short-term ones and wondered where the job at Mr. Peters's business would eventually lead. His interest in becoming a military officer, business owner, or other type of manager also led him to favor staying in school.

Session 3

The *goals* were as follows:

- To discuss the previous night's results
- To look again at the alternatives available to Ted at this time

- To discuss the basic strengths and weaknesses of each alternative
- To discuss the "next steps" in making a decision

The major *elements* were as follows: problem/goal resolution and taking action.

No *counselor preparation* was required.

In the *interview session,* the counselor explored with Ted what were now seen to be the options in front of him. These were as follows:

- Stay in school and go into auto body repair after graduation
- Stay in school, then go to a technical school with auto body repair training
- Stay in school and enter the military after graduation
- Stay in school, then try to get into a community college and take business courses in hopes of going into business for himself
- Quit school now and take the job with Mr. Peters

As they discussed each option's strengths and weaknesses, it was obvious that quitting school had many disadvantages and that finishing high school would be difficult but important. The next question was to explore the options associated with staying in school. Ted was concerned about his study habits and lack of motivation. After exploring reasons for both, the counselor agreed to continue working with Ted on these concerns.

Based on the information he read in the career resource books, Ted did not believe that going into auto body work without any additional training would provide the job security or chances of advancement that were important to him. This led to a discussion focusing on the pros and cons of going to a vocational-technical school or attending the local community college.

As they discussed these options, the counselor pointed out how the time frame had changed from a decision that needed to be made almost immediately to a decision that now could be made over a period of a few months, when new information gathering and career planning could take place. Ted was relieved that he really would not have to make a final decision for a while, because this would give him time to talk with his family and the admissions officers of the schools he was considering. It would also give him time to talk at length with the local military recruiters and his brother about the different options associated with military service.

Case analysis and conceptualization indicate Ted would make good use of his time. Together with the counselor, Ted decided to use the next few months to locate information about the schools and their curricula, talk with the schools' placement officers about their ability to find employment for their students, and then talk to the schools' academic advisers to identify possible courses.

He also planned to visit the recruiting office of each armed services branch and receive as much information as possible on the different options. He planned on using the *Military Career Guide* throughout the remaining months of high school in weighing the programs offered by each branch. The recruiters would help him in this process. He was especially interested in his chances of becoming an officer with his educational background and what he could do to improve his chances. Ted arranged to meet with the counselor later in the month to discuss his career plans again.

Session 4

The *goals* were as follows:

- To review what has happened since Ted's last visit
- To discuss additional information collected by Ted
- To make Ted aware of other career exploration activities
- To review academic progress

The major *elements* were as follows: evaluation and goal resolution.

Counselor preparation involved evaluating Ted's academic progress.

In the *interview session,* the counselor and Ted discussed his satisfaction with the decision to stay in school that he had made three weeks earlier. Ted stated that staying in school was a good choice and that his performance in class has improved. He thought this progress was due to a clearer idea of his reasons for being in school.

Together they reviewed the information Ted had gathered regarding vocational-technical training and military opportunities. The counselor helped Ted evaluate the information, particularly the separation of "recruitment" information from hard facts.

Ted told the counselor that his plans included finishing high school and taking a few more industrial arts classes during the second semester. During that second semester he would decide between voc-tech school and the military, since by then he would have thoroughly researched the opportunities in each.

The counselor commended Ted on following through on his action plan, and she inquired about his parents' reaction to his decision. He told her that having all the information about the options made it easier to talk with them and that they fully supported his plan.

The counselor also told Ted about some other opportunities to explore potential careers, including a computerized career exploration system and a career exploration group that she was beginning for students needing help in exploring their options. Ted assured her that if his plans fell through, he would be back to talk with her and maybe use the computer or join the group.

Before Ted left her office, the counselor encouraged him to continue exploring career options, and she emphasized that career development is a never-ending process.

Turning to *case analysis and conceptualization,* the information research paid dividends by providing Ted with vital information he could use in making his decision. The occupational descriptions helped him compare his interests and skills with various career fields, the employment projections helped him plan with some hope that a job in auto body repair would be available to him on completion of his training, and the training/education/advancement information helped him to plan for his preparation to enter his chosen field. Because advancement in his career was very important to Ted, the information helped him to see that without additional training or education, his chances of owning his own business were limited.

Establishing a new time frame with new goals helped Ted to put his dilemma in perspective. For once he felt he had some breathing room and had time to research his options and eventually narrow them down even more. The immediate challenge for Ted, and for those supporting him at home and at school, was to change his attitude toward school. The counselor agreed to work with him on his study skills and general motivation; however, it would be Ted who would need to take on the responsibility of finishing his assignments and completing all graduation requirements.

The counselor and Ted ended on a positive note, even though a final, specific decision regarding his future career had not been made. Having the opportunity to check in with the counselor on a regular basis provided some continued involvement with the counseling process. The career resource books were constantly available to him as he learned that current and accurate information was indispensable in making good career decisions.

The Case of Paulette
by Mary Heppner*

Paulette felt that she "fell into" teaching as a career. Having grown up in a traditional family, she had not been exposed to many other fields. She was socialized to think in gender-stereotyped ways. Teaching, social work, and nursing were seen by her family as a way out of the blue-collar life of many

*Mary Heppner is Assistant Director, Career Planning and Placement Center, University of Missouri, Columbia.

of her neighbors. The career made sense at the time. She felt it was important to be a role model for young people. Teaching would provide an excellent vehicle for doing so. Paulette's strength was communication. She liked teaching concepts, and working with the students on an individual basis was especially rewarding. For the first few years, teaching seemed to provide what Paulette needed in a job.

After her marriage to Michael, however, Paulette left the medium-sized town in which she had been working and moved to a big city. She got a job in a large high school. Her experience was not nearly so positive. Basically, Paulette felt unappreciated and unsupported by her administration. She had difficulty with the students—especially around the issue of discipline. When she attempted to take a strong stand, she felt that her principal did not back her up. The students were also apathetic. Far from the view of herself as a professional role model, she felt she got little respect at all. On and off for four years, Paulette had considered leaving teaching. But then summer would draw near and she would rationalize that maybe next year would be better. It was not until a financial crisis hit—Michael lost his job—that Paulette seriously considered a career change. They simply could not make it on her salary. Now would be a good time to change— but to what? Paulette had really only considered teaching; she had not thought of doing anything else. And more important, she was not sure she *could* do anything else. She had read about people her age and older who had made dramatic career changes, but she had never pictured herself as one who would.

Paulette had heard a woman talk at one of her church meetings about changing careers. The woman worked for a community agency that helped people plan careers. She decided to call and schedule an appointment.

Session 1

The *goals* were as follows:

- To determine if the goals of the client and the goals of her employer are congruent

- To develop the beginnings of a relationship: trust, rapport, sharing
- To make explicit the counselor and client's roles
- To begin the self-exploration process
- To conduct a personal and work history to determine relevant information
- To gain an understanding of what preexisting information and knowledge bases the client has regarding herself, the work world, and the career transition process

The major *elements* were as follows: relationship development and problem/goal identification.

No counselor preparation was required.

Paulette arrived early for the *interview session* at the New Horizons Center. She felt excited but also a little apprehensive. She had never worked on career planning before, and she was really not sure what to expect. She was hoping that her counselor would be able to test her and tell her what career she would be best suited for. Perhaps the counselor could identify a career that would use all her unique skills in a way she had never considered before.

But together with this hope and optimism came the thoughts, "Why am I here?" "I should just stay with teaching, where I have a secure job." "I don't think I am one of those people who can make a career change successfully." As she was waiting, the receptionist encouraged her to browse through some of the resources in the career library. Diane, her counselor, came out to greet her.

Paulette liked Diane from the start. They were both about the same age. Diane asked what precipitated Paulette's visit. Paulette described her dilemma. Diane asked Paulette what she hoped to get by coming to the New Horizons Center.

Paulette said tentatively, "Well, I was hoping you could give me a test to determine what I'm best at and what I could find happiness in doing."

Diane responded that she was not a mind reader and did not have a crystal ball. She explained that some form of assessment might be a helpful vehicle to start her thinking about other career fields, but that a test, in and of itself, would not provide a magic answer.

Through this initial conversation, Diane was able to help Paulette understand what the New Horizons Center could and could not do. Diane explained that the center helped people examine themselves: their values, interests, abilities, and skills. The center had many career information resource materials that would help Paulette learn about career fields. Diane said she could also help Paulette learn about résumé writing, interviewing skills, and active job-hunting strategies. But the center could not find the perfect job for Paulette, write her résumé for her, or line up job interviews. Those responsibilities were Paulette's. Paulette started to get a clearer picture of what would be involved in this career planning process. It sounded like a lot of work, but also like an interesting and revealing way to learn more about herself and the world of work.

First, Diane explained that in order to help Paulette with her career planning, she needed to get to know her better, and would try to do so by asking a variety of questions regarding herself, her husband, her work, and the like. Diane explained that her perspective on career planning was that it is really *life planning:* "I don't believe it is possible, or even desirable, to separate career counseling from the personal or emotional aspects of life. I find that people's work is so integral to their overall feelings of self-esteem and identity that it is critical to effective career planning to consider these aspects as well. Career transitions, in particular, affect the lives of many significant people in the changer's life. That is, one person changing in a system will precipitate impact in ways never expected. Because of this close interconnection between work and the rest of one's life, I believe that any of these issues are 'fair game' in these sessions. If you have worries or fears about anything, feel free to bring them up."

With this said, Diane went on to ask Paulette about her childhood, her parents and other early role models, her interests growing up, how these early interests had been reinforced by family members in gender-specific occupations, important "trigger points" in her life, how her husband's loss of employment was affecting her, how she typically dealt with stress, and how she typically made decisions. From her years of experience, Diane knew this type of interview needed to be conducted in an informal and conversational way. Clients must never feel interrogated by such questions, but rather must feel the counselor's sincere and genuine interest in helping them.

Paulette and Diane also began talking about Paulette's reasons for wanting to leave teaching. Diane helped Paulette organize her thoughts by jotting down "reasons I like teaching" and "reasons I dislike teaching." As Paulette talked, Diane wrote appropriate notes in each column. She also probed, pushing Paulette to be more specific about both her likes and dislikes. For example, Paulette made the statement, "I have a great deal of difficulty with discipline and it is the most unsatisfactory part of my job." Diane probed: "Give me an example of when it was difficult." "What made it difficult?" "Who did you have to reprimand?" Diane used these specific examples to look for general themes.

During this time, Diane was also assessing the preexisting information with which Paulette came to counseling. This entailed carefully listening, but also asking questions around three specific domains: information Paulette was bringing to counseling regarding herself, the work world, and the career transition process. Did it seem like Paulette was motivated? How much did she believe in her ability to make a career change successfully? How much information did Paulette have about occupational options? Was she operating under gender-role stereotypes or faulty information? Has Paulette had role models who have gone through the career transition process successfully? What does it mean to her to make a career change? Using her sensitivity and counseling skills, Diane's objective in this process was to "get inside Paulette's head" and understand how she was *thinking and reasoning* about the career change.

Through this conversation, both Diane and Paulette had a clearer understanding of the reasons for change. Diane explained that the next session would entail more of this self-exploration process. She emphasized that assessing Paulette's interests, skills, and work values was the first step. Paulette agreed, but was a bit resistant: "I don't have any skills; I teach—that's one skill—but I've never really developed any others."

Diane responded that Paulette was selling herself short. She explained that everyone has skills, but few people can identify these skills exactly. Through two homework assignments, Diane said Paulette would gain more knowledge about her skills. She asked Paulette to write about five positive life experiences in which she had felt good about herself and the skills she had used. These experiences could be from her personal or professional life. Diane emphasized that Paulette should make the experiences as specific as possible. For example, Paulette had done some fundraising for her church. Diane asked her to think of one specific fundraiser and what her own specific role had been in the project. After Paulette had written about these five experiences, Diane directed her to use a skills checklist and indicate which skills had been used in each activity.

The second homework assignment was to take Holland's Self-Directed Search (SDS) as a gauge of basic interest patterns. Diane gave a description of Holland's typology and asked that the Self-Directed Search be completed by the next session.

Case analysis and conceptualization are appropriate at this point. Diane saw Paulette as being motivated but not as having a strong belief in her ability to make a career change successfully. She saw Paulette as being somewhat externally oriented, wanting someone else to tell her what to do. Paulette seemed naive about both what she and the work world had to offer. From Paulette's history, Diane realized how limited her information had been when she made her initial career choice, and how little that information base had expanded in the ensuing years. She also recognized that Paulette had many strengths. She had excellent communication skills, was poised, and most of all was truly a likable person.

Session 2

The *goals* were as follows:

- To examine Paulette's skills assessment
- To examine Paulette's SDS in order to determine basic interest patterns
- To begin a tentative list of possible occupational areas
- To expose Paulette to the career library
- To assess the way the client was thinking and reasoning about herself, the work world, and the career change process
- To assess how the client was encoding or "making personal meaning" out of the information she was receiving from the assessment exercises

The major *elements* were as follows: problem/goal clarification and specification.

Counselor preparation included reviewing case notes from the last session and developing a plan for strategically assisting Paulette with her belief in her ability and her perceptions of internal control.

Paulette came to the *interview session* armed with her skills assessment and SDS. She handed them to Diane. Diane handed them back to her, saying, "Tell me what you learned about yourself from these instruments, Paulette."

Through this simple exchange, Diane again emphasized a point she had made in her first session—that Paulette was in charge of her own learning and that Diane was a counselor and facilitator, not a fortune-teller. Also, by presenting her own self-assessment, Paulette was learning the language of how to describe herself, her skills, and her interests. This would not only be important in future informational and job interviews, but in general would help increase her self-esteem and confidence.

Paulette was a bit taken back, but she began. From the skills experience she learned that she did in fact have skills— a lot of them. Through Diane's probing she discovered that there were patterns to these skills. For example, in each of the experiences she had used language and communication skills, organizational skills, and management skills. In three of the five she had used performing and leadership skills. She found that in the experiences she listed, she tended to be working with people in an organizing, teaching, and leadership role. She discovered that she really liked being in charge and being creative in front of people. She liked thinking of unique ways of getting her point across.

Paulette's SDS showed her interests to be social, enterprising, conventional. She very much agreed with that assessment of herself. She saw herself as verbal, liking to work with people, and often had been described as being persuasive and showing leadership ability. She did possess a number of conventional skills and interests as well. She saw herself as highly organized and attending well to details.

Diane helped Paulette look for areas of consistency and conflict between the skills inventory and the SDS. By examining both instruments, Paulette got a much better idea of her skills and interests. The two of them were able to come up with a list of eight occupations that they both felt were worthy of further exploration: director of a social service agency, employment interviewer, YWCA director, training and development coordinator, adult education instructor, personnel director, hotel manager, and insurance salesperson.

After reviewing the results of the skills and interests assessments, Diane took some time to process with Paulette what meaning she was deriving from the new information. She wanted to understand what Paulette had encoded about this information, how it was fitting into her preexisting knowledge bases, and generally what impact this information was having on how she was perceiving herself, the work world, and the career transition process. In Diane's language, she was assessing whether Paulette's cognitive structure or "schema" had changed, given the infusion of new information.

From this conversation she learned that Paulette had never realized how many skills she had and that this was really increasing her self-confidence. She also learned that

Paulette was feeling overwhelmed by the choices; she had never thought of herself in these roles, knew nothing about them, and thus felt fearful. Diane normalized these fears and reassured her that there were a number of ways to get the information she needed.

After talking about what kinds of information Paulette needed about these career areas, Diane gave her a tour of the career resource center. Diane particularly focused on two resources: The *Occupational Outlook Handbook (OOH)* and the *Dictionary of Occupational Titles (DOT)*. Diane gave Paulette instructions on how to use both resources. She also encouraged Paulette to explore occupations in the *DOT* that were closely related to the occupations on her list of eight.

Paulette's homework this week was to research these eight occupations and to add a few more occupations to her list. Diane instructed her to take notes on each, and to spend some time reflecting on how each of these occupations might fit Paulette's values, interests, and abilities. Diane told her that she wanted Paulette to become familiar enough with these occupations that she could report on each at next week's session.

Along with this exercise, which really focuses on what is referred to as the "content" of career planning, Diane also wanted to focus on the "process" of career planning. She asked Paulette to get a notebook and during the week jot down any and all feelings she was having about the career transition process. Did she find herself daydreaming about the careers she was researching? What were the feelings associated with those daydreams? Did she feel fear, anxiety, excitement, confusion, grief at leaving teaching, lack of confidence? What messages or self talk was she engaging in? Paulette was also instructed to bring this to the next session, but was assured that she would only be expected to share what she felt comfortable sharing.

Case analysis and conceptualization are in order now. Diane saw Paulette as motivated and hardworking. She also saw her as having enough conventional interests to expect that she would carry through on the fairly detailed homework assignment. There had been a rather dramatic change already in Paulette's self-assessment. She had gone from saying "I don't have any skills" to beginning to be able to articulate a long list of skills and interests.

Session 3

The *goals* were as follows:

- To review what occupational information had been learned
- To determine what additional questions Paulette had
- To talk about informational interviewing
- To have Paulette begin informational interviewing
- To review what feelings Paulette had experienced regarding the career transition process

The major *elements* were as follows: problem/goal clarification and specification.

Counselor preparation included planning and conceptualizing what particular interventions might be helpful in increasing Paulette's self-confidence, as well as collecting handouts from the career resource library that would be helpful for Paulette as she conducts informational interviews.

The *interview session* unfolded as follows. Paulette had done a good amount of research in the career library. At least on a superficial level, she could describe various occupations. When Diane asked more detailed questions, especially those that she felt (from past sessions) would have relevance to her client, Paulette found that she needed more information. Diane and Paulette made a list of questions she needed to answer. Diane asked Paulette to share from her "career transition journal." In doing so, Paulette discussed a variety of fears and negative self-talk that she was experiencing. Many of these thoughts and feelings came when she was researching career information. For example, as she read about the position of training and development coordinator and realized that often travel was required, she had fears about Michael's response to this information. Michael was pretty traditional and wanted

Paulette at home to cook the meals and take care of the house. This led to a discussion of Paulette and Michael's communication pattern, the expectations each had for the other, and the impact of the career transition on Michael. They discussed the need for open communication about this and other aspects of Paulette's career change. With this matter discussed and a plan of action agreed on, Diane turned to the career information side of the process once again.

Diane asked Paulette to reflect on what, given her knowledge about these career fields, she would like and dislike about each one. From this research and discussion, Paulette did some tentative prioritizing and discarding. The three occupations that kept resurfacing as being of interest were (1) training and development coordinator, (2) adult education coordinator, and (3) hotel manager. Diane told Paulette about both the Standard Occupational Classification (SOC) system and the Standard Industrial Classification (SIC) system as ways of looking at these and other occupations. In addition to these paper resources, Diane explained the process of informational interviewing.

She also helped Paulette to identify some people who were working in occupations of interest whom she could interview for more information. Although Paulette had excellent communication skills, Diane asked Paulette to practice her informational interview skills by conducting an informal interview with her. This way Diane was able to observe and give direct feedback on Paulette's interviewing skills. Her homework for this week consisted of (1) finding answers to some of her unanswered questions through further exploration in the career information library; (2) interviewing three individuals, one in each of the identified occupations; and (3) writing follow-up notes, thanking these contacts for their time and information.

Turning to *case analysis and conceptualization*, although Paulette had gained very useful information in the possible career fields, she needed to explore further. She had to integrate this information about herself and about the world of work to see what kind of conflicts or consistencies she might expect. She also could benefit from more personal information. The national labor information in the *OOH* and *DOT*, and exposure to the SOC and SIC systems, had given her valuable information to use in formulating questions during her informational interviews. Paulette also had to integrate her new ideas about careers into her personal life. She needed to do much more talking and clarifying with Michael about how these changes would have an impact on both of them.

Session 4

The *goals* were as follows:

- Review information gathered in informational interviews
- Begin looking at possible places of employment
- Begin preparing a functional résumé

The major *elements* were as follows: problem/goal clarification, specification, and beginning of resolution.

Counselor preparation included reviewing past session case notes, and continuing to conceptualize Paulette's dynamics and thinking about what specific counseling strategies would be most beneficial.

In the *interview session*, Paulette revealed that she had conducted informational interviews with two of the three people. She interviewed a man who was in charge of training and development for a hospital complex and a woman who coordinated adult education courses at a community college. Both had provided her with information and valuable contacts for her to interview. Both positions seemed to be interesting and seemed to use the skills she was most interested in using. The adult education coordinator told her about a job she knew of that consisted of training businesspeople in the use of computer systems. Paulette was excited about this possible job lead. The lead also motivated her to put a résumé together, which she had never done before. Diane discussed with Paulette the two major forms of résumés: functional and chronological.

The functional résumé seemed to be the best way to emphasize Paulette's transferable skills from teaching to training adults in the use of computer equipment. Diane emphasized the need to adapt the résumé as much as possible to this specific job. To do this, Paulette should again use some of the information resources in New Horizons' career library. Training and development and computer information in the *DOT* provided some information on what skills were needed in the job and that thus should be highlighted on Paulette's résumé. Paulette also used the state career information delivery system to obtain more localized information.

Her homework for this week was to draft a résumé specifically for this job. She was also to do some research at the library that would help her become familiar with the company with which she would be interviewing. The next session was scheduled for that same week so that Diane could critique Paulette's résumé and help her strengthen it. Diane also scheduled some time in the next session to assist Paulette with her interviewing skills. In preparation for the practice interview, Diane asked Paulette if there were any questions or areas of questioning that caused her anxiety. Paulette confided that questions related to salary made her very anxious. With further exploration, Diane helped Paulette see that most of her anxiety came from lack of information. That is, Paulette did not know what a realistic range for a given occupation was. Diane showed Paulette another useful resource in the career library—the local *Wage Surveys.* By looking through these, Paulette got a much better idea of what was reasonable to ask for during salary negotiations.

Diane again processed with Paulette how she was integrating all of this new information into her conception of herself. Specifically, Diane probed about how this information was changing Paulette's view of herself, the work world, and the transition process. She also talked with Paulette about her conversation with Michael. Paulette had found out that she had been operating under some false assumptions about how Michael would view the possibility of her having to travel. While he would not want Paulette traveling frequently, he certainly understood that a new career might require some travel, and he felt it was about time he learned to do some things, like cooking, for himself.

Now for *case analysis and conceptualization*. Paulette was obviously highly motivated at this point. She lacked some information but was generally self-confident. The position for which she was applying certainly would utilize her strengths: strong communication and organizational skills. Diane viewed Paulette as having a variety of strengths that would be assets to her in this time of career transition. Her perception of the transition was a positive one. She viewed it as a gain rather than a loss. She had thought about the change for some time, and so even though Michael's job loss led to some urgency, it was not perceived as a great shock or crisis. Diane also viewed Paulette as being competent and resourceful, both of which were strengths in this time of transition.

Session 5

The *goals* were as follows:

- To review and strengthen Paulette's functional résumé
- To give her practice with job interviewing
- To talk with her about her role in interviewing with the company as well as the company interviewing her
- To terminate the counseling relationship

The major *elements* were as follows: problem/goal resolution and next steps.

No *counselor preparation* was required.

Paulette brought her résumé to the *interview session*. Diane reviewed it and helped her write a strong career objective. Diane also helped her make the skills section on the résumé more specific and less abstract. In doing so, she was also giving Paulette some more impressive ways of discussing her skills in the job interview.

In addition, Diane talked with Paulette about her role

in the interview process. The company would be attempting to determine if she were the best person for the job. But Diane pointed out that she needed to assess the merits of the company as well. Diane reminded Paulette of her list of the parts of teaching she liked and disliked. How might she assess whether this company would better fit her skills and interests? Would she find more administrative support and reinforcement in this new setting than she did in the schools? Diane helped Paulette develop a number of questions and ways of assessing this type of information during the interview. Paulette hoped she would make a better choice this time and would get into a career she really enjoyed. The rest of this session was spent in helping Paulette try out some questions and answers in a practice job interview. Diane allowed ten minutes at the end of the session to formally terminate the counseling relationship. She gave Paulette additional feedback about how she perceived her changing during their relationship. She asked Paulette for any perceptions of the counseling: What was most helpful? least helpful? critical incidents? She also reassured Paulette that if she needed additional assistance with her planning, to feel free to contact the center.

This brings us to our final *case analysis and conceptualization* remarks. Paulette was able, with Diane's help, to synthesize much of what she knew about herself with career information. Like many adults at this developmental stage, Paulette had many life questions—especially about past decisions. Even though Diane had talked with her about the normalcy of career change, and the probability that this would not be her last change, Paulette was still placing a lot of emphasis on making "the right choice."

Immediately after the interview, Diane called Paulette. She felt the interview had gone very smoothly. She had been able to gain a lot of information about the organization and thought it seemed like an excellent match for her skills and interests. Although the interviewer did not make her a firm offer, there was every indication that one would be forthcoming. Instead of waiting passively, Diane encouraged Paulette to send a thank-you note and express her continued interest in the position.

A week later Diane got another call. Paulette had been hired. She was now a trainer for Computer Systems, Inc. Although her starting salary was not much higher than when she was in teaching, there was much more room for career advancement. The job looked like it would fully utilize Paulette's skills and interests.

15

█▞█▞█▞█▞█▞█▞█▞█▞█▞█▞█▞█▞█▞█▞█

Working with
Structured Groups

█▞█▞█▞█▞█▞█▞█▞█▞█▞█▞█▞█▞█▞█▞█

Traditionally, group-work techniques and methods were used extensively in counseling for career development. In schools, group work (group guidance) often was synonymous with vocational guidance as it took place in homerooms and other classes. In colleges and universities, freshman orientation classes relied on group work to reach students with career information (Baruth and Robinson, 1987). Today, group-work techniques and methods are increasingly popular modes of sharing career information with clients of all ages and circumstances.

Group-work techniques and methods and their purposes often are defined in terms of group type. George and Cristiani (1981) classified groups as guidance groups, counseling groups, therapy groups, encounter or sensitivity groups, and T-groups. Shertzer and Stone (1980) identified the categories of task groups, guidance groups, training groups, counseling groups, personal growth groups, and therapy groups. In this chapter, we will focus on a combination of guidance-group and counseling-group methods, since these are the most common in career information settings.

Baruth and Robinson (1987) reported that a group type that combines guidance-group and counseling-group approaches has evolved. This combination is called a *structured group*. According to these authors, "The structured group is similar to group guidance in its concentration on sharing information, but the focus is both more specific within each group and wider ranging in terms of topics between different groups" (p. 120). These groups "provide for the acquisition of both knowledge and skills, and the group structure allows for the sharing of information and the practice of new behaviors in a supportive environment" (p. 120). Drum and Knott (1977, p. 14) stated that "a structured group is a delimited learning situation with a predetermined goal, and a plan designed to enable each group member to reach this identified goal with a minimum of frustration and maximum ability to transfer the new learning to a wide range of life events."

Because of these features, structured groups are ideal for the use of career information in counseling for career development. Predetermined career topics and information can be introduced and emphasized, and career exploration, planning, and decision skills can be learned and practiced in a supportive atmosphere, all with the needs and concerns of clients in mind. We call structured groups that feature career issues and information *career information structured groups*.

This chapter first presents guidelines for the design and implementation of career information structured groups. Then it features a sample program that emphasizes the use of career information in structured groups.

Designing and Implementing
Career Information Structured Groups

We first discuss the conditions and issues that need to be considered in designing and implementing structured groups. Then we touch on the sequencing of the content of career information structured groups using the learning theory concepts of perceptualization, conceptualization, and generalization. Finally, the importance of the setting in which career information structured groups take place is emphasized.

Conditions and Issues

Pfeiffer and Jones (1973, pp. 173–179) felt that before structured groups could be designed and implemented, data were needed about a number of important conditions and issues. They identified the following conditions and issues as being important:

1. *The Contract.* Specifying the goals of the structured group so that clients would know why they were there and would know what to expect.
2. *The Length and Timing of the Structured Group.* Specifying the amount of time involved; one evening, two days, three days over a period of one week and so forth.
3. *The Location and Physical Facilities.* A retreat setting vs. an on-site setting with specific attention to room size and the ability to arrange and rearrange tables and chairs.
4. *The Familiarity of Participants with Each Other.* Are icebreakers needed or not? Capitalizing on previous relationships and backgrounds.
5. *The Training Experience of the Participants.* Do they know how to function as members of a structured group or will they need time and instruction to learn?
6. *The Availability of Qualified Staff.* It is necessary to take into account the qualifications of the leaders in structured-group design.
7. *The Number of Participants.* The number of participants who will be in a structured group must be known to plan for the structure and nature of the large- and small-group interaction.
8. *Access to Materials and Other Aids.* Access to training materials and other aids (availability, budget, convenience) is necessary, particularly if the participants need to use these materials during the structured group.
9. *The Opportunity for Follow-Through.* What can be anticipated to happen after the structured group is over so that transfer and generalization of skills and knowledge can be encouraged and reinforced?

Sequencing Events

Once information about these conditions and issues is available, the next step is to design the structured-group experiences, paying particular attention to the sequencing of events—that is, the logical flow of activities in the group. The following suggested sequencing of events was adapted from Pfeiffer and Jones (1973, pp. 188–189).

1. *Getting Acquainted.* Establishing some familiarity of the participants with each other.
2. *Closing Expectation Gaps.* Clarifying the goals of the structured group; making them explicit so that there are no misunderstandings about the intent of the structured group.
3. *Legitimizing Risk Taking.* Making it known that risk taking (expressing feelings and thoughts) is expected in a structured group.
4. *Learning About Feedback.* Providing instruction in feedback so that effective group sharing can take place to show that it is expected and should be experienced freely.
5. *Developing an Awareness of Process.* Stopping the structured group periodically to process the information and patterns that are beginning to emerge.
6. *Integrating Conceptual Models.* Looking at some theoretical models of personal, group, and career development to help participants begin to integrate the affective and behavioral data of the structured group.
7. *Experimenting with Self-Expression.* Using expressive techniques (nonverbal exercises) periodically to heighten growth in the awareness of self and others.
8. *Planning Back-Home Applications.* Helping participants to accept responsibility for back home and actually having them begin to develop individual action plans.
9. *Assisting Reentry.* Providing closure activities to help participants to move back into their normal routine, to their reality.

On reflection, we can see that this sequence of events can be conceptualized in terms of learning theory. Wellman and Moore (1975) hypothesized that learning moves from a beginning level of awareness and differentiation (*perceptualization*), to the next level of awareness and differentiation (*conceptualization*), to the highest level of behavioral consistency and effectiveness from the standpoint of both internal and external evaluation (*generalization*). For our purposes, we have grouped events 1–5 under the perceptualization level, event 6 under the conceptualization level, and events 7–9 under the generalization level. When the events are organized in this way, learning theory can provide reference points or cues to a better understanding of how clients may or may not be assimilating the career knowledge being presented and may or may not be gaining the career skills being practiced. Let us look more closely at how these concepts can play this role.

Perceptualization Level. The structured-group activities to be used and the client competencies to be achieved in career information structured groups at this beginning level of learning (events 1–5) emphasize the acquisition of knowledge and skills, and focus attention on selected aspects of the environment and self. The knowledge and skills most relevant are those clients need in making life-role decisions. Attention is the first step toward the development and maturation of interests, attitudes, and values. Competencies at the perceptualization level reflect accuracy of perceptions, ability to differentiate, and elemental skills in performing functions appropriate to the client's level of development. Competencies at this level fall into two major categories, *environmental orientation* and *self-orientation*.

Competencies classified under environmental orientation emphasize the client's awareness and acquisition of knowledge and skills needed to make life-role decisions and to master the demands of life-career settings and events. The competencies at this level are essentially cognitive in nature and have not necessarily been internalized to the extent that the client attaches personal meaning to the acquired knowledge and skills. For example, clients may acquire appropriate job interview skills and knowledge, but it does not necessarily follow that they will use these skills and knowledge in their job interview behavior. However, such knowledge and skills are considered to be prerequisites to behavior requiring them. Thus, the acquisition of knowledge and skills required to make growth-oriented decisions and to cope with environmental expectations is viewed as the first step in clients' development, regardless of whether subsequent implementation emerges. A primary goal of structured groups at this level of learning is the development of knowledge and skills to enable clients to understand and meet the expectations of their social environment and to recognize the values underlying social limits.

Competencies classified under self-orientation focus on the development of accurate self-perceptions. One aspect of an accurate awareness of self is the knowledge of one's abilities, aptitudes, interests, and values. An integral part of identity is clients' ability to understand and accept the ways that they are alike and different from other clients. Attention to life-career decisions and demands relevant to immediate adjustment and future development are considered a prerequisite to an understanding of the relationships between self and environment. An awareness and perhaps an understanding of feelings and motivations is closely associated with self-evaluation of behavior, with the formation of attitudes and values, and with voluntary, rationally based modification of behavior. A second goal of structured groups at this level is to help clients make accurate assessments of self so that they can relate realistically to their environment in their decisions and actions. Thus, the overall focus of structured groups at this level is clients' development of self-awareness and differentiation that will enable appropriate decision making and mastery of behavior in the roles, settings, and events of their lives.

Conceptualization Level. Activities to be used and client competencies to be considered for career information structured groups at this learning level (event 6) emphasize action based on the relationships between perceptions of self and perceptions of environment. The types of action sought are categorized into personally meaningful growth decisions and adaptive and adjustive behavior. The general goal at this level of learning in structured groups is that clients will (1) make appropriate career choices, decisions, and plans that will move them toward personally satisfying and socially acceptable development; (2) take action necessary to progress within developmental career plans; and (3) develop behavior to master their life settings, which includes work. The two major classifications of conceptualization competencies are *directional tendencies* and *adaptive and adjustive behavior*.

Directional tendencies relate to clients' movement toward socially desirable goals consistent with their potential for development. These competencies are indicators of directional tendencies as reflected in the career choices, decisions, and plans that clients are expected to make in ordering the course of their educational, occupational, and social growth. The acquisition of knowledge and skills covered by competencies at the perceptual level is a prerequisite to the pursuit of competencies at this level, although the need to make career choices and decisions may provide the initial stimulus for considering perceptual competencies.

The expected emergence of increasingly stable interests and the strengthening and clarification of value patterns constitute additional indicators of directional tendencies. Persistent attention to particular persons, activities, or objects in the environment to the exclusion of others (selective attention) is an indication of the development of interests through an evaluation of the relationships of self to differentiated aspects of the environment. Competencies that relate to value conceptualization, or the internalization of social values, complement interest development. Here clients are expected to show increased consistency in giving priority to particular behavior that is valued personally and socially. In a sense, the maturation of interests represents the development of educational and occupational individuality, whereas the formation of value patterns represents the recognition of social values and the normative tolerances of behavior.

The second major category of competencies at the conceptualization level includes competencies related to the application of self-environment concepts in coping with environmental pressures and in the solution of problems arising from the interaction of clients and their environment. Competencies in this area of functioning are designated as adaptive and adjustive behavior.

Adaptive behavior refers to clients' ability and skill to manage their life settings (with normative tolerances) to satisfy self-needs, to meet environmental demands, and to solve problems. There are two types. First, clients may, within certain prescribed limits, control their environmental transactions by selection. For example, if they lack the appropriate social skills, they may avoid transactions and choose those where existing abilities will gain the acceptance of the social group. Second, clients may be able to modify their environment to meet their needs and certain external demands.

Adjustive behavior refers to the ability and flexibility of clients to modify their behavior to meet environmental demands and to solve problems. Such behavior modification may include the development of new abilities or skills, a change of attitudes, or a change in method of operation or approach to the demand situation. The basic competencies in this area involve clients' ability to demonstrate adaptive and adjustive behavior in dealing with social demands and in solving problems that restrict the ability to meet such demands. The competencies may be achieved by applying existing abilities or by learning new ways of meeting demands.

Generalization Level. Competencies at the generalization level of career information structured groups (events 7–9) imply a level of functioning that enables clients to (1) accommodate environmental and cultural demands; (2) achieve personal satisfaction from environmental transactions; and (3) demonstrate competence through mastery of specific tasks and through the generalization of learned behavior, attitudes, and values to new situations. Behavior that characterizes the achievement of generalization-level competencies may be described as purposeful and effective by one's own or intrinsic standards and by societal or extrinsic criteria. Clients should be able to demonstrate behavioral consistency, commitment to purpose, and autonomy in meeting educational, occupational, and social demands. Clients exhibiting such behavior therefore are relatively independent and predictable.

Client competencies at this level are classified as *accommodation, satisfaction,* and *mastery.* The concept of sequential and positive progress implies a continuous process of internalization, including applicational transfer of behavior and a dynamic, rather than a static, condition in the achievement of goals. The achievement of generalization competencies may be interpreted as positive movement (at each level of development) toward the ideal model of an effective person (self and socially derived) without assuming that clients will ever fully achieve the ideal.

Accommodation competencies relate to the consistent and enduring ability to solve problems and to cope with environmental demands with minimum conflict. Accommodation of cultural and environmental demands requires that clients make decisions and take action within established behavioral tolerances. The applicational transfer of adaptive and adjustive behavior, learned in other situations and under other circumstances, to new demand situations is inferred by the nature of the competencies classified in this category. The achievement of accommodation competencies can probably best be evaluated by the absence of, or the reduction of, unsatisfactory coping behavior. The wide range of acceptable behavior in many situations suggests that clients who perform within that range have achieved the accommodation competencies for a particular demand situation, whereas if they are outside the range, they have not achieved these competencies.

Satisfaction competencies reflect the internal interpretation that clients give to their environmental transactions. Client interests and values serve as criteria for evaluating the decisions made and the actions taken within the structured-group experience. Although the evaluations of peers and authority figures may influence clients' interpretations (satisfactions), these competencies become genuine only as they are achieved in congruence with the motivations and feelings of clients. The description of satisfaction competencies consistent with structured-group programming at this level should include clients' evaluation of affiliations, transactions, and adjustments in terms of personal adequacy, expectations, and congruency with a perceived ideal life-style. Expressed satisfaction, as well as behavioral manifestations from which satisfaction may be inferred, such as persistence, would seem to be appropriate criterion measures. Also, congruency between measured interests and voluntarily chosen career activities should be considered.

Mastery competencies include the more global aspects of achievement and generalization of attitudinal and behavioral modes. Long-range goals, encompassing large areas of achievement, are emphasized here rather than the numerous short-range achievements that may be required to reach a larger goal. In the social area, competencies relate to social responsibility and to clients' contributions to social affiliations and interactions appropriate to their developmental level. All of the competencies in this category are framed in the context of self and social estimates of potential for achievement. Therefore, criteria for the estimation of achievement of mastery competencies should be in terms of congruency between independent behavioral action and expectations for action as derived from self and social sources.

The Setting

The setting in which career information structured groups take place is critical. Boone and Reid (1978, p. 253) made this point when they stated that "the selection of an appropriate physical setting for a workshop is a critical variable in the learning process." The selection of the site and the arrangements at the site are often the most overlooked details of designing and implementing career information structured groups.

Boone and Reid (1978) emphasized the importance of considering such factors as the location of the site, the type of setting, and room-and-board arrangements if required. They also urged that attention be given to the psychological setting.

They pointed to such variables as privacy, comfort, meeting-room size, the normal use of the site, the philosophy of the site management, and negotiating and contracting for the best site possible. "Thoughtful choices, attention to details, and hard negotiation will help make the site a positive contribution to the success of the workshop," they summed up (p. 257).

Career Information Structured Groups: An Example

Because of the popularity of structured groups, there are many examples available from which to draw. The purpose of this section is to provide one example of how practitioners have developed and used structured-group activities featuring career information in working with their clientele. The example presented is the Career Options for Missouri Farm Families Workshop. The workshop content and format were selected and organized by staff of the Career Planning and Placement Center, University of Missouri, Columbia.

Career Options for Missouri Farm Families

Career Options for Missouri Farm Families is an umbrella designation for various programs and services for farm families in transition in Missouri (Hughey, Heppner, Johnston, and Rakes, 1989). Among the programs offered is the Career Options workshop. The workshop format combines a series of structured-group activities with individual test interpretation sessions over a period of two-and-a-half days. The workshop includes activities and career information related to participant interests, skills, and values as well as résumé writing, preparing cover letters, job interviewing, job search tips, and networking. Exhibit 15.1 shows how the structured-group activities are organized and carried out in the Career Options workshop.

Exhibit 15.1. Career Options Workshop Agenda.

Day One

8:30–9 A.M.	**Registration**
9–9:30 A.M.	**Workshop Orientation and Overview, Career Planning and Career Change Process** Review workshop schedule and goals. Explain the career planning and career change process. Participants get more comfortable with one another during an acquaintance exercise.
9:30–10:15 A.M.	**Your Work Plans** Exploring participants' individual work values through a group exercise utilizing job descriptions. Helps participants identify what is most important to them in a job.
10:15–10:30 A.M.	**Break**
10:30–11:15 A.M.	**Your Career Interests** Explain the six major areas of career interests and the occupations that fit those interests. Exercise helps participants self-assess their career interest patterns and how those interests fit past, present, and future jobs.
11:15 A.M.– 12 noon	**Your Transferable Skills** Through an extensive assessment inventory, participants identify their transferable skills. These skills then reinforce the six major career areas and provide skill words for career planning, résumés, applications, and job interviews.
12 noon–1 P.M.	**Lunch**
1–1:45 P.M.	**Finding Career Information and Informational Interviewing** Describe how to locate written and people sources for information on careers and employers. Participants do a practice informational interview with one another. Also provide a brief overview of current national, state, and local labor market trends. Participants are provided a copy of *A Missourian's Guide to Financial Aid Sources for Education & Training* and the *Missouri Guide to Career Information & Resources*.
1:45–2:15 P.M.	**Writing Your Cover Letters** Handouts and discussion on the most appropriate ways of writing cover letters in job hunting.

Exhibit 15.1. Career Options Workshop Agenda, Cont'd.

2:15–2:30 P.M.   **Break**

2:30–5 P.M.   **Writing Your Résumé**
Numerous handouts strengthen the presented material on the varied aspects of current résumé-writing concepts. Participants then work on their résumé worksheets that help gather and organize each person's résumé information. Staff helps critique and polish résumé drafts. At end of workshop, résumés are left with staff for final polishing, are word processed and laser printed, and are mailed to each participant.

5–7 P.M.   **Dinner**

7–10 P.M.   **Evening Session**
A. One-hour individual counseling appointments with trained career counselors for feedback on the Self-Directed Search assessment and discussion of other career concerns.
B. Complete Myers-Briggs Type Indicator (MBTI).
C. Completion of résumé worksheets.
D. Use of career resource library.

Day Two

7–8:30 A.M.   **Breakfast**

8:30–9:30 A.M.   **Interviewing for Jobs**
Present current information on preparing for a job interview, what to expect during a typical interview, and how to follow up. Includes questions to anticipate, questions to ask, appropriate attire, and so on.

9:30–10:00 A.M.   **Completing Job Applications**
Describe appropriate methods of completing job applications.
Provide handouts and a generic application.

10 A.M.–12 noon   **Practice Job Interviews**
Participants rotate into thirty-minute sessions for individual practice job interviews. A fifteen-minute interview is videotaped, then fifteen minutes are provided for feedback and viewing of the videotape. Interviewers are local employers and Career Options staff.

10:30–10:45 A.M.   **Break**

Exhibit 15.1. Career Options Workshop Agenda, Cont'd.

10:45 A.M.–   **Job Hunting and Networking**
12 noon   This section provides participants with information
                about how to put their own job hunt together, identify
                potential employers, gain job leads through networking
                within their field, and so on.

12 noon–1 P.M. **Lunch**

1–2:15 P.M.   **MBTI, Part 1**
                The MBTI is a brief inventory that provides some indica-
                tion of people's natural preferences in how they focus
                their attention, take in information, make decisions, and
                adopt a life-style and working style. This first section on
                the MBTI helps participants understand the eight differ-
                ent preferences and the opportunity to estimate their own
                type.

2:15–2:30 P.M. **Break**

2:30–3:30 P.M. **MBTI, Part 2**
                Participants are given their individual MBTI scores and
                information about their type preferences. Any differences
                between their estimates and the inventory are discussed,
                along with implications for their job choices, communi-
                cation style, and career development.

3:30–4 P.M.   **Summary and Evaluation**
                Participants summarize for the group what they see as
                next steps for themselves and complete an anonymous
                evaluation of the workshop.

Registration. Prior to attending a workshop, participants complete a packet of information and assessment forms,
including Holland's Self-Directed Search, and My Vocational
Situation as well as our Career Development Plan. Registration and other information are handled through the Missouri
Career Information Hotline.

Follow-Up. Approximately two weeks following each
workshop, staff follow up on each participant by telephone

to answer further questions, assess future needs, and so on. A more formal written follow-up is mailed to each participant six months after each workshop. Each participant is mailed a monthly *Career Options Newsletter* with further career and employment information. The Missouri Career Information Hotline is a toll-free source of continued information and support for all participants.

Analysis of the Career Options Workshop Example

Corey (1990, p. 11) stated that structured groups serve such purposes as "imparting information, sharing common experiences, teaching people how to solve problems, offering support, and helping people learn how to create their own support systems outside of the group settings." Note in the Career Options Workshop example how these purposes are achieved. The participants are provided with self and career information. They learn about themselves in terms of work world–connected traits. They learn the skills of how to relate their traits to possible career options in the planning and decision-making process. The participants share experiences, discuss issues and concerns, and participate in job-seeking skill-building exercises. They also learn about the importance of support systems. And, they learn about a follow-up system they can use on completion of the workshop.

As we stated in the opening paragraphs of this chapter and as was shown in the Career Options Workshop example, structured groups are ideal for the use of career information in counseling for career development. The structured group process is a powerful medium that merges the didactic and experiential learnings clients need to gain the problem-solving life skills they require to achieve their goals or resolve their problems. As has been shown, too, the structured group format and its content connects participating clients directly to one of the major purposes of using career information— education.

To Sum Up

As we have seen through the conditions and issues, sequencing, and setting discussions, and the presentation of the examples, career information structured groups are an excellent way to educate and motivate clients in counseling for career development. There are a number of reasons why this is the case. First, career information structured groups are systematic in design, structured in organization, and skill-training oriented in focus. They have a direct, concrete orientation. Second, career information structured groups demystify the process for clients because the goals to be reached are clear and the activities to be used are explained (Rudestam, 1982). Clients can review the format and activities and see the connections between their goals and the goals of the structured group. Third, career information structured goals are time-limited. This is advantageous because clients can see a beginning and an end to the process. Finally, clients who are involved in dealing with career issues not only find out that the structured group process provides them with the career information they need and the structure to assist them to integrate and use the information, but also offers them a safe place to test their ideas and to receive supportive feedback from the group leader and other group members.

Resource

National Career Development Association Guidelines

Guidelines for the Preparation and Evaluation of Career and Occupational Information Literature

National Career Development Association

These *Guidelines* are destined to be used by both the publishers and the consumers of career and occupational information literature. Because career and occupational literature is often an individual's initial (and sometimes only) exposure to a specific occupation or occupational field, it is very important that this information be accurately and comprehensively conveyed to the user. The *Guidelines* represent the National Career Development Association's (NCDA) views of what constitutes good career and occupational literature. The Association encourages the use of these *Guidelines* by publishers to ensure quality control in their publications and by those who select and use career and occupational literature to ensure maximum value from their purchases.

Helping individuals obtain, evaluate, and use career and occupational information is within the scope of NCDA's mission to facilitate the career development of individuals. The revision of these *Guidelines* is one of the services pro-

Note: This 1991 edition of the Guidelines is a revision of the guidelines for career and occupational literature previously published by NCDA/NVGA. This revision was prepared under the direction of Jennifer B. Wilson, Ph.D., University of Wisconsin-La Crosse, Wisconsin (Chairperson of the CIRS Subcommittee on Print Materials), with the assistance of the Career Information Review Service Committee, chaired by Roger Lambert, Ph.D., University of Wisconsin-Madison. The Guidelines were approved by the NCDA Board of Directors April, 1991.

vided by NCDA to encourage the development of accurate and reliable information by publishers, and the informed use of this information by consumers and clients.

The nature of career information has changed considerably in its content and its delivery since NCDA was founded in 1913, as the National Vocational Guidance Association. However, the need for career and vocational information as an important consideration in career planning has remained constant. As recently as 1989, 65% of the adults who participated in the NCDA Gallup Survey indicated that if they could plan their work lives again, they would try to get more information about career choices and options.

In addition to their evaluative use locally, these *Guidelines* also form the basis for the ratings of current career and occupational literature by the Career Information Review Service of NCDA. These ratings appear in *The Career Development Quarterly* to assist professionals in their selection of quality career and occupational information literature.

Definition of Terms

The first step in any evaluation process is to determine that all parties concerned are using terms that communicate the same meaning to all. To address this issue of clarity, the following *Guidelines* have been designed to be used for occupational literature and for career literature. The content and purpose of these two types of literature are closely related but differ in some important aspects. Therefore, the terms occupation, occupational field, career, and career progression have been used in these *Guidelines* to refer to the specific type of information being discussed. Occupation refers to a specific job, usually indicated by a job title and/or number. Occupational field refers to a group or cluster of related occupations, often but not necessarily requiring similar skills, knowledge, and abilities and sharing similar working conditions. Career is a more encompassing term that includes, but is not limited to, the series of occupations one might expect to hold in the course of his or her working history. Career progression refers to the series of occupations that might be held during one's work history, each involving increasing levels of decision making, responsibility, status, and compensation.

General Guidelines

This section discusses items related to the general preparation and presentation of career and occupational literature.

1. Dating and Revisions

The date of publication should be clearly indicated. Because of rapid changes in employment outlook and earnings, material should be revised at least every three to four years to stay current and accurate. This is particularly important in highly technical and skilled occupations and less a factor in unskilled or semiskilled occupations.

2. Credits

Credits should include (a) publisher, (b) consultants, (c) sponsor, and (d) sources of any statistical data. Photographs and original artwork should be accompanied by the name of the photographer/artist, photographic outfit, and copyright mark (if any).

3. Accuracy of Information

Information should be accurate and free from distortion caused by self-serving bias, sex stereotyping, or dated resources. Whenever possible, resources over five years old should be avoided. Information should be secured from and/or reviewed by knowledgeable sources within the occupation, the occupational field, or career research. Reviewers should be selected to reflect different viewpoints germane to an occupation (e.g., business and labor) and be trained in the evaluation process. Reviewers must not use the literature to promote their own concerns or viewpoints. Data such as earnings and employment projections should be based on current, reliable, and comprehensive research.

4. Format

The information should be conveyed in a clear, concise, and interesting manner. Although information from the Content Guidelines should appear in all publications, publishers are encouraged to vary the manner of presentation for the sake of stimulation and appeal. A standard style and format for grammar should be adopted and utilized throughout the document.

5. Vocabulary

The vocabulary of the information should be appropriate to the target group. Career and occupational information is used by people of varying ages and abilities. Information designed for a specific age range or for any other clearly identifiable group should be clearly identified as such. Information designed for broader use should be comprehensible to younger persons but suitable in style for adults. Technical terminology or jargon should be either fully explained or avoided. The use of nonsexist language is essential.

6. Use of Information

The intended purpose, the target audience, and the potential use of the information should be clearly identified in the introduction to the material. Reviews should specify the intended audience, such as elementary schools, middle/junior high schools, high schools, vocational schools, community college, colleges/universities, employment/training programs, rehabilitation agencies, correctional agencies, libraries, or specify other audiences. Persons often do not have the opportunity to thoroughly review materials until after the materials have been purchased. The authors and publishers should help potential purchasers determine whether the materials present useful information.

7. Bias and Stereotyping

Care should be taken in all publications to eliminate bias and stereotyping against persons with a disability, or based on gender, race, social status, ethnicity, age, or religion. Job title and information should be bias-free. Particular care should be taken to ensure the use of gender-free language. If graphics are used, people of different races, ages, sexes, and physical abilities should be portrayed at various occupational levels. Where applicable, data, information, or resources relevant to equal opportunity for women, minorities, or persons with a disability should be included.

8. Graphics

Graphic displays, when used, should enhance the value of the narrative information. Pictures should be current and portray individuals engaged in activities primary to the occupation or unique to it. Again, the importance of portraying individuals of different sexes, races, ages, and physical abilities in a variety of roles cannot be overemphasized.

Content Guidelines

This section discusses guideline items that deal with the content of information on occupations and/or occupational fields. Reviews of nonoccupational materials will rely primarily on the previously discussed criteria.

1. Duties and Nature of the Work

The career and occupational literature should describe in a clear and interesting fashion: (a) the purpose of the work, (b) the activities of the worker, (c) the skills, knowledge, interests, and abilities necessary to perform the work, and (d) any specializations commonly practiced in the occupation. Literature that describes occupational fields should also include: (a) the overall function and importance of the field, (b) the variety of

occupations available, (c) the common skills, knowledge, interests, and abilities shared by members of the field or industry,
and (d) contrasts among the various occupations represented
in the field.

2. Work Setting and Conditions

The portrayal of the work setting and conditions should include a description of the physical and mental activities and
the work environment. Where applicable, the information
should include the full range of possible settings in which
the work may be performed. The range of typical physical
and mental activities should be described. Environmental characteristics should include the physical surroundings, the psychological environment, and the social environment. In
addition to these characteristics, other conditions related to
the performance of the work, such as time requirements or
travel requirements, should be described.

Aspects of the work that might be regarded as undesira-
ble are as crucial to realistic decision making as those that
are generally considered desirable; therefore, care should be
taken to make descriptions as comprehensive as possible.
Because different individuals may view a given work condition as either positive or negative, the descriptions should be
free of the author's bias and present a balanced picture. The
variety and similarity of settings should be discussed. Specific
geographic locations related to employment in the occupational field should be included.

3. Preparation Required

The preparation required for entrance into the occupation,
or into various levels of an occupation, should be clearly
stated. The length and type of training required and the
skills, knowledge, abilities, and interests of successful students
or trainees should be indicated. Typical methods of financial
support during training should be included. Alternative
means of obtaining the necessary preparation or experience

should be stated where applicable. Readers should be informed of any preferred employer selection criteria over and above minimal preparation requirements. In literature that describes a range of occupations in a career progression, the various levels of preparation required for employment in each successive occupation should also be highlighted.

4. Special Requirements or Considerations

Bonafide Physical Requirements. Bonafide physical requirements that are necessary for entrance into a particular occupation should be included. Only bonafide occupational qualifications should be addressed. Consideration should be given to addressing job accommodations that can and are legally required to open opportunity to all the members of our society.

Licensing, Certifications, or Membership Requirements. Licenses, certifications, or memberships in unions or professional societies may also be required for some occupations. These requirements should be indicated and the process necessary for achieving any of these requirements should be described.

Personal Criteria. The listing of qualities desired of any worker (e.g., honesty, dependability) is not particularly valuable to individuals attempting to differentiate various career possibilities. On occasion it may be useful and appropriate to consider personal criteria, if available, regarding unique skills, knowledge, mental and physical abilities, and interests. The basis for the information should be clearly identified.

Social and Psychological Factors. Participation in an occupation has important effects on the lifestyle of the individual (and his or her family), and these effects should receive appropriate consideration in the presentation of information. When these factors are determined to be appropriate to the use of the material, the source of the information presented on social and psychological factors should be clearly identified.

5. Methods of Entry

The variety of means for typical entry into the occupation should be indicated, as well as any preferred avenues for entry. Alternative approaches should be described where applicable—particularly for those occupations where experience can be substituted for education and other formal preparation or where education can be substituted for work experience.

6. Earnings and Other Benefits

Current data on entry wages, average earnings, and the typical range of earnings in the occupation should be presented. In addition, variations in average earnings by geographic region should be reported if available. Fringe benefits have become an increasingly important aspect of total compensation, and ample coverage of both typical benefits and those that are unique to the occupation or occupational field should be given.

7. Usual Advancement Possibilities

The typical and alternative career progressions related to the occupational field should be presented. The supplementary skills, knowledge, and abilities necessary for advancement and the alternative means for acquiring them should be indicated. Issues such as the role of job change, availability of training, and seniority should be discussed as they pertain to advancement in the particular occupational field.

8. Employment Outlook

Statements concerning the employment outlook should be realistic and include both the short-range and the long-range outlook for the occupation and occupational field. Mention of the past record of the occupation may be useful in completing its outlook picture. A broad range of factors that may have an impact on the employment outlook, including economic, demographic, technological, geographic, social, and political factors, should be considered. Current U.S. Department of Labor or other expert research should be consulted. Realism is essential, but readers should not be discouraged from entering highly competitive fields if they have the ability, interest, and motivation to succeed.

9. Opportunities for Experience and Exploration

Literature should list opportunities for part-time and summer employment; opportunities for internships, apprenticeships, and cooperative work programs; and opportunities for volunteer work. Pertinent clubs and organizations, as well as school-related activities and programs, should be described. Publishers are encouraged to give sufficient attention to this heading because these career-related possibilities can be acted on immediately and thus have high motivational value.

10. Related Occupations

Occupations that share similar requirements on aptitudes, interest patterns, or work environments with the occupation under consideration should be listed. In addition to its value in early exploration, this information is particularly useful to adults considering lateral occupational changes.

11. Sources of Additional Information

Reference should be made to additional sources of information such as professional or trade organizations and associations, specific books or pamphlets, journals or trade publications, audiovisual materials, and literature available from public agencies. For students, the assistance of school guidance counselors or college career counselors is recommended.

Career and Occupational Literature
Reviewer's Rating Form—1991

Rating: _____ Type (Code Number): _____ Setting/Population: _____

GENERAL PUBLICATION DATA:

1. Title: _____

2. Author (s): _____

3. Publisher name: _____

4. Publisher address: _____

5. Year of publication: _____ 6. Number of pages: _____ 7. Price: _____

SETTING/POPULATION(s)

- ☐ 1. Elementary Schools
- ☐ 2. Middle/Junior High Schools
- ☐ 3. High Schools
- ☐ 4. Vocational Schools
- ☐ 5. Community Colleges
- ☐ 6. Colleges/Universities
- ☐ 7. Employment/Training Programs
- ☐ 8. Rehabilitation Agencies
- ☐ 9. Correctional Institutions
- ☐ 10. Libraries
- ☐ 11. Other: _____

TYPE OF PUBLICATION:

- ☐ **1. Vocational**
  - ☐ a. Occupations
  - ☐ b. Trends and Outlook
  - ☐ c. Job Training
  - ☐ d. Employment Opportunities

- ☐ **2. Educational**
  - ☐ a. Status and Trends
  - ☐ b. Schools, Colleges
  - ☐ c. Scholarships, Fellowships, Grants, and Loans

- ☐ **3. Career/Personal**
  - ☐ a. Planning (resume, how to look for a job, career planning, etc.)
  - ☐ b. Adjustment
  - ☐ c. Theory
  - ☐ d. Assessment (Interest, Aptitude testing, etc.)

CONTENT:
5=Outstanding   4=Good   3=Satisfactory   2=Poor
1=Unsatisfactory   0=Does not apply

5	4	3	2	1	0	Date of publication is indicated on material
5	4	3	2	1	0	Appropriate credits are given in the material
5	4	3	2	1	0	Information accurate, free from distortion
5	4	3	2	1	0	Clear, concise, interesting
5	4	3	2	1	0	Vocabulary appropriate to age group and occupational level
5	4	3	2	1	0	Intended purpose/population/use is clearly identified
5	4	3	2	1	0	Free of bias (racial, sexual, age, physical ability, etc.)
5	4	3	2	1	0	Illustrations/graphic displays are current, enhance material
5	4	3	2	1	0	Duties and nature of work (purpose, activities, skills, etc.)
5	4	3	2	1	0	Conditions of work (work setting, physical activities, environment)
5	4	3	2	1	0	Preparation required (length and kind of training)
5	4	3	2	1	0	Special requirements (license, certification, degrees, memberships, personal/social criteria, etc.)
5	4	3	2	1	0	Methods of entry (typical, preferred, any alternative means)
5	4	3	2	1	0	Earnings and other benefits (figures should be current and represent range)
5	4	3	2	1	0	Usual advancement opportunities (any requirements for advancement)
5	4	3	2	1	0	Employment outlook (current, realistic, short- and long-term)
5	4	3	2	1	0	Opportunities for experience and exploration
5	4	3	2	1	0	Related occupations indicated
5	4	3	2	1	0	Sources of education and training
5	4	3	2	1	0	Sources of additional information

The following items are applicable only when the publication is a bibliography, directory, or financial assistance publication.

Bibliography

5	4	3	2	1	0	Publication date(s) listed
5	4	3	2	1	0	Price(s) available
5	4	3	2	1	0	Reference to author(s)
5	4	3	2	1	0	Annotation of materials

Financial Assistance

5	4	3	2	1	0	Sources of financial aid
5	4	3	2	1	0	Amount of aid available
5	4	3	2	1	0	Qualification requirements

Directories

5	4	3	2	1	0	Content
5	4	3	2	1	0	Format	_____ **TOTAL SCORE**

Reviewer's Overall Rating for Listing—Circle Your Choice
5=Outstanding 4=Good 3=Satisfactory 2=Poor 1=Unsatisfactory

COMMENTS: Recommendations and suggestions for the authors/ publishers. (If there is an apparent discrepancy between the total score and your evaluation, please document your evaluation decision.)

Evaluation prepared by: _____ Date: _____

Career Software
Review Guidelines

National Career Development Association

Introduction

The National Career Development Association (NCDA) has a long history of evaluating career materials. The Association's career information reviews have for years helped counselors and career center coordinators select from available career information books and pamphlets.

In the last decade, several professional groups have developed evaluation criteria for career software. As computers came into use to help individuals access career information, the United States Department of Labor and then the National Occupational Information Coordinating Committee provided start-up grants so individual states could implement systems of career information. State system operators formed the Association of Computer-Based Systems for Career Information (ACSCI) and adopted standards for the operation of such systems, publishing them periodically since 1980. In 1985, ACSCI also published guidelines for the effective use of computer-based systems for career information.

Several states conducted or commissioned evaluations before adopting a system for state operation, and several individuals and research centers have published guidelines for

Note: The 1991 edition of the Career Software Review Guidelines was prepared under the direction of Bruce McKinlay, Ph.D., University of Oregon, Eugene, Oregon (chairperson of the CIRS Subcommittee on Software Resources), with the assistance of the Career Information Review Service Committee, chaired by Roger Lambert, Ph.D., University of Wisconsin-Madison. The Guidelines were approved by the NCDA Board of Directors April, 1991.

system selection or guides to available career information delivery software. In 1988, the American Association for Counseling and Development published a comprehensive guide to counseling software.

Several educational organizations, including the International Society for Technology in Education, publish guides to instructional software and guidelines for evaluation of instructional software.

The existing standards provided ample precedence for these NCDA guidelines. All of them help clarify important issues regarding career development software while equipping professionals to choose software appropriate for their counseling practices or their school's or agency's service needs. The purpose here is not to compile all of the good guidelines or to supersede well-established software standards and evaluations, but to reinforce them with NCDA's efforts.

These NCDA guidelines apply to software that individuals use in planning their own careers. Because the computer is an information tool and its major use in career development is for information delivery, the guidelines are specific about the content, orientation, and coverage of occupational and educational information. The computer is not just an information storage and retrieval device, however, nor is career planning based solely on facts about work and schooling. Computers are also used to organize information about the individual and to aid decision making. Criteria for the evaluation of those career development programs are also included in the guidelines. By selecting the applicable criteria, a reviewer can evaluate special purpose programs as well as comprehensive career information systems.

Useful software rarely consists only of computer programs and data. User guides, coordinator manuals, evaluation reports, and implementation strategies are all valuable and are covered by the guidelines.

Many career software programs have companion publications or refer users to other information sources. Similarly, software developers are beginning to add other visual and electronic media to their career programs. Therefore, these software review guidelines rely on and are designed to complement two other sets of NCDA guidelines—those for print and those for media.

These guidelines are written for use by NCDA members and others in selecting and using career software. They can also be useful to NCDA in reviewing career software and to developers in producing career planning software.

The guidelines have two parts: (a) a format for describing the software and (b) criteria for evaluating the program. These two parts can be used separately or together, depending on the purposes of the user.

References

Association of Computer-Based Systems for Career Information. (1982). *Handbook of Standards for Computer-Based Career Information Systems*. Eugene, OR: ACSCI Clearinghouse.

Association of Computer-Based Systems for Career Information. (1985). *Guidelines for the Use of Computer-Based Career Information and Guidance Systems*. Eugene, OR: ACSCI Clearinghouse.

Herlihy, B., & Golden, L. (1990). *Ethical Standards Casebook*. Alexandria, VA: American Association for Counseling and Development.

National Career Development Association Career Information Review Service. (1987). *Instructions for CIRS Committee - Career Information Review Service*. Alexandria, VA: Author.

Northwest Regional Educational Laboratory (1988). *Evaluator's Guide for Microcomputer-Based Instructional Packages*. Eugene, OR: International Society for Technology in Education (formerly International Council for Computers in Education).

Walz, G., & Bleuer, J. (1990). *Counseling Software Guide: A Resource for the Guidance and Human Development Professions*. Alexandria, VA: American Association for Counseling and Development.

Part 1: Software Description

Title: _____ Version: _____
Developer: _____
Hardware Requirements: _____
Topics: _____
_____

User Materials Provided: _____
_____

Applicable to the Following Career Development Activities:
- ☐ Career Awareness
- ☐ Career Exploration
- ☐ Skill & Knowledge Development
- ☐ Career Decision Making

- ☐ Career Growth
- ☐ Career Change
- ☐ Other: _____

Applicable in:
- ☐ Instruction
- ☐ Counseling

- ☐ Job Search
- ☐ Human Resource Development

Appropriate for Settings such as:
- ☐ Elementary Schools
- ☐ Middle & Junior High Schools
- ☐ High Schools
- ☐ Vocational Schools
- ☐ Community & Junior Colleges
- ☐ Colleges & Universities

- ☐ Rehabilitation Agencies
- ☐ Counseling Agencies
- ☐ Correctional Institutions
- ☐ Job Placement Services
- ☐ Personnel Offices
- ☐ The Work Place
- ☐ Libraries & Resource Centers
- ☐ Job & Training Programs

Cost:
Software for: Single-User Computer $ _____
Networked or Time-Shared Computer $ _____

Consumable Materials: $ _____ per _____

Licensing provisions for multi-user installations (networks, computer labs, etc.) _____

_____

_____

Field tested data are available:
   ☐ On Request   ☐ With the Program   ☐ Not Available

Objectives:
   ☐ Stated by Developer   ☐ Inferred

_____

_____

_____

_____

Prerequisites for successful use:
   ☐ Stated by Developer   ☐ Inferred

_____

_____

_____

_____

Content and Structure:

_____

_____

_____

_____

Potential Uses:

_____

_____

_____

_____

Description prepared by: _____ Date: _____

Part 2: Software Evaluation Criteria

You can evaluate five aspects of a program with these criteria categories:

- information in the program,
- career development process,
- user interaction,
- technical aspects of the software and materials, and
- support services.

There are few software programs, even comprehensive career information systems, to which you would apply all 67 of the criteria listed. You will need to omit the criteria that are not appropriate to the type of program you are evaluating.

Some of the criteria are standards of quality that any career development software program should meet. These include such standards as nondiscriminatory language, current and valid information, user control of decision making, program reliability, and availability of technical assistance. Use these important standards of quality to rate every program.

Other criteria (e.g., inclusion of test results or appropriateness for small group use) are features which may not be important for a particular type of program. Do not rate items that are not applicable to the kind of product you are evaluating; cross out their rating scales instead.

If you are rating one program and doing it yourself, you can select criteria and do the rating at the same time. However, if you are comparing several programs, or if several people are doing independent ratings, you first need to make several copies of the rating form. In that case, cross out the criteria that are not applicable, then make copies of the rating form.

For each applicable criterion, rate the program:

5=Outstanding   4=Good   3=Satisfactory   2=Poor   1=Unsatisfactory

After you have finished rating the program, you can construct a summary score for it. If you want a summary score, sum

the points assigned and divide the total points by the number of
items rated, omitting the items you decided were not applicable.
Use the overall numeric score only as a guide. If an essential criterion is rated unsatisfactory, you may decide to reject the program
even if some of its features are attractive.

Information in the Program

These information criteria cover the following aspects of the program: relevance to the audience, appropriate language, organization
of the information, and information quality.

                                                              Outstanding   Unsatisfactory

1. The information is clear, concise, and informative
   to the intended audience 5 4 3 2 1
2. The language is nondiscriminatory. Content is
   free from race, ethnic, gender, age, and other
   stereotypes 5 4 3 2 1
3. The content is free from spelling and grammatical
   errors 5 4 3 2 1
4. All subjects are covered in a comprehensive man-
   ner. For example, if information about all types
   of occupations is presented, it covers 90% of total
   employment in the area where the program is
   being used. Or, if the information applies specifically to one field of training, it covers all relevant
   instructional programs 5 4 3 2 1
5. The information for each topic encourages com-
   parisons among schools or occupations 5 4 3 2 1
6. Occupational information covers standard occupational categories, duties, abilities, skills, working conditions, equipment, earnings, employment,
   outlook, training, and methods of entry. It identi-
   fies related occupations 5 4 3 2 1
7. Information about educational programs covers
   program objectives, specialties, degrees conferred,
   sample courses, and schools offering the pro-
   gram 5 4 3 2 1

8. Information about schools includes general information, admissions, programs of study, housing, costs, financial aid, and student service 5 4 3 2 1

9. The program lists only schools that meet basic licensing requirements. It reports accreditation by recognized organizations 5 4 3 2 1

10. The information is based on empirical data that are current and valid 5 4 3 2 1

11. Updated information is distributed promptly, at least yearly 5 4 3 2 1

12. In a personal search questionnaire, there is a clear, empirical relationship between characteristics of the user and those of the occupations, schools, or other activities being sorted 5 4 3 2 1

13. In a program using off-line or computer-administered assessment instruments, those instruments conform to accepted standards of validity and reliability 5 4 3 2 1

14. Advice is clearly distinguished from factual information. The sources of advice are identified 5 4 3 2 1

15. Statements made in one component are consistent with those made in other components of the program 5 4 3 2 1

16. If the program produces only lists of titles, it effectively refers users to specific sources of accurate information 5 4 3 2 1

17. Published information sources are readily available, for example, in local career information centers 5 4 3 2 1

18. To supplement objective information, the program suggests interviewing individuals about their personal career histories, including how they feel about their schools or jobs 5 4 3 2 1

Career Development Process
These criteria evaluate the compatibility of the program with important career development principles.

Outstanding   Unsatisfactory

19. The program motivates individuals to develop their own career plans 5 4 3 2 1

20. The program fosters self-knowledge relevant to work and learning 5 4 3 2 1

21. The program helps individuals to integrate and develop their values, interests, abilities, skills, and goals 5 4 3 2 1

22. Using the program broadens an individual's awareness of current options for employment and education 5 4 3 2 1

23. If there is a search process, it broadens the outlook of individuals regardless of their race, ethnic group, gender, or age 5 4 3 2 1

24. The program supports informed decision making by helping individuals generate ideas, obtain necessary information, and evaluate alternatives in responsible and personally relevant ways 5 4 3 2 1

25. The program encourages the user to get appropriate counseling and advice in making long term decisions 5 4 3 2 1

26. Using the program integrates planning with previous experiences 5 4 3 2 1

27. The user, not the program, controls the decision making 5 4 3 2 1

28. The structure of the program demonstrates that career planning is a developmental, lifelong process 5 4 3 2 1

29. The program is appropriate for individual use 5 4 3 2 1

30. The program is appropriate for small group use 5 4 3 2 1

31. The program can be a useful resource in a counseling program 5 4 3 2 1

32. The program provides information that can be useful in instruction 5 4 3 2 1
33. The program can be a useful resource in a job search program 5 4 3 2 1
34. Using the program contributes to a person's career development 5 4 3 2 1

User Interaction

These criteria cover the user's interaction with the program, the objectives and features of the program, and your analysis of it.

Outstanding Unsatisfactory

35. The purpose of the program is well defined and clearly explained to the user 5 4 3 2 1
36. The organization is clear, logical, and effective, making it easy for the intended audience to understand 5 4 3 2 1
37. The language in the program and in the user's guide is clear to the intended audience 5 4 3 2 1
38. User materials are easy to use, appealing to users, and readily available 5 4 3 2 1
39. Prerequisites are identified and instruction is provided in the software or in the user guides so individuals can run the program and understand its results 5 4 3 2 1
40. The individual has the choice of going directly to desired information or using a structured search to identify relevant topics 5 4 3 2 1
41. The individual can operate the program independently, creating his or her own sequence of presentation and review 5 4 3 2 1
42. The program acknowledges input. Feedback on user responses is employed effectively 5 4 3 2 1
43. Invalid commands are handled constructively. The program tolerates variations in command formats (e.g., upper or lower case, extra spaces, etc.) 5 4 3 2 1

44. Individuals can easily start and exit the program. It is easy to back up, change answers, and give commands 5 4 3 2 1

45. If there are "help" and "hint" messages, they are easy to access 5 4 3 2 1

46. If the program contains tests of knowledge or skill, it reports which items were missed and which were correct 5 4 3 2 1

47. The program is attractive and interesting. It motivates users to continue using the program and exploring career options 5 4 3 2 1

48. The program is demonstrably effective with the intended audience, including people of varying abilities and experiences 5 4 3 2 1

49. The program can be used by various cultural groups 5 4 3 2 1

50. The program achieves its purpose 5 4 3 2 1

Technical Aspects of the Software and Materials
These criteria cover aspects of the computer hardware and programs.

Outstanding   Unsatisfactory

51. The system uses standard equipment that is reliable, widely available, and applicable to a variety of uses 5 4 3 2 1

52. Computer capabilities such as graphics, color, or sound are used for appropriate instructional reasons 5 4 3 2 1

53. If the program requires special equipment, the requirements are minimal and clearly stated by the developer 5 4 3 2 1

54. The program is reliable in normal use. Software is bug free 5 4 3 2 1

55. The program provides a copy or summary of its basic information to the user for future reference 5 4 3 2 1

56. Printouts are clear and well organized. The print-
outs are dated 5 4 3 2 1
57. Updates can be loaded easily into the system 5 4 3 2 1
58. If any processing in the program is based on assessment scores, course grades, or other client records,
the program explains to the user how the records
are being used 5 4 3 2 1
59. If the program uses client records, it does not
restrict an individual in exploring any of the infor-
mation in the program 5 4 3 2 1
60. If the program creates a permanent record for a
user, that record is secure and confidential. There
is provision for erasing the record when the information is no longer valuable in providing ser-
vices 5 4 3 2 1

Support

These criteria cover aspects of support for professionals who implement the program: written materials, staff training, service, and cost.

Outstanding Unsatisfactory

61. The site coordinator's manual explains the content and process for updating information 5 4 3 2 1
62. Print or computer materials explain the content
and effective use of the program to local site
coordinators 5 4 3 2 1
63. Training on appropriate and effective use of the
program is provided regularly 5 4 3 2 1
64. There is a system of communication between user
sites and the system developer which may include
newsletters, telephone assistance, and annual
evaluations 5 4 3 2 1
65. On-site technical assistance is available for effec-
tive program use 5 4 3 2 1
66. Evaluations of the program's effectiveness are
available to site coordinators 5 4 3 2 1

67. The cost per user makes it feasible to serve most
    clients who can benefit from the program 5 4 3 2 1

Summary Comments
Major Strengths:

_____
_____
_____
_____
_____

Major Weaknesses:

_____
_____
_____
_____
_____

Other Comments:

_____
_____
_____
_____
_____

Evaluation prepared by: _____ Date: _____

References

Allen, F. J. "The Need for Clearing Information on Occupational Studies and Possible Ways of Organizing a Clearance Service." *Vocational Guidance Magazine,* 1925, *3,* 235–238.

American Council on Education. *Guide to External Degree Programs in America.* Washington, D.C.: American Council on Education, 1980.

American Legion. *Need A Lift? Educational Opportunities, Careers, Loans, Scholarships, Employment.* (40th ed.) Indianapolis: National Emblem Sales, 1990.

American Trade Schools Directory. Jericho, N.M.: Croner Publications, 1990 (and continually updated).

Anderson, N. *Man's Work and Leisure.* Leiden, The Netherlands: Brill, 1974.

Arbona, C. "Hispanic Employment and the Holland Typology of Work." *Career Development Quarterly,* 1989, *37,* 257–268.

Association of Computer-Based Systems for Career Information. *1991 Directory of State-Based Career Information Delivery Systems.* Eugene, Oreg.: Association of Computer-Based Systems for Career Information Clearinghouse, 1990.

Astin, H. S. "The Meaning of Work in Women's Lives: A Sociopsychological Model of Career Choice and Work Behavior." *Counseling Psychologist,* 1984, *12*(4), 117–126.

Auster, C., and Auster, D. "Factors Influencing Women's Choice of Nontraditional Careers: The Role of Family, Peers, and Counselors." *Vocational Guidance Quarterly,* 1981, *29*(3), 253–263.

Avasthi, S. "Hispanics in the 90's—Breaking Through Barriers to Reach Hispanic Immigrants." *Guidepost,* 1990, *33*(1), 1.

Ayala-Vazquez, N. "The Guidance and Counseling of Hispanic Females." *Journal of Non-White Concerns,* 1979, 7(3), 114–120.

Ayers, M. L. "Counseling the American Indian." *Occupational Outlook Quarterly,* 1977, *21*(1), 22–29.

Bailey, L. J. *Career and Vocational Education in the 1980's: Towards a Process Approach.* Carbondale: Southern Illinois University Press, 1976.

Barrett, L. A., and Chick, G. E. "Chips off the Ol' Block: Parents' Leisure and Their Children's Play." *Journal of Leisure Research,* 1986, *18*(4), 266–283.

Bartlett, W. E., and Oldham, D. "Career Adjustment Counseling of 'Young-Old' Women." *Vocational Guidance Quarterly,* 1978, 27(2), 156–164.

Baruth, L. G., and Robinson, E. H. *An Introduction to the Counseling Profession.* Englewood Cliffs, N.J.: Prentice-Hall, 1987.

Berman, J. J., and Munson, H. L. "Challenges in a Dialectical Conception of Career Evaluation." *Personnel and Guidance Journal,* 1981, *60*, 92–96.

Biggs, D. A., and Keller, K. E. "A Cognitive Approach to Using Tests in Counseling." *Personnel and Guidance Journal,* 1982, *60*(9), 367–371.

Bloland, A., and Edwards, P. "Work & Leisure: A Counseling Synthesis." *Vocational Guidance Quarterly,* 1981, *30*(2), 101–108.

Bloomfield, M. *Readings in Vocational Guidance.* New York: Ginn, 1915.

Bolles, R. N. *The Three Boxes of Life.* Berkeley, Calif.: Ten Speed Press, 1981.

Boone, T. A., and Reid, R. A. "Selecting Workshop Sites." In

J. W. Pfieffer and J. E. Jones (eds.), *The 1978 Annual Handbook for Group Facilitators.* San Diego, Calif.: University Associates, 1978.

Borow, H. (ed.). *Man in a World at Work.* Boston: Houghton Mifflin, 1964.

Bowen, M. *Key to the Genogram.* Washington, D.C.: Georgetown University Hospital, 1980.

Bradley, R. W. "Editor's Introduction—Discussion of Multicultural Counseling." *Counselor Education and Supervision,* 1987, *26*(3), 162-163.

Brayfield, A. H. "Putting Occupational Information Across." *Educational and Psychological Measurement,* 1948, *8,* 493-495.

Brewer, J. M. *The Vocational-Guidance Movement.* New York: Macmillan, 1922.

Brolin, D. E. "Introduction to Career Development for Special Needs Learners." *Journal of Career Development,* 1987, *13*(4), 3-4.

Brolin, D. E., and Elliott, T. R. "Meeting the Lifelong Career Development Needs of Students with Handicaps: A Community College Model." *Career Development for Exceptional Individuals,* 1984, *7,* 12-21.

Brolin, D. E., and Gysbers, N. C. "Career Education for Students with Disabilities." *Journal of Counseling and Development,* 1989, *68*(2), 155-159.

Brooks, L. "Career Counseling Methods and Practice." In D. Brown, L. Brooks, and Associates, *Career Choice and Development: Applying Contemporary Theories to Practice.* (2nd ed.) San Francisco: Jossey-Bass, 1990.

Brooks, L. "Counseling Special Groups: Women and Ethnic Minorities." In D. Brown, L. Brooks, and Associates, *Career Choice and Development: Applying Contemporary Theories to Practice.* San Francisco: Jossey-Bass, 1984b.

Brooks, L., and Haring-Hidore, M. (eds.). *Journal of Career Development,* 1985, *14*(4). (A special issue of the *Journal of Career Development* titled "Career Interventions with Women.")

Brown, D. "Trait and Factor Theory." In D. Brown, L. Brooks, and Associates, *Career Choice and Development:*

Applying Contemporary Theories to Practice. (2nd ed.) San Francisco: Jossey-Bass, 1990.

Brown, D., and Brooks, L. *Career Counseling Techniques.* Needham Heights, Mass.: Allyn & Bacon, 1991.

Brown, D., Brooks, L., and Associates. *Career Choice and Development: Applying Contemporary Theories to Practice.* San Francisco: Jossey-Bass, 1984.

Brown, D., Brooks, L., and Associates. *Career Choice and Development: Applying Contemporary Theories to Practice.* (2nd ed.) San Francisco: Jossey-Bass, 1990.

Brown, D., and Minor, C. (eds.). *Working in America: A Status Report on Planning and Problems.* Alexandria, Va.: National Career Development Association, 1989.

Bucher, D. E., Brolin, D. E., and Kunce, J. T. "Importance of Life-Centered Career Education for Special Education Students: The Parents' Perspective." *Journal of Career Development,* 1987, *13*(4), 63–70.

Bureau of the Census, Department of Commerce. *U.S. Census of Population, 1980: Alphabetical Index of Occupations and Industries.* (Final ed.) Washington, D.C.: U.S. Government Printing Office, 1982a.

Bureau of the Census, Department of Commerce. *U.S. Census Population, 1980: Classified Index of Industries and Occupations.* (Final ed.) Washington, D.C.: U.S. Government Printing Office, 1982b.

Bureau of Economic Analysis, Department of Commerce. *Survey of Current Business.* Washington, D.C.: U.S. Government Printing Office, 1989.

Bureau of Industrial Economics, Department of Commerce. *1990 U.S. Industrial Outlook: Prospects for Over 350 Industries.* Washington, D.C.: U.S. Government Printing Office, 1990.

Bureau of Labor Statistics, Department of Labor. *Occupational Outlook Handbook (1990–1991).* Washington, D.C.: U.S. Government Printing Office, 1990a.

Bureau of Labor Statistics, Department of Labor. *Occupational Projections and Training Data.* Washington, D.C.: U.S. Government Printing Office, 1990b.

Bureau of Labor Statistics, Department of Labor. *Outlook 2000.* Washington, D.C.: U.S. Government Printing Office, 1990c.

Burge, P. L. *Career Development of Single Parents*. Columbus, Ohio: ERIC Clearinghouse on Adult, Career, and Vocational Education, National Center for Research in Vocational Education, 1987.

Campbell, R. E., and Cellini, J. V. "A Diagnostic Taxonomy of Adult Career Problems." *Journal of Vocational Behavior*, 1981, *79*, 175-190.

Career Information Review Service Committee. "Current Career Literature." *Career Development Quarterly*, 1991, *39*(4), 372-379.

Carlsen, M. B. *Meaning-Making: Therapeutic Processes in Adult Development*. New York: W. W. Norton, 1988.

Chatham, H. E. "Afrocentricity and Career Development for African-Americans." *Career Development Quarterly*, 1990, *38*(4), 334-346.

Christensen, T. E. "Functions of Occupational Information in Counseling." *Occupations*, 1949, *28*(1), 11-14.

Coelho, R. J., and Wilkins, D. M. "Evaluation of Occupational Literature: A Guide for Use with Minorities." *Journal of Non-White Concerns*, 1980, *9*, 3-9.

Cole, H. P. *Process Education*. Englewood Cliffs, N.J.: Educational Technology Publications, 1972.

Cole, H. P. *Approaches to the Logical Validation of Career Development Curricula Paradigms*. Carbondale, Ill.: Career Development for Children Project, Department of Occupational Education, Southern Illinois University, 1973.

Collison, M. "Unique Program Guides Black 8th Graders Out of High School and on to College." *Chronicle of Higher Education*, July 1, 1990, p. 14.

Commission on Precollege Guidance and Counseling, The College Board. *Keeping the Options Open: Recommendations*. New York: College Board, 1986.

Corey, G. *Theory and Practice of Group Counseling*. (3rd ed.) Pacific Grove, Calif.: Brooks/Cole, 1990.

Corre, M. P. "Proceedings of the Occupational Research Section." *Vocational Guidance Magazine*, 1926, *4*(7), 307-309.

Crites, J. O. *Career Counseling: Models, Methods, and Materials*. New York: McGraw-Hill, 1981.

Crosby, F. "Job Satisfaction and Domestic Life." In M. D.

Lee and R. N. Kanungo (eds.), *Management of Work and Personal Life*. New York: Praeger, 1984.

Curnow, T. C. "Vocational Development of Persons with Disability." *Career Development Quarterly*, 1989, *37*, 269–278.

Cutler, B. "Where Does the Time Go?" *American Demographics*, 1990, *12*(11), 36–39.

Dagley, J. *A Vocational Genogram*. Athens: University of Georgia, 1984 (Photocopied).

Dahl, P. R. "Counteracting Stereotypes Through Career Education." *Career Development for Exceptional Individuals*, 1981, *4*, 13–24.

D'Alonzo, B. J., Marino, J. F., and Kauss, M. W. "Mesa Public Schools' Comprehensive Career and Vocational Education Program for Disabled Students." *Career Development for Exceptional Individuals*, 1984, 7, 22–29.

Davis, H. V. *Frank Parsons: Prophet, Innovator, Counselor*. Carbondale: Southern Illinois University Press, 1969.

de Grazia, S. *Of Time, Work, and Leisure*. New York: Twentieth Century Fund, 1962.

Department of Defense. *Military Career Guide*. Chicago, Ill.: U.S. Military Entrance Processing Command, 1988.

Department of Leisure Studies, University of Illinois. *Annual Report of Research, 1988–1989*. Urbana-Champaign: Department of Leisure Studies, University of Illinois, 1990.

de Vries, B., Birren, J. E., and Deutchman, D. E. "Adult Development Through Guided Autobiography: The Family Context." *Family Relations*, 1990, *39*, 3–7.

Dinkmeyer, D. C., Pew, W. L., and Dinkmeyer, D. C., Jr. *Adlerian Counseling and Psychotherapy*. Pacific Grove, Calif.: Brooks/Cole, 1979.

Drier, N. "Career Information for Youth in Transition: The Need, Systems, and Models." *Vocational Guidance Quarterly*, 1980, *24*, 135–143.

Drum, D., and Knott, J. *Structured Groups for Facilitating Development: Acquiring Life Skills, Resolving Life Themes, and Making Life Transitions*. New York: Human Sciences Press, 1977.

Dudley, G., and Tiedeman, D. V. *Career Development: Exploration and Commitment.* Muncie, Ind.: Accelerated Development, 1977.

Dumazedier, J. *Toward a Society of Leisure.* New York: Free Press, 1967.

Duvall, E. M. "Family Development's First Forty Years." *Family Relations,* 1988, *37,* 127–134.

Edwards, P. *Leisure Counseling Techniques.* (3rd ed.) Los Angeles: Constructive Leisure, 1980.

Eisenberg, G. G. *Learning Vacations.* (6th ed.) Princeton, N.J.: Peterson's Guides, 1989.

Employment and Training Administration, Department of Labor. *Dictionary of Occupational Titles.* (4th ed.) Washington, D.C.: U.S. Government Printing Office, 1977.

Employment and Training Administration, Department of Labor. *Guide for Occupational Exploration.* Washington, D.C.: U.S. Government Printing Office, 1979.

Employment and Training Administration, Department of Labor. *Selected Characteristics of Occupations Defined in the Dictionary of Occupational Titles.* Washington, D.C.: U.S. Government Printing Office, 1981.

Employment and Training Administration, Department of Labor. Supplement to the *Dictionary of Occupational Titles* (4th ed.) Washington, D.C.: U.S. Government Printing Office, 1986.

Fain, T. "Self Employed Americans: Their Number Has Increased Between 1972–79." *Monthly Labor Review,* 1980, *103*(11), 3–8.

Farmer, H. S. "A Shiny Fresh Minted Penny." *Counseling Psychologist,* 1984, *12*(4), 141–144. (Response to Astin's paper in the same issue.)

Field, F. L. "A Taxonomy of Educational Processes, the Nature of Vocational Guidance, and Some Implications for Professional Preparation." Unpublished manuscript, National Vocational Guidance Association, 1966.

Figler, H. "The Emotional Dimension of Career Counseling." *Career Waves,* 1989, *2*(2), 1–11.

Fisher, I. "Midlife Change." Unpublished doctoral dissertation, Teachers College, Columbia University, 1989.

Flanders, R. "The Evolution of the NOICC-SOICC Programs: 1977-1987." *Journal of Career Development*, 1988, *14*(3), 145-159.

Frederickson, R. H. *Career Information.* Englewood Cliffs, N.J.: Prentice-Hall, 1982.

Freeman, R. B. "The Work Force of the Future: An Overview." In C. Kerr and J. W. Rosow (eds.), *Work in America: The Decade Ahead.* New York: Van Nostrand Reinhold, 1979.

Freeman, S. C., and Haring-Hidore, M. "Outplacement for Underserved Women Workers." *Journal of Career Development*, 1988, *14*(4), 287-293.

Friedman, D. E. "Work vs. Family: War of the Worlds." *Personnel Administrator*, 1987, *32*(8), 36-39.

Fullerton, H. N., Jr. "Labor Force Projections 1986 to 2000." *Monthly Labor Review*, 1987, *110*(9), 19-29.

Gallup, G., and Newport, F. "1989 Gallup Leisure Audit." *Gallup Poll Monthly*, Apr. 1990, pp. 27-29.

Gelatt, H. B. "Positive Uncertainty: A New Decision Making Framework for Counseling." *Journal of Counseling Psychology*, 1989, *36*(2), 252-256.

Gelatt, H. B. "Decision-Making: A Conceptual Frame of Reference for Counseling." *Journal of Counseling Psychology*, 1962, *9*, 240-245.

George, R. L., and Cristiani, T. S. *Theory, Methods, and Processes of Counseling and Psychotherapy.* Englewood Cliffs, N.J.: Prentice-Hall, 1981.

Germain, R. (ed.). *National Avocational Organizations.* (7th ed.) Washington, D.C.: Columbia Books, 1987.

Ginzberg, E. *Good Jobs, Bad Jobs, No Jobs.* Cambridge, Mass.: Harvard University Press, 1979.

Ginzberg, E., Ginsburg, S. W., Axelrod, S., and Herma, J. L. *Occupational Choice: An Approach to a General Theory.* New York: Columbia University Press, 1951.

Glaser, R. "Experts Defined." *Centergram.* National Center for Research in Vocational Education, 1986, *21*(1), 1-4.

Goldhammer, K. "Career Education: An Humane Perspective on the Functions of Education." *Journal of Career Education*, 1975, *2*, 21-26.

Goldhammer, K., and Taylor, R. E. *Career Education: Perspective and Promise.* Columbus, Ohio: Merrill, 1972.

Gordon, E. W. "Vocational Guidance: Disadvantaged and Minority Populations." In E. Herr (ed.), *Vocational Guidance and Human Development.* Boston: Houghton Mifflin, 1974.

Gordon, V. N. "The Undecided Student: A Development Perspective." *Personnel and Guidance Journal*, 1981, *59*, 433-438.

Gottfredson, G. D., and Holland, J. L. *Dictionary of Holland Occupational Codes.* (2nd ed.) Odessa, Fla.: Psychological Assessment Resources, 1989.

Greenhaus, J. H. "The Intersection of Work and Family Roles: Individual, Interpersonal, and Organizational Issues." *Journal of Social Behavior and Personality*, 1988, *3*(4), 23-44.

Griffin, A. R. "Justification for Black Career Development." *Journal of Non-White Concerns*, 1980, *8*(2), 77-83.

Griffin, A. R. "Career-Entry Issues for Minority Professionals." *Journal of Non-White Concerns*, 1987, *6*(4), 183-190.

Gutek, B. A. (ed.). *Enhancing Women's Career Development.* New Directions for Education, Work, and Careers, no. 8. San Francisco: Jossey-Bass, 1979.

Gutek, B. A., and Larwood, L. (eds.). *Women's Career Development.* Newbury Park, Calif.: Sage, 1987.

Gysbers, N. C., and Moore, E. J. *Career Guidance, Counseling, and Placement.* Columbia: University of Missouri, 1974.

Gysbers, N. C., and Moore, E. J. "Beyond Career Development: Life Career Development." *Personnel and Guidance Journal*, 1975, *53*, 647-652.

Gysbers, N. C., and Moore, E. J. *Improving Guidance Programs.* Englewood Cliffs, N.J.: Prentice-Hall, 1981.

Gysbers, N. C., and Moore, E. J. *Career Counseling: Skills and Techniques for Practitioners.* Englewood Cliffs, N.J.: Prentice-Hall, 1987.

Gysbers, N. C., and Associates. *Designing Careers: Counseling to Enhance Education, Work, and Leisure.* San Francisco: Jossey-Bass, 1984.

Hall, D. T., and Hall, F. S. "Stress and the Two-Career Couple." In C. L. Cooper and R. Payne (eds.), *Current Concerns in Occupational Stress.* New York: Wiley, 1980.

Hansen, L. S. "Interrelations of Guidance and Career." In Gysbers, N. C., and Associates, *Designing Careers: Counseling to Enhance Education, Work, and Leisure.* San Francisco: Jossey-Bass, 1984.

Harmon, L. W. "What's New? A Response to Astin." *Counseling Psychologist,* 1984, *12*(4), 127–128.

Harmon, L. W. "The Life and Career Plans of Young Adult College Women: A Followup Study." *Journal of Counseling Psychology,* 1989a, *28*, 416–427.

Harmon, L. W. "Longitudinal Changes in Women's Career Aspirations: Developmental or Historical?" *Journal of Vocational Behavior,* 1989b, *35*, 46–63.

Harris, S. (ed.). *Accredited Institutions of Postsecondary Education, 1990–91.* Washington, D.C.: American Council on Education, 1991.

Hartman, J. S., and Askounis, A. C. "Asian-American Students: Are They Really a Model Minority?" *School Counselor,* 1989, *37*(2), 109–112.

Hawley, P. *Sex-Fair Career Counseling.* Washington, D.C.: National Vocational Guidance Association, 1980.

Hedges, J. "The Workweek in 1979: Fewer But Longer Workdays." *Monthly Labor Review,* 1980, *103*(8), 31–33.

Hedges, J., and Taylor, D. "Recent Trends in Worktime: Hours Edge Downward." *Monthly Labor Review,* 1980, *103*(3), 3–11.

Heinl, P. "The Image and Visual Analysis of the Genogram." *Journal of Family Therapy,* 1985, *7*(3), 213–229.

Hellmich, N. "Many Fathers Seek Ways to Have It All." *USA Today,* June 15, 1990, p. D-2.

Heppner, P. P. "Identifying the Complexities Within Clients' Thinking and Decision Making." *Journal of Counseling Psychology,* 1989, *36*(2), 257–259.

Heppner, P. P., and Krauskopf, C. J. "An Information-Processing Approach to Personal Problem Solving." *Counseling Psychologist*, 1987, *15*(3), 371-446.

Herr, E. L. (ed.). *Vocational Guidance and Human Development*. Boston: Houghton Mifflin, 1974.

Herr, E. L. *Counseling in a Dynamic Society: Opportunities and Challenges*. Alexandria, Va.: American Association for Counseling and Development, 1989.

Herr, E. L., and Cramer, S. H. *Career Guidance and Counseling Through the Life Span*. Glenview, Ill.: Scott, Foresman, 1988.

Herring, R. D. "Attacking Career Myths Among Native Americans: Implications for Counseling." *The School Counselor*, 1990, *38*(1), 13-18.

Hill, R. L. "Life Cycle Stages for Types of Single-Parent Families: Of Family Development Theory." *Family Relations*, 1986, *35*, 19-29.

Hitchner, K. W., and Hitchner, A. *Making a Difference in College Admission*. West Uyac, N.Y.: Center for Applied Research in Education, 1989.

Holland, J. L. *Making Vocational Choices: A Theory of Vocational Personalities & Work Environments*. Englewood Cliffs, N.J.: Prentice-Hall, 1985a.

Holland, J. L. *The Self-Directed Search Professional Manual*. Odessa, Fla.: Psychological Assessment Resources, 1985b.

Hoppock, R. F. *Occupational Information*. (4th ed.) New York: McGraw-Hill, 1976.

Hotchkiss, L., and Borow, H. "Sociological Perspectives on Career Choice and Attainment." In D. Brown, L. Brooks, and Associates, *Career Choice and Development: Applying Contemporary Theories to Practice*. (2nd ed.) San Francisco: Jossey-Bass, 1990.

House, E., and Katzell, M. E. (eds.). *Facilitating Career Development for Girls and Women*. Alexandria, Va.: American Association for Counseling and Development, 1975. (A monograph of the National Vocational Guidance Association.)

Hoyt, K. B. "The Career Status of Women and Minority Persons: A 20-Year Retrospective." *Career Development Quarterly*, 1989, *37*, 202-212.

Hughey, K. F., Heppner, M. J., Johnston, J. A., and Rakes,

T. D. "Farm Families in Career Transitions: Descriptive Characteristics and an Intervention." *Journal of Counseling and Development,* 1989, *67,* 475–477.

Isaacson, L. E. *Basics of Career Counseling.* Needham Heights, Mass.: Allyn & Bacon, 1985.

Isaacson, L. E. *Career Information in Counseling and Career Development.* (4th ed.) Needham Heights, Mass.: Allyn & Bacon, 1986.

Izzo, M. V. "Career Developments of Disabled Youth: The Parents' Role." *Journal of Career Development,* 1987, *13*(4), 47–55.

Jepsen, D. A. "Relationship Between Career Development Theory and Practice." In N. C. Gysbers and Associates, *Designing Careers: Counseling to Enhance Education, Work, and Leisure.* San Francisco: Jossey-Bass, 1984.

Johnson, C. A., and Figler, H. E. "Career Development and Placement Services in Postsecondary Institutions." In N. C. Gysbers and Associates, *Designing Careers: Counseling to Enhance Education, Work, and Leisure.* San Francisco: Jossey-Bass, 1984.

Jones, G. B., and others. *Planning, Developing, and Field Testing Career Guidance Programs.* Palo Alto, Calif.: American Institutes for Research, 1972.

Jordaan, J. P. "Life States as Organizing Modes of Career Development." In E. L. Herr (ed.), *Vocational Guidance and Human Development.* Boston: Houghton Mifflin, 1974.

Jordaan, J. P., and Heyde, M. B. *Vocational Maturity During the High-School Years.* New York: Teachers College Press, 1979.

June, L. N., and Fooks, G. M. "Key Influences on the Career Directions and Choices of Black University Professionals." *Journal of Non-White Concerns,* 1980, *8*(3), 157–166.

Kahl, M. C. (ed.). *Directory of External Graduate Programs 1987–1988.* (4th ed.) Albany, N.Y.: Regents College Degrees, The University of the State of New York Cultural Education Center, 1987.

Kalleberg, A. L., and others. *Indianapolis/Tokyo Work Commitment Study: Preliminary Results.* Bloomington: Institute for Social Research, Indiana University, 1983.

Kapes, J. T., and Mastie, M. M. (eds.). *A Counselor's Guide to Career Assessment Instruments.* (2nd ed.) Alexandria, Va.: National Career Development Association, 1988.

Kaplan, M. *Leisure Theory and Practice.* New York: Wiley, 1975.

Katz, M. "The Name and Nature of Vocational Guidance." Unpublished manuscript, National Vocational Guidance Association, 1966.

Kazalunas, J. R. "Counseling and Testing Procedures for Chicano Students." *Journal of Non-White Concerns,* 1979, 7(3), 108-113.

Keller, F. J. "Accomplishments of NOC." *Occupations,* 1937, 15, 324-327.

Keller, K. E., Biggs, D. A., and Gysbers, N. C. "Career Counseling from a Cognitive Perspective." *Personnel and Guidance Journal,* 1982, 60(6), 367-371.

Kelly, J. R. "The Centrality of Leisure." *National Forum,* 1982a, 62, 19-21.

Kelly, J. R. *Leisure.* Englewood Cliffs, N.J.: Prentice-Hall, 1982b.

Kelly, R. *Leisure Identities and Interactions.* London: Allen & Unwin, 1983.

Kerka, S. *Single Parents: Career-Related Issues and Needs Digest 75.* Columbus, Ohio: ERIC Clearinghouse on Adult, Career, and Vocational Education, National Center for Research in Vocational Education, 1988.

Kimeldorf, M. *Pathways to Leisure.* Bloomington, Ind.: Meridian Education Corporation, 1989.

Kinnier, R. T., Brigman, L., and Noble, F. C. "Career Indecision and Family Enmeshment." *Journal of Counseling and Development,* 1990, 68, 309-312.

Kinnier, R. T., and Krumboltz, J. D. "Procedures for Successful Counseling." In N. C. Gysbers and Associates, *Designing Careers: Counseling to Enhance Education, Work, and Leisure.* San Francisco: Jossey-Bass, 1984.

Kleibert, D., Larson, L., and Csikszentmihalyi, M. "The Experience of Leisure in Adolescence." *Journal of Leisure Research,* 1986, 18, 169-176.

Knefelkamp, L. L., and Slepitza, R. "A Cognitive-Development Model of Career Development: An Adaptation of The Perry Scheme." *Counseling Psychologist,* 1976, *6*(3), 53–58.

Kortering, J. J., and Edgar, E. B. "Vocational Rehabilitation and Special Education: A Need for Cooperation." *Rehabilitation Counseling Bulletin,* 1988, *31,* 178–184.

Krumboltz, J. D. *Private Rules in Career Decision Making.* Columbus, Ohio: National Center for Research in Vocational Education, 1983.

Lane, M. R. "The Content, Volume, and Uses of Occupational Studies." *Vocational Guidance Magazine,* 1927, *6*(1), 30–40.

Lane, M. R. "Outlines Used in Preparing Occupational Studies." *Vocational Guidance Magazine,* 1931, *9,* 356–359.

Leatherman, C. "Promises of College Tuition Found to Keep Many Students in School." *Chronicle of Higher Education,* July 18, 1990, p. A-3.

Lee, C. C. "Needed: A Career Development Advocate." *Career Development Quarterly,* 1989, *37,* 218–220.

Lefkowitz, B. *Breaktime.* New York: Hawthorn, 1979.

Leonard, P. Y. "Vocational Theory and the Vocational Behavior of Black Males: An Analysis." *Journal of Multicultural Counseling and Development,* 1985, *13*(1), 91–104.

Leong, F.T.L. "Career Development of Asian Americans." *Journal of College Student Personnel,* 1985, *26*(6), 539–546.

Leong, F.T.L. "Career Development Attributes and Occupational Values of Asian American and White American College Students." *Career Development Quarterly,* 1991, *39*(3), 221–230.

Levitan, S. A., and Johnson, W. B. *Work Is Here to Stay, Alas.* Salt Lake City, Utah: Olympus, 1973.

Lewis, R. A., and Gilhousen, M. R. "Myths of Career Development: A Cognitive Approach to Vocational Counseling." *Personnel and Guidance Journal,* 1981, *59*(5), 296–299.

Loesch, L. C. *Leisure Counseling.* Ann Arbor: ERIC/CAPS Clearinghouse, University of Michigan, 1980.

Loesch, L. C., and Wheeler, P. T. *Principles of Leisure Counseling.* Minneapolis, Minn.: Educational Media Corporation, 1982.

Love, M., Galinsky, E., and Hughes, D. "Work and Family: Research Findings and Models for Change." *ILR Report,* 1987, *25*(1), 10–12.

Low, A. *Mental Health Through Will Training.* (14th ed.) Boston: Christopher, 1966.

McCormac, M. E. "The Use of Career Information Delivery Systems in the States." *Journal of Career Development,* 1988, *14*(3), 205–215.

McDaniels, C. "Vocation: A Religious Search for Meaning." *Vocational Guidance Quarterly,* 1965, *14*(1), 31–35.

McDaniels, C. "The Role of Leisure in Career Development." *ACTES Proceedings of the Fifth World Congress of the International Association for Educational and Vocational Guidance.* Quebec, Canada: International Association for Educational and Vocational Guidance, 1973.

McDaniels, C. "The Role of Leisure in Career Development for Girls and Women." In E. House and M. E. Katzell (eds.), *Facilitating Career Development for Girls and Women.* Alexandria, Va.: American Association for Counseling and Development, 1975. (A monograph of the then National Vocational Guidance Association.)

McDaniels, C. (ed.). *Leisure and Career Development at Mid Life.* Blacksburg: Virginia Polytechnic Institute and State University, 1976a. (ED 155 577)

McDaniels, C. (ed.). *Occupational Information Dissemination Project.* Blacksburg: College of Education, Virginia Polytechnic Institute and State University, 1976b. (Department of Labor contract no. 99-6-816-08-101.)

McDaniels, C. "Leisure and Career Development at Mid-Life: A Rationale." *Vocational Guidance Quarterly,* 1977, *25*(4), 356–363.

McDaniels, C. "Comprehensive Career Information Systems for the 1980's." *Vocational Guidance Quarterly,* 1982a, *30*(1), 344–350.

McDaniels, C. *Leisure: Integrating a Neglected Component in Life Planning.* Columbus, Ohio: ERIC Clearinghouse on Adult, Career, and Vocational Education, National Center for Research in Vocational Education, 1982b.

McDaniels, C. "The Role of Leisure in Career Development." *Journal of Career Development*, 1984a, *11*(2), 64–71.

McDaniels, C. "Work and Leisure in the Career Span." In N. C. Gysbers and Associates, *Designing Careers: Counseling to Enhance Education, Work, and Leisure.* San Francisco: Jossey-Bass, 1984b.

McDaniels, C. "Virginia VIEW: 1979–1987." *Journal of Career Development*, 1988, *14*(3), 169–176.

McDaniels, C. *The Changing Workplace: Career Counseling Strategies for the 1990s and Beyond.* San Francisco: Jossey-Bass, 1989.

McDaniels, C., and Hesser, A. "Career Services for Adult Workers at Virginia Tech." *Career Planning and Adult Development Newsletter*, 1982c, *4*(11), 1–2.

McDaniels, C., and Hesser, A. "Outplacement: An Occasion for Faculty Career Development." In Walz, G. E. (ed.), *Outplacement Counseling.* Ann Arbor: ERIC/CAPS Clearinghouse, University of Michigan, 1983.

McDaniels, C., and Hummel, D. *Unlocking Your Child's Potential.* Reston, Va.: Acropolis, 1982d.

McDaniels, C., and Puryear, A. "The Face of Career Development Centers for the 1990s and Beyond." *The School Counselor*, 1991, *38*(5), 324–331.

McDaniels, C., Snipes, J. K., and Peevy, E. S. *A Feasibility Study for a Career Information System for Virginia.* Prepared for the Virginia Occupational Information Coordinating Committee, Richmond, Va., June 1980.

McDaniels, C., and Watts, G. A. "Cooperation: Key to Employee Career Development Programs." *Career Development Quarterly*, 1987, *36*(2), 170–175.

McDavis, R. J., and Parker, W. M. "Strategies for Helping Ethnic Minorities with Career Development." *Journal of Non-White Concerns*, 1981, *9*(4), 130–136.

McDowell, C. F., Jr. *Leisure Counseling: Selected Lifestyle Processes.* Eugene, Oreg.: Center for Leisure Studies, University of Oregon, 1976.

McGoldrick, M., and Gerson, R. *Genograms in Family Assessment.* New York: W. W. Norton, 1985.

McKay, M., Davis, M., and Fanning, P. *Thoughts and Feelings: The Art of Cognitive Stress Intervention.* Richmond, Calif.: New Harbinger, 1981.

McKinlay, B. "Oregon's Contribution to Career Information Delivery, 1972–1987." *Journal of Career Development,* 1988, *14*(3), 160–168.

Macklin, E. D. "Nontraditional Family Forms: A Decade of Research." *Journal of Marriage and Family,* 1980, *42*(4), 175–192.

Martin, E. S., and Schurtman, R. "Termination Anxiety as It Affects the Therapist." *Psychotherapy,* 1985, *33*, 583–591.

Martin, G. M. "A Guide to Setting up a Career Resource Information Center." *Occupational Outlook Quarterly,* 1980, *24*, 12–17.

Martin, G. M., and Fountain, M. C. "Matching Yourself with the World of Work." *Occupational Outlook Quarterly,* 1982, *31*, 2–12.

Masnick, G., and Bane, M. J. *The Nation's Families: 1960–1990.* Cambridge, Mass.: School of Public Health and Joint Center for Urban Studies, Harvard University, 1980. (ED 198 929)

Matthews, E. E."Counseling Girls and Women in the Year 2000." In E. A. Whitfield and A. Gustav (eds.), *Counseling Girls and Women over the Life Span.* Alexandria, Va.: American Association for Counseling and Development, 1972. (A monograph of the former National Vocational Guidance Association.)

Matthews, E. E. "The Vocational Guidance of Girls and Women in the United States." In E. L. Herr (ed.), *Vocational Guidance and Human Development.* Boston: Houghton Mifflin, 1974.

Miller, D., and Form, W. *Industrial Sociology.* New York: HarperCollins, 1951.

Miller, J. V. *The Family-Career Connection: A New Framework for Career Development.* Columbus, Ohio: ERIC Clearinghouse on Adult, Career, and Vocational Education, National Center for Research in Vocational Education, 1984.

Miller, J. V. "The Family-Career Connection: A New Component for Career Development Programs." *Journal of Career Development,* 1985, *12*(1), 8–22.

Minor, C. W. "Career Development: Theories and Issues." In Z. B. Leibowitz and H. D. Lea (eds.), *Adult Career Development: Concepts, Issues, and Practices.* Alexandria, Va.: National Career Development Association, 1986.

Moore, G., and Hedges, J. "Trends in Labor and Leisure." *Monthly Labor Review,* 1971, *94*(2), 3–11.

Mortimer, J. T., Lorence, J., and Kumka, D. S. *Work, Family and Personality: Transition to Adulthood.* Norwood, N.J.: Ablex, 1986.

Mosak, H. H. "Lifestyle." In A. G. Nikelly (ed.), *Techniques for Behavior Change.* Springfield, Ill.: Thomas, 1971.

Mundy, J., and Odum, L. *Leisure Education: Theory and Practice.* New York: Wiley, 1979.

Murphy, J. *Concepts of Leisure.* (2nd ed.) Englewood Cliffs, N.J.: Prentice-Hall, 1981.

Myers, G. E. *Principles and Techniques of Vocational Guidance.* New York: McGraw-Hill, 1941.

Myers, J. R., and Scott, E. W. *Getting Skilled, Getting Ahead.* Princeton, N.J.: Peterson's Guides, 1989.

National Association of College Admission Counselors. "Guide to College Guides—Students' Edition." *The Journal of College Admissions,* 1989, Summer (124), 22.

National Association of College Admission Counselors. *Statement on Precollege Guidance and Counseling* and *The Role of the School Counselor.* Alexandria, Va.: National Association of College Admission Counselors, 1990.

National Center for Education Statistics, Department of Education. *A Classification of Instructional Programs.* Washington, D.C.: U.S. Government Printing Office, 1981.

National Center for Education Statistics, Department of Education. *The Condition of Education, 1989.* Vol. 2: *Postsecondary Education.* Washington, D.C.: U.S. Government Printing Office, 1989a.

National Center for Education Statistics, Department of Education. *Digest of Education Statistics, 1988.* Washington, D.C.: U.S. Government Printing Office, 1989b.

National College Counseling Project. *Frontiers of Possibility.* Burlington: Instructional Development Center, University of Vermont, 1986. (A project sponsored by the National Association of College Admissions Counselors.)

National Occupational Information Coordinating Committee. *Vocational Preparation and Occupations.* Washington, D.C.: National Occupational Information Coordinating Committee, 1982.

National Occupational Information Coordinating Committee. *Status of the NOICC/SOICC Network—1989.* Administrative report no. 14. Washington, D.C.: National Occupational Information Coordinating Committee, 1990.

National Recreation and Park Association. *Life. Be in It.* Alexandria, Va.: National Recreation and Park Association, 1981.

National Vocational Guidance Association. "Distinguishing Marks of a Good Occupational Monograph." *Occupations,* 1939, *18,* 129-130.

National Vocational Guidance Association. "Content of a Good Occupational Monograph—The Basic Outline." *Occupations,* 1940, *19,* 20-23.

National Vocational Guidance Association. "Standards for Use in Preparing and Evaluating Occupational Literature." *Occupations,* 1950, *28,* 319-324.

National Vocational Guidance Association. "Guidelines for Preparing and Evaluating Occupational Materials." *Vocational Guidance Quarterly,* 1964, *12,* 217-227.

National Vocational Guidance Association. *Guidelines to Preparation and Evaluation of Occupational Films.* Washington, D.C.: National Vocational Guidance Association, 1966.

National Vocational Guidance Association. *Guidelines for the Preparation and Evaluation of Career Information Media.* Washington, D.C.: National Vocational Guidance Association, 1971.

National Vocational Guidance Association. *Position Paper on Career Development.* Washington, D.C.: National Vocational Guidance Association, 1973.

National Vocational Guidance Association. "Guidelines for

the Preparation and Evaluation of Career Information Literature." *Vocational Guidance Quarterly,* 1980, *28,* 291–296.

Neimeyer, G. J. "Personal Construct Systems in Vocational Development and Information." *Journal of Career Development,* 1989, *16*(2), 83–96.

Neulinger, J. *Introduction to Leisure.* Needham Heights, Mass.: Allyn & Bacon, 1981.

Newlon, B. J., Nye, N. K., and Hill, M. S. "Career Awareness Workshops for Disadvantaged Youth." *Journal of Career Development,* 1985, *11*(4), 305–315.

Nieva, V. F., and Gutek, B. A. *Women and Work: A Psychological Perspective.* New York: Praeger, 1981.

Norris, W., Hatch, R. J., Engelkes, J. R., and Winborn, B. B. *The Career Information Service.* (4th ed.) Skokie, Ill.: Rand McNally, 1979.

Obleton, N. B. "Career Counseling of Black Women in a Predominantly White Coeducational University." *Personnel and Guidance Journal,* 1984, *62*(6), 365–368.

Office of Federal Statistical Policy and Standards, Department of Commerce. *Standard Occupational Classification Manual.* Washington, D.C.: U.S. Government Printing Office, 1980.

Office of Management and Budget, Executive Office of the President. *Standard Industrial Classification Manual.* Washington, D.C.: U.S. Government Printing Office, 1972.

Office of Management and Budget, Executive Office of the President. *Standard Industrial Classification Manual: 1977 Supplement.* Washington, D.C.: U.S. Government Printing Office, 1977.

Okiishi, R. W. "The Genogram as a Tool in Career Counseling." *Journal of Counseling and Development,* 1987, *66*(2), 139–143.

Osipow, S. "What Do We Really Know About Career Development?" In N. C. Gysbers and D. Pritchard (eds.), *National Conference on Guidance, Counseling, and Placement in Career Development and Educational-Occupational Decision-Making.* Columbia: University of Missouri, 1969. (ED 041 143)

Osipow, S. H. "Research in Career Counseling: An Analysis

of Issues and Problems." *Counseling Psychologist,* 1982, *10,* 27–34.

Overs, R. P., Taylor, S., and Adkins, C. *Avocational Counseling Manual.* Washington, D.C.: Hawkins Associates, 1977.

Parker, S. *The Future of Work and Leisure.* New York: Praeger, 1971.

Parsons, F. *Choosing a Vocation.* Boston: Houghton Mifflin, 1909.

Paterson, D. G., and Darley, J. G. *Men, Women, and Jobs: A Study in Human Engineering.* Minneapolis: University of Minnesota Press, 1936.

Peevy, E. "Leisure Counseling: A Life Cycle Approach." Unpublished doctoral dissertation, College of Education, Virginia Polytechnic Institute and State University, 1981.

Perry, W., Jr. *Intellectual and Ethical Development in the College Years.* Troy, Mo.: Holt, Rinehart & Winston, 1970.

Personick, V. A. "Industry Output and Employment Through the End of the Century." *Monthly Labor Review,* 1987, *110*(9), 30–45.

Peterson, D. W. "Information Review Service Is Ready." *Vocational Guidance Quarterly,* 1956, *4,* 100–102.

Pfeiffer, J. W., and Jones, J. E. "Design Considerations in Laboratory Education." In J. W. Pfeiffer and J. E. Jones (eds.), *The 19th Annual Handbook for Group Facilitators.* San Diego, Calif.: University Associates, 1973.

Philip, F. W., and Bradley, R. W. "Black and White Students' Assessments of Counseling Services in American Overseas High School." *Journal of Non-White Concerns,* 1980, *8*(4), 193–198.

Picou, J. S., and Campbell, R. E. (eds.). *Career Behavior of Special Groups: Theory, Research, and Practice.* Columbus, OH.: Merrill, 1975.

Pieper, J. *Leisure: The Basis of Culture.* New York: Pantheon, 1964.

Prediger, D. J., and Swaney, K. B. *Role of Counselee Experiences in the Interpretation of Vocational Interest Scores.* Research report no. 86. Iowa City, Iowa: American College Testing Program, 1985.

Pritchard, D. H. "The Occupational Exploration Process: Some Operational Implications." *Personnel and Guidance Journal,* 1962, *40*(8), 19–27.

Rapaport, R., and Rapaport, R. *Leisure and the Family Life Cycle.* New York: Routledge, 1975.

Raskin, P. M. *Vocational Counseling: A Guide for the Practitioner.* New York: Teachers College Press, 1987.

Raspberry, W. "Role Models and the Education of Black Boys." *Washington Post,* August 24, 1990, p. A-27.

Reardon, R. C. "Use of Information in Career Counseling." In H. D. Burck and R. C. Reardon (eds.), *Career Development Interventions.* Springfield, Ill.: Thomas, 1984.

Research and Forecasts, Inc. *Where Does the Time Go? The United Media Enterprises Report on Leisure in America.* New York: United Media Enterprises, 1982.

Research and Forecasts, Inc. *The Miller Lite Report on American Attitudes Toward Sports.* Milwaukee, Wis.: Miller Brewing Company, 1983.

Rest, J. R. "Development Psychology as a Guide to Value Education: A Review of 'Kohlbergian' Programs." *Review of Educational Research,* 1974, *44,* 241–259.

Richmond, L. J., Johnson, J., Downs, M., and Ellinghaus, A. "Needs of Non-Caucasian Students in Vocational Education: A Special Minority Group." *Journal of Non-White Concerns,* 1983, *12*(1), 13–18.

Roberts, K. *Leisure.* (2nd ed.) White Plains, N.Y.: Longman, 1981.

Roe, A. *The Psychology of Occupations.* New York: Wiley, 1956.

Roper Organization. "The 1990's from Promise to Performance." Roper Report. *Public Pulse,* Jan. 1990, pp. 2–3.

Rosenthal, N. "More Than Wages at Issue in Job Quality Debate." *Monthly Labor Review,* 1989, *112*(12), 4–8.

Rounds, J. B., Jr., and Tinsley, H.E.A. "Diagnosis and Treatment of Vocational Problems." In S. D. Brown and W. W. Lent (eds.), *Handbook of Counseling Psychology.* New York: Wiley, 1984.

Rounds, J. B., and Tracey, T. J. "From Trait-and-Factor to Person-Environment Fit Counseling: Theory and Process."

In W. Bruce Walsh and S. H. Osipow (eds.), *Career Counseling: Contemporary Topics in Vocational Psychology.* Hillsdale, N.J.: Erlbaum, 1990.

Rudestam, K. E. *Experiential Groups in Theory and Practice.* Pacific Grove, Calif.: Brooks/Cole, 1982.

Rusalem, H. "New Insights on the Role of Occupational Information in Counseling." *Journal of Counseling Psychology,* 1954, *1*(2), 84–88.

Schlossberg, N. K. *Counseling Adults in Transition.* New York: Springer, 1984.

Schumacher, E. F. "Good Work." In D. W. Vermilye (ed.), *Relating Work and Education: Current Issues in Higher Education.* San Francisco: Jossey-Bass, 1977.

Sears, S. "A Definition of Career Guidance Terms: A National Vocational Guidance Association Perspective." *Vocational Guidance Quarterly,* 1982, *31*(2), 137–143.

Sekaran, U. *Dual-Career Families: Contemporary Organizational and Counseling Issues.* San Francisco: Jossey-Bass, 1986.

Sekaran, U., and Hall, D. T. "Asynchronism in Dual-Career and Family Linkage." In M. B. Arthur, D. T. Hall, and B. S. Lawrence (eds.), *Handbook of Career Theory.* Cambridge, England: Cambridge University Press, 1989.

Seligman, K. *Assessment in Developmental Career Counseling.* Cranston, R.I.: Carroll Press, 1980.

Shertzer, B., and Stone, S. C. *Fundamentals of Counseling.* (3rd ed.) Boston: Houghton Mifflin, 1980.

Sinick, D. "Problems of Work and Retirement for an Aging Population." In N. C. Gysbers and Associates, *Designing Careers: Counseling to Enhance Education, Work, and Leisure.* San Francisco: Jossey-Bass, 1984.

Smith, E. J. "Career Development of Minorities in Nontraditional Fields." *Journal of Non-White Concerns,* 1980, *8*(2), 141–155.

Snyder, C. R., Higgins, R. L., and Stucky, R. J. *Excuses: Masquerades in Search of Grace.* New York: Wiley, 1983.

Steinhauser, L. "Career Counseling with the Handicapped— the Final Stage: Some Unique Approaches." *Journal of Employment Counseling,* 1983, *12*(2), 73–80.

Stephens, W. R. *Social Reform and the Origins of Vocational Guidance.* Washington, D.C.: National Vocational Guidance Association, 1970.

Stern, B., and Best, F. "Cyclic Life Patterns." In D. W. Vermilye (ed.), *Relating Work and Education: Current Issues in Higher Education.* San Francisco: Jossey-Bass, 1977.

Stone, G. L. "Cognitive-Behavioral Theory and Its Application to Career Development." In L. W. Harmon (ed.), *Using Information in Career Development: From Cognitions to Computers.* Columbus, Ohio: ERIC Clearinghouse on Adult, Career, and Vocational Education, National Center for Research in Vocational Education, 1983.

Subich, L. M. "A Challenge to Grow: Reaction to Hoyt's Article." *Career Development Quarterly,* 1989, *37,* 213–217.

Sue, D. W. "Asian Americans: Social Psychological Factors Affecting Their Lifestyles." In J. S. Picou and R. E. Campbell (eds.), *Career Behavior of Special Groups: Theory, Research, and Practice.* Columbus, Ohio: Merrill, 1975.

Super, D. E. "A Theory of Vocational Development." *American Psychologist,* 1953, *8,* 185–190.

Super, D. E. *The Psychology of Careers.* New York: Harper-Collins, 1957.

Super, D. E. "Some Unresolved Issues in Vocational Development Research." *Personnel and Guidance Journal,* 1961, *40,* 11–15.

Super, D. E. "A Reconceptualization of Vocational Guidance." Unpublished manuscript, National Vocational Guidance Association, 1966.

Super, D. E. "Emergent Decision Making in a Changing Society." *Proceedings of the International Seminar on Educational and Vocational Guidance.* Lisbon: Portuguese Psychological Society, 1975.

Super, D. E. *Career Education and the Meanings of Work.* Department of Health, Education, and Welfare. Washington, D.C.: U.S. Government Printing Office, 1976.

Super, D. E. "A Life-Span, Life-Space Approach to Career Development." *Journal of Vocational Behavior,* 1980, *16,* 282–298.

Super, D. E. "Assessment in Career Guidance: Toward Truly Developmental Counseling." *Personnel and Guidance Journal,* 1983, *61,* 555–562.

Super, D. E. "Career and Life Development." In D. Brown, L. Brooks, and Associates, *Career Choice and Development: Applying Contemporary Theories to Practice.* San Francisco: Jossey-Bass, 1984.

Super, D. E. "Coming of Age in Middletown: Careers in the Making." *American Psychologist,* 1985, *40,* 405–414.

Super, D. E. "A Life-Span, Life-Space Approach to Career Development." In D. Brown, L. Brooks, and Associates, *Career Choice and Development: Applying Contemporary Theories to Practice.* (2nd ed.) San Francisco: Jossey-Bass, 1990.

Super, D. E., and Bachrach, P. B. *Scientific Careers and Vocational Development Theory.* New York: Teachers College Press, 1957.

Super, D. E., and Bohn, M. J., Jr. *Occupational Psychology.* Belmont, Calif.: Wadsworth, 1970.

Super, D. E., and Overstreet, P. L. *The Vocational Maturity of Ninth-Grade Boys.* New York: Teachers College Press, 1960.

Super, D. E., and others. *Vocational Development: A Framework for Research.* New York: Teachers College Press, 1957.

Tennyson, W. "Comment." *Vocational Guidance Quarterly,* 1970, *18,* 261–263.

Thompson, S. D. "Data-People-Aspirations: The Career Information Delivery System the Maine Way." *Journal of Career Development,* 1988, *14*(3), 177–189.

Tiedeman, D. V., and O'Hara, R. P. *Career Development: Choice and Adjustment.* New York: College Board, 1963.

Tifft, S. "Diamonds in the Rough." *Time,* Aug. 6, 1990, pp. 58–59.

Tindall, L. W., and Gugerty, J. J. "Careers for Persons with Disabilities." *Journal of Career Development,* 1987, *13*(4), 47–55.

Tinsley, H.E.A., and Teaff, J. D. *The Psychological Benefits of Leisure Activities for the Elderly: A Manual and Final Report of an Investigation.* Carbondale: Southern Illinois University Press, 1983.

Tinsley, H.E.A., and Tinsley, D. J. "A Holistic Model of Leisure Counseling." *Journal of Leisure Research,* 1982, *14*(2), 100–116.

Tyler, L. E. *Individuality: Human Possibilities and Personal Choice in the Psychological Development of Men and Women.* San Francisco: Jossey-Bass, 1978.

Veblen, T. *The Theory of the Leisure Class.* New York: Viking Penguin, 1935. (Originally published 1899.)

Voydanoff, P. *Work and Family Life.* Newbury Park, Calif.: Sage, 1987.

Voydanoff, P. "Work and Family: A Review and Expanded Conceptualization." *Journal of Social Behavior and Personality,* 1988, *3*(4), 1–22.

Wahalee-Lynch, R. "Americans with Disabilities Act Pending in Congress." *Guidepost,* 1990, *33*, 1, 4.

Walsh, W. B., and Osipow, S. (eds.). *Career Counseling.* Hillsdale, N.J.: Erlbaum, 1990.

Watts, G. A. "Identifying Career Orientations of Female Non-Managerial Employees at Virginia Tech." Unpublished doctoral dissertation, Department of Education, Virginia Polytechnic Institute and State University, 1989.

Wellman, F. E., and Moore, E. J. *Pupil Personnel Services: A Handbook for Program Development and Evaluation.* Washington, D.C.: U.S. Department of Health, Education, and Welfare, 1975.

Wells, J. H., and Ready, B. C. (eds.). *The Independent Study Catalog: NUCEA's Guide to Independent Study Through Correspondence Instruction.* Princeton, N.J.: Peterson's Guides, 1989.

White, L. S. "Career Planning: A School Guidance Model for Minority Female Youth." *Journal of Non-White Concerns,* 1979, *7*(4), 170–175.

Whitfield, E. A., and Gustav, A. (eds.). *Counseling Girls and Women Over the Life Span.* Alexandria, Va.: American Association for Counseling and Development, 1972. (A monograph of the National Vocational Guidance Association.)

Wilhelm, W. "Career Development in Changing Times." *Career Planning and Adult Development,* 1983, *1*(1), 9–14.

Williamson, E. G. *How to Counsel Students: A Manual of Techniques for Clinical Counselors.* New York: McGraw-Hill, 1939.

Williamson, E. G. *Vocational Counseling.* New York: McGraw-Hill, 1965.

Wolfe, D. M., and Kolb, D. A. "Career Development, Personal Growth, and Experimental Learning." In J. W. Springer (ed.), *Issues in Career and Human Resource Development.* Madison, Wis.: American Society for Training and Development, 1980.

Wolleat, P. L. "Reconciling Sex Differences in Information-Processing and Career Outcomes." *Journal of Career Development,* 1989, *16*(2), 97–106.

Wooley, W. W. "The Career Information Program in Florida: A Personal Perspective." *Journal of Career Development,* 1988, *15*(2), 100–109.

Yankelovich, D., and Lefkowitz, B. "American Ambivalence and the Psychology of Growth." *National Forum,* 1982a, *62*(3), 12–15.

Yankelovich, D., and Lefkowitz, B. "Work and American Expectations." *National Forum,* 1982b, *62*(2), 3–5.

Yost, E. B., and Corbishley, M. A. *Career Counseling: A Psychological Approach.* San Francisco: Jossey-Bass, 1987.

Zedeck, S., and Mosier, K. L. "Work in the Family and Employing Organization." *American Psychologist,* 1990, *45*(2), 240–251.

Name Index

A

Adams, J. P., 320
Adkins, C., 148, 293
Adler, A., 72, 79, 171–172
Allen, F. J., 273
Anderson, N., 136, 333
Arbona, C., 280
Askounis, A. C., 286
Astin, H. W., 283
Auster, C., 284
Auster, D., 284
Avasthi, S., 286
Ayala-Vazquez, N., 286
Ayers, M. L., 286

B

Bailey, L. J., 9
Bailey, R. L., 236
Bane, M. J., 160
Barrett, L. A., 149
Bartlett, W. E., 284
Baruth, L. G., 368–369
Basta, N., 322
Bauer, B., 234, 320
Bear, J., 234
Berger, S. L., 320

Berman, J. J., 79
Betz, N. E., 282
Biggs, D. A., 22, 60, 64
Birnbaum, M., 234, 320
Birren, J. E., 180
Bleuer, J., 318, 402
Bloch, D. P., 322
Bloland, A., 148
Bloomfield, M., 5
Bohn, M. J., Jr., 8
Bolles, R. H., 15, 322
Boone, T. A., 377–378
Borow, H., 41, 106
Bowen, M., 174
Bowlsbey, J., 249
Bradley, R. W., 286
Brayfield, A. H., 326
Brewer, J. M., 5
Brigman, L., 79
Brolin, D. E., 293, 294
Brooks, L., 17, 84–85, 176, 280, 282
Brown, D., 16, 31, 32, 84–85, 106, 176, 280, 282, 316–317
Brown, S. T., 316–317
Burge, P. L., 161
Bush, G., 289
Butterworth, A. S., 320

C

Campbell, R. E., 81
Carlsen, M. B., 10, 67
Cass, J., 234, 320
Cellini, J. V., 81
Chapman, R., 323
Chick, G. E., 149
Christensen, T. E., 326
Coelho, R. J., 268-269, 270-271
Cole, H. P., 9
Collison, M., 289
Corbishley, M. A., 17, 18
Corey, G., 381
Corre, M. P., 273
Cramer, S. H., 15, 22, 41, 268, 326
Cristiani, T. S., 368
Crites, J. O., 17, 23, 24, 32, 81,
  382
Croner, U.H.E., 319
Crosby, F., 167
Csikszentmihalyi, M., 151
Curnow, T. C., 292-293
Cutler, B., 139

D

Dagley, J., 176, 180, 181
Dahl, P. R., 293
D'Alonzo, B. J., 291
Daley, J. G., 28
Davis, H. V., 4
Davis, M., 330
de Grazia, S., 136
Deutchman, D. E., 180
Devon, C. S., 322
de Vries, B., 180
Dilts, S. W., 234, 319
Dinkmeyer, D. C., 72, 171
Dinkmeyer, D. C., Jr., 72, 171
Downe, B. J., 321
Downs, M., 287
Drier, N., 243
Drum, D., 369
Dudley, B., 56
Dumazedier, J., 136
Durgin, R., 250
Duvall, E. M., 164, 165

E

Edgar, E. B., 292-294
Edwards, P., 148, 156, 237
Eisenberg, G. G., 122, 237
Elfin, M., 234, 320
Eliot, C., 5
Ellinghaus, A., 287
Elliot, T. R., 293
Engelkes, J. R., 326
Erikson, E., 149

F

Fabish, V., 236
Fanning, P., 330
Farmer, H. S., 283
Feodaroff, P. L., 322
Field, F. L., 7, 67
Figler, H. E., 314-315, 318
Fine, S., 317
Fisher, I., 48
Fiske, E. B., 234, 320
Fitzgerald, L. F., 282
Flanders, R., 240, 246, 255
Fooks, G. M., 287
Form, W., 42
Fountain, M. C., 201
Frankel, R., 322
Frederickson, R. H., 32
Friedman, D. E., 160, 161
Fullerton, H. N., Jr., 109n, 110 n

G

Galinksy, E., 160
Gallup, G., 139
Gault, J., 237
Gelatt, H., 56, 58-59
George, R. L., 368
Germain, R., 233, 237
Gerson, R., 174, 176
Gilhousen, M. R., 80, 330
Gillespie, G. A., 237
Ginzberg, E., 6
Glaser, R., 328
Golden, L., 402
Goldhammer, K., 9

Goldstein, S. E., 321
Gordon, E. W., 14–15, 288
Gottfredson, G. D., 328
Greenhaus, J. H., 162, 165
Griffin, A. R., 286, 288
Gruber, G. R., 320
Gugerty, J. J., 294
Gupta, G. R., 321
Gustav, A., 283
Gutek, B. A., 282
Gysbers, N. C., 9–10, 17, 18, 60, 64, 71, 79, 106, 159, 174, 176, 280, 294

H

Hall, D. T., 158, 162–163, 164
Hall, F. S., 162–163
Hansen, L. S., 282–283
Hansen, R., 342
Haring-Hidore, M., 282
Harmon, L. W., 82, 282–283
Harris, S., 131, 134, 234, 319
Harrower, G., III, 319
Hartman, J. S., 286
Hatch, R. J., 326
Havighurst, R. J., 149
Hawkes, S., 317
Hayden, T. C., 235
Hedges, J., 143, 144
Hedrick, H. L., 321
Heinl, P., 174, 176
Hellmich, N., 162
Heppner, M. J., 318, 352, 378
Heppner, P. P., 58
Herlihy, B., 402
Herr, E. L., 15, 22, 41, 106, 160, 268, 280, 326
Herring, R. D., 286
Heyde, M. B., 48
Higgins, R. L., 332
Hill, M. S., 287
Hill, R. L., 164
Hitchner, A., 223
Hitchner, K. W., 223
Holland, J. L., 28, 33–34, 36, 38–40, 68, 80, 82, 175n, 306, 328, 347, 357, 381
Hopke, W. E., 213

Hoppock, R. F., 271, 273, 326
Hotchkiss, L., 41
House, E., 284
Hoyt, K. B., 280–281, 288
Hubbard, M., 317
Hughes, D., 160
Hughey, K. F., 378

I

Isaacson, L. E., 70, 268
Izzo, M. V., 294

J

Jacobs, J. E., 319
Jacobsen, D. J., 322
Jepsen, D. A., 64
Johnson, C. A., 314–315, 318
Johnson, J., 287
Johnson, J. A., 318
Johnson, M., 323
Johnston, J. A., 378
Jones, G. B., 9
Jones, J. E., 370, 371
Jordaan, J. P., 9, 48
June, L. N., 287

K

Kalleberg, A. L., 146
Kapes, J. T., 32
Kaplan, M., 136
Katz, M., 7
Katzell, M. E., 284
Kauss, M. W., 291
Kaye, K. R., 319
Kazalunas, J. R., 286
Keller, F. J., 273
Keller, K., 22, 60, 64
Kelly, J. R., 136, 145, 146–147, 149, 237
Kerka, S., 161
Kimeldorf, M., 230, 322
Kinnier, R. T., 17, 20–21, 79
Kleibert, D., 151
Knefelkamp, L. L., 61
Knott, J., 369

Kolb, D. A., 13
Kortering, J. J., 292, 293–294
Krannich, R. L., 322
Krauskopf, C. J., 58
Krumboltz, J. D., 17, 20–21, 82
Kumka, D. A., 165

L

Lambert, R., 387n, 400n
Lane, M. R., 273
Lang, E., 289
Larson, L., 151
Larwood, L., 282
LaVeck, J., 322
Leatherman, C., 288
Lee, C. C., 281, 288, 297
Lefkowitz, B., 147
Leider, A., 237, 321
Leider, R., 237, 321
Leonard, P. Y., 287
Leong, F.T.L., 286, 297
Lester, J., 255
Levinson, D., 149
Lewis, R. A., 80, 330
Lindquist, C. L., 322
Loesch, L. C., 148, 156, 237
Lorence, J., 165
Love, M., 160
Low, A., 329

M

McCormac, M. E., 248, 249, 251n
McDaniels, C., 7–8, 111, 138, 149,
   229, 237–238, 239, 242, 243, 244,
   246, 247, 285, 300, 322
McDavis, R. J., 287
McGoldrick, M., 174, 176
McKay, M., 330
McKinlay, B., 247, 400n
Macklin, E. D., 160
Mangrum, C. L., 321
Marino, J. F., 291
Martin, D. L., 319
Martin, E. S., 86
Martin, G. M., 201, 243
Masnick, G., 160
Mastie, M. M., 32

Matthews, E. E., 283
Migliare, S. A., 320
Miller, D., 42
Miller, J. V., 160, 181
Minor, C. W., 10, 106
Moll, R., 235
Moore, E. J., 9–10, 17, 18, 71, 79,
   159, 174, 176, 372
Moore, G., 143
Mortimer, J. T., 165
Mosak, H. H., 72, 174
Mosier, K. L., 158–159, 160, 162,
   166, 167–168, 170–171, 174
Mundy, J., 145, 146
Munson, H. L., 79
Murphy, J., 136
Myers, G. E., 6
Myers, J. R., 119, 322

N

Naisbitt, J., 111
Neimeyer, G. J., 60–61
Neulinger, J., 136, 145
Newlon, B. J., 287
Newport, F., 139
Nieva, V. F., 282
Noble, F. C., 79
Norris, W., 326
Nye, N. K., 287

O

Odum, L., 145, 146
O'Hara, R. P., 56, 83
Okiishi, R. W., 176
Oldham, D., 284
Ollies, H., 255
Osipow, S. H., 16, 17, 42, 283
Overs, R. P., 148, 293
Overstreet, P. L., 48
Owen, J., 145

P

Parker, S., 136
Parker, W. M., 287
Parsons, F., 4–5, 6, 17, 28–29, 30, 31
Paterno, J., 236

Paterson, D. G., 28
Peevy, E. S., 148, 243
Perry, W., Jr., 61
Personick, V. A., 110n
Peterson, D. W., 274
Petras, K., 322
Petras, R., 322
Pew, W. L., 72, 171
Pfeiffer, J. W., 370, 371
Philip, F. W., 286
Pieper, J., 136
Prediger, D. J., 327
Pritchard, D. H., 334, 341
Puryear, A., 300

R

Rakes, T. D., 378
Rapaport, R., 149
Rapaport, R., 149
Rapoza, R. S., 282, 283
Raskin, P. M., 17
Raspberry, W., 287
Re, J. M., 321
Ready, B. C., 319
Reardon, R. C., 17, 255
Reid, R. A., 377-378
Renetzky, A., 322
Rest, J. R., 60
Richardson, B. L., 297
Richmond, L. J., 287
Roberts, K., 136
Robinson, E. H., 368-369
Roe, A., 6-7, 304-305
Rogers, C., 31
Rosenblatt, R., 321
Rosenthal, N., 106
Rounds, J. B., Jr., 28, 33, 80
Rudd, H., 322
Rudestam, K. E., 382
Rusalem, H., 326
Rushing, B. C., 321
Russell, J. J., 321

S

Sacharov, A., 323
Sampson, J. P., 255
Schlacter, G. A., 237, 321

Schlossberg, N. K., 28, 51-55, 252
Schneider, L., 321, 323
Schumacher, E. F., 146
Schurtman, R., 86
Schwartz, J., 321
Scott, E. W., 119, 322
Sears, S., 137, 138
Sekaran, U., 158, 162, 163, 164
Seligman, K., 17
Shaw, Mrs. Q. A., 4
Shertzer, B., 27, 368
Sinetar, M., 238
Sinick, D., 78
Slepitza, R., 61
Smith, E. J., 288
Snipes, J. K., 243
Snyder, C. R., 332
Steele, J. V., 321
Steinbrecher, P., 320
Steinhauser, L., 292
Stephens, W. R., 4
Stone, G. L., 82
Stone, S. C., 27, 368
Straughn, B. L., 235
Straughn, C., 235
Strichart, S. S., 321
Stucky, R. J., 332
Subich, L. M., 281
Sue, D. W., 286
Super, D. E., 7, 8, 10, 11, 17-18, 28,
    32, 43-44, 48-51, 68, 77, 79, 82,
    138, 252, 327
Swaney, K. B., 327

T

Taylor, D., 144
Taylor, R. E., 9
Taylor, S., 148, 293
Teaff, J. D., 147
Tennyson, W., 14
Thompson, S. D., 248
Tiedeman, D. V., 56, 83
Tindall, L. W., 294
Tinsley, D. J., 148
Tinsley, H.E.A., 80, 147, 148
Toffler, A., 111
Torregrosa, C. H., 235
Tracey, T. J., 28, 33

Tifft, S., 289
Tyler, L. E. 15–16

V

Veblen, T., 136
Von Vorys, B., 319
Voydanoff, P., 160, 165–166

W

Walsh, W. B., 17
Walz, G. R., 318, 402
Ware, C., 323
Watts, G. A., 285
Weber, R. D., 321
Wegmann, R., 323
Weiss, S. C., 317
Well, J. H., 319
Wellman, F. E., 372
Wells, J., 323
Wheeler, P. T., 148, 156, 237

White, L. S., 286
Whitfield, E. A., 283
Wilhelm, W., 24–25
Wilkins, D. M., 268–269, 270–271
Williamson, E. G., 17, 28, 31
Wilson, J. B., 387n
Winborn, B. B., 326
Wolfe, D. M., 13
Wolleat, P. L., 60
Wooley, W. W., 247

Y

Yankelovich, D., 147
Yost, E. B., 17, 18

Z

Zedeck, S., 158–159, 160, 162, 166,
    167–168, 170–171, 174
Zidik, M. A., 319
Zytowski, D., G., 64, 283

Subject Index

A

Academy of Model Aeronautics, 123

Accommodation: in decision making, 57–58; in groups, 376

Accreditation/approval, for education options, 130–132, 133, 134

Action, taking: in counseling framework, 19, 24; for families, 181–182; and theoretical constructs, 81–83

Adaptive and adjustive behaviors, in groups, 375

Administration, in work-family counseling, 169–170, 173, 176–180

Administrative support occupations, trends in, 99, 104

Adolescence, leisure exploration stage in, 151–152

Adult career development transition model, basic tenets of, 51–55

Adult education, options in, 118, 224

Adulthood: educational options in, 223–227; leisure implementation stage in, 154; women's career development in, 285

Affect issues, in closing relationship, 85

African Americans: career development for, 285–289; employment opportunities for, 280; in higher education, 128; in labor force, 93, 95; mentoring for, 284, 287, 289; in single-parent families, 161

Age groups: in higher education, 127–128; in labor force, 92–94; leisure in, 150–156

Agricultural, forestry, fishing, and related occupations, trends in, 99

Agricultural education, as option, 218

Air Force, Community College of the, education options, 121

Alaskan Natives, in labor force, 95

American Association for Counseling and Development (AACD), 133, 258, 266, 287, 291, 297

American Association of Retired Persons, 230

American Association of University Women (AAUW), 266

American College of Sports Medicine, 318

American College Personnel Association, 258

American College Testing (ACT) Program, 236, 249, 253

American Council on Education, 125, 234

American Education Week, 302

American Guidance Service, 197

American Indians: career development for, 286; in labor force, 95

American Institute of Banking, education by, 124

American Legion, 130, 227, 228, 236, 320

American Library Association, 317

American Management Association, training by, 123

American Psychological Association, 258, 259

American Rehabilitation Association, 291

American Rehabilitation Counseling Association, 258, 291

American School Counselor Association, 258

American Vocational Association (AVA), 8, 258, 259, 266

Americans with Disabilities Act of 1990 (Public Law 101-336), 280, 289-290

Analysis, in work-family counseling, 169-172, 173-174, 180-181

Anticipation phase, in decision making, 56-57

Appalachian Educational Laboratory, 207; Career Information System of, 306, 307-308

Appalachian Mountain Club, 123

Apprenticeships: local survey of, 264-265; options in 119-120, 224; state information on, 246

Arizona: disabled students program in, 291-292; ethnic diversity in, 285, 287

Arizona, University of, minority workshop at, 287

Armed Services Vocational Aptitude Battery (ASVAB), 345, 347

Artistic: environment, 37, 306; personality, 35

Asian Americans: career development for, 286; in higher education, 128; in labor force, 93, 95. *See also* Special populations

Association for Adult Development and Aging, 258

Association for Counselor Education and Supervision, 133, 258

Association for Higher Education, 143

Association for Humanistic Education and Development, 258

Association for Measurement and Evaluation in Counseling and Development, 258

Association for Multicultural Counseling and Development, 258

Association for Religious and Value Issues in Counseling, 258

Association for Specialists in Group Work, 258

Association of Computer-Based Systems for Career Information, 245, 248, 249, 254, 400, 402

Associations: civic and service, 123-124, 266; financial aid from, 228; professional, and career information, 257-259, 272-275; resources from, 311; training sponsored by, 123

Auburn University, correspondence study from, 121

B

Basic Assistance Grant (BAG), 241-242

Behavior: client, in counseling framework, 19, 22-23; interview for understanding, 78-79; and personality and environment types, 38-39

Bennet Occupations Filing Plan and Bibliography, 304

Boston Vocation Bureau, 4

Boundary differences, in dual-career families, 163

BPWC, 266

Breaktime, and satisfaction, 147

Bureau of Economic Analysis, 138

Bureau of Industrial Economics, 205
Bureau of Labor Statistics: and career development centers, 312, 319; and career development centers, 312, 319; and career information delivery systems, 244; resources from; resources from 198, 200, 201, 207, 212; and world of work, 92, 94n, 96, 98n, 101n, 102n, 111, 112
Bureau of the Census, 206, 212, 244, 312
Business education, option of, 218-219

C

California: ethnic diversity in, 285; mentoring in, 289
Canada Systems Group, 250
Canadian Career Information Resource Advisory Group, 317
Career adaptability, constructs of, 48
Career assessment, interview on, 72-74
Career counseling: leisure counseling and work counseling related to, 148; life-span approach to, 156-157
Career development: aspects of, 3-26; aspects of foundations for, 89-182; background on, 3-4; broader concepts of, 9-11; concepts of, 3, 4-13; counseling framework for, 16-26; and counseling practice, 14-16; defined, 138, 159; and education and training, 114-134; and family, 158, 182; formative concepts of, 4-6; future concepts of, 11-13; leisure in, 135-157; life-span, life-space approach to, 43-51; resources for, 183-276; segmental model of, 44; transitional concepts of, 6-9; transitional model of, 51-55; and work world, 91-113
Career development centers (CDCs); advisory group for, 311; aspects of, 298-323; automated systems

in, 303; background on, 298-300; films and tapes in, 302; firsthand observations in, 300-318; and multimedia approach for, 300, 304; organizing, 304-308; and placement, 312-316; print media in, 302-303; resources for, 311-312, 316-323; user range for, 308-311; videos and films in, 301; visual displays in, 302
Career Development Plan, 381
Career Development Quarterly, 11, 136, 283, 287, 291
Career Development Software, 211
Career Genogram, for work-family counseling, 174-181
Career information: aspects of renewing and evaluating, 256-276; and community development, 265, 266-267; conclusion on, 275-276; content review of, 270; distorting, 328-332; educational purposes of, 326-332; and equal opportunity factors, 270-271; evaluating, 268-275; in individual counseling, 324-334; and information development, 261-266; motivational purpose of, 333; from occupational card sort, 334-341; place of, 325-326; and professional development, 257-260; and renewal plan for, 256-268; structure and organization of, 269-270; in structured groups, 368-383; use of, 333-334
Career information delivery systems (CIDS): aspects of, 239-255; background on, 239-242; in career development centers, 303, 307, 309, 312, 315; concept of, 239; delivery modes for, 244-245; elements of, 242-246; key resources on, 254-255; locations for, 243; multimedia used for, 242-243; range of sources for, 244-246; software systems for, 248-254; state systems for, 246-248; user appeal of, 243-244
Career Information Review Service Committee, 274-275, 287n, 388, 400n, 402

Career Information System (CIS), 247, 250, 303
Career maturity: and general adjustment, 82; and life-span, life-space theory, 46, 48; and testing, 77
Career myths, 330
Career Options for Missouri Farm Families, 378-381
Career Pattern Study, 7, 48
Career plans. *See* Individual career plans
Career Research and Testing, 213
Career Software Review Guidelines, 400-413; for Software Description, 403-404; and Software Evaluation Criteria, 405-412
Career (publisher), 209, 213
Careers: aspects of, 3-26; background on, 3-4; broader concepts of, 9-11; concepts of, 3, 4-13, 137, 388; and counseling practice, 14-16; formative concepts of, 4-6; future concepts of, 11-13; transitional concepts of, 6-9; understanding theories of, 27-64; work and leisure related to, 7, 138, 146, 148, 214, 215-216, 229, 297
Carnegie Corporation, 273
Census of Population, 206, 212
Center for Research in Vocational Technical Education, 143
Certification/licensure: for leisure counseling, 156; requirements for, 132-134
Childhood, leisure awareness stage in, 150-151
Choice, and taking action, 82
CHOICES, 247, 248, 250, 303
Chronicle Guidance Publications, 209, 213, 259, 303, 305
Civic and service organizations, and education options, 123-124, 266
Civic Service House, 4
Civitan, 266
Classification of Instructional Programs, 205, 212
Client-centered counseling, impact of, 31
Client goal or problem: in counsel-

ing framework, 18-19, 20-23; and interactions, 67; resolving, 19, 23-26
Clients: counseling and theory in interaction with, 65-68; understanding information and behavior of, 19, 22-23
Clubs, education options of, 123. *See also* Associations
Cognitive schemas: elimination of, 63; as structural organizer, 60-61
Cognitive theory: basic tenets of, 60-64; and diagnoses, 80-81; implications of, 63-64; organizers in, 60-63
College Blue Book, 236
College Board, 222, 227, 235, 237, 320
College Placement Council, 315, 320
College Research Group, 320
College Scholarship Financial Aid, 129
Colorado, University of, correspondence study from, 121
Commission on Precollege Guidance and Counseling, 222
Community colleges, options in, 117-118, 121, 224
Community development, and career information, 265, 266-267
Compensation theory, of work and family, 167
Competencies: in counseling, 15-16; in structured groups, 373-377
Comprehensive Employment and Training Act (CETA), 120, 225
Computer technology occupations, growth of, 100
Conflict theory, of work and family, 167-168
Congruence, of personality and environment, 39
Consistency, of personality and environment, 40
Conventional: environment 38, 306; personality, 36
Cooperative Extension Service, 121-122
Cooperative Office Education, 218-219

Coordinate Occupational Information Network, 250

Coping resources, for transitions, 54-55

Correspondence study, options in, 121, 225

Council for Accreditation in Counseling and Related Education Professionals, 133

Council for Exceptional Children, Division of Career Development of, 291

Council on Postsecondary Accreditation (COPA), 131, 134

Counseling: applications of, 277-383; applications of theory for, 65-87; and career development centers, 298-323; career theory in, 1-87; and careers and career development, 14-16; certification for, 132-133, 156; clients and theory in interaction with, 65-68; conclusion on, 26; framework for, 16-26; future for, 86-87; individual, 324-367; interview in, 71-79; for leisure, 148-149; multicultural, 286; process of, 16-18, 31; for special populations, 279-297; in structured groups, 368-383; for work-family relationship, 168-181

Counseling Psychologist, 148, 283

Counselors: advisory committees for, 267; as career development advocates, 288, 296; networks for, 259-260; occupational classifications of, 190-192, 194, 196-197; professional development by, 257-260; and special populations, 295; and termination issues, 85-86

Current Population Survey, 98n

D

Davidson College, Love of Learning at, 289

DECA, 220

Decision making: acquiring skills for, 82; basic tenets of, 55-60; concept of, 58; and diagnoses, 81; implications of, 59-60; phases of, 56-58; as rational and intuitive, 58-59; and taking action, 83

Deficiencies, in counseling, 15

Delivery systems. *See* Career information delivery systems

Department of Commerce, 138

Department of Defense, 202, 212, 320

Department of Education, 227

Department of Labor: and career information, 239, 247, 259; and guidelines, 400; resources from, 188, 290, 312

Department of Leisure Studies, 143

Department of Rehabilitative Services, 225

Development: in cognitive theory, 61-62; in counseling, 14-15, 18-26; and general adjustment, 82. *See also* Career development

Developmental assessment model, for counseling, 17-18

Developmental meaning-making, and counseling process framework, 67

Diagnoses, making: in counseling framework, 19, 23; for families, 181-182; and theoretical constructs, 80-81; types of, 23

Dictionary of Occupational Titles (DOT): and career development center organization, 304, 305, 306; in individual counseling, 328, 360, 363, 364; and world of work, 187-193, 194, 196, 198, 200, 202, 206, 212

Differentiation, of personality and environment, 40

Directional tendencies competencies, in groups, 374-375

Disabilities, persons with: career development for, 289-294; defined, 290; placement for, 315-316; programs for, 291-294; sources on, 290-291

DISCOVER, 248, 249, 250, 252-254, 303

E

East Carolina Teacher's College, change of, 126
East Carolina University, size of, 126
Education: accreditation/approval for, 130-132, 133, 134; in adulthood, 223-227; aspects of, 114-134; background on, 114-116; in career assessment, 73-74; evaluating information, 271-272; key resources on, 234-237; as leisure option, 216; and licensure/certification requirements, 132-134; life-span tree of learning, 115-116; occupational trends in, 103; options in, 117-125; and preparation for leisure, 145-146; progress in, 114-115; required for work, 103-105; resources on, 216-229; role in, 84; school sources on, 216-218; undergraduate and graduate, 121, 125-128; vocational, 218-221. *See also* Higher education
Educational Testing Service, 251
ELDERHOSTELS: and career development centers, 310; options in, 122, 225, 233, 234
Empire State College, impact of, 126
Employment and Training Administration: and career development centers, 319; and individual counseling, 328; and world at work, 188, 192, 194, 197, 212
Employment Service, 188
Enterprising: environment, 38, 306; personality, 36, 347
Entrepreneurship, in future, 112
Environment: personality related to, 39-40; types of, 36-38; variables of, 54-55; and vocational personalities, 33-44
Environmental orientation competencies, in groups, 372-373
Equal opportunity factors, in career information, 270-271
Ethnic groups, career development for, 285-289

Evaluation: of career information, 268-275; in counseling framework, 19, 25; theoretical constructs for, 84-85
Executive, administrative, and managerial occupations, trends in, 96-97, 104
External degrees, extent of, 125-126

F

Fabricators jobs, trends in, 100, 104
Family: aspects of integrating careers and, 158-182; backgrounds on, 158-160; counseling for work and, 168-181; crises and transitions for, 165-166; diagnosis and action for, 181-182; dual-career, 162-163; issues and trends in, 160-166; and leisure, 140, 142, 149, 150, 152, 154; life cycle and tasks of, 164-165; role in, 84; single-parent, 161-162; structures of, 160-163; work related to, 166-181
Financial aid: changes in, 128-130; resources on, 227-229, 236-237; state information on, 246
Fishing and forestry occupations, trends in, 99
Florida: career information delivery system in, 247, 249; ethnic diversity in, 285
Florida State Department of Education, Bureau of Career Development in, 247
Florida State University, Center for the Study of Technology in Counseling and Career Development at, 255
4-H, and leisure, 152
Free universities, options in, 124
Future Business Leaders of America, 219
Future Homemakers of America, 220

G

Gallup organization, 106, 139
Garrett Park Press, 210, 213, 259

General Accounting Office, 288
General Aptitude Test Battery, 346
General Education Development (GED), 118, 224
GI Bill, 125
Government: career information resources from, 240–242; resources on work from, 187–201
Government Printing Office, 208
Groups, structured: aspects of, 368–383; background on, 368–369; concept of, 369; conceptualization level in, 373–375; conditions and issues for, 370; designing and implementing, 369–378; example of, 378–381; generalization level in, 375–377; perceptualization level in, 372–373; purposes of, 381–382; sequencing events for, 371–377; setting for, 377–378; summary on, 382–383
Guaranteed Student Loans, 129
Guidance Associates, 212
Guidance Information System (GIS), 248, 251, 303
Guide for Occupational Exploration (GOE), 193–194, 195–197, 212, 344–345, 346, 347
Guided career fantasy exploration, use of, 62
Guidelines for the Preparation and Evaluation of Career and Occupational Information Literature, 387–399; for content, 391–395; definition of terms in, 388–389; in general, 389–391; and Reviewer's Rating Form, 396–399

H

Health Occupations Students of America, 219
Health-related training, options in, 119, 219, 226
Health services occupations, growth of, 100, 103
Hexagon, for personality-environment model, 39–40
High School Equivalency, 118

Higher education: age groups in, 127–128; correspondence study in, 121; financial aid for, 128–130, 227–229, 236–237, 246; foreign students in, 128; institutional size and scope in, 126; minority enrollment in, 128; sources on, 221–223, 224, 234–237; state information on, 246; work resources from, 207
Hispanics: career development for, 285–286; employment opportunities for, 280; in labor force, 93, 96. See also Special populations
Holland occupational codes, 35–38, 306, 328, 347
Home economics education, 219–220
Houghton Mifflin Company, 251

I

I Have a Dream Foundation, 289
Illinois at Urban-Champaign, University of: Leisure Behavior Research Laboratory at, 143; leisure scholar at, 145
Impact Publications, 210, 213
Individual career plans: and closing relationship, 85; in counseling framework, 19, 24–25; theoretical constructs for, 83–84
Individual counseling: aspects of, 324–367; career information in, 324–334; cases of, 341–367; occupational card sort in, 334–341
Information on client gathering: in counseling framework, 18–19, 21–22; methods for, 71–77. See also Career information
Institute of International Education, 321
Instrumental theory, of work and family, 167
Interactionism, in cognitive theory, 62–63
International Association of Marriage and Family Counselors, 258
International Society for Technology in Education, 401

Interview, in counseling, 71–79
Investigative: environment, 37, 306; personality, 35

J

James Madison University, size of, 126
Jaycees: and community development, 266, 267; and education, 123
JIST Works, 212
Job Corps, 225
Job Training Partnership Act (JTPA): and career development, 120, 225; and career information, 243, 245, 250, 252; and placement, 316
Journal of Career Development, 8, 136, 246, 254, 255, 283, 291, 294, 318
Journal of Counseling and Development, 136, 291, 294
Journal of Employment Counseling, 283, 315
Journals: and career and career development concepts, 7, 8, 11; on career development centers, 318; on leisure, 136, 148, 157; on placement, 315; on special populations, 283, 286–287, 291, 292, 294

K

KANSAS CAREERS, 251
Kansas State University, software system from, 251
Kiwanis, 266

L

Labor force: age groups in, 92–94; changes in, 158–159; civilian, 108–109; composition of, 92–96; and population changes, 93–94; racial groups in, 95–96
Labor Markets Information, 203
Laborers jobs, trends in, 100, 104
League of Women Voters, and education, 124

Learning, theory of, and structured groups, 372
Learning vacations, options in, 122, 225
Leisure: activities for, 139–141; in age groups, 150–156; analysis of resources on, 214–238; aspects of, 135–157; awareness stage of, 150–151; background on, 135–137, 214–216; career and work related to, 7, 138, 146, 148, 214, 215–216, 229, 297; in career assessment, 74; changing attitudes toward, 214–215; concepts of, 137, 229; conclusion on, 157; and definitions of terms, 137–138, 144–145; education as option for, 216; exploration stage in, 151–152; and families, 140, 142, 149, 150, 152, 154; findings on, 142; implementation stage of, 154; involvement and reassessment stage of, 155; issues of, 143–149; key resources on, 237–238; life-span approach to, 149–156; local sources on, 263; national sources on, 233–234; preparation for, 145–146, 152–154; reawareness and reexploration stage of, 155–156; role in, 84; satisfaction from, 146–147, 154, 155; sources of information on, 229–234; spending on, 138–139; status of, 138–142; time for, 139; trends in, 143–144
Leisure counseling: career counseling and work counseling related to, 148; life-span approach to, 156–157
Leisure Education Advancement Project (LEAP), 146
Licensed Professional Counselor, 132, 156
Licensure. *See* Certification/licensure
Licensure training programs, as option, 226
Life-Career Assessment (LCA): applications of, 71–79, 327; and Typical-Day Assessment, 171

Life-career development: concept of, 9–10; factors in, 12
Life-career rainbow, elements of, 48–49
Life-career themes, information from, 72, 173–174
Life-Role Analysis, for work-family counseling, 168–172
Lifelong Career Development Project, 293
Life-span, life-space approach: basic tenets of, 43–51; to career and leisure counseling, 156–157; and education, 115–116; implications of, 51; to leisure and work, 149–156; propositions in, 43–47
Lions: and community development, 266; and education, 124
Listening: in counseling framework, 22–23; for distortions, 328–332; in interview, 78
Local Job Survey From, 261–262
Local sources: on financial aid, 228–229; information development from, 261–266; on leisure, 230, 232; on wages, 364
Local training programs, as option, 225

M

McDaniels Leisure Development Inventory, 230–232
Madison College, change of, 126
Maine, career information delivery system in, 248, 249, 250
Managerial occupations, trends in, 96–97, 104
Manpower Defense Training Act (MDTA), 120, 225
Marketing and sales occupations, trends in, 97
Marketing education, as option, 220
Maryland, minority counseling in, 287
Mastery competencies, in groups, 377
Mentors: for counselors, 259–260; for special populations, 284, 289, 296

Mesa, Arizona, disabled students program in, 291–292
Michigan, career information delivery system in, 246
Mid-America Quilt Exhibit, 233
Middletown, New York, life-span study in, 48
Midlife, leisure involvement and reassessment stage in, 155
Military Career Guide, 202–203, 212, 345, 347, 350
Military Educators and Counselors Association, 258
Military service: education options in, 120–121, 225; recruitment numbers of, 213; state information on, 246
Milwaukee, Wisconsin, rehabilitation counseling in, 293
Minorities. *See* Special populations
Missouri: Career Information Hotline in, 381; Career Options workshop in, 378–381; VIEW system in, 303
Missouri at Columbia, University of: Career Planning and Placement Center at, 378; correspondence study from, 121
Missouri at Kansas City, University of, size and scope of, 126
Missouri at St. Louis, University of, size and scope of, 126
Missouri State Chamber of Commerce, 207
Motivation: career information for, 333; toward work, 106–107
My Vocational Situation, 381
Myers-Briggs Type Indicator (MBTI), 380–381

N

National Alliance of Business, 259
National Association of College Admission Counselors, 222, 235–236, 271–272
National Association of Student Financial Aid Administrators, 321
National Association of Trade and Technical Schools, 119

National Board of Certified Counselors, 132, 156

National Career Development Association (NCDA): Commission on Leisure and Career Development of, 136; guidelines from, 385–413; and leisure, 135, 137, 143; and National Vocational Guidance Association, 11, 30; and professional development, 258, 266; and professional standards, 226, 256, 268, 269–270, 275, 276; publications of, 106, 317; and special populations, 280–281, 283

National Career Development Week, 266

National Career Guidance Week, 302

National Center for Education Statistics, 125, 127n, 205, 212

National College Counseling Project, 222

National Crosswalk Service Center, 242

National Defense Education Act (NDEA), 128, 129

National Education Association, 145

National Employment Counselors Association, 258

National Employment Mental Health Counselors Association, 258

National Gardening Association, 123

National Governors' Association, 280

National Occupational Conference, 273

National Occupational Information Coordinating Committee (NOICC): and career information, 240–242, 244–245, 254; and guidelines, 400; Training Support Center of, 242; and world of work, 205

National Public Radio, 302

National Recreation and Park Association, 145–146

National University Continuing Education Association, 121

National Vocational Education Week, 266

National Vocational Guidance Association (NVGA): concepts from, 6, 7, 8; Guidance Information Review Service of, 274; guidelines of, 275; and leisure, 135, 137; and National Career Development Association, 11, 30, 388; Occupational Research Section of, 273–274; and special populations, 282, 283, 285

Nationally Certified Counselor, 132, 156

Native Americans: career development for, 286; in labor force, 95

New Careers Center, 210, 213

New England Fall Foliage Tours, 233

New Horizons Center, 354–367

New Mexico, ethnic diversity in, 285

New Orleans Jazz Club Meeting, 233

New York: ethnic diversity in, 285; life-span study in, 48

New York University, leisure scholar at, 145

Nondirective counseling, impact of, 31

Nonprint media: in career development centers, 301–302; leisure sources in, 233–234; work resources in, 211–212

North Carolina, minority enrichment in, 289

North Carolina at Chapel Hill, University of, Center for Competitiveness and Employment Growth at, 207

Northwest Regional Educational Laboratory, 402

Nova University, impact of, 126

O

Occupational card sort: applications of, 327, 334–341; learning from, 341; themes in, 335–341

Occupational Outlook Handbook (OOH): and career development centers, 302–303, 309; and career information, 239; in individual counseling, 344, 346, 347, 360, 363; and world of work, 198–200, 208–209, 212

Occupational Outlook Quarterly, 200–201, 212, 243

Occupations: concepts of, 5, 6–7, 8, 188, 189, 388; employment trends in, 96–103; fastest-growing, 100–101; largest-growing, 101–103; local sources on, 263–264; state information on, 245

Office of Federal Statistical Policy and Standards, 203, 213

Office of Management and Budget, 204, 213

Ohio State University, size of, 126

On-the-job training, options in, 120, 224

Opening: in counseling framework, 18, 20–21; presenting statements for, 70–71

Operators, fabricators, and laborers jobs, trends in, 100, 104

Optimist Club, 266

Oregon, Career Information System in, 247

Oregon, University of: Leisure Fair at, 153; software system from, 250

P

Pacific Islanders, in labor force, 95

Pacific New Car Show, 233

Paralegal occupations, growth of, 101

Parks and recreation departments, and education, 124

Paulette's case, 352–367

Pennsylvania Higher Education Assistance Agency, 228

Pennsylvania State University: coach from, 236; correspondence study from, 121

Perkins Loans, 129

Personalities: environment related to, 39–40; types of, 34–36; vocational, 33–44, 80

Personnel and Guidance Journal, 7, 283

Peterson's Guides: and career development centers, 319, 320, 321, 322, 323; and education, 227, 234, 235, 237, 238

Placement: activities for, 312–316; with employment agencies and self-help techniques, 316; in-school, 313–314; institutional and agency, 315–316; postschool, 314–315

PLUS loans, 129

Plus-one staging, and cognitive theory, 64

Population changes: and labor force, 93–94; racial and ethnic, 285–286

Precision production, craft, and repair jobs, trends in, 99–100

Prediction, in counseling, 14

President's Commission on Employment of People with Disabilities, 290

Print media: in career development centers, 302–303; on leisure, 233; work resources in, 208–211

Private career/proprietary school, options in, 119, 224

Professional specialty occupations, trends in, 96, 97, 104

Project Reconceptualization, 7

Psychometric movement, and trait-and-factor theory, 30

Public Broadcasting System, 301

Public Law 101–336, 280, 289–290

Public Offender Counselor Association, 258

R

Racial/ethnic groups, career development for, 285–289

Rational emotive therapy, use of, 62–63

Rationale, in work-family counseling, 168–169, 171–172, 176

Reagan recovery, 215

Realistic: environment, 37, 306; personality, 34–35, 347

Red Cross, and education, 123

Regents College of the State University of New York, 125

Relationship: in counseling framework, 19, 21, 25–26; tasks in closing, 84–86

Research and Forecasts, 139–140, 146

Resources: applications of, 277–383; background on, 185–187; for career development, 183–276; for career development centers, 311–312, 316–323; career information delivery systems for, 239–255; for coping with transitions, 54–55; for education and leisure, 214–238; renewing and evaluating, 256–276; on special populations, 282–284, 286–287, 290–291; systems for organizing, 304–308; for work world, 185–213

Retail trade, growth of, 103

Retirement, leisure reawareness and reexploration stage in, 155–156

Richard Rosen Press, 209

Role models, for African Americans, 287

Roper Organization, 214–215

Rotary: and community development, 266; and education, 124

S

Satisfaction: competencies of, in groups, 376–377; job, 107–108; leisure, 146–147, 154, 155; in lifespan, life-space theory, 47

Scouts, and leisure, 152

Segmentation theory, of work and family, 167

Selected Characteristics of Occupations, 193–194

Self-control, cognitive, 63

Self-Directed Search (SDS), 34, 357, 358, 359, 380, 381

Self-instruction, use of, 63

Self-orientation competencies, in groups, 373

Service occupations, trends in, 99, 109–110

Small Business Administration, 312

Small businesses: in future, 112; local survey of, 265–266

Social: environment, 37–38, 306; personality, 35–36

Socioeconomic systems theories: basic tenets of, 41–43; and diagnoses, 81; implications of, 42–43; variables in, 41–42

Software systems: for career information delivery, 248–254; review guidelines for, 400–413

South Carolina, software system in, 250

Southeastern Regional Iris Show, 233

Southern Illinois University: Leisure Exploration Services at, 153; leisure studies at, 147

Southern Living, 211, 233

Southern Regional Education Board, 207

Special populations: aspects of counseling, 279–297; background on, 279–297; background on, 279–281; career development centers for, 309; defined, 279; disabled persons as, 289–294; interventions for, 295–296; racial/ethnic groups as, 285–289; suggestions for, 284–285, 294–297; theoretical issues for, 296–297; women as, 281–285

Spillover theory, of work and family, 166

Staff-sponsored programs, for education and training, 24

Standard Industrial Classification (SIC) *Manual*, 202, 203–205, 213, 362, 363

Standard Occupational Classification (SOC) *Manual*, 200, 202, 203, 213, 362, 363

State occupational information coordinating committees (SOICCs), 240–242, 245–246, 248, 254, 267

States: agencies of, and community development, 267; financial aid from, 227–228; leisure resources from, 232–233; placement services by, 315–316

Stimulus, in counseling, 15

Strengths and obstacles, interview on, 74–76
Structure, in cognitive theory, 60–61
Structured groups. *See* Groups, structured
Summary, in counseling interview, 76–77, 84–85
Sunburst Communications, 212
System of Interactive Guidance and Information (SIGI), 251, 303

T

Talent Search, 287
Technicians and related support occupations, trends in, 96, 97
Technology education, option of, 220–221
Ted's case, 342–352
Television and video, and education options, 122–123
Ten Speed Press, 210, 213
Termination, premature, 85
Testing: in counseling framework, 19, 22; in counseling interview, 77–78; and trait-and-factor theory, 30
Texas, ethnic diversity in, 285
Texas Woman's University, Leisure Resources Room at, 153
Theories, career: of adult career development transitions, 51–55; aspects of, 1–87; of careers and career development, 3–26; clients and counseling in interaction with, 65–68; cognitive, 60–64, 80–81; concept of, 27; for counseling clients, 65–87; of decision making, 55–60; and learning theory, 372; of life-span, life-space approach, 43–51; need for, 27–28, 64; of socioeconomic systems, 41–43, 81; and special population issues, 296–297; trait-and-factor, 28–33, 80; understanding, 27–64; of vocational personalities and work environments, 33–44
Thinking, distorted, 330–332
Tours, alumni/organization-sponsored, 225

Trade and industrial education, 219
Training. *See* Education
Trait-and-factor theory: assumptions in, 32; basic tenets of, 28–33; and diagnoses, 80; implications of, 33; new approaches to, 31–33
Transitions: in adult career development model, 51–55; and client interactions, 65–66; coping resources for, 54–55; for families, 165–166; process of, 53–54; type and context of, 52–53
Treatment, in counseling, 15
Two-Dimensional Occupational Classification Scheme, 304–305
Typical day, interview on, 74
Typical-Day Assessment, for work-family counseling, 171–174

U

Upjohn Institute for Employment Research, 143
Upward Bound, 287
USA Today, 210, 233

V

Vacations, option of learning from, 122, 225
Veterans Administration, 245, 291
Virginia: Career Information Delivery System in, 246–247, 303; sources for, 318–323
Virginia Association of Manufacturers, 207
Virginia Employment Commission, 315
Virginia Health Careers Council, 207
Virginia Polytechnic Institute and State University, Counselor Education Programs of, 307–308
Vocational Biographies, 209, 213
Vocational development, in transitional years, 7
Vocational education: options in, 117; postsecondary, 224; sources on, 218–221

Vocational Education Week, 302, 311
Vocational guidance: concept of, 6; in formative years, 4-6; process of, 29-30; and trait-and-factor theory, 28
Vocational Guidance Manuals, 209, 213
Vocational Industrial Clubs of America, 219
Vocational personalities: assumptions on, 33-34; and general adjustment, 82; implications of, 40; and interactions, 68; theories of, 33-44
Vocational-technical colleges, options in, 117-118

W

Washington, disability counseling in, 292
Washington State University, correspondence study from, 121
Wayne State University, leisure scholar at, 145
Wildlife of the Deserts of the Southwest United States, 233
Wisconsin, rehabilitation counseling in, 293
Women: career development for, 281-285; with disabilities, 290; in higher education, 126-127; in labor force, 92, 94-95, 108-110; proposed solutions for, 284-285
Women's Network, 266
Work: analysis of resources for, 185-213; aspects of world of, 91-113; background on, 91-92; career and leisure related to, 7, 138, 146, 148, 214, 215-216, 229, 297; in career assessment, 73; commercial sources on, 208-212; coun-

seling for family and, 168-181; coverage of sources on, 187-188, 193, 195, 198, 200; defined, 137; educational requirements for, 103-105; environments and vocational personalities, 33-44; families related to, 166-181; in future workplace, 111-113; government resources on, 187-201; history of sources on, 188-189; at home, 113; information types on, 189-193, 195-197, 198-199, 200-201; issues and trends in, 160-166; key resources on, 212-213; labor force for, 92-96; life-span approach to, 149-156; local sources on, 208; long-term changes in, 108-110; in nonprint media, 211-212; occupational groups in, 96-103; in print media, 208-211; reasons for, 105-108; regional sources on, 207; role in, 83; state sources on, 207-208; supplemental sources on, 201-206; trends in, 143-144
Work counseling, career counseling and leisure counseling related to, 148
Work force. *See* Labor force
Work-in-America Institute, 143
Work-study programs, and financial aid, 129-130
World Future Society, 143, 267

Y

Yankee, 211, 233
YMCA and YWCA: and community development, 266; and education, 124; and leisure, 152
Young adulthood, leisure preparation stage in, 152-154
Young Black Scholars, 289
Youth Clubs, and leisure, 152